KU-730-863

PUBLIC RECORD OFFICE HANDBOOKS

No 25

Development of the Welfare State 1939–1951

A Guide to Documents in the Public Record Office

Andrew Land, Rodney Lowe and Noel Whiteside

LONDON: HMSO

© Crown copyright 1992

Applications for reproduction should be made to HMSO

First published 1992

ISBN 0 11 440249 3

British Library Cataloguing in Publication Data

A CIP catalogue of this book is available from the British Library

HMSO publications are available from:

HMSO Publications Centre
(Mail and telephone orders only)
PO Box 276, London, SW8 5DT
Telephone orders 071-873 9090
General enquiries 071-873 0011
(queuing system in operation for both numbers)

HMSO Bookshops
49 High Holborn, London, WC1V 6HB   071-873 0011 (Counter service only)
258 Broad Street, Birmingham, B1 2HE   021-643 3740
Southey House, 33 Wine Street, Bristol, BS1 2BQ   0272-264306
9–21 Princess Street, Manchester, M60 8AS   061-834 7201
80 Chichester Street, Belfast, BT1 4JY   0232-238451
71 Lothian Road, Edinburgh, EH3 9AZ   031-228 4181

HMSO's Accredited Agents
(see Yellow Pages)

And through good booksellers

Univ Wales Swansea
UNIVERSITY COLLEGE
WITHDRAWN LIBRARY STOCK
SWANSEA

Contents

		Page
List of Abbreviations		vi
Acknowledgements		vii
Introduction		viii

1	**The Central Direction of Welfare**	1
1.1	Introduction	3
1.2	Wartime reconstruction planning 1939-1945	3
1.3	The central co-ordination of welfare under Labour 1945-1951	9
1.4	Bibliography	13

2	**Social Security**	15
2.1	Introduction	17
2.2	The Beveridge Report and wartime planning	18
2.3	National insurance	22
	2.3.1 General	22
	2.3.2 Sickness benefit	25
	2.3.3 Unemployment benefit	27
	2.3.4 Widows' and retirement pensions	29
	2.3.5 Miscellaneous benefits	32
2.4	National assistance	33
2.5	Family allowances	37
2.6	Industrial injuries and diseases	40
2.7	War pensions and allowances	43
2.8	Bibliography	45

3	**Housing and Town and Country Planning**	47
3.1	Introduction	49
3.2	The wartime emergency	49
3.3	The genesis of town and country planning	54
	3.3.1 Wartime developments	54
	3.3.2 Postwar legislation	61
	3.3.2.1 The New Towns Act 1946	61
	3.3.2.2 The Town and Country Planning Act 1947	65
	3.3.2.3 National Parks and Access to the Countryside Act 1949	68
3.4	The postwar housing programme	69
	3.4.1 General	69
	3.4.2 Wartime planning	70
	3.4.3 Short-term measures	72

	3.4.4	The postwar housing programme: the growth of the council sector	76
	3.4.5	The private sector: owner-occupied and rented accommodation	81
	3.4.6	The supply of labour and raw materials	84
3.5	Bibliography		87

4   **The National Health Service**   **89**

4.1	Introduction		91
4.2	War and the emergency medical services		92
	4.2.1	Introduction	92
	4.2.2	The Emergency Medical Service	93
		4.2.2.1 General	93
		4.2.2.2 EMS: accommodation, equipment, staff	95
	4.2.3	Wartime local authority health services	100
		4.2.3.1 ARP casualty services	100
		4.2.3.2 Antenatal and postnatal care, child health	103
4.3	Planning a National Health Service		105
4.4	The National Health Service Act 1946		111
	4.4.1	Policy proposals and discussions	111
	4.4.2	Implementation of the Act	113
		4.4.2.1 General	113
		4.4.2.2 Central administration	114
		4.4.2.3 Hospital and specialist services	116
		4.4.2.4 Local health authority provision: health centres; maternity and child welfare; domiciliary and other services	121
		4.4.2.5 'Practitioner' services: GPs; dentists; opticians; chemists	124
		4.4.2.6 Mental health services	127
	4.4.3	The financial crisis	129
4.5	Bibliography		133

5   **Education**   **135**

5.1	Introduction		137
5.2	Wartime policy and the shaping of the 1944 Education Act		138
5.3	Primary and secondary education		142
	5.3.1	Wartime problems	142
	5.3.2	Implementation of the principles of the 1944 Act	146
	5.3.3	School building programme	150
	5.3.4	Supply of teachers	153
	5.3.5	Special services	157
		5.3.5.1 School meals and milk	157
		5.3.5.2 School medical service	160
		5.3.5.3 Special educational treatment	162

5.4 Further and higher education 165
    5.4.1 Technical, further and adult education 165
        5.4.1.1 General 165
        5.4.1.2 Technical education 165
        5.4.1.3 Day continuation schools 168
        5.4.1.4 Further education 169
    5.4.2 The universities 170
5.5 Youth service 172
5.6 Bibliography 176

6 Other Local Government Services 177
6.1 Introduction 179
6.2 Local government reform 179
6.3 The elderly 182
    6.3.1 Wartime services 182
    6.3.2 Wartime planning and the National Assistance Act 1948 186
6.4 Children 188
    6.4.1 Pre-war service and the war emergency 188
    6.4.2 Nursery provision 191
        6.4.2.1 Day nurseries 191
        6.4.2.2 Residential nurseries 194
    6.4.3 Child care reform proposals and the Curtis Committee 197
    6.4.4 The Children Act 1948 and its implementation 199
6.5 The physically disabled 203
6.6 Bibliography 205

Appendices 207
A Rationing of food, clothing and domestic fuel 207
B Details of committees referred to in more than one section 213
C Chairmen of committees 221

Index 227

Abbreviations

AB	Assistance Board
ARP	Air Raid Precautions
BDA	British Dental Association
BMA	British Medical Association
CEPS	Central Economic Planning Staff
CYEE	Central Youth Employment Executive
EMS	Emergency Medical Service
ETS	Emergency Training Scheme
GP	General Practitioner
HMC	Hospital Management Committee
HORSA	Hutting Operation for the Raising of the School Leaving Age
LEA	Local Education Authority
NAB	National Assistance Board
NACTST	National Advisory Council on the Training and Supply of Teachers
NEC	National Executive Council
NHI	National Health Insurance
NHIS	National Health Insurance Scheme
NHS	National Health Service
NI	National Insurance
NUT	National Union of Teachers
PAC	Public Assistance Committee
PAI	Public Assistance Institution
PRD	Prevention and Relief of Distress (Scheme)
PRO	Public Record Office
RHB	Regional Hospital Board
ROSLA	Raising of the School Leaving Age (Scheme)
SSEC	Secondary Schools Examination Council
TUC	Trades Union Congress
UAB	Unemployment Assistance Board
UGC	University Grants Committee
UISC	Unemployment Insurance Statutory Committee
UNESCO	United Nations Educational, Scientific and Cultural Organization
WEA	Workers' Educational Association
WVS	Women's Voluntary Service
YMCA	Young Men's Christian Association
YWCA	Young Women's Christian Association

Acknowledgements

This handbook was compiled by Andrew Land under the supervision of Dr Noel Whiteside and Dr Rodney Lowe of the University of Bristol.

We would like to thank a number of people for their comments and advice on specific chapters: chiefly, Dr Charles Webster, Dr Kevin Jefferys, Professor J H Veit Wilson, Professor Roy Parker and Professor Alan Murie. We wish especially to thank Jacqui Rose and Dorothy Maxwell for their extensive editorial work on the final manuscript and Dr Anita Travers for compiling the index.

Finally, the authors and the Public Record Office would like to acknowledge the generous financial assistance of the Economic and Social Research Council, without which this handbook could not have been compiled.

AL, RL, NW.

Introduction

The outbreak of war in 1939 initiated a revolution in the relationship between state and society. The duration of the conflict—and its scope—forced the central government to assume control over all national resources. As a result, the machinery of government expanded to manage the crisis and the central state became involved in the day to day lives of its citizens to an unprecedented extent. Much of this new involvement centred on questions of welfare: how, for example, children and the elderly should be protected in the blitz, or how limited supplies of food, clothing and medical care could best be utilized to protect the well-being of the population without damaging the war effort. As it was vital to maintain civilian morale, attention was given to questions of equity and social justice when allocating 'fair shares' for all from very limited resources. Reconstruction plans for postwar Britain carried these principles forward, proposing how wartime experiments might be adapted for peacetime purposes and co-ordinated with existing services which had slowly evolved over the past century.

When many of these reconstruction plans were implemented by the 1945-51 Labour government, the range of services provided by the public sector became collectively known as the 'welfare state'. Government intervention, however, was based at both a central and local level on a rather haphazard collection of statutes. Both the purpose and the extent of the 'welfare state' were ill-defined. Was its main aim the 'abolition of want', as implicit in the famous 1942 Beveridge Report (Cmd 6404), or the creation of a more egalitarian society as propounded by such social scientists as T H Marshall? Should it embrace the management of the economy in order to guarantee a high level of employment, as Beveridge implied in his report (pp 163-165), or should it be confined solely to a range of social services—such as social security, health, education and housing—as subsequently became the convention? The confusion over the exact definition of the 'welfare state' is with us still.

The welfare state has at intervals become a political issue provoking widely differing approaches and interpretations. In 1950, Labour ministers were convinced that the positive promotion by the state of everyone's welfare was an electoral asset; Attlee, as prime minister, started openly to champion the 'foundation of the welfare state' as one of the prime achievements of his government. In recent years, however, this 'achievement' has been thrown into question, as the extension of state welfare has come to be interpreted less as a triumph of a civilized society and more as an unnecessary burden which undermines individual initiative and saps the roots of economic prosperity and growth. This new characterization of a 'nanny state' has underlain the rerouteing of official welfare provision away from the universalist principles supported by Beveridge towards more selective services 'targeted' on those in need.

This shift in policy has been described as 'radical' by many of its adherents but, as the records identified in this handbook reveal, it has merely revived a long-standing debate on the relative merits of state intervention and the market; a debate which had been particularly active in the 1940s. Many counter-arguments to more recent orthodoxies can be found in these records. State welfare was seen by many then not as destructive of economic efficiency, but as conducive to its future development.

Similarly, the provision of welfare through official channels was not perceived as wasteful, bureaucratic and cumbersome. On the contrary, it was proposed as a solution to the problems arising out of private systems of welfare, in which provision was uneven, unco-ordinated and inconsistent. The re-examination of the 1940s debate can therefore help to place current discussion on the future of the welfare state in its full historical context and assist in a more balanced judgment.

The records

The sheer volume of records in the Public Record Office has, in the past, frequently discouraged their effective use. In the study of government policy, for example, researchers have been tempted to confine their attention to the papers of the Prime Minister's Office, the Cabinet and the Treasury, which document activity only at the apex of the decision-making process. Further, those primarily interested in the history of a given locality, institution or client group have often failed to take full advantage of the wealth of information amassed by central government in the course of both the making of policy and its implementation. Consequently, the primary purpose of the handbook is to introduce those interested in welfare to the full range of departmental records relating to specific areas of policy and, secondly, to demonstrate the potential of government papers to those with a broader interest in social conditions and social change.

Whilst later chapters will emphasize the richness of the records preserved at the PRO, it is perhaps appropriate here to identify some of their main limitations. First, there is the obvious point that not all records relevant to the study of social policy are held at the PRO. The existence of both the Scottish Office and the Northern Ireland government, for example, restricted the administrative coverage of departments in Whitehall. In Scotland, the Scottish Development Department was responsible for housing; the Scottish Education Department for schools, universities, further education and probation; the Home and Health Department for all welfare, health services and hospitals; and the Scottish Economic Planning Department for the location of new towns. All these records, together with papers of the Association of County Councils in Scotland, are held in the Scottish Record Office in Edinburgh. Similarly, all records of the Northern Ireland government—including those of its Ministry of Health and Social Services (which cover housing as well as the named areas of responsibility) and its Ministry of Education—are held in the Public Record Office of Northern Ireland in Belfast. Moreover, although central government records hold large quantities of material relating to local conditions—such as plans for future development, reports on local conditions and copious correspondence on issues ranging from the provision of schools to home helps for the elderly—the archives of local government itself are not to be found in the PRO, but in the county record offices and city and district archives all round the country. Another important source outside the PRO is the records of individual hospitals incorporated within the National Health Service since 1948. A recent project, funded by the Wellcome Institute of the History of Medicine in co-operation with the Public Record Office, is locating those records available for public inspection and use. Finally, there are the private papers of those involved in policy-making, which often reveal much which the official record was designed to hide. A prime example is the Beveridge Collection held by the British Library of Political and Economic

Science. The location of other, similar collections of private documents can be identified through the Royal Commission on Historical Manuscripts.

The location of material that is held outside the PRO is one problem. The absence of material that one might expect to find there is another. Most of the records of government departments relating to the Second World War were transferred rather hastily, following a decision to open files for the 1941-45 period to public inspection in 1972, before all were thirty years old. Moreover, after the Second World War, there was a considerable reorganization of government and file series were switched from department to department. Consequently there has been some separation of collections that arguably belonged together, the temporary loss of some material less immediately concerned with the prosecution of the war— and the apparently permanent disappearance of some file series belonging to wartime ministries which were subsequently wound up. An example in this last category came to light during the research for this handbook: the files of the Ministry of Supply relating to medical equipment and drugs for the Emergency Medical Service have not all been traced, although a few policy files were re-registered as Ministry of Health records. Similarly, some departmental papers relating to the work of particular committees could not be located. What is presented in the handbook necessarily reflects the contents of the PRO at the time of writing, but it is quite possible that this might be augmented by future transfers of records from government departments to the PRO. More specifically, 'particular instance papers', containing material of a personally sensitive nature on individuals, are closed to public inspection for up to 75 years and cannot be covered in detail by this handbook. Hence, conscription papers are not included, nor are any personal records relating to claims to social security or any form of wartime compensation, to individual children in care, and so on. If preserved, such records may eventually be open to public inspection, subject to the normal review procedure, but not in the immediate future.

The final caveat concerns the very nature of official records. They are not, it must be remembered, a full and disinterested record of government policy-making. Rather, they are the working papers of state departments from which decisions (and the reasons for them) might be deliberately excluded, information might be suppressed rather than revealed, and in which the views expressed by politicians and officials alike might be tailored to suit a particular political situation or a given audience. Moreover, decisions may be unrecorded because they were taken over the telephone or at informal meetings (Dale 1941 p 116), or at formal meetings where minutes were deliberately not taken (Gaitskell 1983 p 130).

It is factors such as these which make an exclusive dependence on records documenting the apex of the decision-making process inadvisable. Cabinet minutes, for example, are particularly uninformative because the opinions of individual ministers are usually omitted and the summary of decisions taken is extremely brief. These restrictive conventions were established as early as the 1920s. 'Once upon a time', recorded the then deputy secretary to the Cabinet, 'we wrote speeches of Ministers very fully and under their own names. Objection was taken to this as it was possible to confront individual Ministers today with what they had said last week or last month' (Jones 1969 p 293). Better guides to ministerial and departmental thinking are to be found in the minutes of Cabinet committees, be they permanent 'standing' committees or *ad hoc* committees created in response to specific circumstances. Even here, however, the political sensitivity of an issue might lead to the distortion of the record. Individual opinions, for example, were deliberately excluded from the minutes of the 1951 *ad hoc* Committee on the Expenditure on the Social Services (CAB 130/66) and the accuracy of the minutes of the standing Committee on the National Health Service aroused political controversy (CAB 21/2027). The papers of the secretariats which serviced Cabinet and other interdepartmental committees form a further valuable source of debates within government—and one that is sadly under-used. The secretariats most relevant to the study of welfare policy in the 1940s are those of the Cabinet itself, the Reconstruction Committee and the Lord President's Committee. Details of these papers are in chapter 1.

Too great a reliance on the records from the centre of government can lead to other distortions. Many vital policy decisions are not taken explicitly by ministers and senior civil servants but, in reality, by relatively low-level officials during the implementation of policy. Hence the records of individual departments often contain the most important evidence. It is a specific objective of this handbook to encourage their greater use. Departmental records themselves, however, have their own pitfalls. They are frequently at their most voluminous when policy changes threaten the interests of a department, or of a particular division within a department. Such bureaucratic wrangling may generate vast amounts of paperwork, but this does not in itself signify that the issue is of intrinsic importance. There is, therefore, a danger that the wood may be lost for the trees and time and trouble spent disentangling a dispute that can be shown to have exerted little influence on subsequent events. Consequently, to maintain a balanced perspective on the issues documented in the files, it is essential—wherever possible—to balance official records with other written and oral testimony.

The handbook

In accordance with the approach outlined above, the aim of this handbook is to bring together records from all departments of government, held in the Public Record Office, pertaining to specific policy issues in the field of social welfare. The format broadly follows that of the Public Record Office *Current Guide* Part 1. However, in this instance, the handbook is arranged by subject areas (cross-referenced as necessary) rather than by administrative agencies. Each chapter is divided into discrete subsections; policy files of central significance are cited in the text in brackets and additional records relating to the issue in question are described at the end of each section. These descriptions are arranged to present general documentation of the subject first, followed by references to files covering particular aspects of it. In most cases, reference is made to whole classes (file series) of records. Readers with an interest in specific topics within a given area will then be able to locate the individual documents they require from the class lists which are to be found on the Search Department shelves at the Public Record Office at Kew.

After the first chapter on the machinery of central planning, the handbook follows a conventional approach to the description of state welfare, by examining the main social services in turn: social security, housing (including town and country planning), health, education and, finally, other local authority services. Records documenting wartime and postwar domestic rationing—of fuel, food and clothing—are included in Appendix A. A select bibliography is appended to each of the main chapters. These bibliographies will inevitably become out of date in a relatively short space of time. Indeed, the handbook will have failed if it does not stimulate further work in this field. It was felt, however, that a list of published works that have used the public records quite extensively would be valuable, as in themselves they provide guidance to the different types of record involved.

Guidance to committees has presented particular problems. Owing to the extent of the war emergency—and thus to the scope of postwar reconstruction—a multiplicity of interdepartmental bodies were created, both to co-ordinate action between agencies, suddenly pushed into close co-operation, and to develop and implement programmes of postwar reform. Committees whose scope included policy areas covered in more than one section of this handbook are noted in the text by an asterisk and described in Appendix B. Here the reader will find details of the committee, including the chairman, the secretary, the date of its first meeting, the references to its papers (minutes, correspondence, interim reports etc) and to its published reports (if any). Cross-references from the chairman's name to the formal title of the committee or subcommittee can be found in Appendix C. The index includes references under the committee's name to the chapter and section where its work is discussed and, where relevant, to Appendix B.

Finally, it will be noted from the structure of the handbook that the narrower, conventional definition of the welfare state has been adopted—rather than the broader definition indicated at the start of this introduction. Economic policy has been excluded, as the relevant records are covered in a companion handbook, *Economic Planning 1943-51: a guide to documents in the Public Record Office*, which is being prepared simultaneously. Reference is made in chapter 1 to records on taxation policy, which clearly had a substantial impact on the distribution of resources and therefore on welfare. The vast bulk of official records, however, are concerned with the development of the five main social services. As this handbook is not a comprehensive history but a guide to the holdings of the PRO, it has naturally to reflect this fact.

Bibliography

H E Dale, *The higher civil service in Great Britain* (1941)

The diary of Hugh Gaitskell 1945-1956, ed P M Williams (1983)

T J Jones, *Whitehall diary*, vol 1, ed K Middlemas (1969)

R Lowe, 'The Second World War, consensus and the foundation of the welfare state', *Twentieth Century British History*, vol I (2) (1990) pp 152-182

T H Marshall, *Social policy* (1965)

H Pelling, *The Labour governments* 1945-51 (1984)

Record repositories in Great Britain: a geographical guide (8th edition, 1987)

Chapter 1 – THE CENTRAL DIRECTION OF WELFARE

1.1 Introduction

1.2 Wartime reconstruction planning 1939-1945

1.3 The central co-ordination of welfare under Labour 1945-1951

1.4 Bibliography

1.1 Introduction

The purpose of this chapter is to provide an introduction to the broad political and administrative context within which welfare policy evolved between 1939 and 1951. Its three principal objectives are therefore to note briefly the major political crises that influenced, or were influenced by, welfare policy; to describe the distribution of power within the committee structure of the Cabinet; and to identify those debates on the purpose and funding of the welfare state which transcended the individual policies that are to be examined in later chapters.

As noted in the introduction, the slow gestation of the term 'welfare state' is testimony to the fact that there was little concerted welfare planning between 1939 and 1951. Consequently anyone hoping to locate in the public records regular debates on the purpose, development or impact of welfare policy will be disappointed. There were admittedly certain occasions on which some of the broader principles of welfare were discussed. For example the Beveridge Committee on Social Insurance and Allied Services* provided the forum for such a debate between June 1941 and November 1942, and the Reconstruction Committee* of the Cabinet produced a flurry of White Papers on each of the 'core' social services after November 1943. The former, however, was concerned largely with a single welfare measure, whilst the latter was as much concerned with papering over the cracks in the wartime coalition as with developing practical blueprints for postwar reform.

After the war, not even the 'official birthday' of the welfare state—the Appointed Day of 5 July 1948 on which the National Health Service and national insurance became operative—occasioned a major debate within Whitehall on the underlying objectives of state welfare. Such co-ordination as was attained was achieved by information officers trying to maximize the impact of individual policies which were running 'to different timetables and designed to meet very different objectives' (Wildy 1985 p 206). Rather it was crises, such as that in 1951 over National Health Service expenditure which led to the resignation from the Cabinet of Aneurin Bevan, Harold Wilson and John Freeman, that stimulated explicit debate. Such crises, however, were infrequent and hardly conducive to balanced judgment.

1.2 Wartime reconstruction planning 1939-1945

1939-January 1943

During the first phase of the Second World War from September 1939 to the spring of 1940, the so-called 'phoney war', the expectation of a speedy Allied victory was widespread. The priority for the Chamberlain administration in the field of social welfare was, therefore, to discuss and approve only those measures deemed essential to the war effort. Taxation was increased, the first wave of evacuation from the cities involving some 1.5m people was implemented, an emergency medical service was set up, and other welfare services such as unemployment assistance were amended. Projected pre-war welfare reforms and initiatives, such as the raising of the school leaving age and an investigation into workmen's compensation, were abandoned.

Once it became more apparent that the war was not going to end swiftly, popular and parliamentary discontent with the government began to mount. Chamberlain was perceived to lack the necessary qualities of leadership to unite the country and win the war. He was succeeded in May 1940 by Winston Churchill, who formed a coalition government which included leading members of the Liberal and Labour Parties. Each of the political parties agreed to observe an electoral truce for the duration of the war.

The Labour ministers were given primary responsibility for the home front and, after Dunkirk and the Battle of Britain in June and July 1940, the attitude of central government towards welfare policy appeared to change. A War Aims Committee was set up under Attlee's chairmanship (CAB 87/90) 'to consider means of perpetuating the national unity achieved in this country during the war through a social and economic structure designed to achieve equality of opportunity and service among all classes of the community'. Then, in June 1941, Churchill issued with Roosevelt the Atlantic Charter which contained, at the insistence of the Cabinet, a commitment to postwar social security (Churchill 1950 pp 392-5). Such grandiose initiatives, however, achieved little of political value. The former failed to reach an agreed declaration and the latter has been dismissed as 'nothing more than a press release' (Calder 1971 p 304).

Little practical progress was achieved. Churchill personally was hostile to social reform and, in particular, opposed anything which detracted from the immediate waging of the war (PREM 4/89/2). His views were shared by the Conservative majority in the House of Commons, inherited from the 1935 general election, which formed a formidable parliamentary barrier to reform. Moreover, for both political and personal reasons, the position of the Labour ministers in the coalition was relatively weak and their responsibility for the home front was gradually assumed by the Lord President's Committee* (Addison 1975 pp 279-280). For example, the responsibility of Arthur Greenwood (the Labour Party's deputy leader) for the Production Council and the Economic Policy Committee* was transferred to the lord president in January 1941 and that of Attlee (the Labour Party leader) for the Food Policy Committee* and the Home Policy Committee* in February 1942. The Lord President's Committee* thus gradually became the effective cabinet for domestic affairs and significantly it was chaired by Sir John Anderson who, in his interwar role as a civil servant, had used his immense administrative expertise to discourage radical reform.

Greenwood, admittedly, was compensated for his loss of power with the chairmanship of the potentially important Reconstruction Problems Committee*. However, it met only four times before his dismissal in February 1942 and he was replaced by the equally ineffective Sir William Jowitt. The Reconstruction Secretariat, for which they were successively responsible, also failed to make any significant impact on Whitehall (CAB 117/27; Lee 1980 p 130). 'It is wrong', remarked R A Butler in 1942, 'to put failures into reconstruction' (Dalton 1986 p 150).

A final impediment to reform was the Treasury, which remained politically influential during the first years of the war. However, the increasing shift in priority away from finance and towards the management of resources meant that other departments, such as the Board of Trade and the Ministry of Labour, grew in political and administrative importance. Further, the appointment of Keynes as a Treasury adviser in 1940 and the establishment of an Economic Section within the War Cabinet in 1941 (Cairncross and Watts 1989) provided government with an alternative source of economic advice which, as will be seen, was potentially more sympathetic to the development of welfare policy.

Relative inactivity at the centre disguised considerable activity at a lower political and administrative level. As later chapters will show, the immediate needs of wartime administration led to decisions which set important precedents for postwar welfare policy. For example, the stigma associated with state relief was reduced with the abandonment of the household means test in 1941 (see chap 2.4); and the new universal nature of welfare policy was advanced by the approval of free subsidized milk to mothers and children under five in June 1940 (see chap 4.2.3.2). Many official enquiries, such as the Beveridge Committee*, were instituted which were to provide the consensus of expert advice on which later reconstruction plans were based. Individual government departments, which already had plans to rectify perceived weaknesses in interwar policy, were stimulated into further action, if only to control the more radical ideas which were developing outside government. Finally there was an explosion of unofficial enquiries into reconstruction. The Nuffield College surveys on various aspects of social welfare had a politically strong impact on government thinking (CAB 124/440-441; CAB 117/157-174; T 161/1135/S50805/01; T 161/1134/S50805) although the Treasury typically dismissed the social survey as 'an extraordinarily valueless document' (T 161/1164/S48497/2: 25 Sept 1942). Other proposals were framed by such groups as the National Council for Social Services and Political and Economic Planning, local authorities which often established their own reconstruction committees, and a number of individuals (CAB 117; T 161/1461/S52276). All these developments coincided with, and helped to consolidate, a marked shift in public opinion in favour of reform (INF 1/864; PREM 4/88/4).

January 1943-May 1945

The publication of the Beveridge Report in November 1942 revolutionized the Cabinet's handling of reconstruction. Public opinion, released from the fear of defeat by Britain's first major victory (El Alamein, Oct 1942) gave it an enthusiastic reception (see chap 2). This strengthened the resolve of leading Labour ministers, in particular Bevin and Morrison, to demand reform (CAB 87/13: PR (43)2,15). It also led to a major backbench revolt against the coalition when ministers gave the report a lukewarm reception during the parliamentary debate in February 1943. These pressures proved too strong even for the combined opposition of the Treasury and the Conservative Party and, in a broadcast on 2 March, Churchill was forced publicly to commit himself to a programme of reform. The publication of the report, therefore, proved to be a significant landmark in the development of a welfare state, not just because it laid down the basic framework for social security for the next thirty years, but because it symbolized popular hopes for a different and more just world, and revolutionized perceptions of what was politically possible (Harris 1977 chap 17).

The initial forum for the ensuing debate within government on the future nature of welfare policy was the ministerial Reconstruction Priorities Committee*. This had been set up in January 1943 to consider the Treasury's objections to the Beveridge Report and to determine the line the government should take in the forthcoming parliamentary debate. The committee gave the report a guarded welcome (CAB 66/34: WP(43)58)

5

but all its reservations were swept away in the debate's aftermath. Accordingly, two subcommittees were established to plan the Beveridge Report's implementation: the Sheepshanks Committee to deal with the social insurance provisions and the Steering Committee on Postwar Employment which looked at Beveridge's 'assumption' of full employment.

By the autumn of 1943 reconstruction planning had generated such party controversy within the coalition that there had to be a major restructuring of political and administrative responsibilities. All existing ministerial reconstruction committees were dissolved and a new Reconstruction Committee* was established under a non-party, if not exactly neutral, minister of reconstruction, Lord Woolton. For the remainder of the war it was at this Committee, and its various ministerial and official subcommittees that all major issues of principle were discussed before the publication of reconstruction White Papers. The Lord President's Committee*, therefore, lost its primacy over reconstruction issues, although it retained responsibility for any immediate wartime measure and any agreed postwar policy (such as the 1944 Education Act) which required enactment during the war.

The political and administrative changes in 1943 signified that, unlike earlier years, 'reconstruction was being treated as a matter of first rate importance in Whitehall, worthy of the energies of some of the most powerful politicians and civil servants'. (Addison 1975 p 221). Amongst the latter were two officials who were to dominate postwar Whitehall—E E Bridges and Norman Brook—and it was Brook, who, as joint secretary of the Reconstruction Priorities Committee* and then permanent secretary at the Ministry of Reconstruction, was the driving force behind reconstruction policy for the rest of the war (Dalton 1986 p 684). The streamlining of the Cabinet committee structure in 1943, however, ensured neither harmonious nor business-like policy-making. Indeed the reality was that in the absence of political and administrative consensus, the committee system often became a forum for delay as much as for reform (Dalton 1986 pp 696, 769).

Administrative resistance to welfare reform centred on the Treasury, where opposition to the Beveridge Report had been fundamental from the start. In relation to the report's proposals on social security, it objected to the overall cost, which it feared would result in high taxation and thus a diminishing of individual freedom and entrepreneurial initiative, to the very principle of universal social security, which it considered would undermine work incentive, and to the priority social security was given over competing needs such as defence, increased exports, and other welfare policies including education (CAB 87/3: RP (43) 5; CAB 87/13: PR (43) 8; T 273/57). It also attacked Beveridge's third assumption of full employment as theoretically unsound and, in practice, unattainable.

On this last issue, the Treasury came directly into conflict with the Economic Section of the War Cabinet and a major battle developed between the two on the Steering Committee on Postwar Employment, which was responsible for the initial drafts of the famous 1944 *Employment policy* White Paper (Cmd 6527; Peden 1988 chap 6). The Treasury's fundamental belief was that in the annual budget, government expenditure and income should balance. Such a belief was justified by classical economic theory and the need to maintain a strict political and administrative discipline, so that public expenditure could be kept under control (Peden 1988 chaps 3-4). However the problem with this was that, in a depression, welfare expenditure had to be cut just when it was urgently needed. Keynes in *The general theory* (1936) had challenged the theoretical assumptions of this policy and, in *How to pay for the war* (1940), he popularized a new approach to economic policy which required the budget to balance not the government's accounts but aggregate demand and supply within the economy as a whole. This new approach was further developed by the Economic Section and had potentially revolutionary consequences for welfare policy. To offset a depression and to generate full employment, for example, demand could be increased by either increasing welfare expenditure (eg on the building of hospitals and schools) or reducing taxation (in particular national insurance contributions; see chap 2.2). Welfare policy, in short, could be brought into constructive partnership with economic policy and could, moreover, be expanded when it was most needed.

Because of Treasury opposition, however, there was no 'Keynesian' revolution during the War. The *Employment policy* White Paper, despite its commitment to a 'high and stable level of employment', was full of unresolved contradictions (Glynn and Booth 1987 chap 13); and little serious thought was given to the constructive interdependence of economic and social policy.

Most of the Treasury's objections to welfare reform were instinctively shared by the Conservatives and by Churchill (see chap 2.2). He tried initially to stifle debate on the Beveridge Report. Then, in February 1943, he established the principle that no major commitment to increased expenditure should be made until after the end of the war when a new parliament could be elected and the country's resources properly judged (CAB 66/34: WP(43)65). Finally, in November 1943, he instructed the new minister of reconstruction that policy should be based on the principle of 'anything that is essential for the transition [from war to peace], whether it be controversial or not: nothing which is not essential for the transition unless it commands a broad measure of support' (CAB 124/566). Even then he tried to delay agreed recommendations of the Reconstruction Committee* by referring them to Beaverbrook and Bracken. Labour tried to counter this disruption, with Attlee remonstrating with Churchill to particularly good effect in February 1943 and January 1945 (K Harris 1982 pp 241-4). Attlee, Bevin and Morrison also provided powerful voices in the call for postwar planning (CAB 66/38, 26 June 1943; PREM 4/87/4). However, whilst Labour were able to ensure that postwar reconstruction and finance was debated, they were often unable to secure political agreement (PREM 4/87/9; T 172/2007; T 230/15, 96-98).

Differences over the principles of policy remained substantial. R A Butler spoke of fundamental disagreements between Conservative and Labour ministers 'on any matters which involve property or the pocket' (Jefferys 1987 p 140; see also Lee 1980 for a refutation of Addison's thesis of wartime consensus). This dissension was particularly noticeable in relation to the 1942 Uthwatt Committee on Compensation and Betterment* which, by proposing nationalization of the development rights of land, posed a fundamental threat to the rights of private property and thus to the distribution of power within Britain (see chap 3). So intense, indeed, did the Labour Party's suspicion eventually become of the Conservative's sincerity towards welfare reform that the Labour ministers were forced to resign from the coalition in May 1945 before the ending of the war against Japan. There then followed a Caretaker government under Churchill's premiership (23 May-26 July 1945), in which the decreased priority accorded to reform was signified by the winding up of the Reconstruction Committee*. In its place the Lord President's Committee*—temporarily renamed the Home Affairs Committee*— became once again the decisive Cabinet committee for domestic policy.

* for committee references see Appendix B

7

Records

PREM 1 (Chamberlain) and PREM 4 (Churchill) contain Prime Minister's Office files on issues of particular and general relevance to welfare policy which were of sufficient political importance to require the prime minister's attention.

The CAB classes contain all the relevant records of the Cabinet and its various ministerial and interdepartmental official committees. The minutes and memoranda of the War Cabinet are at CAB 65-CAB 66. CAB 67 contains Cabinet memoranda of a less secret nature which received a wider distribution between 1939 and 1941, whilst CAB 68 contains reports by various departments to the War Cabinet between 1939 and 1942. The minutes and memoranda of the Home Policy Committee are at CAB 75. Minutes of *ad hoc* committees set up to look at single issues are at CAB 78. Cabinet Office papers which often contain important background information on committees, such as the reasons for the choice of membership and discussion of internal disputes, can be found at CAB 21. The Lord President's Committee papers are at CAB 71, with those of its secretariat at CAB 123. Papers of the various Reconstruction Committees are at CAB 87 and those of the Reconstruction Secretariat at CAB 117. The Cabinet's Historical Section, which was responsible for writing the official war histories and for gathering together some of the most important wartime files, is at CAB 102.

The Economic Section of the Cabinet which was established in January 1941 and not absorbed into the Treasury until 1957 was staffed by a small group of economists who offered the Cabinet independent expert advice on a wide range of issues including welfare policy. Its papers are at T 230, and are listed in full in the PRO handbook, *Economic planning 1943-1951: a guide to documents in the Public Record Office*. Papers of the Committee on Postwar Employment are at CAB 87/63, 70; BT 64/3345-3346; and LAB 8/733.

Treasury files are important not just for the Treasury's own views on welfare policy but also for the co-ordination and prioritizing of policy in the light of scarce resources. They were restructured and decentralized after 1948. Files under the old system which were still current in 1948 were reclassified under the new system. Therefore the decentralized files often contain pre-1948 papers. Treasury files can be most easily grouped under four headings:

Finance: the budget and finance bill papers are at T 171. The more routine finance files before 1948 are in T 160 and thereafter in T 233.

Supply: these papers contain details of negotiations between the Treasury and individual departments on their estimates and expenditure and are at T 161 before 1948 and T 227 thereafter. These often contain the most useful and illuminating documents.

Establishments: these files document Treasury control over the organization and staffing levels of individual departments. Decisions on organization frequently occasioned debate on the purpose of policy. The pre-1948 files are at T 162 and thereafter at T 214. In 1942 the Organization and Methods Division was set up to achieve greater efficiency and its files are at T 222. Blue notes containing a complete and regularly updated description of each department's history, responsibilities and estimates are at T 165.

Miscellaneous: these classes were never registered in the main series but were retained by individual ministers and officials. The most important of these are the chancellor of the Exchequer's papers at T 172 and those of Sir Edward Bridges (Cabinet secretary 1938-1947 and permanent secretary 1945-1956) at T 273. The Keynes papers relating to his period as a Treasury adviser between 1940-1946 are at T 247 (see also various volumes of the Macmillan edition of *The collected works of John Maynard Keynes* for reproductions of the major memoranda).

INF 1/862-864 charts the growing importance of social policy in the statements on war aims by the government during the war.

The Reconstruction Joint Advisory Council provided a forum between 1942 and 1945 for representatives of labour and industry to discuss general policy arising out of postwar reconstruction. Its papers are at CAB 123/49; BT 168/219; CAB 87/19; CAB 117/203-207; CAB 124/299; BT 64/3087, 3151.

Treasury papers dealing with reconstruction issues in Northern Ireland are in T 160/1327/F14464/043/04.

1.3 The central co-ordination of welfare under Labour

The central co-ordination of welfare policy under the two postwar Labour governments also falls into two distinct phases, with 1947 as the watershed. Throughout the whole period, it is true, the Cabinet itself debated and took far more key decisions than had been the case during the war. It decided, for instance, to alter the balance between central and local government by nationalizing hospitals (CAB 128/1: 18 October 1945), to spurn retrenchment in 1947 by reaffirming the raising of the school leaving age (CAB 128/9: 16 Jan 1947) and, conversely, to accept the need for economy by sanctioning charges in the NHS in 1951 (see chap 4). The Lord President's Committee* also remained the court of appeal below the Cabinet in domestic issues whilst, at the Legislation Committee, crucial decisions were taken on the timing and detailed content of forth-coming bills. However, before 1947 most planning of welfare policy continued—as in wartime—to take place within the relevant departments and only two major committees attempted greater co-ordination. These were the Social Services Committee*, which in fact was only concerned with national insurance and assistance and (briefly) the NHS; and the Housing Committee*, chaired by Attlee in a vain attempt to achieve success in an area of major electoral interest.

This somewhat relaxed approach was destroyed by a succession of economic and political crises in 1947. There were three main economic crises (Cairncross 1985). The US loan, upon which Britain had been dependent since 1945 to finance both welfare policy and essential imports, began to run out and was not replaced by Marshall Aid until the summer of 1948. The convertibility of sterling (which had been a condition of the US loan) almost eliminated Britain's gold and dollar reserves in August 1947 and had to be abandoned precipitately. Inflation also began to increase at an alarming rate. Politically, the Great Freeze and the subsequent fuel crisis, which severely restricted power to industry and homes in February and March, damaged the reputation of a government committed to planning. Attlee's leadership came under direct challenge from Dalton and Cripps respectively in July and September, and Dalton himself was forced to resign as chancellor of the Exchequer after a budget leak in November. There also appeared in Cabinet an increasing division between the majority of ministers, led by Morrison, who wanted to consolidate their past achievements and a minority, personified by Bevan, who wished to press on with socialist reforms (PREM 8/428). To the public, the government started to appear as ageing, ineffectual and divided, and its popularity accordingly waned.

The economic crises were also used by those who had always been opposed to the extension of welfare policy as a pretext for demanding its contraction. S P Chambers of the Inland Revenue, for example, in a paper, *The economic crisis 1947*, identified high taxes, low industrial investment and the lack of incentives for savings as the main cause of the crisis, and blamed national insurance for these problems (T 172/2023). These views were shared by many in the Treasury. The reasons for its opposition to welfare policy have already been noted and they were reinforced by the perceived need to maintain the confidence of the City and overseas financiers, upon whom the funding of the national debt and the support of sterling were deemed to depend. Such underlying administrative assumptions led to a certain crisis of confidence between Dalton and his officials, as it was to do again in 1949 when Cripps was chancellor (Dalton 1986; Williams 1983 chap 3).

For a number of reasons, therefore, there was a radical overhaul of the machinery of central decision-making in 1947—as had, in fact, long been planned in Whitehall (CAB 21/1701-1703; Hennessy 1986 pp 36-43). The first major innovations, in the spring of 1947, were the creation of a Central Economic Planning Staff (CEPS) under Sir Edwin Plowden and the appointment of an Economic Planning Board to involve industrialists and trade unionists in policy-making (T 229/28-39; CAB 134/210-214). The role of the former was to plan and implement more effectively the use of scarce resources both through the drafting, with the Economic Section of the Cabinet, of an annual *Economic survey* and through the related work of a number of new Cabinet committees. In September, Cripps was appointed to the new post of minister of economic affairs to overview this machinery and he thus became in effect the new 'planning minister' in place of Morrison (Pelling 1984 pp 178-180). In this capacity he was appointed also to the two new major co-ordinating Cabinet committees set up in October. These were the Economic Policy Committee* chaired by Attlee, in which the 'big five' of Attlee, Morrison, Bevin, Dalton and Cripps were grouped to discuss mainly long-term and international economic issues, and the Production Committee*, chaired by Cripps himself, responsible largely for short-term decisions on the domestic economy. When Dalton resigned as chancellor, Cripps succeeded him and took the CEPS into the Treasury.

These changes (which are described in more detail in the handbook *Economic planning 1943-1951*) had major repercussions for welfare policy. The Social Services* and Housing Committees* were dissolved and the requirements of all policies, but especially those relating to housing, education and health (which required heavy capital expenditure and supplies of imported materials such as timber) were placed under stricter economic scrutiny. Restrictions were ordered on school building, for example, in order to economize on imported timber and to release manpower for the export drive (T 227/150). Most important of the new committees for welfare policy was arguably the Investment Programmes Committee*, and its working party, in which estimates were made of the resources required by various policies; of the need for economies and how to implement them; and occasionally of the social implications of such cuts (e.g. CAB 134/448: IPC(WP)(48)132). Much of the preparatory work for the committee was undertaken by the CEPS and its papers contain much of importance on welfare policy. The committee's reports were also examined by such advisory bodies as the Economic Planning Board and by executive committees such as the Production Committee*, and

10

so their papers are also of considerable relevance (see, for example, criticism of the proposed educational building programme 1950-1952 in CAB 134/642: PC(49)61).

Despite the increased emphasis on the greater co-ordination of policy, explicit reviews of the general principles, cost, and consequences of welfare policy were still extremely rare. 'It is remarkable', wrote Norman Brook in 1950, 'that the present government have never reflected upon the great increase in public expenditure and the subsequent changes in its pattern, which has come about during the past five years in consequence of their policies in the field of the social services' (CAB 21/1626). The debates that did take place were occasioned by specific crises such as devaluation in September 1949 and the increase in defence expenditure and inflation in 1950 consequent upon the Korean War. Hence Cripps circulated a memorandum to the Production Committee* in July 1948 seeking to veto any increase in social services capital investment expenditure in an attempt to boost industrial investment (CAB 134/638: PC(48)98); and he circulated a further series of memoranda on public expenditure to the Economic Policy Committee* between July and December 1949 which resulted in three important debates in October 1949 and May 1950 (CAB 134/220: EPC(49)34, 35; CAB 134/224: EPC(50)12). In 1950 the seriousness of the situation was stressed by the chancellor when he wrote that 'we cannot confine ourselves to administrative changes, important though these are. We must face the necessity for changes in policy too if the reductions in expenditure are to be in the least adequate' (T 227/401).

The most renowned battle over welfare policy was that over the finance of the NHS, which started in 1949 and concluded with Bevan's resignation from the Cabinet in April 1951 (see chap 4). A wide range of personal and political issues were involved in this dispute but principal amongst them were those identified by the Treasury at the time of the Beveridge Report: the Treasury's own concern for budgetary discipline and a limit to social expenditure, the need to establish priorities within welfare policy (with Bevan's colleagues growing increasingly resentful of the disproportionate resources consumed by the NHS) and the need, with the expansion of defence expenditure, to redraw the balance between social and other public expenditure (CAB 130/60:GEN 357).

Finally there were three broad, if subsidiary, issues to which attention was paid throughout the period 1945 to 1951: the public reaction to welfare policy, the relationship between welfare policy and taxation, and parallel international developments. Under the Labour government the cost of home publicity increased tenfold and eventually aroused such parliamentary concern that a committee of enquiry, the French Committee, had to be appointed in 1949. It recommended major economies (Cmd 7836; Crofts 1987). Most of the money was spent on providing the public with factual information, such as how to register with an NHS doctor; but the government was concerned also to identify public attitudes to welfare policy, mould public opinion and monitor the effectiveness of its own publicity campaigns. The agency responsible for the first and last of these objectives was the Social Survey, an official polling organization which carried out numerous individual surveys (to which reference will be made in later chapters) culminating in a general survey of public knowledge and opinion on the social services in May 1950 (RG 23/111).

General publicity policy itself was the responsibility of the lord president. He worked through a ministerial and an official committee on home information, the latter served by a subcommittee on social publicity and supported by an official committee on economic information. Differences of opinion are revealed in these committees' deliberations on the planning of publicity for the Appointed Day, on 5th July 1948 (CAB 134/458; CAB 124/1015-1016; Wildy 1985). Some ministers, including Bevan, wanted to publicize the virtues of individual policies rather than their collective significance. Others demanded a more inspirational campaign which would counter escalating wage claims and complaints against bureaucracy by stressing the increasing value of the social wage and its redistributive effects. In the end a low-key theme was chosen. As the lord president was advised, 'it is more important to counter not just the working-class view of taxation as "robbery", but also the equally dangerous middle class delusion that taxes paid by them financed the social services' (CAB 124/1015). Thus the 'value for money' of state welfare in relation to any comparable package of private insurance was stressed. So too was the fact that the services were not 'free' but had to be earned by everyone through higher productivity.

The relationship between taxation and welfare policy was a subject which, as the last quotation illustrates, lay just beneath the surface throughout the 1940s, and gained political prominence in 1951 with the appointment of a Royal Commission on the Taxation of Profits and Income. It aroused interest for two very different reasons. On the one hand, in line with the Treasury's critique of welfare policy, the high rates of taxation needed to finance increased expenditure were adjudged to diminish individual welfare by discouraging investment and hard work, and thus economic growth. On the other hand, it was argued that taxation could have important social consequences and should be used deliberately to redistribute income and wealth. Thus Keynes in 1942 had called for a 'social policy' budget which would increase taxes on luxury goods whilst modifying direct taxes in favour of women and children (T 171/360, 362). Such proposals were opposed by the Inland Revenue and Treasury on the grounds that taxation should be equitable between individuals, simple, and easy to administer. Any element of 'social engineering', it was held, would make the collection of taxes more difficult. Moreover, the Inland Revenue lacked the staff to plan, implement and monitor such a policy (T 273/100; Hogwood 1987 p 141). As a result, whenever a tax change was proposed in the drafting of a budget, its social consequences were rarely considered (T 171, *passim*).

By 1948, however, there was such public opposition to high taxation—especially amongst the middle classes—and such concern within the Treasury and the Economic Section about discouragement of economic growth by the tax system, that the momentum for a general enquiry mounted (T 171/394-395; T 171/400: BC(50)5 and 14; T 171/405). It climaxed with an exceptional review by the Inland Revenue which examined, amongst other things, the social consequences of taxation and admitted that 'the social and economic effects of taxation are so great and the possibility of the deliberate use of taxation to achieve social and economic ends so important that it is no longer possible to deal with taxation purely...in a fiscal sense' (T 171/427). Attlee was therefore persuaded to appoint a royal commission (PREM 8/1182). It was eventually to report in 1955, the same year that saw the publication of Titmuss's article on the 'social division of welfare' which argued that in the 'real world of welfare' fiscal and occupational welfare were as important as the conventional social services (Cmd 9474; Titmuss 1958).

Finally, as economic and political problems mounted in the late 1940s, and as a consequence of Marshall Aid, the Labour government became increasingly interested in welfare developments abroad. From 1948 to 1951 there was a Cabinet Committee on Social Services in western Europe (CAB 134/704-705; LAB 13/611), and in January 1951 the Economic Policy Committee* received a memorandum on economic and social policy in Australia and New Zealand (CAB 134/229: EPC (51) 51). Typically, however, most comparative information was accumulated and assessed not collectively but—as later chapters will show—by individual departments seeking solutions to particular problems.

* for committee references see Appendix B

Records

Papers of the Prime Minister's Office are in PREM 8.

Cabinet minutes and memoranda are in CAB 128-CAB 129. Standing committees are at CAB 134 and *ad hoc* committees at CAB 130. Cabinet Office Papers are at CAB 21. Papers of the Lord President's Committee are at CAB 132, with its secretariat at CAB 124. It continued to play an important co-ordinating role in peace time although, after Morrison's serious illness in 1947 and the accompanying economic crisis, it was relieved of many of its responsibilities for economic policy.

The papers of the CEPS are at T 229 and are listed in full in the PRO handbook, *Economic planning 1943-1951*. For the main Treasury files see chap 1.2.

Individual files of interest include Investment Working Party calculations on capital expenditure programme for each service between 1946 and 1948 (T 161/1370/S53555/03); notes on the probable future growth of expenditure on reconstruction and the social services in 1946 (T 171/386). Attlee's file on government expenditure 1949-1951 is at PREM 8/1415 and the Lord President's Secretariat at CAB 124/1110. T 269/1 contains the permanent secretary to the Treasury's papers on the 1949 devaluation crisis and its consequences.

Papers of the Ministerial Committee on Home Information Services which sat from 1946-1948 are at CAB 134/354. It was renamed the Information Services Committee, and its papers for 1948 to 1951 are at CAB 134/458-460. The Official Committee on Home Information's papers are at CAB 134/355-360, with other departmental papers relating to it, and its subcommittee on social publicity, at MH 79/579, 588, 591, 603 and INF 12/309-315. Papers of the Economic Information (Official) Committee which was responsible for the 1950 Survey on the Social Services, are at CAB 134/361-373.

Files on public attitudes towards welfare policy, collected by the Ministry of Information and the Social Survey, are at INF 12, RG 23 and RG 40.

1.4 Bibliography

P Addison, *The road to 1945* (1975)

C Barnett, *The audit of war* (1986)

A Cairncross, *Years of recovery* (1985)

A Cairncross and N Watts, *The economic section, 1939-1961* (1989)

A Calder, *The people's war* (1971)

W S Churchill, *The Second World War:* vol 3, *the grand alliance* (1950)

W Crofts, *Coercion or persuasion?* (1989)

H Dalton, *The Second World War Diary 1940-1945*, ed B Pimlott (1986)

The diary of Hugh Gaitskell 1945-1956, ed P M Williams (1983)

S Glynn and A Booth, *The road to full employment* (1987)

J Harris, *William Beveridge* (1977)

K Harris, *Attlee* (1982)

P Hennessy, *Cabinet* (1986)

P Hennessy, *Whitehall* (1989)

B Hogwood, *From crisis to complacency* (1987)

K Jefferys, 'British politics and social policy during the Second World War', *Historical Journal*, 30 (1987), p 128

K Jefferys, *The Churchill coalition and wartime politics, 1940-1945* (1991)

J M Lee, *The Churchill coalition* (1980)

R Lowe, 'The Second World War, consensus and the foundation of the Welfare State', *Twentieth-Century British History*, vol 1 (2) (1990)

K Morgan, *Labour in power 1945-51* (1984)

G C Peden, *Keynes, the Treasury and British economic policy* (1988)

H Pelling, *The Labour governments 1945-51* (1984)

R S Sayers, *Financial policy 1939-1945* (1958)

R Titmuss, 'The social division of welfare', in *Essays on the welfare state* (1958)

T Wildy, 'Propaganda and social policy in Britain' (1985) (unpublished Leeds University Phd thesis)

Chapter 2 – SOCIAL SECURITY

2.1 Introduction

2.2 The Beveridge Report and wartime planning

2.3 National insurance

    2.3.1   General

    2.3.2   Sickness benefit

    2.3.3   Unemployment benefit

    2.3.4   Widows' and retirement pensions

    2.3.5   Miscellaneous benefits

2.4 National assistance

2.5 Family allowances

2.6 Industrial injuries and diseases

2.7 War pensions and allowances

2.8 Bibliography

2.1 Introduction

Before the Second World War, responsibility for social security had been divided between various government departments. The principal ones involved were: the Ministry of Labour (unemployment insurance); the Ministry of Health (national health insurance, contributory old age and widows' pensions, public assistance); the Home Office (workmen's compensation); the Ministry of Pensions (war pensions); the Unemployment Assistance Board (unemployment assistance); and the General Post Office (non-contributory old age pensions).

During the early years of the war, little was done to reform this structure. Priority was given to policies directly affecting the conduct of the war and, because of the impact of wartime inflation and the blitz, these included amendments to features of the pre-war social security system. This led to the raising of benefits and assistance rates, the amending of the system of means testing and the extension of state help to those who had suffered damage either to themselves or their property due to enemy action. Reform of the unsatisfactory structure of the system was not placed on the political agenda until 1941 when an increasing awareness in government of the need to boost public morale, by planning for a better postwar world, coincided with pressure from Labour Party members within the coalition, a number of back-bench Tory MPs and numerous outside organizations.

Social security was an obvious area for reform. Administration was badly organized. Benefits were inconsistent and often overlapped. The large expansion of war pension schemes and benefits further complicated the issue. The Royal Commission on Workmen's Compensation (see chap 2.6) which sat from 1938 to 1940 had exposed the difficulties involved in attempting to reform one branch of the system without affecting the rest. Consequently in June 1941 the Interdepartmental Committee on Social Insurance and Allied Services* under the chairmanship of Sir William Beveridge was appointed to look at the whole issue. Its report was to play a central part in the postwar reform and in welfare state folklore for the next forty years. This was due in part to its author who ensured the document was more than simply an investigation into insurance, and to the popular reception the report received. Whilst both major political parties adopted the scheme into their postwar plans, it was the Labour Party which seemed the more committed to the proposals and the Tories who prevaricated. Whilst intervention by the Treasury and other interested groups ensured the proposals were eroded, nevertheless the scheme introduced by the Labour government between 1945 and 1951 was based on the framework of the Beveridge Report.

Records

Because of the centrality of social insurance in postwar welfare reform policy discussions on the subject took place at the highest level. Therefore all the major central domestic committees like the Lord President's Committee*, and the various committees on reconstruction, identified in chapter 1, contain detailed discussions on social security policy.

administration of the scheme eventually came under the direction of the Ministry
...onal Insurance, and so the bulk of records referring to the various schemes are
...PIN classes. However, numerous other departments kept files on the subject.
...e administration of the scheme remained with the central authority, rather than
...assed on to a local authority (as was the case with education, for example), there
are few local reports of implementation.

* for committee references see Appendix B

2.2   The Beveridge Report and wartime planning

The Interdepartmental Committee on Social Insurance and Allied Services* was
appointed in June 1941 under the chairmanship of Sir William Beveridge. It consisted
of middle ranking officials from each of the seven departments concerned with social
insurance together with the government actuary and representatives of the Treasury,
the Registry of Friendly Societies and the Ministry of Reconstruction. Despite the
Treasury's belief that the committee was simply to carry out a tidying up exercise, and
because of the ambiguous nature of the committee's terms of reference, Beveridge was
able to stamp his authority on it immediately and to ensure that the whole issue of
social insurance was fundamentally reassessed: 'the interdepartmental committee was so
evidently outpaced by its chairman that its inquiries rapidly took on the character of
a personal mission' (Webster 1988 p 35).

The Beveridge Report, *Social insurance and allied services*, was published the following year. Its central recommendations comprised the creation of a unified and
universal system of social insurance. This would provide cash benefits to protect those
in employment and their dependants against all interruptions in earnings 'from the
cradle to the grave'. In return for a flat rate contribution from the state, the employer
and the employee, the state would pay subsistence level benefits to the unemployed,
the sick, the retired and those suffering from industrial injuries and diseases. A new
ministry would be created to administer the scheme. For those who failed to contribute,
national assistance would be available on a means-tested basis (but one considerably
more lenient than the 'household test' of the 1930s). The remnant of the Poor Law
responsibility for income maintenance, which had been vested in the public assistance
committees, was to end. To underpin his insurance plans, Beveridge assumed the
creation of a national health service, the maintenance of a high level of employment,
and the introduction of family allowances.

The meetings of the committee had proved surprisingly uncontentious, due in part
to Beveridge's dominance. A large number of organizations consulted agreed with the
proposals or had developed their own policies along similar lines. Even organizations
like the Federation of British Industry accepted the basis of the plan, although they
wanted it postponed until the end of the war (Harris 1977 pp 401-402, 414-415).

In December 1942, the Committee on Reconstruction Problems* appointed an Official Committee on the Beveridge Report*, chaired by Sir Thomas Phillips, to consider
its recommendations (CAB 87/2: 13 Dec 1942). Whilst accepting the principle of a
comprehensive health service, the committee was highly critical of a number of important

aspects of the scheme. They argued the reform of the existing system would pamper the feckless class of people for whom it had acted as a deterrent. They questioned the need for family allowances and argued for payment in kind rather than cash, an approach Beveridge rejected. Most importantly of all they dismissed the principle of 'adequacy', arguing that a standard level of subsistence was impossible to find, considering the different costs of living in different parts of the country. The report of the Phillips Committee was to play a crucial role in undermining many aspects of Beveridge's scheme.

A small central staff was appointed under the minister without portfolio (Jowitt) to co-ordinate policy between the various government departments that would be affected by the social security reforms, to hear deputations and to examine the scheme in a more detailed fashion (PIN 8/1-82). This body was primarily responsible for the initial drafting of the two White Papers (Cmd 6550, 6551 1943-44) which contained the government's eventual legislative proposals for social security reform (see below).

Within the Churchill Cabinet, the question of the cost of the Beveridge proposals was the focal point of concern (CAB 123/45, 242-244). As with all areas of social reform Churchill wanted to delay action until the end of the war, to avoid both distractions and expensive postwar commitments (CAB 66/44: 15 Feb 1943; PREM 4/89/1-2). The total cost of the proposals, including family allowances and a universal health service was estimated at £535m in the first year of which £302m would fall on the Exchequer, a 300% increase in the cost of an equivalent service in 1941. This helps explain the attempts to suppress the report. Before publication the Cabinet had warned Beveridge against making public statements on the subject (CAB 65/28, 16 Nov 1942). Brendan Bracken, minister of information, feared that 'some of Beveridge's friends are playing politics and that when the report appears there will be an immense amount of ballyhoo about the importance of implementing the recommendations without delay' (T 172/2093). In March 1943 Beveridge's proposed visit to the USA to discuss the plan was officially opposed, especially by Bracken (FO 371/34098: A2492). Despite this, Beveridge succeeded in drawing attention to himself and his proposals.

Opposition to the report also came from a number of MPs. Sir Waldron Smithers, for example, quoted St Luke 14: 28-30 (T 161/1193):

> For which of you, intending to build a tower,
> Sitteth not down first, and counteth the cost,
> Whether he have sufficient to finish it ?
> Lest haply, after he hath laid the foundations,
> and is not able to finish it, all that behold
> it begin to mock him.
> Saying, This man began to build and he is not able
> to finish it.

In particular, opposition rallied around the Phillips Committee's hostility to subsistence payments (MH 57/221; T 230/104). In December 1942 a secret committee was set up under Ralph Assheton to ascertain the Conservative Party's views on Beveridge. Representing the views of about 90% of MPs, it emphatically rejected the idea of subsistence benefit, as too expensive and undermining the incentive to work (Deacon 1983 p 43).

All three wartime chancellors, Simon (28 May 1937-10 May 1940), Wood (12 May 1940-24 Sep 1943) and Anderson (29 Sep 1943-26 July 1945) were naturally suspicious of welfare expenditure. Wood feared any expansion of welfare would be at the expense of economic growth (PREM 4/89/1). The Treasury was concerned at the long-term financial implications of the scheme for itself—it unsuccessfully attempted to pass its burden of national insurance contribution back onto the public (T 161/1193/S48497/017)—and for the postwar economy. In particular, it doubted the ability of the scheme to remain funded by contributions and feared the fiscal implications of the expenditure involved (T 171/367). Even if the scheme could be maintained by contribution, Gilbert, under-secretary at the Treasury, feared that employers would pass national insurance costs on in higher prices and so would make British goods less competitive in the world market (T 161/1164/S48497/2). In the autumn of 1942 the Treasury issued a memorandum entitled the *Social security plan*, which outlined its main financial objections. These included the future cost of international security, the difficulty of abolishing unemployment immediately after the war and the inability of national income growth to keep pace with the scheme in cost (T 273/57). It saw the system as a threat to work incentives, entrepreneurial initiative and freedom from high taxation (CAB 87/3: RP(43)5; CAB 87/13: RP(43)8). Treasury objections were to lead to cuts in both the level and duration of benefits in the programme put forward in the White Papers (PIN 8/59).

The position of women within the scheme also caused a number of problems. Beveridge had long been concerned with securing fairer treatment of women. The report therefore recommended that single employed women be given the equivalent insurance status to men, and married women a wide range of benefits based on their husbands' contributions. Married women workers received a choice of these options though, much to the annoyance of some women's organizations, rates of benefit were to be lower than those for employed men (PIN 8/65). Beveridge argued they were less likely than their husbands to pay rent and household maintenance costs. For non-working housewives he proposed, in return for husbands' contributions, maternity grants and benefits not only in widowhood but also on divorce and separation. Sickness benefits were to be allowed in the form of payments for domestic help. Beveridge argued that the work of the housewife was as important economically and socially as waged work and should therefore receive the same recognition under the social security system.

The Treasury concluded that many of the proposals were unnecessary and a waste of resources. Benefits for divorced and separated wives were successfully opposed on the grounds that the government was 'subsidizing sin' (PIN 8/137). Beveridge was also forced to drop his proposals for sickness allowances for housewives. Alternative proposals put forward by the National Council of Women for a regular allowance paid to all housewives, equivalent to a wage, was opposed by Beveridge as impractical (PIN 8/48). Beveridge therefore found himself sandwiched between the demands of some women's organizations for the further extension of benefits, and ministerial demands for cutbacks. Consequently, most of Beveridge's plans for women failed to be fully implemented (PIN 8/136; Harris 1977 pp 402-406).

Yet despite this opposition, the report's basic proposals were carried through on a wave of national feeling. The Ministry of Information reported that the plan had been 'welcomed with almost universal approval by people of all shades of opinion and by all sectors of the community' and that it was seen as 'the first real attempt to put into practice the talk about the new world' (INF 1/864). They wisely began using the report as positive propaganda rather than resisting its distribution. Within parliament the Labour Party was in support of the proposals and willing to fight within the coalition for their implementation (see chap 1.2). The Liberal Party and Liberal MPs overwhelmingly endorsed it. The Tory Reform Committee (consisting of 45 Conservative MPs) supported the immediate setting up of a Ministry of Social Security (Barnett 1986 pp 27-31).

The scheme gained the support, on economic as well as social grounds, of J M Keynes (T 247/80). The Economic Section of the Cabinet Office was particularly keen to use national insurance contributions as a means of quickly and directly regulating demand (CAB 87/63, 16 Oct 1943, 23 Oct 1943; T 230/16, 20, 21, 101-102, 105). A system was developed by J E Meade, chief assistant in the Economic Section, which linked social security rates to unemployment in order to stabilize demand (PIN 19/42; ACT 1/697). Whilst no precise scheme was worked out, the principle was established during the bill stage of the National Insurance Act 1946 (PIN 3/70).

Problems surrounding the Beveridge proposals encouraged those involved in analysing them to look abroad for guidance. Family allowance schemes were studied in other countries (T 161/1116/S43697/1); the New Zealand system of social security contributions was looked at as a way of solving the problem of the rate of contribution within Britain (T 161/1193/S48497/017); even the German system was assessed (FO 371/34435: C9370). From 1945 onwards social security systems were kept under continuous review (AST 7/806).

In preparation for the introduction of reform, a new Ministry of National Insurance was created in 1944 (PIN 3/62). This subsequently absorbed staff and responsibilities from the Ministries of Labour and National Service and Health, and from the approved societies. Its creation was met with concern from the secretary of state for Scotland that his department would lose control to the new Ministry (PIN 8/156).

The first reform which, arguably, owed its origin to the Beveridge Report was the Family Allowances Act, passed by the Caretaker government in 1945 (see chap 2.5). In the following year, and in accordance with election promises, the Labour government introduced the National Insurance Act (see chap 2.3) and the National Insurance (Industrial Injuries) Act (see chap 2.6) which contained the bulk of the new social insurance programme. In 1948 the National Assistance Act extended and rationalized the work of the existing Assistance Board (see chap 2.4). The majority of benefits became available on the 'Appointed Day', 5 July 1948. Family allowances were introduced early in August 1946, as were retirement pensions in the winter of that year.

* for committee references see Appendix B

Records

Discussions on the Beveridge Report and representations from interested parties are at PIN 8.

Treasury files on the Committee, report, and discussions following its publication can be found in the T 161/S48497 series. General files are at T 161/1164/S48497/1-2 and T 161/1165/S48497/3. T 161/1423/S48497/01/1-3 contain various enquiries following the report and T 161/1165/S48497/026 contains comments on the White Paper. T 161/1193/S48497/17 deals with the financing of the plan. T 161/1193/S48497/017, 025 contain discussions on the timetable and machinery. A file on the setting up of the

Ministry of National Insurance is at T 161/1198/S52103. T 161/1242/S48497/010, T 161/1251/S53086/022 and T 171/388 deal with the taxation of benefit. T 230/104 deals with benefit rates and subsistence needs. The Chancellor of the Exchequer's Office file on Beveridge is at T 172/2093. Calculations by the government actuary on the cost of the scheme are at ACT 1/692-708, with contributions to the Committee at ACT 1/681-691. Calculations used in drafting the White Paper are at ACT 1/762-768.

The Prime Minister's Office files on the Beveridge Report are at PREM 4/89/1-4, and on the White Paper at PREM 4/89/5. PREM 4/89/6 refers to the setting up of the Ministry of National Insurance. A file assembled by Sir Edward Bridges, secretary to the Cabinet, on the scheme is at T 273/57. Files of the Economic Section of the Cabinet are at T 230/100, 103-104 and CAB 21/588. The Lord President's Secretariat files are at CAB 123/43, 45, 242-244, with files of the Committee on Reconstruction Problems* at CAB 21/2295.

Bill papers relating to the setting up of the Ministry of National Insurance are at PIN 3/62, with Ministry of Health papers at PIN 8/156. PIN 23 relates to the staffing and organization of the Ministry. Establishment and staffing files are at PIN 19. A Treasury blue note listing the administrative history of the Ministry is at T 165/269.

The Reconstruction Committee appointed a subcommittee on Social Insurance to draft a White Paper based on the Beveridge proposals. Its papers are at CAB 87/11.

Ministry of Health papers on the legislative timetable for the social insurance legislation are in HLG 68/71. Papers relating to the standard of subsistence are at MH 57/221.

Actuarial papers giving advice to Northern Ireland's Ministry of Labour on Beveridge's scheme are in ACT 1/709-713.

2.3   National insurance

2.3.1   General

The responsibility for drawing up the National Insurance Bill lay with the Ministry of National Insurance. The ministry was established in November 1944 following the introduction and passing of the Ministry of Social Security Bill earlier that year. Sir William Jowitt became its first minister. In April 1945 it assumed the health insurance and pensions functions of the Ministry of Health and the Department of Health for Scotland, and the unemployment insurance and assistance functions of the Ministry of Labour and National Service and the Assistance Board. Administration of unemployment payments and assistance continued under agency arrangement with local offices of the Assistance Board, to give the ministry time to develop its own network.

After the election success of the Labour Party in July 1945, James Griffiths was appointed minister of national insurance. He had been a leading critic of the Churchill government in February 1943 for its failure to give the Beveridge Report a full and enthusiastic reception. He was, therefore, a firm supporter of many of the proposals and was keen to secure their earliest possible implementation.

The first government proposals for a national insurance scheme appeared in February 1946. One consolidated insurance scheme would bring together sickness, unemployment, and old age benefits, as well as maternity and widows' benefit. Insured men, together with their spouses, and insured women were covered. The scheme was to be administered directly by the state rather than by the approved societies. Finance of the scheme was to be based on a central fund filled by national insurance contributions. Few amendments were made to these proposals and the National Insurance Act was passed on 1 August 1946. The bulk of the scheme came into operation on the Appointed Day, 5 July 1948, along with the National Health Service (see chap 4).

At the national level the scheme remained the responsibility of the minister of national insurance. His position was somewhat weakened by the fact that the portfolio did not carry with it a place in the Cabinet. A National Insurance Advisory Committee* was appointed in 1947 to give advice and assistance to the minister in relation to his duties under the Act. This was supplemented by local advisory committees which advised him on any local problems that needed his attention.

Central supervision of the day to day administration of the schemes (including family allowances) was moved to a new office in Newcastle upon Tyne in October 1946. This resulted in considerable savings in administrative costs. The great bulk of administrative work, however, was carried out on a regional basis. Ten English regions were each given a controller, deputy and assistant regional controllers, nine senior medical officers and a regional finance officer. Their functions were to supervise their own area offices, to collect contributions, and to evaluate claims to benefit. Local offices dealt directly with claims to benefit and arranged for payments.

The provision of local services caused a number of problems initially (PIN 8/4). Because of the lack of an existing structure, the Ministry of National Insurance was forced to use the offices of the Ministry of Labour and National Service (LAB 12/545) and the Assistance Board (AST 7/808) on an agency basis. A Joint Standing Committee of the Ministry of Labour and National Service and Ministry of National Insurance (PIN 7/329; LAB 12/509), and the Padmore Committee on the Organization of the Local Work of the Ministry of National Insurance and the Assistance Board co-ordinated the arrangements between the Ministries. The 'How to Pay' Committee (PIN 19/14) looked at the various ways of paying benefits with the interdepartmental Committee on the Payment of Pensions and Allowances through the Post Office looking specifically at payment over the Post Office counter (PIN 18/158; T 222/383-384; T 233/1122-1123).

Applications for benefit were first considered at the local offices. Appeals could be made to local tribunals. Any subsequent appeal went to the National Insurance Commissioners, an independent authority appointed by the Crown under the 1946 legislation, and finally to the minister.

Pensions, at the full rate, were introduced ahead of the main scheme in the winter of 1946 (see chap 2.3.4). This marked a major step away from the insurance principle. Beveridge had argued that retirement pensions should be phased in over a twenty year period to allow national insurance contributions to accumulate; but the government bowed to pressure from its supporters and the electorate at large.

Despite the early introduction of retirement pensions, by 1949 there was a large surplus in the national insurance account. This was due mainly to the low level of postwar unemployment which had remained below the 8.5% rate assumed for the purpose of calculations by the government actuary (see chap 2.3.3). Under the provisions of the 1946 Act, contribution rates were due to be raised in 1951. The surplus therefore led to mounting calls for this increase to be abandoned. This was resisted by the Treasury which argued that the likely scale of future national insurance commitments—as the population aged and an increasing number of claimants became dependant on a relatively decreasing number of contributors (CAB 128/17: 1 Oct 1951)—made it impossible to consider such a move. Bridges commented that they were faced with 'an embarrassingly large immediate surplus and an embarrassingly large future deficit' (T 227/236: 30 Nov 1950). Mounting pressure to make use of the surplus, however, necessitated some action from the Treasury. The value of old age pensions had gradually been eroded throughout the late forties, and many pensioners had been compelled to resort to national assistance (see chap 2.3.4). This was coupled with a severe labour shortage which made it desirable to encourage elderly people to stay in employment. Consequently an increase in the retirement pensions at 70 to forty-one shillings was proposed. Whatever its advantages, this marked the first substantial departure from the principle of uniform and universal flat rate benefits.

Under the provisions of the 1946 Act, quinquennial reviews were to be carried out to look at benefit rates and contribution levels, and to make appropriate adjustments. The first review was held in 1952, and led to the increase of benefits and contribution rates in the National Insurance Act 1952 and the Family Allowances Act 1952 (T 227/119-121).

The measures introduced by the National Insurance Act 1946 were reinforced by the National Insurance (Industrial Injuries) Act 1946 which for the first time extended the insurance principle to cover a risk previously omitted from the general insurance scheme (see chap 2.6), and by the National Assistance Act 1948 which provided means-tested benefits to those who were no longer covered by the insurance scheme (see chap 2.4).

The importance of national assistance grew markedly in the late forties and early fifties. Beveridge's proposals of 1942 had been framed on the assumption that postwar prices would be rigorously controlled. Therefore rates were only to be reviewed at five yearly intervals. In the event between 1946 and 1957 the price of basic commodities rose by more than 50%. Under the 1948 National Assistance Act, however, means-tested benefit was continually readjusted to account for this. Consequently national assistance played an important role not just in providing for those outside the insurance scheme, but also for topping up increasingly inadequate insurance payments (see chap 2.4).

* for committee references see Appendix B

Records

The National Insurance Bill papers are at PIN 3/62, 64, 69-72. PIN 19/8 contains information on the preparation of the Bill by the health and pensions divisions of the Ministry of National Insurance. Ministry files on financial policy and procedure in relation to the legislation are at PIN 18. Papers relating to the establishment of the Ministry of National Insurance include PIN 3/62.

Treasury papers leading up to the Bill are at T 161/1249/S53086/2, with financial resolutions at T 161/1249/S53086/06. Actuarial calculations on the Bill are at ACT 1/762-768, 788-792. PIN 18/27 contains correspondence between the Ministry of National Insurance and the Treasury and government actuary. The main discussions on the problems of the National Insurance Fund surplus are at T 227/235-239. Treasury Home Finance Division files are at T 233/420. A file on the problem of the Economic Section of the Cabinet is at T 230/262.

The Prime Minister's Office papers relating to the Bill are at PREM 8/290. The Lord President's Secretariat papers are at CAB 123/46. Lord Chancellor's Office papers are at LCO 2/3102-3103.

The papers of the National Insurance Advisory Committee are in PIN 60. Papers of the various local committees are at PIN 30.

A selection of Ministry of National Insurance files dealing with the problems arising out of the implementation of the Act are at PIN 32. The papers of the Newcastle office dealing with all aspects of the administration of the scheme are at PIN 23. Staff organization within central offices was also looked at by a Pensions Organization Committee. Its papers include PIN 32/29 and PIN 46/4. Publicity material is at BN 10/1-5.

PIN 44 deals with the adjudication policy and procedure under the Act. PIN 16 contains the papers of the insurance commissioners charged with the question of adjudication. PIN 55 deals with overlapping benefits and anomalies. A Ministry of Pensions file on the same subject is at PIN 15/3757. PIN 43 is concerned with all aspects of National Insurance contribution, but includes the classification and liability of classes of insured persons and the policy of enforcement and prosecution in cases of fraud. Local tribunal papers are in PIN 49. Those of the National Insurance Commissioners are at CT 1-CT 5. Appeals considered by the minister are at PIN 54. Lord Chancellor's Office papers relating to the appointment of local tribunal chairmen are at LCO 2/4766.

Papers of the Interdepartmental Committee on the Organization of the Local Work of the Ministry of National Insurance and the Assistance Board are in T 222/50; T 214/26; AST 7/808; AST 9/104, 114; PIN 23/22.

A number of reciprocal agreements were arranged with other countries to provide social security cover when abroad. The main files are at PIN 34, but others include ACT 1/796-806; FO 371/79288; MH 79/634; PIN 7/332; PIN 46/35.

2.3.2 Sickness benefit

Before the implementation of the National Insurance Act, the National Health Insurance Scheme (NHIS) in Britain covered all workers earning less than £240 per annum. It granted each the right to basic medical care from a general practitioner and a cash sickness benefit in return for a tripartite contribution from employer, employee and the state. The scheme was administered by 'approved societies'; these were essentially private agencies registered for the purpose by the Ministry of Health, consisting principally of industrial insurance companies, friendly societies and a handful of trade unions. The contributor was free to chose his or her society; similarly the societies were at liberty to reject applicants. Those who were not covered were called 'deposit contributors' and subscribed to a state scheme run by the General Post Office.

By the late 1930s, the scheme was being widely criticized. It had a tendency to distort the distribution of medical care in inverse proportion to claimant's needs. The biggest societies attracted the 'best lives' (healthiest workers) and used their profits to extend the range of medical services available to their members. Conversely, the poorest societies were overburdened with recruits from unhealthy trades (for example mining and heavy industry) and could only offer the minimum statutory treatment to those who needed something better. The scheme did not cover the families of contributors, thus leaving working-class housewives without any access to state sponsored medical care. Further, substantial overlap and confusion existed between claimants to workmen's compensation, to war pensions and to health insurance; the societies were constantly complaining that they were liable for the maintenance of those who should properly have been the responsibility of other agencies. Finally sickness benefits were substantially lower than unemployment benefits; this, coupled with the absence of dependant's allowances meant that chronic cases were forced to top up on means-tested public assistance.

At the start of the war, the dislocation caused by the shift in manpower and the expansion of the armed services made it necessary to amend existing legislation governing contributory health insurance and pensions (PIN 3/59). The Beveridge Report sought to reform the system more permanently by separating the right to medical treatment from the issue of income maintenance (see chap 4 for the development of the National Health Service). Under the report's proposals, insurance was extended to the whole waged workforce. The same level of benefit was to be made available to all claimants, irrespective of the cause of their loss of wages, in an attempt to remove the difference between sickness benefit and workmen's compensation. Hence, under the National Insurance Act, dependants' allowances were introduced for those who claimed sickness benefit. The basic level of benefit for the unemployed and the sick was made the same, fixed at 3% above Rowntree's 1936 poverty level, and subject to a quinquennial review. Although the right to medical treatment under the National Health Service was no longer attached to any contributory record, it was commonly supposed that a proportion of the new national insurance contribution would go towards funding for the NHS. This was expected to cover 1/5 of the cost of the service, a figure greatly overestimated; by 1957 national insurance contributions provided just 1/17 of NHS funds (PREM 11/1805; see chap 4.4.3).

Under the new legislation, the approved society system was abolished. Beveridge himself had wanted to incorporate the friendly societies into the new scheme but to exclude the more commercially orientated industrial insurance companies (whom he accused of exploiting their position under the old scheme to promote the sales of their highly profitable life insurance policies to those who could not afford the premiums). In the event such a distinction proved impractical. In spite of their repeated protests (PIN 8/62; PIN 32/2) the friendly societies, the industrial insurance companies and the other approved societies were excluded as administrative agencies under the 1946 Act; all benefit payments were determined by the newly formed Ministry of National Insurance through its local offices. Advice on the transfer of services from the approved societies to the Ministry of National Insurance was given by an Advisory Committee on the Absorption of the Approved Societies (PIN 32/21; PIN 23/68-71). The consequences of abolition on the health services are dealt with elsewhere (see chap 4).

Following the passage of the postwar legislation, the new provisions operated without any unforeseen difficulties. On the whole, the level of claims and benefits remained well below the level predicted by the government actuary at the end of the war. Some controversy did arise over the connection between absenteeism and sickness benefit. The postwar labour shortage and need to implement compulsory overtime in a number of industries, so increasing cost, made employers more sensitive to the issue. This was particularly true of the coal industry where stocks were falling dangerously low. Whilst loss of output was blamed in part on the introduction of the five-day week and extended holiday provisions under the Miner's Charter, the growth in the level of absenteeism caused increasing concern. Sickness benefit, and in particular the method of doctors' certification, was mainly held to be responsible (COAL 26/166; PREM 8/1238). A Committee on Involuntary Absenteeism in the Coalmining Industry was appointed by the prime minister to look at the problem. It found, however, that whilst the change in the law relating to sickness benefit had increased the degree of absenteeism, in the vast majority of cases the absence from work was perfectly reasonable (POWE 37/86-88). This was supported by a report from the minister of labour in 1949 which found no connection between sickness benefit and absenteeism (CAB 128/15: 26 Nov 1949).

Records

Bill papers on the issue are at PIN 3/72, with two relevant Ministry of National Insurance files at PIN 19/95, 101. Planning files on disability benefit include PIN 8/101. Central staff discussions on sickness benefit are at PIN 8/11, with resolutions from friendly societies at PIN 8/62 and insurance companies at PIN 8/160. Other deputation files include PIN 8/88-100, 160.

Actuarial calculations on the likely cost of sickness benefits are at ACT 1/685, 700, 764-766.

Later discussions by the Reconstruction Committee* (1944) and the Social Services Committee* (1945-46) are at CAB 87/5, 9 and CAB 134/697-698. Other major files detailing the formation, passage and implementation of the National Insurance Act 1946 are described elsewhere (see chap 2.2 and chap 2.3.1).

Records referring to the provisions of the Industrial Assurance and Friendly Society Act, which clarified the position of the societies following the 1946 legislation, include T 233/980-981 and T 227/298. The transfer of approved society records and payments are detailed at PIN 23 and T 214/399; questions of staffing are dealt with in PIN 18/8, PIN 23/68, T 214/27, 158. Payment of benefit in the interim period is dealt with at PIN 32/15.

PIN 35 contains benefit files on problems arising out of the 1946 Act in relation to sickness benefit. National Insurance Commissioners' decisions on sickness benefit claims are at CT 5. PIN 39 contains the papers of the medical department of the Ministry of Health which include general medical advisory services and the control of sick absenteeism.

The main class of files dealing with the earlier National Health Insurance Scheme is PIN 4; further material can be found in ACT 1, MH 49, MH 62, MH 65, MH 81, PIN 2, and PIN 19. A complete list of approved societies is at PIN 32/15 and selected records of two societies 1912-1948 are in PIN 24.

* for committee references see Appendix B

2.3.3 Unemployment benefit

Unlike national health insurance, unemployment insurance had been subject to continual reassessment and modification throughout the interwar period. By 1939, state support for the unemployed was divided between two national agencies: the Unemployment Insurance Statutory Committee (UISC) and the Unemployment Assistance Board (UAB) (see chap 2.4). The former administered unemployment benefits, available as of right to those complying with the statutory requirements of the unemployment insurance acts. The latter, whose clients were the long-term unemployed, administered assistance whose level was determined according to the resources of the household in the much hated 'household means test'. Both schemes included dependants' allowances and both, like health insurance, were confined to workers earning less than £240 per annum. A few groups, including domestic servants, could not claim under the UISC because they were not identified as 'insured trades'.

Beveridge, who had himself chaired the UISC during the 1930s, recommended extensive alterations in the rate, coverage and duration of unemployment benefits in his 1942 report. The recommendation that all those in work should be covered by the scheme was eventually accepted, but the rate at which benefits should be paid was reduced below the subsistence minimum that Beveridge had wanted (see chap 2.2). One of the main objections to high benefits was that this would reduce the incentive to work. However, with the introduction of family allowances the problems of wage overlap became less pressing, allowing a more generous view of benefit levels.

Beveridge also proposed that the unemployed be given benefit for as long as they remained out of work. This, however, was to be conditional on availability for retraining, itself a radical new proposal. The financial, economic and social implications of this were serious. Hale and Gilbert, the Treasury officials responsible for social services expenditure argued that 'it is unquestionable that prolonged sickness or unemployment tends to produce a state of mind in which effort can only be made in response to a stimulus, and for this reason it has hitherto been thought necessary to put the long-term case into a position in which he has to ask for assistance if he really is unable to work' (T 161/1249/S53086/1; see also T 161/1448/S48497/013). This position was supported by a number of ministers on the wartime Committee on Reconstruction Priorities* (CAB 87/12). Under the Labour government, the issue again became a major area of disagreement. Pressure from the minister of national insurance to provide fifty-six week's benefit to the unemployed was strongly resisted by the chancellor and Ernest Bevin (CAB 134/698: 15 Jan 1946). At a Cabinet meeting in January 1946, Bevin proposed that the unemployed who had exhausted their claim to unemployment benefit should have recourse to local tribunals in an attempt to gain an extension of benefit (CAB 128/5: 17 Jan 1946). This was agreed at a follow up meeting (CAB 130/8). The 1946 Act therefore imposed a 6 month restriction on claims but allowed extensions of benefit to be given by local tribunals. Beveridge's idea of compulsory retraining was therefore dropped.

Married women workers were permitted to choose whether or not they wished to be covered by the National Insurance Act. Those who elected to stay within its provision paid a reduced contribution and received a lower rate of benefit (see chap 2.2). Similarly, the self-employed, such as shopkeepers and some categories of professional workers, were not covered for unemployment benefit. Around 1.5m fell within this group after the war. Special provisions were made for particular groups, notably shore fishermen and seamen (PIN 22), whose pattern of employment did not fit easily within the provisions of the scheme.

Most of the disqualifications pertaining to the interwar unemployment scheme were retained after 1946. Those who left voluntarily or who were deemed incapable of or unavailable for work, for example, were disqualified from claiming. Major debates arose around the issue of benefits for those unemployed because of industrial action, for those receiving training, and for workers who were sacked (PIN 7/309, 364; LAB 10/825). This was particularly relevant in 1947 considering the national fuel crisis and the possible laying off of workers (PREM 8/618). Adjudication on these and similar questions was determined by the National Insurance Advisory Committee* and the unemployed claimant could appeal through the tribunal procedure (see chap 2.3.1). The responsibility for the administration of unemployment benefits remained with the employment exchanges, which were run by the Ministry of Labour and National Service in co-operation with the Ministry of National Insurance.

As demand for labour remained high after the war, the scheme operated without any major difficulties. Indeed, thanks to the unexpectedly low level of unemployment (the government actuary had estimated 8.5% for the purposes of calculating the rate of contribution in 1940) the National Insurance Fund found itself with an embarrassingly large surplus by 1950 (see chap 2.3.1). Although inflation had by then caused national assistance rates to overtake national insurance benefits, the Treasury were wary of using this surplus for the benefit of short-term claimants, preferring instead to make changes in the provision for pensioners, and savings in the Exchequer contribution to the fund.

* for committee references see Appendix B

Records

Central staff discussions on unemployment benefit are at PIN 8/15. Government actuary calculations on unemployment benefit within the Beveridge scheme are at ACT 1/685. Later files are at ACT 1/762-768, 794-795.

A file relating to the cost of administering the scheme between 1946 and 1947 to calculate a charge on the national insurance fund is at PIN 18/48. T 227/9 contains a Treasury file on the position of the unemployment fund. Central Statistical Office unemployment statistics are at CAB 139/28-29.

Other major files outlining the formation, passage and implementation of the 1946 legislation are dealt with elsewhere (see chap 2.2 and 2.3.1).

Records on unemployment exchanges and unemployment insurance, including those of the UISC are in PIN 7. Decision books and case files pertaining to the Office of the Umpire until 1948 are in PIN 29. LAB 9 contains a number of files on the financial side of the pre-1948 unemployment insurance schemes. LAB 12 contains files on the administration of the scheme. LAB 9/148 looks at the relationship of the Ministries of Labour and National Insurance in the adjudication and payment of claims under the new scheme.

Papers of the Unemployment Insurance Statutory Committee are at PIN 7/212-221, 299, 182, with a Treasury file at T 227/9.

2.3.4 Widows' and retirement pensions

The earliest state pensions had been introduced in 1908 and 1925. The first act had provided a non-contributory old age pension to all claimants over the age of 70 whose income fell below a certain annual limit, with particular disallowances for specific types of annuity and friendly society benefit. The second act was contributory and provided pensions for widows, orphans and workers aged 65 to 70. The creators of the latter piece of legislation had hoped that the contributions so raised would eventually finance all state pensions—a hope crushed by the impact of the interwar recession on the scheme's income. Neither scheme made pensions conditional on retirement from the labour force.

The value of both types of pension was well below the subsistence level throughout the interwar period and pensioners had frequently to apply for means-tested supplementation from the public assistance committees of local government. One of the conditions of the Labour Party joining the coalition government in 1940 was the more generous payment of supplementary pensions by the Unemployment Assistance Board; and the name of the UAB was consequently changed to the Assistance Board (see chap 2.4). Another of the Labour Party's interwar policies was to make pensions conditional upon retirement. This idea had first been mooted at the start of the century and the purpose then, as in the 1930s, was to reduce competition for work in an overcrowded labour market. The retirement condition was one of the options reviewed by the Beveridge Committee* when it reviewed the whole field of social insurance (see chap 2.2).

In the event, the Beveridge Report recommended the payment of old age pensions at subsistence level conditional on the retirement of the applicant. These pensions were to be funded from the National Insurance Fund and so were to be phased in slowly over twenty years, allowing time for the fund to grow. During the period, Beveridge argued, means-tested supplementary pensions would have to continue in order to bridge the gap, with qualification based on the Determination of Needs Act (see chap 2.4).

The main area of controversy centred around the issue of pensions being conditional on retirement. In his report Beveridge argued that pensions should be paid at a higher level for those who continued beyond the minimum retirement age, 65 for men and 60 for women, hoping that elderly people would continue to work for as long as they were physically fit. This went against the opinions of the TUC, which had argued that retirement benefits should be used as a means of encouraging the elderly to leave the labour market, so creating work for younger people. Beveridge strongly opposed the view that the elderly should be kept out of the labour market (Harris 1977 p 394; CAB 87/77: 14 Jan 1942; CAB 87/79: 17 Apr 1942). In the context of the postwar labour shortage, especially amongst skilled and experienced workers, the Beveridge proposals had obvious appeal. They were therefore incorporated into the 1946 legislation and were reinforced by an earnings disregard for those continuing part-time work after retirement (CAB 134/697: 22 Nov 1945).

The 1944 White Paper *Social insurance* had called for the immediate payment of pensions from the start of the scheme, rather than phasing them in over twenty years as Beveridge had recommended. This move was widely criticized at the time, especially as other measures, such as family allowances, were set at lower rates than Beveridge had recommended. *The Times* argued that it seemed 'to reflect the fact that pensioners have votes while children have not' (Deacon 1983 p 45). Under pressure from its supporters (CAB 128/1: 16 Oct 1945) the Labour government decided to support this policy (CAB 134/697: 3 Sep 1945). Retirement pensions were therefore introduced immediately, in the winter of 1946 in advance of the rest of the National Insurance Act, so undermining the contributory principle of the scheme.

From the start, the pensions scheme proved to be the main problem for politicians and administrators alike, mainly because the elderly provided the main bulk of social security claimants in the postwar period. The rate of pension payments was therefore an important issue. The levels set under the 1946 legislation proved insufficient to withstand postwar inflation. As national assistance payments were adjusted regularly to the level of inflation, whilst national insurance payments were amended only every five years, the latter began to fall behind. Consequently after 1948 a high proportion of the elderly were resorting to means-tested supplementation to their pensions. This led to an increase in the pressure to raise the rate of contributory pensions.

By 1949 the Treasury was facing, as has been seen, a large surplus on the National Insurance Account. Further, contribution rates were due to be raised the following year in accordance with the provisions of the 1946 Act. Moves to use the surplus to avoid increasing contributions were resisted by the Treasury on the grounds of future financial commitments (CAB 128/17: 1 Oct 1951). Pressure for pension increases had been mounting towards the end of the decade as inflation began to bite. The National Federation of Old Age Pensioners, for example, were calling for a forty-shilling pension for all at 60 (PIN 46/14, 20). However this provided a major problem for the Treasury. Pensioners were the largest group of claimants and their number was likely to increase in the years to come. Rising life expectancy was seen as a major threat to the long-term viability of the whole insurance scheme. However the Treasury felt it impossible to resist some alleviation in favour of pensioners and a four-shilling increase was agreed (see chap 2.3.1).

Widows' allowances had been introduced in the 1925 Act. This had entitled the wives of insured contributors (the coverage was the same as for the health insurance scheme) to a low weekly pension on the death of the husband. Additional allowances were available for children. In the event of remarriage or cohabitation, the pension ceased. In addition the Ministry of Pensions provided widows' war pensions to those women who had lost husbands in the armed forces (see chap 2.7).

The Beveridge Report proposed widows' benefit for all payable at the same rate as maternity benefit (50% greater than unemployment benefit) for up to thirteen weeks, and guardian benefits for those with children. Under the 1946 National Insurance Act, three types of widows' benefit were introduced. All widows received a pension for three months after the death of their spouse. Thereafter this pension continued only for those women over 50 and for those mothers in charge of dependant children, and was subject to an earnings rule in these cases. Women with a claim to the old pensions but not to the new continued to claim as before. As was the case with retirement pensions, postwar inflation badly eroded the new benefits, and widows and their families became prominent among claimants for means tested national assistance in the late forties.

* for committee references see Appendix B

Records

The main files on retirement pensions arising out of the discussions on Beveridge are at PIN 8/117-119 and on widows' benefit at PIN 8/108-110. Central staff papers on widows' benefit are at PIN 8/26. PIN 8/64 contains correspondence and resolutions from old age pensioners' associations. Treasury files on widows' pension proposals include T 161/1448/S48497/05 and on retirement pensions T 161/1448/S48497/03. Actuarial calculations are at ACT 1/683, 697. Major files and classes on the formation, passage and implementation of the 1946 legislation are discussed elsewhere (see chap 2.2 and 2.3.1).

The main file series dealing with the administration of widows' and old age pensions after 1948 are in PIN 46. Records relating to the administration of all pension schemes mentioned in this section with specific reference to supplementation are in AST 7. Papers on the transfer from the old to the new scheme are at PIN 4/90.

Central Statistical Office papers relating to the payment of pensions are at CAB 141/69.

National Insurance Commissioners' decisions on retirement cases are at CT 3.

Files relating to schemes outside the national insurance provisions include MH 108 on the NHS superannuation scheme, T 227/329 on teachers' superannuation, and COAL 26/178-193 on miners' pensions.

Records relating to non-contributory old age pensions are at AST 15. Documents on the pre-war administration of contributory and non-contributory old age pensions and widows' and orphans' schemes are at PIN 4.

2.3.5   Miscellaneous benefits

The Beveridge Report also introduced a number of smaller scale proposals which, nevertheless, were an important part of the overall scheme.

A number of changes were proposed in the treatment of married women. On entering marriage the report considered the woman 'a new person, acquiring new rights and not carrying on into marriage claims to unemployment or disability benefit in respect of contributions made before marriage' (Cmd 6404 1943 p 131). Qualifications for pension rights were now accrued through the husband's payments. A number of measures were introduced to compensate the housewife for this loss of benefit, and to recognise her status as an important figure within the economy. A marriage grant was proposed paying £1 for every £40 contributed before marriage up to a £10 maximum. This was seen as desirable both from the point of view of compensation for loss of benefit rights and as a way of receiving prompt notification of marriage for national insurance and tax purposes.

The maternity benefit system was also improved. Under the old system, approved societies had been obliged to pay a lump sum on the birth of a child to the wife of a contributor, doubling the amount for a woman who was insured in her own right as well. The Beveridge Report proposed a maternity grant payable to all married women, whether gainfully employed or not. This would not cover the whole cost of maternity. In addition, for married women who were gainfully employed there was to be a maternity benefit given for a period of up to thirteen weeks on condition of giving up work. This was intended to 'make it easy and attractive for women to give up gainful occupation at the time of maternity'. This approach has subsequently been criticised. 'This proposed reward for maternity', Elizabeth Wilson has argued, for example, 'was of a piece with the moral basis for Beveridge's proposals for family allowances... Beveridge, that is, was a good imperialist, dismayed, as many had been before him, by the falling birthrate and therefore anxious to get women back into the home' (Wilson 1977 p 151).

To compensate for the loss of sickness benefit Beveridge proposed the provision of home helps for housewives in time of sickness in order to release them from their domestic duties and allow them to obtain appropriate medical attention. For women facing divorce, legal separation, desertion or voluntary separation, he proposed that benefit should be available where the circumstances arose through no fault of the woman concerned.

Very few of these proposals reached the statute book. The National Insurance Act 1946, influenced by international conventions about the conditions of work for married women, did introduce a maternity allowance which was designed to enable women to give up work well before they were due to be confined. It also provided an attendance allowance for four weeks for women who could not claim maternity allowance. However the remainder of the scheme withered away. The provision of domestic help to cover sickness was successfully resisted by the Treasury on financial grounds. The policy of payment of benefits to divorced or separated women was seen as 'subsidizing sin' (see chap 2.2).

Beveridge's proposals on unemployment benefit included a strong emphasis on retraining. He proposed, for example, that unemployment benefit should be payable subject to compulsory retraining (see chap 2.2). He therefore proposed a training benefit, payable to those not eligible for unemployment benefit, at the same rate as the latter, and to include a dependant's allowance, up to a maximum of twenty-six weeks, to encourage retraining and provide help in finding employment. However moves to limit the duration of unemployment benefit led to the dropping of compulsory training proposals during the post-Beveridge Report discussions.

The provision of a death grant was a major innovation designed to help the poorest sectors of the community avoid the disgrace normally associated with a pauper funeral. Payment was based upon contributions by the deceased, their father or widowed mother, or husband. Whilst originally intended to cover all the costs involved, the impact of inflation in the postwar period eroded the value of the provision fairly quickly and made it necessary for an increasing number of claimants to turn to the Assistance Board for help (AST 7/840).

Records

Actuarial calculations for Beveridge on the death grant are at ACT 1/685, with a wartime planning file at PIN 8/155. A wartime Treasury file on the subject is at T 161/1448/S48497/04. The National Insurance Bill papers on the death grant are at PIN 3/73. Records relating to the administration of the grant are at PIN 37.

Wartime planning files on the maternity benefit are at PIN 8/127-128. Actuarial calculations for the National Insurance Bill are at ACT 1/764-766. Files on the provision of the benefit are at PIN 52. A review of the scheme between 1948 and 1952 is at PIN 19/40. Papers arising out of the National Insurance Advisory Committee report on maternity benefit are at PIN 60/63.

2.4   National assistance

Traditionally, the relief of destitution had been the responsibility of the Poor Law. By the outbreak of the Second World War, however, this function had passed to other agencies. The long-term unemployed (see chap 2.3.3) could claim relief from the Unemployment Assistance Board (UAB), under the household means test. For those not active in the labour market—the old, the very young, the sick, or the disabled—recourse had to be made to the local public assistance committee of the relevant local authority, which administered what remained of the old system of outdoor relief, also on a means-tested basis.

With the advent of war, the administration of this type of assistance underwent a change. The emergency enlarged the UAB's clientele because claimants whose destitution was primarily the result of wartime conditions, were forced to turn to the state for help. At the outset of the war, the Board became responsible for the administration of the Prevention and Relief of Distress Scheme (PRD). This was designed to cover those who were in need because of the war, and who would otherwise be forced to apply for public assistance. It allowed the UAB to provide assistance to groups like evacuees (AST 11/29-64) and those who had lost their livelihood but had no recourse to unemployment benefit. The Board could also give immediate grants to people whose homes had been damaged by enemy action.

In 1939 the UAB was charged with the assessment and the provision of emergency relief to those civilians injured by bomb attacks, as an agency of the Ministry of Pensions under the Personal Injuries (Civilian) Scheme (see chap 2.7). It also became responsible for the advance payment of compensation for war damage, as agent for the Treasury, although this was restricted to cover replacements for business tools, essential clothing and furniture.

In 1940 the passing of the Old Age and Widows' Pension Bill led to the UAB changing its name to the Assistance Board (AB) and to its responsibility for the administration of a nationally funded income supplement for those on fixed incomes whose resources were being depleted by wartime inflation. This followed a 1939 enquiry into old age pensions, which had concluded that supplementation was essential if the viability of the insurance schemes was to be maintained (ACT 1/467-477). The Treasury argued that any person requiring assistance could already resort to the Poor Law, and that the lack of applicants showed that the level of existing benefits was satisfactory. The chancellor of the Exchequer, Sir John Simon, however, was proved to be very mistaken when he said that 'it is difficult to believe that there are still any very large number who prefer destitution to the alleged indignity of applying for public assistance' (CAB 67/4: WP (G)(40)5). The number of claimants under the new provisions, particularly from people in receipt of widows' pensions, old age pensions and workmen's compensation, was far higher than expected and illustrated the degree of stigma attached to the old public assistance system (AST 7/451).

The Old Age and Widows' Pension Act 1940 included a provision that the Board should conduct its administration 'in such a manner as may best promote the interest of pensioners'. In the autumn of 1941 the Board launched an investigation into the circumstances of pensioners and particularly into the proportion who were infirm or living alone (AST 12/13). The Board increasingly came to see itself as the champion of the pensioners' interests. In 1942 it launched a major enquiry into clothing needs, visiting all those living solely on a pension and making additional grants. It also began to develop its own 'Welfare Service', through public assistance committees. This included daily visits to pensioners considered to be isolated (AST 7/710). It also referred pensioners to other agencies providing appropriate services, and became increasingly involved in the provision of old people's homes, home helps and meals on wheels (AST 7/627, 634, 663, 664, 750, 756, 781; see chap 6.4).

A key condition for the Labour Party joining the 1940 coalition government was the abolition of the household means test. Many of Labour's leading figures had been prominent in the campaign against it in the 1930s. This was particularly true of Ernest Bevin who had then been general secretary of the Transport and General Workers Union. On top of this, the expansion of services required a major reassessment of the way these cases were judged. Under the Determination of Needs Act (1941) the household means test was abandoned and a more generous system introduced. This abolished the concept of the 'liable relative', which in certain cases had given children the statutory obligation to help their parents, and based the means test solely on the resources of the applicant and spouse, a principle which continued in the postwar years.

By the end of the war, therefore, the new Board had acquired a range of additional duties. By 1945, there were 1.5 million supplementary pensioners, representing a quarter of all people over pensionable age. It had also become an agent for a number of departments in assessing means and providing local administrative services. It acted as local agent for the Ministry of Pensions in assessing dependants' allowances, for example, and the Ministry of National Insurance in assessing claims to benefit at the local level (AST 11/122-157).

The Beveridge Report, basing its recommendations on the idea that state benefit should be available as of right, reflected the distaste with which the means test was popularly regarded during the 1930s. This was reinforced by the experiences of many people in the Second World War when poverty became seen less as a personal failing and more as a consequence of external circumstances. The continuation of means testing, therefore, came to be bitterly resented (Deacon 1983 p 31; Harris 1977 pp 381-382). The Beveridge Report envisaged an ever decreasing role for means-tested benefits in the postwar period, with the exception of short-term old age pensions. Its popularity can be partly ascribed to this.

This popular conception was not, however, shared by all. In particular a large percentage of Tory MPs argued that the payment of subsistence benefits, as Beveridge had recommended, would undermine work incentives and prove costly (chap 2.2), and called instead for some degree of means testing. This was supported by the Phillips Committee*, which argued that subsistence varied from area to area and so could not be provided by a flat-rate national benefit.

The 1944 White Paper, *Social insurance* (Cmd 6550 1944), contained major departures from Beveridge's idea of subsistence and accepted the need for means testing. Benefit was to provide a 'reasonable insurance against want' whilst taking account of the 'maximum contribution which the great body of contributors can properly be asked to bear'. The 1946 National Insurance Act gave, in the words of the minister of national insurance, 'a broad subsistence basis to the leading rates'. However these rates proved to be well below subsistence level and necessitated recourse by many people to means-tested benefit (see below).

The failure to implement Beveridge's subsistence principle was based on two factors. Firstly, the level of rent varied considerably from area to area making it difficult to establish a set definition of subsistence. More important, however, was the fact that the scheme was financed by flat rate contributions and had to be affordable to the lowest paid worker. The government therefore argued that the rate required to pay subsistence benefits would be politically unacceptable. It was further unwilling to pass on the cost to the Exchequer or industry (Deacon 1982 p 290).

In 1948 the National Assistance Act was passed. This abolished the final remnants of the Poor Law, transferring responsibility for public assistance claimants to the new National Assistance Board, thereby uniting the various branches of what had hitherto been known as 'outdoor relief', unemployment and public assistance. Local authorities, therefore, lost their responsibility for Poor Law administration, although in practice reception centres for vagrants continued to be run by local authorities who acted as agents for the Board. Another important area of local authority responsibility was nationalized under the postwar legislation. The NAB inherited responsibility for those disabled whose condition was attributable neither to industrial injury nor to the consequences of war (AST 7/85; see chap 2.6 and 2.7). The new board also took on more new agency roles. Thus under the 1949 Legal Aid and Advice Act the NAB became responsible for investigating the financial position of claimants (AST 2; AST 20).

Considering the level of debate surrounding the means test of the 1930s, its continuation in the form of the 1948 legislation proved remarkably uncontentious. After the war it was no longer seen as a gauge of poverty and shame by many policy makers but, instead, as a supplement to existing benefit; a supplementary system which had worked well in relation to pensions. Consequently there was little opposition to the proposals from either side of the House of Commons (Deacon 1982 p 302). Nevertheless, in the public's mind the shadow of the Poor Law remained and the take-up of means-tested benefit remained a long-term problem.

As National Insurance benefits were fixed by statute and the cost of living continued to rise, an ever increasing number of claimants 'topped up' their income under the national assistance scheme. In 1947, for example, 4% of unemployment benefit was supplemented, in 1948 this had risen to 7%, by July 1949 10% and by early 1950 to more than 10% (PIN 17/322: 19 Jan 1950). By 1949 national assistance scales were higher than statutory insurance benefit levels; as a result long-term claimants to state benefit, notably pensioners, were reverting habitually to the NAB. This led many, including the lord president, to conclude that the Determination of Needs Act should be reconsidered and that applicants for assistance from well-to-do households should be disqualified (CAB 130/20: 20 Oct 1947). However, national assistance was considered to be less of a burden to public finances than the universal raising of benefits in line with the cost of living. This guaranteed means-tested assistance would continue to play a major role in the British social security system.

Records

The main series of files referring to the activities of the UAB and its successors can be found at AST 7. The main public assistance files which refer to vagrancy, poor law relief and related matters, including the formation and operation of the National Assistance Act 1948, are at MH 57.

Bill papers of the 1948 legislation are at MH 80/47-52. Assistance Board papers relating to the Bill are at AST 7/921. Lord President's Committee reports on the Bill are at CAB 21/1712. Treasury papers are at T 227/12. The Bill was prepared by the Committee for the Breakup of the Poor Law*. Files relating to the Bill and its effects on public assistance are at MH 57/426-446.

Bill papers relating to the Old Age and Widows' Pension Act 1940 are at PIN 3/57-58. Departmental papers relating to the Bill include Board of Customs and Excise papers on the arrangement for the payment of supplementary pensions at AST 15/135-136,146; government actuary papers at ACT 1/667-668; Ministry of Health files at MH 57/218, 387, 391, 396, PIN 23/179 and PIN 19/35; Ministry of Labour papers include LAB 9/46, LAB 16/29, LAB 17/137; Ministry of Pensions files are at PIN 15/2187-2189; Unemployment Assistance Board papers include AST 7/418, 444, 448, 457-460, 526, 591, and those at AST 30. AST 15 deals with the Board's role in supplementary pensions. Treasury files on the subject include T 161/994/S45029/1-3; T 161/995/S45029/4-7; T 161/999/S46053/1-2; T 161/1002/S47149/1; T 161/1420/S46112/5-7. Papers relating to non-contributory pensions after the war include T 227/14; T 161/1250/S53086/023/1; CAB 124/941; AST 7/784; and PIN 32/11.

Unemployment Assistance Board papers relating to the Determination of Needs Act 1941 include Bill papers at AST 7/454, 470, 530, with implementation files at AST 7/591, 714, 552, and AST 11/145. Ministry of Health files include MH 57/402, 413-414. Post Office papers on the effect of the Act on holders of National Savings Certificates include NSC 11/315, 470, and NSC 21/185-197. Registry of Friendly Societies papers on the bill include FS 23/166. A Lord President's Secretariat file on the means test is at CAB 123/10, with Treasury files on the Bill at T 161/1135/S51016/1-2.

Establishment files of the UAB and its successors are at AST 9. Minutes of meetings, annual reports and local reports are at AST 12. AST 13 contains instructions and circulars to local offices. Case papers and applications for allowances to the NAB are at AST 1. A UAB blue note for 1939 is at T 160/F6139/0152 and for the NAB at T 165/290. Files on the Board's role in implementing the 1948 legislation are at MH 57/447-478.

Files relating to the administration of wartime functions are in AST 11, with related papers at AST 14. Assistance Board financial estimates for 1940-41 are at T 160/1024/F13852/41. War damage payments are detailed at AST 11/158-217, with an official history at CAB 102/736. Board involvement in Polish resettlement is detailed at AST 7/953, with a few further files in AST 18. Refugees in general are dealt with at AST 11/65-103. Preparations for the war emergency include LAB 25/37.

* for committee references see Appendix B

2.5   Family allowances

The idea of family endowment in the form of a public subsidy to families with children had been under consideration in policy-making circles since the First World War. The idea was perceived as a cure for a variety of ills. By eliminating poverty amongst large families it appealed to the pro-natalist lobby concerned with Britain's 'falling population' at a time when population growth was seen as 'vital to our future as a nation' (T 171/363: 12 Aug 1942). Social welfare groups were also in support, especially as the level of child poverty had been shown to be surprisingly high in a number of surveys carried out in preparation for wartime evacuation (CAB 89/12). Its universal coverage also enabled the income gap between those in work and the unemployed to be maintained, thereby safeguarding work incentives whilst minimizing risks to family health.

In the early 1940s, wartime conditions caused the issue to assume increased significance as one means by which pressure on wages might be eased as prices began to rise. In *How to pay for the war* (1940) Keynes argued the case for progressive taxation and strict price and wage control. However this raised the problem of the income of large families for, if wages were fixed high enough to meet their needs, the results would be inflationary. Family allowances were a way of overcoming these difficulties. A survey of economic and financial plans, carried out by Lord Stamp, supported this, arguing that family allowances would buy off the pressure for wage increases (CAB 89/22-23). At this stage a number of Treasury officials proved undecided about the scheme, arguing that 'any proposal must be judged by one criterion alone, namely whether it will help win the war. In relation to family allowances this means that if their effect would be, on balance, deflationary they should be adopted, if inflationary they should not be adopted' (T 161/S43697/1: April 1940).

In June 1941 an all party deputation of MPs submitted a memorandum to the chancellor of the Exchequer asking for an investigation into the introduction of a scheme of family allowances (PIN 8/163; T 161/1116/S43697/2), after a Commons motion welcoming a national scheme received 152 MPs' signatures. The investigation was carried out by Hale at the Treasury (T 161/1073/S43697/02/1) and led to the publication of a government White Paper by the chancellor of the Exchequer (Cmd 6354 1942).

The publication of the paper, however, opened up a number of major problems which were to delay the passing of legislation until 1945. For a number of Labour ministers, the White Paper did not go far enough in providing a clear statement of what such a scheme would entail. Debate now centred around three major issues: first, whether the new benefit should be universal or selective. Central to this debate was the question of cost. Many in the Treasury believed that the scheme should be limited in eligibility, arguing that the low paid labourer with the large family was an exception and so universal payment was financially wasteful (T 161/1116/S43697/1). Others like the chancellor supported a universal flat rate system but argued any scheme should be put off until the end of the war (CAB 71/9: 29 May 1942). The second debate centred around whether the scheme should be contributory or non-contributory. The Conservatives favoured contributions, whilst the Labour Party and the TUC were only prepared to support a universal non-contributory scheme. Thirdly, strong arguments were put forward for provision in kind rather than cash payments, particularly in the form of milk and school meals. One Treasury official argued that cash payments to households would simply increase 'their expenditure in beer and tobacco', and that 'the only effective way of securing [healthy children] will be direct provision through the school without the intervention of the parent at all' (T 161/1116/S43697/3). This was reinforced with the support of the farmers' lobby, and the Board of Education which saw in these proposals the opportunity to safeguard the school meals service after the war (T 161/1073/S43697/02/1; PIN 8/116: 11 Dec 1942; see chap 5.3.5.1). The provision of welfare foods to mothers and young children through the Ministry of Food's scheme further strengthened this argument (MH 57/377).

In December 1942, the Beveridge Report insisted on family allowances as one of its assumed conditions for the existence of a social insurance system. Allowances were to be non-contributory, universal and graduated by age. Beveridge estimated nine shillings would be needed per child, minus one shilling covered by school meals and milk, leaving eight shillings payment. The first child of each family was excluded from the scheme, partly in response to Treasury concern about cost. The provision of benefit was further eroded when the Phillips Committee* recommended a five shilling rate. In February 1943 the chancellor announced the government's intention to introduce family allowances. He denied the lower rates were a consequence of financial cutbacks and argued the case for payments in kind.

A final major disagreement occurred over whether payment should be to the father or to the mother (PIN 17/4). The White Paper had proposed payments to the father. This was supported by the Home Office, which argued that payment must always be to the legal custodian (HO 45/20674) and by some Treasury officials, one of whom argued that 'it would be interesting to know whether a mother who squandered the allowances in dress or drink could be prosecuted for failure to apply them to the benefit of children. I should imagine not, as the primary responsibility must continue to rest on the father and his wages. It always seemed to me that this was a point on which sentiment was dangerous' (T 161/1165/S49497/026; 18 Jan 1944). A number of women's organizations, on the other hand, were in favour of payment to the mother both as the best means of reaching children and in recognizing the economic rights of women (PIN 8/7, 65-66). The position of other organizations was more ambiguous. The TUC in general favoured payment to mothers but the Ministry of Labour, normally sensitive to TUC opinion, favoured payment to the father as legal guardian (PIN 8/7; PIN 17/2; MacNichol 1980 pp 192, 210). Finally, the War Cabinet decided that, because of the political and public strength of feeling, the only solution was a House of Commons free vote on the issue (CAB 65/49: 6 Mar 1945). The Family Allowances Act reached the statute book in June 1945. Saved from the means test and, eventually, safeguarded for the housewife, it was to be the final achievement of the Caretaker government.

The scheme was inaugurated in August 1946 and covered all children in each family except the first, at a flat rate below the level originally prescribed by Beveridge. The scheme pre-dated the full introduction of the new scheme of social insurance and so provoked a number of problems at the local level, especially in relation to other benefits (PIN 19/62, 86; T 161/1248/S52494/06). A number of local Assistance Board offices, for example, were found to be decreasing supplementary allowances in direct proportion to the new family allowance (AST 7/817; MH 57/418-420). In relation to residential special schools, parents were still claiming family allowances for children who did not live at home, encouraged by the education authorities who wanted to maintain parental responsibility (ED 31/631). Problems also occurred over checking the status of children. Schools were resistant to extra work being placed upon their teachers in verifying the attendance of individual children (ED 147/424).

By the late 1940s, there was a growing concern over the rate at which the allowance was being paid. Owing to the devaluation of the pound, moreover, the agreement between government and the TUC on wages was coming under increasing pressure as inflation rose. Raising family allowances appeared to offer an alternative solution. The Royal Commission on Population, reporting in 1949, recommended that the scheme should include the eldest child, and that the allowance be increased for older children, made payable from confirmation of pregnancy and exempt from taxation. Although these proposals were given serious consideration by the minister of national insurance (PIN 17/55; PIN 18/49; PIN 36/77), their overall cost was exorbitant and this undermined their appeal. In any case, a high postwar birth rate rendered pro-natalist arguments inappropriate. Family allowances were raised within the existing structure in 1951 (T 227/237-239). However, pressure to remedy the situation and to clarify early anomalies did not generate fresh legislation until 1952, after the return of the Conservative Party to power.

Records

Papers of the Ministry of National Insurance and its predecessors relating to the general proposals on family allowances and their transformation into legislative form are at PIN 17. Bill papers are at PIN 3/63, 65 and PIN 17/69-72. Further papers include PIN 19/7,12. Papers on the overpayment of allowances are at PIN 18/38.

Treasury files on the issue are at T 161/1073/S43697/02/1-2 and T 161/1248/S52494/1-3. Agriculture and Food Division papers relating to family allowances and payment in kind are at T 223/15. Actuarial calculations on the cost of the scheme are at ACT 1/664-665.

The Prime Minister's Office files include PREM 1/438 and PREM 4/89/7. Lord President's Secretariat papers are at CAB 123/47. The question of family allowances as part of the Beveridge Scheme came under the scrutiny of the Phillips Committee* and the central staff of the Committee on Reconstruction Problems* (PIN 8/16, 68, 132, 163).

Other departmental contributions to the debate include general wartime planning files of the Ministry of Health (MH 79/525) and the Assistance Board (AST 7/390). The issue of school meals and milk in relation to family allowances is discussed in a chapter of E.K. Ferguson's official war history, *The nutrition of the school child*, at CAB 102/245. Board of Education files include ED 136/370-375, ED 50/402, and ED 31/545, 631. A Ministry of Food file on the subject is at MAF 101/530 and interdepartmental meetings on the subject are recorded at PIN 18/12. Home Office discussions on the payment of allowances to children in institutions are at MH 102/1303-1313, 1621, with other papers at HO 45/20674. Lord Chancellor's Office papers on the Act are at LCO 2/3084. Ministry of Pensions files on their own child allowance scheme for children of men in the armed forces and its relation to the new general scheme are at PIN 15/2749-2750, 2755, 2993, 3362, 4019. Admiralty files include ADM 1/19065, with Air Ministry papers at AIR 2/9286. General Register Office papers are at RG 41/40.

Administration of the scheme was centred at the Ministry's offices at Newcastle upon Tyne; the relevant file series is PIN 36. Treasury staffing files for the administration of the scheme are at T 214/29. National Insurance Commissioners' decisions on family allowance claims are at CT 6. Publicity for the scheme is at BN 10/7.

* for committee references see Appendix B

2.6   Industrial injuries and diseases

The basic pre-war system for helping workers incapacitated by an industrial accident or a specified industrial disease dated back to the late nineteenth century. Under the Workmen's Compensation Acts, an employer was obliged to pay financial compensation to any employee whose inability to work was due either to an accident at work, for which the workman himself was not responsible, or to his having contracted an illness which was legally judged to have been caused by the nature of his employment. Compensation might be in the form of a lump sum, or a weekly payment lasting until recovery was complete. The amount of cash was determined in relation to previous earnings; all obligations ceased when the worker was deemed fit enough to work, even if he was permanently prevented from following a previous occupation. Government responsibility for the scheme rested with the Home Office.

The system was far from popular and it was criticized particularly by the trade union movement which became heavily involved in promoting its reform. As the whole scheme operated through the courts (damage to workers' labour power being regarded in much the same way as damage to private property), gaining compensation was a time consuming, costly and complicated business. Trade unions themselves were much involved in fighting cases on their members' behalf; indeed without considerable private means it was not possible for a worker to fight a case without such support. Although not demanded by legislation, most employers insured themselves privately against the risk of court action. Hence unions found themselves pitted against the considerable resources of the industrial insurance companies, which had strong commercial reasons for limiting their liability and engaged the best medical experts to ensure that their interests were served.

Following the report of the Stewart Committee in 1938 (Cmd 5657) entitled *Certain questions arising under the Workmen's Compensation Acts*, a royal commission, under Sir Hector Hetherington, was set up to look at these issues. However, the problem proved to be a complicated one. Approved societies were eager for reform as workers deprived of their rightful compensation claimed from them under the National Health Insurance Scheme. The same was true of the Public Assistance Committees. However, the government were nervous about enforcing employers' liability in this area too strictly for fear of the implications for insurance premiums and industrial costs. Employers were able to claim that the outbreak of war meant that they were unable to prepare evidence properly and in July 1940 the commission's investigation was ended. Its minutes of evidence were published during the course of the proceedings, but its winding up report was not issued until 1945 (Cmd 6588). The government was able to argue that the appointment of the Beveridge Committee* was an illustration of its continuing commitment to reform.

The Beveridge Report sought to unravel the knot by transferring responsibility for compensation from the individual employer to the state. It argued that the causes of physical disability were irrelevant, and that workmen's needs were the same whether earnings were interrupted through industrial injury or some other form of accident. It was strongly opposed to lump sum payments and critical of the continuous legal procedure (CAB 87/76: 11 Dec 1941). Under the new scheme, compensation was to become part of the general social insurance programme; a worker's right to help was secured by his being an insured contributor. He was to be entitled only to a flat rate benefit in line with all other social insurance claimants.

This solution, not surprisingly, was opposed by the commercial and mutual insurance interests whose position would be undermined. Strong opposition came also from the TUC. Earnings related compensation, which could be as high as forty-eight shillings a week, was to be reduced to subsistence level (CAB 87/77: 14 Jan 1942). Further, the TUC believed it unjust that workers should pay contributions to cover employer's negligence and felt that the punishment aspect of the compensation would be lost, leading to more accidents (CAB 87/77: 11 Mar 1943). At the other end of the scale, officials within the Treasury were questioning the need for industrial injury payments at all. Gilbert, for example, argued that to pay compensation in work and not outside it would lead to ludicrous consequences. He argued workmen's compensation should be abolished and classed as sickness (T 161/1164/S48497/2: 2 Apr 1943).

As a result of this opposition, the proposals for the reform of the compensation scheme became detached from the rest of the social insurance programme and eventually reached the statute book as a separate act. Differences over the scheme became polarized over whether payments should be based on loss of earnings or severity of injury. The TUC continued to press for higher rates of payment and compensation based on loss of earnings (PREM 8/291; PIN 8/72; PIN 21/68). This was opposed by the Ministry of Pensions whose war pensions compensation scheme was based on severity of injury, which might lead to potentially embarrassing comparisons (CAB 134/697: 1 Oct 1945; see chap 2.7). This view was shared by the Treasury who wanted benefit linked directly to contributions (T 161/1248/S52183/3), and by the British Employers' Confederation who 'understood and sympathized with the worker's desire for security but [were] alarmed at the increase in benefit. It was doubtful whether a Bill conferring such high benefits could be carried by the country without economic disaster' (PIN 21/1: 31 Aug 1945).

From 1943 a Workmen's Compensation Advisory Committee assisted in the shaping of the scheme of compensation. This was followed by a White Paper on the subject, drafted by the home secretary and considered by a Workmen's Compensation Subcommittee of the Reconstruction Committee*. In response to union pressure, flat rate benefits, payable for the first thirteen weeks of industrial injury, were set at forty-five shillings a week, compared with just twenty-six shillings for sickness and unemployment benefits (CAB 134/697: 8 Oct 1943). However, the TUC lost its battle to get long-term disability benefits based on previous earnings. The National Insurance (Industrial Injuries) Act 1946 based long-term benefit on the medically assessed severity of injury, and created an administrative structure to operate the scheme along these lines.

In April 1947 a medical department was set up in the Ministry of National Insurance to deal with medical questions arising from the provisions of the National Insurance and National Insurance (Industrial Injuries) Acts. These included the diagnosis of prescribed diseases and the assessment of disablement claims for industrial benefit. At the local level, assessment of disability was carried out by medical boards, with appeals heard by medical tribunals, all working under the direction of the Ministry of National Insurance. An Interdepartmental Committee on Assessment of Disablement due to Specified Injuries considered these issues during 1946 (PIN 15/2734-2736, 2989; PIN 21/75-76).

Arising out of the need to classify the severity of injury, central government started more extensive investigations into the provenance and nature of specific diseases to determine the degree of disability involved and their association with particular trades and industries through the Departmental Committee on Industrial Disease (PIN 20/5, 9, 11-18, 22-23, 30-31, 43). This followed pressure from the BMA which argued that the distinction between industrial injuries and diseases was archaic (PIN 21/20).

Although the new legislation transferred responsibility for the compensation of injuries as Beveridge had intended, this did not automatically overcome some of the difficulties associated with the earlier legislation. Instead of arguing cases with the industrial insurance companies, the trade unions found themselves going through the same procedure with the state, which had its own reasons for wishing to contain claims made under the new Act.

Records

The main policy files relating to industrial injury proposals arising out of the Beveridge Committee* are at PIN 8. Miscellaneous papers of the committee referring specifically to industrial injury are at PIN 21/65. PIN 21/67 contains papers relating to the White Paper. The Bill papers of the National Insurance (Industrial Injuries) Act 1946 are at PIN 3/66-68, 126-130. PIN 21/8-17 contain correspondence on drafting the Bill.

Treasury files relating to the White Paper and the Bill are at T 161/1247/S52183/1-2 and T 161/1249/S52183/4-6. Actuarial calculations for the Beveridge Committee* on industrial injury benefit are at ACT 1/681-682, and on the Bill at ACT 1/769-779 and PIN 18/23. Treasury papers on industrial disease include T 248/291.

The Prime Minister's Office files on the White Paper are at PREM 4/89/5, and PREM 4/89/8 relates to the Bill. Lord President's Secretariat files include CAB 123/243 on the Beveridge proposals and CAB 123/47 on the Bill.

Other departments' files include a Ministry of Pensions file on the Bill at PIN 15/2391, with implementation papers at PIN 15/2869-2870. Board of Trade concerns about the effect of the Bill on their compensation scheme are in BT 15/288/F1863/48. Coal industry files are at COAL 26/131-132, 139-140. Lord Chancellor's Office papers on the White

Paper are at LCO 2/3776; those on the Act are at LCO 2/3053-3057, 4252-4256, 5510, 6223-6225. Files dealing with workmen's compensation before the Act are at LCO 2/4242-4251. LAB 18/239 deals with the implementation of the Act in relation to training and rehabilitation. Papers of the Board of the Inland Revenue on the Act are at IR 40/13380, with Board of Trade workmen's compensation cases at BT 15/288. A Colonial Office file is at CO 859/149/2, and Ministry of Education papers at ED 31/622.

Papers of the Workmen's Compensation Advisory Committee are at PIN 8/18, PIN 21/66, and T 161/1247/S52183/1. Papers of the subcommittee on Workmen's Compensation are at CAB 87/11 and PIN 8/21.

A Departmental Committee on Alternative Remedies looked at the effect of the Act on payment for personal injury caused by negligence. Its papers are at PIN 12/85,101; PIN 21/48; PIN 15/3363; CAB 128/6; T 227/10; AST 7/891; LCO 2/3775, 3777-3780.

Ministry of National Insurance files on the drafting and administration of the Act are in PIN 20 and PIN 21; PIN 20 refers specifically to industrial diseases; other files on this area can be found at PIN 12/90-98 and COAL 26/153-157. PIN 32 relates to problems arising directly out of implementation. The papers of the medical section of the Ministry of National Insurance are at PIN 39. Records of the medical boards and tribunals are at PIN 44. PIN 21/116-124 contains files of the Medical Appeals Tribunal. National Insurance Commissioners' files on industrial injury are at CT 4. Early records on the operation of workmen's compensation are at PIN 12. Problems of administration of the various wartime schemes of compensation are documented at PIN 18. Pre-1946 Bill papers and proposals for reform are in PIN 11 and HO 45.

Papers relating to the Royal Commission on Workmen's Compensation are at PIN 12/105, PIN 7/178, T 161/1036/S43363, PIN 15/3073, and MH 58/312.

* for committee references see Appendix B

2.7   War pensions and allowances

During the First World War, the scale of the conflict and the introduction of military conscription led to the development of a comprehensive system of separation allowances and war pensions, which were payable to the incapacitated and to families of the deceased, administered by a new Ministry of Pensions. With the advent of the Second World War, these responsibilities were taken over by the Ministry of War Transport. The Ministry of Pensions now became responsible for Second World War death and disability pensions and allowances. Whilst these remained outside the wartime consideration of postwar social services, their existence had important effects on discussions on future welfare services. In particular this was true of family allowances (see chap 2.5) and widows' pensions (see chap 2.3.4).

War pensions had a past record of influencing the shape of wider social planning. The comparatively generous nature of the First World War scheme had encouraged the introduction of the first civilian contributory pension scheme for widows and orphans in 1925; it had been difficult to justify the different treatment of families in similar circumstances simply on the basis of cause of death of the bread winner. This was again true in the Second World War.

The establishment of the Personal Injuries (Civilian) Scheme in 1939 had its origins in the difficulties foreseen if men or women were injured or killed whilst working for the war effort in factories or workshops. Although it was essential that factories should continue production despite enemy action, it was considered inappropriate to ask employers to compensate through the workmen's compensation acts for any resulting injury. Under the scheme, therefore, payment of workmen's compensation was forbidden in those cases of injury caused by enemy action. Instead, government payments were made through the Ministry of Pensions, based on severity of injury rather than on loss of income and, as such, set important precedents for the future of compensation for industrial injuries. Attempts made to secure equal compensation for men and women under the scheme were strongly resisted by the Ministry of Pensions. Such a move would have established a precedent which could have led to similar pressure on war pensions (CAB 71/10: 17 Sept 1942).

The payment of separation allowances also had important consequences for civil provision. The system of separation payments was introduced in the First World War and developed further during the Second. The wives of all men in the armed forces received a marriage allowance together with an allowance for each dependant child. The rate of contribution and benefit varied according to rank. It has been argued that the existence of this benefit had important consequences for family allowances. The arrival of American GIs in 1942 drew public attention to the poor pay and conditions of many men in the armed forces and led to a national campaign, organized through the press, for their improvement. At a time when it was considered that taxation had reached its limit, increases in separation allowance for servicemen were given priority over the implementation of a general scheme of family allowances (Land 1975 pp 179-216).

The Ministry of Pensions also developed a number of wartime welfare schemes which were to influence greatly the development of civil schemes. Welfare provisions for the war disabled and their families, and for widows and their dependants, continued after the war. Welfare officers were appointed in 1948 to all the main Ministry of Pensions offices, and at hospitals administered by the Pensions Department. The Ministry was also responsible for children orphaned through the war. The role of the welfare officer was to act as a guide to existing statutory and voluntary services and to direct Ministry services where appropriate. Particular attention was given to the rehabilitation and resettlement of the disabled. Many of the services overlapped with civil services and were therefore included in postwar planning discussions (PIN 8/146; PIN 32/50; T 161/1448/S48497/020). Help for the disabled, for example, was divided between the Ministry of Pensions (PIN 38; PIN 15/2863, 3157-3179, 3963), the Ministry of National Insurance and the Assistance Board. The care of orphaned children was the responsibility of the Ministry of Pensions, the Home Office and the Ministry of Education. This division was the subject of the discussions of the Curtis Committee on the Care of Children* (see chap 6).

The Beveridge Committee recommended disentangling the services by proposing the absorption of the Ministry of Pensions into a new Ministry of Social Insurance. War pensions were not considered as part of the overall scheme of social security, but as a 'temporary provision'. These arrangements were for administrative convenience.

In 1948 the Ministry lost its control of the supply of artificial limbs, surgical appliances and invalid carriages and instead acted as an agency for the newly created NHS. A complete transfer of these services was effected in 1953. Other health functions were transferred to the Ministry of Health; and in 1951 the remaining services were fused with the Ministry of National Insurance to create the Ministry of Pensions and National Insurance.

* for committee references see Appendix B

Records

The main series of documents on war pensions and war pensions policy are to be found in PIN 15.

A number of records exist relating to the Personal Injuries (Civilian) Scheme and the Personal Injuries (Emergency Provisions) Act 1939 which gave it a legislative basis. Assistance Board files are at AST 11/113-120, with Ministry of Home Security files at HO 186/1038, 1315, 1437, 1439, 1483, 2454, 2736, 2745, 2765. Ministry of Pensions files include PIN 15/1194, 2230, 2261-2262, 2267-2272, 2772, 3363. Cabinet Office papers include CAB 123/213, with Prime Minister's Office papers at PREM 4/98/4. Treasury papers can be found in T 164, with others at T 172/2091. Other departmental files include Admiralty files at ADM 1/15020, Air Ministry files at AIR 2/6646, Board of Trade files in BT 58/262, Home Office in HO 45/18527, 20233 and HO 187/945, 949, with Ministry of Health files in MH 76/293-296. An official history of the scheme is at CAB 102/720. The transfer of functions from the Ministry of Pensions to the Ministry of Health is dealt with at MH 79/637.

Files on the War Pensions Committee, who assessed claims, are in PIN 5, PIN 9, and PIN 56. Appeals are in PIN 25 and PIN 40. The Central Advisory Committee of War Pensions records are in PIN 41. Disablement services are dealt with in PIN 38. PIN 59 contains policy files on awards and administration. Specimen files on the payment of war disability pensions are at PIN 45.

The register of appeals against decisions of the Ministry of Pensions in relation to entitlement to benefit is at BF 1. Further papers are at BF 3. J 96 contains appeals made to the Pension Appeals Tribunal, including a number relating to civil claims during the Second World War.

Ministry of Pensions papers dealing with the prevention of overlapping benefits due to the National Insurance Act 1946 are in PIN 15/3757. Papers relating to the National Insurance (Industrial Injuries) Act 1946 are at PIN 15/2391, 2869-2870. Papers relating to the Old Age and Widows' Pension Act 1940 are in PIN 15/2187-2189. Papers on the Ministry's children allowance scheme and its effects on the family allowance scheme are in PIN 15/2755, 2749-2750, 2993, 3362, 4019.

2.8 Bibliography

P Addison, *The road to 1945* (1975)

C Barnett, *The audit of war* (1986)

J Beveridge, *Beveridge and his plan* (1954)

W H Beveridge, *Power and influence* (1953)

J Cutler and J & K Williams, *Keynes, Beveridge and beyond* (1986)

A Deacon, 'An end to the means test? Social security and the Attlee Government', *Journal of Social Policy* II (1982)

A Deacon and J Bradshaw, *Reserved for the poor* (1983)

D Fraser, *The evolution of the welfare state* (1980)

J Harris, *William Beveridge* (1977)

J Harris, 'Social planning in wartime: some aspects of the Beveridge report', in *War and Economic Development*, ed J M Winter (1975)

J Hess, 'The social policy of the Attlee government', in W J Mommsen, *The Emergence of the Welfare State in Britain* (1981)

G King, *The Ministry of Pensions and National Insurance* (1958)

H Land, 'The introduction of family allowances', in *Change, choice and conflict in social policy*, ed P Hall and others (1975)

J S Macnicol, *The movement for family allowances 1918-45* (1980)

E Shragge, *Pensions policy in Britain* (1984)

E Wilson, *Women and the welfare state* (1977)

Social Insurance and Allied Services (the Beveridge report, Cmd 6404 1942)

Chapter 3 – HOUSING AND TOWN AND COUNTRY PLANNING

3.1 Introduction

3.2 The wartime emergency

3.3 The genesis of town and country planning

3.3.1 Wartime developments

3.3.2 Postwar legislation

3.3.2.1 The New Towns Act 1946

3.3.2.2 The Town and Country Planning Act 1947

3.3.2.3 National Parks and Access to the Countryside Act 1949

3.4 The postwar housing programme

3.4.1 General

3.4.2 Wartime planning

3.4.3 Short-term measures

3.4.4 The postwar housing programme: the growth of the council sector

3.4.5 The private sector: owner-occupied and rented accommodation

3.4.6 The supply of labour and raw materials

3.5 Bibliography

3.1   Introduction

The interwar period witnessed an unprecedented growth in public sector housing. Temporary measures to make good the chronic shortages following the First World War had been consolidated by both Conservative and Labour administrations in the course of the following decade. While Labour focused on the expansion of council houses, the Conservatives provided subsidies for all house builders capable of providing basic accommodation at a reasonable cost. Public expenditure constraints in the 1930s forced a revision of this approach. Exchequer subsidies were directed solely at slum clearance. Nonetheless, through the indirect encouragement of building society activity in the area of private housebuilding, central government fostered the expansion of owner occupation among lower income groups. By the outbreak of the Second World War, serious overcrowding had been halved and governments had helped foster some spectacular redevelopment schemes in both the public and private sectors.

Nevertheless, serious problems remained. The majority of the population still lived in privately rented accommodation, often in squalid conditions. This was particularly the case in the depressed industrial north, where social enquiries revealed a continuing saga of urban blight and decay. In such areas, local authorities experienced serious difficulties in raising the revenue necessary for extensive slum clearance projects. At the other end of the country, problems consequent on urban congestion were beginning to be felt. In areas around London particularly, unplanned ribbon development placed severe strains on existing social amenities—notably transport systems, schools, hospitals, shops and recreational facilities. This threatened future economic growth. Nor were houses built by the private sector of particularly good quality; the label 'jerry built' originated in this period. Finally, the inexorable expansion of suburbs in south-east England encroached upon undeveloped agricultural land, provoking opposition from the Council for the Preservation of Rural England, which had been founded in 1926, and an extensive public debate about land usage. The use of the countryside for recreation also increased—via bridleways and public footpaths—a tendency viewed with mounting concern by landowners whose views on the sanctity of private property were frequently challenged by ramblers' associations and others. The creation of a central planning authority was widely understood to be the sole solution to these problems. These and other issues were fully examined in the Barlow Report on the Distribution of the Industrial Population in 1940 (see chap 3.3.1).

3.2   The wartime emergency

The prospect of blitzkrieg had focused the minds of planners on the likely destruction to life and property should war break out. Forecasts of the damage to housing had been high and consequently preparations had been made to deal with the homeless and building repairs. The Housing (Emergency Powers) Act 1939, to be supplemented later by the War Damage Acts of 1941 and 1943, gave local authorities emergency powers, obliging them to find shelter for the homeless, to provide initial help for those who had lost their possessions, and to carry out emergency repairs to property where feasible. To stop private landlords, builders and building societies from using the shortage of accommodation to their own advantage, a Rents and Mortgage (Restrictions) Act 1939 was introduced which froze rents and mortgage repayments at September 1939 levels (HLG 41/104). In Scotland, rents were not frozen until 1943 when the Rent of Furnished Homes Control (Scotland) Bill was passed (T 161/1135/S50870). Private builders had to secure a licence to build housing and in turn had to guarantee the selling price or rental value. In the event the blitz proved less severe than imagined. Nevertheless German bombs entirely destroyed 200,000 dwellings and severely damaged 3,500,000 more, of which 250,000 were rendered uninhabitable.

For most of the war, overall control of the housing programme rested with the Ministry of Works, which was established in October 1940. It was given the responsibilities of the old Office of Works for building, accommodation, and supply, as well as for co-ordinating the government building programme and the control of all civil building. It also co-ordinated the planning for the postwar physical reconstruction of town and country (see also chap 3.3.1).

House repair and building: men and materials

Responsibility for the repair of houses and factories rested with the Directorate of Emergency Works within the Ministry. This was replaced in February 1941 by a Directorate of Emergency Repairs and was in turn merged with the Directorate of Demolition and Recovery to form a Directorate of Emergency Work and Recovery. A Committee on Air Raid Damage provided weekly reports on damage and emergency provisions (CAB 71/23, 24). Other departmental committees supervised specific areas of work. The Ministry of Aircraft Production, for example, established a Coventry Reconstruction Co-ordinating Committee to rebuild the city after the November 1940 air raids (LAB 12/128; HLG 7/189; AVIA 22/381; ADM 116/4904; CAB 89/14).

Co-ordination of the implementation of the government building programme was initially carried out through an interdepartmental central priority organization under the direction of the Ministerial Priority Committee of the War Cabinet. Its Works and Buildings Priority Subcommittee dealt primarily with competing demands for building manpower, while the Central Priority Department of the Ministry of Supply dealt with building materials.

Throughout the war (and after it) civilian building was restricted by a system of licences. This was introduced in October 1940 along with Ministry of Works' powers to regulate design, materials and standards of construction. Not surprisingly priority was given to projects benefiting the war effort. 'It is the essence of war economics', argued H D Henderson, economic adviser to the Treasury, 'that it becomes necessary to take a comparatively short view. We must concentrate our energies, as far as possible, on work that will be of help to us within the next few years' (CAB 89/8). At the end of 1939 a Housing (War Requirements) Committee was established to determine where new housing was needed to accommodate the wartime labour force. From October 1941 all builders and civil engineering contractors were required to register with the Ministry. The allocation of raw materials was implemented by the Central Priority Department of the Ministry of Supply, which carried out the decisions of the Ministerial Priority Committee and its subcommittee. The latter were replaced in May 1940 by the Production Council and in December 1940 by a Production Executive as part of the general reshaping of the control of domestic affairs at Cabinet level. Its functions were to allocate materials and labour and to establish priorities where necessary. In February 1942 a new Office of the Minister of Production, later the Ministry of Production, took over these functions, with the exception of labour. The new ministry, however, was merely a co-ordinating body and responsibility for the actual implementation of policy remained with the Ministry of Supply, with the exception of the allocation of skilled labour which was controlled through the Treasury's manpower budget and arranged through the Ministry of Labour. Mobilization of workers, and the prioritizing of war work, made it difficult to find workers to meet wartime housing needs (see chap 3.4.6). In a number of cases investigators found builders using children to cover for absent labourers (LAB 8/465).

A system of consultative councils provided co-ordination between the building industry, the building materials industry and the government. A Central Council for Works and Buildings was inaugurated in April 1941 (WORK 45/1420) and in September 1942 an Advisory Council of the Building and Civil Engineering Industries was also established to examine problems and policies affecting the industry. The latter, which was renamed in 1943 the National Consultative Council of the Building and Civil Engineering Industries, gradually replaced the former as the main channel of communication between ministers and industry. Other advisory bodies included the National Brick Advisory Council (WORK 45/11; DSIR 4/1822), the Advisory Committee of Specialists and Sub-contractors in the Building Industry, and the Payment by Results Advisory Panel. These various committees produced guidelines concerning the economic use of men and materials, published after the war as Postwar Building Studies. They formed the basis of the new British Standard Codes of Practice.

The use of unorthodox building methods meant that at the end of the war many buildings did not conform to building regulations. In 1944 the Reconstruction Committee* appointed a Subcommittee on the Wartime Contravention of the Building Laws to look at this problem (LAB 87/35; CAB 124/364-365; HLG 68/63; HLG 71/1398).

Research into new materials and techniques was organized through the Ministry of Works, and the Department of Scientific and Industrial Research. The wartime experience established initiatives for improving peacetime building design and production methods (see chap 3.4.6).

Rent controls

One of the most important emergency issues was rent. Over half the population lived in private rented accommodation, and the rent control legislation of 1939 was designed to protect them from exploitation. This measure, however, created problems of its own. Many people with space to rent were discouraged from offering it to tenants because of the low returns. In many cases it was necessary for local authorities to use their powers of requisitioning to take over property (HLG 41/94; HLG 108/8; CAB 71/2: 10 Apr 1941; CAB 71/3: 15 Apr 1941; CAB 71/11: 4 June 1943). Some landlords, however, still managed to circumvent the legislation and, in particular, relations with the American Army became strained when it became clear that landlords were charging exorbitant rents for GIs using furnished accommodation (HLG 41/95).

Air raids and homelessness

Another emergency issue was dealing with the consequences of air raids. Responsibility was divided between a number of agencies. Compensation for damage to property and possessions was administered by the War Damage Commission, which was set up under the War Damage (Compensation) Act 1941. Grants from it could be used for the reconstruction of property, subject to the approval of local planning authorities (HLG 71/239-260). Emergency payments to cover the loss of possessions was the responsibility of the Assistance Board (see chap 2.4). Responsibility for the homeless remained with local authorities, but in September 1940 it passed from their public assistance committees to new specialized committees which established information and administrative centres, extended the provision of rest centres, and mobilized and co-ordinated the work of voluntary groups. Rest centres had been established in evacuation areas and were designed to meet the immediate needs of those whose homes had suffered war damage. They were considered short-term measures; in the longer term people were expected to return to their homes or find a billet. However it soon became clear that, whilst the number of civilian casualties had been overestimated, the damage to property had been underestimated. Consequently rest centres soon became blocked with people.

The problem of homelessness was exacerbated in London by the magnitude of the destruction and elsewhere by the competition for accommodation with war workers. In London, a special commissioner for the homeless was appointed to the Civil Defence Region, assisted by a London Repairs Executive which co-ordinated the work of the Ministries of Works, Health, and Labour, and the War Damage Commission (CAB 139/145-146). The most serious problems were experienced in the exceptionally severe winter of 1944 when, following the flying bomb attacks, an extensive programme of emergency repairs, temporary housing provision, and shelters had to be mobilized. This programme was planned by the Winter Plans Subcommittee of the Civil Defence Committee (CAB 78/28: 27 Nov 1944; CAB 87/9: 30 Aug 1944, 5 Sept 1944; CAB 87/35: 11 Sept 1944; CAB 124/469, 471, 813-814; CAB 108/36-37; MH 79/503; WORK 45/10).

Outside London, the homeless found themselves competing with others for scarce accommodation. In some areas the expansion of munitions production and war work in general saw the building of hostels to house workers. In others, the War Office supervised the building of service camps. Both were given priority over housing for non-essential workers. More seriously, some local authorities were forced to requisition houses. This had been approved by the Housing (War Requirements) Committee which had been established to look at accommodation for war workers (AVIA 46/308; HLG 68/6); and again war workers received priority over the homeless (T 161/1003/S48129). The same was true in rural areas. Evacuation had put a severe strain on rural accommodation (CAB 124/580,125). However, the development of wartime agriculture demanded the building of accommodation for new workers. An emergency scheme was therefore instigated by the Ministry of Health to provide 3,000 cottages through 377 rural district councils to meet these needs (HLG 40).

* for committee references see Appendix B

Records

War Cabinet files relating to civil defence, many of which have implications for housing are in CAB 73. Papers of the Treasury Land and Building Division are at T 226. Ministry of Health files arising out of its special wartime functions are at HLG 68. War diaries relating to housing are at MH 101/23-28.

Prime Minister's Office papers leading up to the War Damage Bill 1941 are at PREM 4/81/1. Treasury papers include T 226/57-58, 73 on the 1941 War Damage Regulations; papers relating to the War Damage Bill 1943 are at T 163/130/12. Ministry of Works files relating to the War Damage Acts are at WORK 22/125-127, with further papers at WORK 12/484 and WORK 19/1087. Ministry of Health papers on the 1941 Act are at HLG 7/459, with further papers at HLG 7/469-470. Inland Revenue files are at IR 62/2464 and IR 63/157. Ministry of Health papers relating to the passing and implementation of the Housing (Emergency Powers) Act 1939 are at HLG 7/952-956, with Bill papers at HLG 29/259 and HLG 54/513. The provisions of loans under the Act are at HLG 48/715. Lord Chancellor's Office papers on the same are in LCO 2/1505. Bill papers of the Rent and Mortgage Interest Restriction Act 1939 are at HLG 29/259, with later papers at HLG 101/282.

The minutes and papers of the War Damage Commission are at IR 33. Policy files are at IR 34 with case files at IR 35-IR 37. Instructions to regional offices are at IR 38 and establishment files at IR 39. A Treasury blue note on the commission is at T 165/435. Under the War Damage (Valuations Appeal) Act 1945 the jurisdiction to decide certain questions arising out of the War Damage Act 1943 passed to a War Damage Valuation Appeals Panel, appointed by the lord chancellor. Its papers are at LT 1.

More generally, Lord President's Secretariat files on repairs to air raid damage can be found in CAB 123/3-5. General papers on wartime housing requirements, including workers' hostels and housing, war damage and public morale are at CAB 123/121. CAB 124/447 contains reports on flying bomb damage. Prime Minister's Office papers relating to homelessness due to war damage include PREM 4/99/1. T 226/104 contains Treasury papers on notifications of war damage after the war. Files dealing with various aspects of wartime housing provision include T 161/1435/S45159/1-6 and T 161/1421/S45159/7-8. Further papers relating to war damage compensation are at T 177/53, 1995 and T 218/117. Ministry of Health files relating to issues such as the repair of air raid damage and London housing policy can be found at HLG 7/1002-1047. Papers relating to the care of the homeless are at HLG 7/338-611, 955. Papers on the redevelopment of specific areas following air raid damage include HLG 68/66, 70. Papers relating to rest centres and the emergency food service are at MH 56/412. Official war histories on homelessness are at CAB 102/724-726 with sources at CAB 102/739-740. Papers on the repair of houses are at CAB 102/722. Papers of the Ministry of Home Security's Research and Experiment Department which include surveys of air raid damage to houses by area are at HO 192. Included in this are HO 192/212 on rest centres in Birmingham, HO 192/1237 on housing and rehousing in Birmingham, and HO 192/1286 on housing in Hull. Files of the Department of Scientific and Industrial Research relating to the repair of war damage are at DSIR 4/2567-2587. Other departmental files on war damage include Admiralty files at ADM 116/4769, Air Ministry at AIR 2/6068, Board of Education at ED 31/491, Board of Trade at BT 64, Home Office files at HO 186, Land Registry files at LAR 1/38, 88, Land Tribunal papers at LT 1-LT 2, Lord Chancellor's Office papers at LCO 2/1506-1508, Ministry of Labour at LAB 16/339, and Assistance Board files at AST 11/158-217, 228.

Files relating to rent control are at HLG 41.

The main papers of the Ministry of Works relating to the construction industry and building matters are at WORK 45. Most files here deal with production, supply and the costing of building materials, although files on training and policy are also included. WORK 46 contains unpublished sources used in C M Kohen's official war history of the Ministry of Works. These relate to the demands on the building industry, the creation of the Ministry of Works, the problems of control, co-ordination of the building programme, control of building materials, repair of air raid damage and other topics. Papers of the Ministerial Priority Committee are at CAB 92 and CAB 21/1198-1199, 1237-1238. HLG 31 contains housing notes and instructions issued by the Ministry of Health to principal housing officers, dealing with temporary houses, building materials, and labour. Ministry of Supply files relating to the war history of individual raw materials are at BT 131/86-115. Files relating to the Central Priority Department of the Ministry of Supply are at T 246. AVIA 22/174 contains papers relating to air raid damage, and AVIA 22/2 on the supply of hutted accommodation for all purposes. AVIA 46/481-494 deals with timber supplies. Other files relating to raw material are in SUPP 14. Preparations for the war history of the building industry are at CAB 103/250 and of wartime works and buildings at CAB 103/398, 490. The Ministry of Labour war history relating to labour aspects of the building and civil engineering industries are at LAB 76/6-17. Further files relating to the supply of labour and materials are listed in chap 3.4.6.

A Treasury file on accommodation for war workers is at T 161/1003/S48129 and on building labour at T 161/1168/S56618. HLG 7/184-94 deals with the billeting of war workers. Papers of the Housing (War Requirements) Committee are at HLG 68/6, HLG 7/1048-1049, HLG 101/230, and CAB 123/121. Ministry of Supply papers on the allocation of labour include AVIA 22/719-720, 1347. War history papers on housing and hostels for war workers at CAB 102/129. Ministry of Agriculture papers relating to the wartime emergency programme in agricultural housing are at MAF 228/67. Other files can be found in MAF 234.

Files on the demarcation of functions between the Ministry of Works and the Ministry of Health include T 161/1168/S56618 and CAB 124/43, and between the Ministry of Supply and Ministry of Works at AVIA 22/187.

Welsh Board of Health files, organized by local authority and referring to wartime housing problems are in BN 11.

3.3   The genesis of town and country planning

3.3.1   Wartime developments

Many of the debates about town and country planning during the war had been examined between 1937 and 1940 by the Barlow Commission on the Distribution of the Industrial Population, which had been set up in the context of the interwar problems of regional depression and the growth of London. Reporting in January 1940 (Cmd 6153), it anticipated the Scott and Uthwatt reports in recommending the establishment of a central planning authority to oversee the dispersal of the population from congested areas, to inspect town planning schemes in the light of national policy, and to encourage the development of the depressed areas.

The war encouraged reconstruction planning on a grand scale and the postwar housing programme tended to become overshadowed by the wider issues of town and country planning. Organizations such as the Town and Country Planning Association, already well established by the outbreak of war, became more vociferous in their demands for change (CAB 21/1583). New organizations like the 1940 Council were established to 'promote the planning of the social environment' (CAB 117/175; HLG 86/1). Government sponsored surveys, like the one carried out by the Nuffield College Social Reconstruction Survey on behalf of the Ministry of Works and Buildings, also advocated extensive new machinery for town and country planning.

Responsibility for town and country planning was initially divided. Under a scheme proposed by the Committee on Reconstruction* in September 1940, the old Office of Works became the Ministry of Works and Buildings under Lord Reith. At the end of 1940 it took responsibility for co-ordinating the planning of postwar reconstruction. Responsibility for planning under housing legislation, however, remained with the Ministry of Health. A committee of the Privy Council, established in July 1941, ensured compatibility between the functions of the two ministries.

Overall reconstruction planning was co-ordinated by a small reconstruction group within the Ministry of Works and Buildings. Advice was provided by a specialist Consultative Panel on Physical Reconstruction established by the Ministry in 1941 (HLG 86/2-20), an Interdepartmental Advisory Committee on Reconstruction to help prepare the formal machinery for postwar planning, and a Committee on the Reconstruction of Town and Country to deal with general issues (CAB 87/21; CAB 117/115; CAB 21/583; CAB 124/129; BT 64/3052H). Finally, to look at specific problems, the minister appointed two committees which were to have an important effect on planning policy over the next few years: the Uthwatt Committee on Compensation and Betterment* and the Scott Committee on Land Utilisation in Rural Areas*.

The Scott Committee was appointed in 1941 to look at rural land usage and the problems of development. Its report (Cmd 6378 1942) represented a compromise between the demands of the Town and Country Planning Association, the Ministry of Agriculture and Fisheries (which felt their views were not being heard in the planning procedure (CAB 21/1583)), and the rural conservationists. The report argued that prime agricultural land (4% of all land) was a major national asset which should be protected from development. It therefore supported Barlow Commission recommendations concerning urban containment through the use of 'green belts' around urban areas. It also proposed the establishment of national parkland to provide extra protection for areas of particular importance, adding weight to the campaigns which had developed during the 1930s (see chap 3.3.2.3).

The Uthwatt Committee was appointed in 1941 to tackle the problems of compensation and betterment. In the case of undeveloped land, the existing lack of standard, national regulations made planning difficult as people refused planning permission in one locality could easily seek permission for a similar development in another. In towns and cities the problem was different, but as serious. The high land values made it difficult for local authorities without unrestricted powers of compulsory purchase to control urban change through the purchase of large quantities of land. The committee saw a need, therefore, to provide local planning authorities with the power to 'cut through the tangle of separate ownership and boundary lines' to allow comprehensive redevelopment. Such powers raised the question of compensation for landowners (who were no longer to be free to develop their land as they wished) and betterment (the increase in the value of property resulting from the granting of permission to develop or through other local development). The issue of betterment proved particularly controversial. Many argued that it should be heavily taxed because the rise in land prices was due not to individual action, but to the action of the community. Others argued that a development was gain enough for the community and that the levy of a tax was unwarranted.

Having considered nationalizing all undeveloped land, and concluded that such a move would be politically dangerous and administratively difficult, the Uthwatt Committee recommended the nationalization of development rights. Any scheme which would alter the condition or use of land would require planning permission from local authorities. Land for development would be purchased by the state and leased back to the developer, with compensation being paid to landowners on the basis of a fixed single payment. In urban areas the Committee also recommended new purchasing powers for local authorities allowing them to buy land required for development at rates not greater than those in March 1939. Finally the Committee came out in support of the levy of betterment at a rate of 75% of any future increase in the annual value of developed land. To administer the scheme it recommended the establishment of a central planning authority.

The formation of a central planning authority was the first issue to be dealt with by the coalition government. Support for such an authority had developed in the 1930s (HLG 52/1206), and the Barlow, Scott and Uthwatt Reports had increased the demand (CAB 117/116-119; CAB 123/42; CAB 124/473; CAB 127/162, 164, 171-172). The idea of a central planning authority, consisting of both an executive council on policy and development and a new department of town and country planning, was duly considered by the Committee on Reconstruction Problems* in October 1941 (CAB 87/1: 31 Oct 1941). It established an Interdepartmental Committee on a Central Planning Authority, which met in June 1942 to look at the issue in detail (CAB 87/20; CAB 117/118). Meanwhile, in February 1942, the War Cabinet decided in the short term to transfer the statutory planning functions of the Ministry of Health to the Ministry of Works and Buildings (CAB 65/25: 9 Feb 1942). Accordingly, in July 1942, the Ministry of Works and Buildings became the Ministry of Works and Planning (HLG 54/458) and, two weeks later, Lord Portal replaced Reith as minister.

An Interdepartmental Advisory Committee on Reconstruction, established to look at long-term policy, failed to put forward any satisfactory proposals; and when the issue returned to the War Cabinet in November 1942 it was decided to create a new government department with responsibility for local planning and the ratification of local planning appeals, and for new town and country development (CAB 65/28: 19 Nov 1942). Whilst having less power of intervention than a central planning authority, it would provide some degree of central co-ordination. In February 1943 the Ministry of Town and Country Planning was duly established. As well as taking on responsibility for the statutory planning functions, the new ministry also became responsible for 'securing consistency and continuity in the framing and executing of national policy controlling the use and development of land in England and Wales'.

At the local level the Ministry established ten regional offices. These were to work closely with local planning authorities, offering them advice, keeping them informed of national developments, and keeping the Ministry informed of any local problems. In Wales, responsibility for town and country planning was transferred from the Welsh Board of Health to its own Welsh Regional Office.

The new Ministry, however, fell far short of a central planning authority as envisaged by its numerous advocates. Responsibility for industrial location remained with the Board of Trade and for housing with the Ministry of Health. Nevertheless, its establishment recognized the importance of town and country planning and guaranteed that the implementation of any legislation resulting from the Scott and Uthwatt reports would be co-ordinated within one ministry.

Together with pressure for a new ministry, supporters of town planning had long argued for an enhanced status for workers in the profession. Following the recommendation of the Scott Committee that local planning authorities must employ qualified personnel and that universities, colleges and professional institutes should draw up training schemes, the issue was passed to the Hankey Committee on Further Education and Training*, and then to the Schuster Committee on the Qualification of Planners (HLG 87). After 1945 professional courses became more widely available (HLG 71/262-264, 1388; HLG 51/870; HLG 87; LAB 8/1229).

Following the creation of the new Ministry, pressure to secure implementation of the Uthwatt and Scott reports increased. The blitz of 1940-41 and the flying bomb attacks on the South East in 1944 had destroyed whole areas of towns and cities. In addition, despite Treasury claims to the contrary (T 161/1136/S51476), there was also the need to redevelop older towns which, whilst having avoided war damage, were unsuited to modern needs. An advisory panel on the redevelopment of city centres (HLG 88/8-15) persuaded the Ministry that more extensive legislation was needed.

Certain ministers, such as Herbert Morrison, advocated an all encompassing bill which would radically alter town and country planning and give local planning authority to counties and county boroughs. Anything less, it was argued, would give the impression that Uthwatt's recommendations were being ignored. Others, like W S Morrison (the Conservative minister of town and country planning), argued that such extensive legislation would take time and that what was needed was an interim measure to control undesirable development during the transition period, using existing machinery (CAB 71/11: 25 Mar 1943; CAB 75/15: 16 Mar 1943). The issue clearly raised intense party conflict within the government. As a first move towards new planning control and after considerable pressure from local authorities (HLG 71/1467), the Town and Country Planning (Interim Development) Act 1943 was passed which established a framework of development control over the whole country for the first time. Once a resolution plan had taken effect, the appropriate local authority acquired certain powers of control over development. It was thus able to take immediate action against any undesirable development.

Longer-term measures were considered by innumerable other committees. In particular a Subcommittee on the Uthwatt Report on Compensation and Betterment (a subcommittee of the Official Committee on Postwar Internal Economic Problems*) saw some heated debate over the questions of the acquisition of land and the payment of betterment CAB 87/57-58). It set up its own subcommittee on the acquisition of land to look at the problem further (CAB 89/59; HLG 81/22-24). After November 1945, much of the debate at ministerial level took place in the Reconstruction Committee*, although many arguments were passed up to Cabinet. Whilst not threatening to nationalize land, the proposals to nationalize development rights was enough to raise the fears of many landowners. For example, Lord Brocket, of the Property Owners' Protection Society, regarded the report as unprovoked aggression. A memorandum from the National Federation of Property Owners to the Reconstruction Committee* expressed 'the opinion that some of the recommendations of the Uthwatt Committee go far beyond the committee's terms of reference as an expert committee. If given statutory effect they will prove to be a fatal deterrent to individual initiative, thrift and enterprise and will reproduce serious political controversy' (PREM 4/92/9). This was supported by the

Central Land Owners' Association (CAB 117/128) and numerous other groups (CAB 117/129-134).

Not surprisingly, such views found much support within the Conservative Party. With Labour politicians pressing hard for the full implementation of Uthwatt, there were serious political clashes. Nevertheless a Conservative Party Committee on the Uthwatt Report recognized the political damage of a purely negative attitude to the control of land use. Therefore, whilst avoiding the development rights scheme, they supported the extension of compulsory purchase powers (HLG 81/38).

A compromise policy was advanced in a government White Paper on the Control of Land Use in 1944 (Cmd 6537 1944). It accepted the Uthwatt Committee's arguments on the public acquisition of land, but argued that its proposals on compensation and betterment were unacceptable. In particular, it disagreed with the differentiation between developed and undeveloped land. The new proposals empowered local authorities to acquire land at March 1939 prices if the land was required for large scale development, subject to ministerial approval. Development rights were to remain with the landowner but could not be exercised without approval from the local planning authority. Betterment was to be paid by the owner of the land, whether developed or undeveloped, at an 80% rate. Compensation for loss of development rights was to be restricted solely to land which in 1939 had some development value. Responsibility for the payment of compensation and collection of betterment would be transferred from local planning authorities to newly appointed land commissioners.

These proposals added fuel to the fire of political debate. In particular, the decision to pay compensation at 1939 prices angered both landowners and some Conservatives (who argued for payment at current land values), whilst Labour politicians saw compensation of any sort as a victory for landed, over public, interests (CAB 124/375). Only intervention by Churchill, and the appointment of a committee under Attlee, secured a compromise. Compensation remained at 1939 prices but a 30% supplement was added to allow for individual circumstances.

The need for further speedy legislation meant that government preparation of a Bill avoided controversial areas and concentrated mainly on creating new powers of public acquisition. Under the Town and Country Planning Bill 1944, local authorities were given the power to redevelop blitzed and blighted areas through the compulsory purchase of land, with compensation payable to the landowner. All development was to be subject to central government approval; plans were to show how land in areas of extensive war damage was to be acquired and redeveloped. Substantial grants were made available. A Central Advisory Committee on Estate Development and Management was established to advise the minister of town and country planning (HLG 88/1-7). The Bill received royal assent in November 1944. More extensive implementation of the planning controls had to await the end of the war and a Labour government.

Following the passing of the Act, local planning authorities began to prepare development plans outlining their proposals. Initially these were prepared by the hundreds of planning authorities up and down the country but, after 1945, the new Labour government was to encourage the creation of Joint Town Planning Committees to secure wider co-operation and economies of scale (HLG 71/155, 283-297). Local planning committees were assisted in their work by the regional organization of the Ministry of Town and Country Planning. Regional controllers had been appointed by the Ministry to the civil defence regions in 1943 but after 1946 much of the work was to be carried out through the interdepartmental regional physical planning committees which they chaired. These were appointed by a conference of regional planning officers in 1946 and were composed of representatives of the various government departments. Overall co-ordination was provided by a Central Interdepartmental Physical Planning Committee (HLG 104/10; MAF 144/43).

With the election of a new Labour government, plans for wider implementation of the Uthwatt proposals began in earnest. In August 1945, ministerial and official subcommittees of the Lord President's Committee* began to plan detailed schemes for dealing with the compensation and betterment aspects of town and country planning (CAB 132/26-27; CAB 124/382-392).

The arguments surrounding the Uthwatt Report, and the moves to implement or resist it, highlighted the political differences within the government in a way which no previous issue had done. Michael Foot has argued that 'the intricacies of parliamentary manoeuvre over the Town and Country Planning Bill cast a gleam of light across the whole field of British politics. The question of ownership of land was the real rock on which the coalition was broken. Here was where property stood its ground against the prevailing sentiment of the age and political accommodation was forbidden' (M Foot, *Aneurin Bevan* vol 2 1973 p 473).

* for committee references see Appendix B

Records

The main papers of the Barlow Commission on the Distribution of the Industrial Population are at HLG 27. Those for the Scott Committee are at HLG 80, and for the Uthwatt Committee at HLG 81. As well as committee papers, these classes include deputations to the committee and subsequent papers. Reconstruction Secretariat correspondence on the Scott Committee is at CAB 117/127. CAB 123/44 contains the Lord President's Secretariat papers relating to the Scott and Uthwatt reports. Prime Minister's Office notes on the Scott, Barlow, and Uthwatt reports are at PREM 4/92/2. Papers of the Chancellor of the Exchequer's Office relating to Uthwatt are at T 172/1993. Board of Education considerations of the implications of Scott and Uthwatt for the education service are in ED 136/331. Home Office papers on the Scott Committee findings are at HO 45/20657. CAB 127/163 contains Jowitt's private papers on Uthwatt. The Bridges papers on the Uthwatt proposals are at T 273/340-341.

Cabinet Office papers relating to the 1943 legislation are at CAB 21/1596-1597. Reconstruction Secretariat papers on town and country planning legislation include CAB 117/133-134 on the Town and Country Planning (Interim Development) Act 1943, whilst those relating to the Town and Country Planning Act 1944 are at CAB 117/131. Lord President's Secretariat papers on the 1943 Act are at CAB 123/51, whilst those on the 1944 Act and subsequent discussions are at CAB 124/371-379. Papers on the Ministry of Town and Country Planning Act 1943 are at CAB 21/1075 and CAB 117/131-132. Prime Minister's Office papers relating to the 1943 Act are at PREM 4/92/1, to the White Paper at PREM 4/92/5, to the 1944 Act at PREM 92/7, and to subsequent discussions at PREM 4/92/8. Treasury files relating to the Town and Country Planning Act 1944 include T 226/7 and T 226/9. Ministry of Town and Country Planning bill papers for the 1943 Act are at HLG 29/268-269, and for the 1944 Act are at HLG 29/272-275. Ministry of Health papers include HLG 29/267 on the Ministry of Town and Country Planning Act 1943; HLG 29/268-269 on the Town and Country Planning (Interim

Development) Act 1943; and HLG 29/272-275 on the Town and Country Planning Act 1944. ED 136/538 deals with the lack of consultation with the Board of Education over the Town and Country Planning (Interim Development) Act 1943, and ED 31/542 and ED 136/539-541 with the 1944 Act. Papers of the Lord Chancellor's Office relating to the town and country planning legislation are at LCO 2/2650, 2658, 3043-3045. Ministry of Agriculture and Fisheries files on town and country planning legislation are in MAF 48. Parallel War Damage Commission papers are at IR 34/1203-1220. Board of Trade papers include BT 64/3112. Land Registry papers are in LAR 1/298, and Ministry of Transport papers are in MT 39/110, 536.

More generally, central policy files include Reconstruction Secretariat papers relating to the debate for a central planning authority at CAB 117/118. Lord President's Secretariat papers on land utilization in rural areas are at CAB 124/836, with papers on the control of land use at CAB 124/374. Relevant papers of the Economic Section of the Cabinet are at T 230/16. Relevant files from the Prime Minister's Office include PREM 4/92/6, relating to ministerial responsibilities for town and country planning. PREM 34/92/9 deals with various issues over the whole period.

Treasury Land and Building Division files are at T 226. Treasury papers on general planning policy are at T 161/1249/S53041. Papers on the control of land use include T 222/131.

Jowitt's personal papers are in CAB 127. These include CAB 127/162 on the central planning authority proposals, CAB 127/164, 169, 171, 172, 176 on administrative changes and debate, CAB 127/181 on compensation, CAB 127/185 on compensation and betterment, and CAB 127/192 on legislative proposals.

The main files of the Ministry of Works and Buildings relating to the reconstruction of town and country planning are at HLG 86. General policy files concerned with various planning functions carried out by the Ministry of Works and Buildings and, from 1943, by the Ministry of Town and Country Planning, are at HLG 71. Earlier Ministry of Health files on the same are at HLG 52 and HLG 95.

The papers of the Interdepartmental Advisory Committee on Reconstruction are at HLG 86/21-26, HLG 52/1420, and CAB 117/114.

The main establishment files of the Ministry of Town and Country Planning are in HLG 86. Files relating to administrative policy following the Act are at HLG 71/320-362, 1396-1397, 2212-2213. Ministry circulars are at HLG 71/1272. Papers of the Ministry of Town and Country Planning's Regional Physical Planning Committee are at HLG 83 and include general policy files, and minutes of meetings. Further papers are at HLG 104/10-15. Papers on the establishment of the Ministry are at HLG 124/20-21.

The main Ministry of Health files on planning and redevelopment are at HLG 104. Policy files are in HLG 101 with other housing files in HLG 68.

Local planning authority development schemes, mainly from before 1944 are at HLG 4. Plans submitted after the 1944 Act are at HLG 79. Other redevelopment proposals can be found at HLG 71/11-15, 1283-1293, 1409-1418. Planning appeals are at HLG 71/273-282, 1389-1390. Welsh development plans are in BD 28. Papers of the Ministry of Town and Country Planning Regional Office are at HLG 107.

Papers relating to the Nuffield College Survey are in HLG 82.

3.3.2 Postwar legislation

Three Acts provided the basis of postwar town and country planning and represented both policy developed by the Labour Party and the continuation and implementation of wartime policy. The New Towns Act 1946, the Town and Country Planning Act 1947, and the National Parks and Access to the Countryside Act 1949 established the administrative framework and approach to policy which were to apply for the next thirty years.

3.3.2.1 The New Towns Act 1946

The concept of new towns, built according to a specific plan to relieve urban congestion in large cities and to provide an attractive environment for their citizens, was an old one, dating back to the Garden City Movement at the beginning of the century. From the 1930s onwards, the uncontrolled growth of London and other urban areas encouraged the development of these ideas into a movement for more co-ordinated town planning. Organizations like the Hundred New Towns Association and the Town and Country Planning Association, whose influence on the Barlow Report was most significant, were established at this time to put pressure on government for change (HLG 90/2-10). Wartime investigations, like that carried out by the Nuffield College Social Reconstruction survey, added weight to their arguments (HLG 82/32, 35). Finally the Barlow Report and the Scott Report (see chap 3.3.1) both argued the case for the development of satellite towns in preference to the continued expansion of urban sprawl.

The formation of definite plans, however, was initially tackled by Professor Patrick Abercrombie. His Greater London Plan, prepared at the request of the minister of town and country planning, was presented in 1944 and published in 1945. The main theme of the plan was decentralization. This was to be achieved through inner-area redevelopment, the expansion of towns outside London, the building of new satellite towns, and the general encouragement of migration. The overall aim was to reduce the population of London by 1.03 million. In addition, urban expansion was to be stopped by a Green Belt, five miles wide, around London. The most radical idea within the report was the building of new towns. These were to accommodate 400,000 people in towns built 20-25 miles from London. In addition a further 600,000 people would be accommodated in small country towns 30-50 miles from London.

The need for the early implementation of the report became clear when some local authorities started to give permission for developments which were contrary to its proposals (HLG 71/146). In addition, industry was looking for sites on which to rebuild (CAB 71/9: 16 Nov 1945). The report had been favourably received by the new Labour administration, and so the new minister of town and country planning and the secretary of state for Scotland appointed a New Towns Committee under Lord Reith in October 1945 to look at the general issues involved.

The committee worked at speed. By January 1946 a first interim report had been prepared, which outlined specific arrangements to allow the development of Stevenage before the passing of the Bill (Cmd 6759 1946). Stevenage had been selected by the coalition government as the first new town with land set aside for development at the end of November 1945 (CAB 71/19: 30 Nov 1945). The announcement of this new town development was made in March 1946. A second interim report appeared in April (Cmd 6794 1946), followed by the final report in July (Cmd 6876 1946).

The final report fully supported Abercrombie in his view of the need for new towns and recommended an optimum population for each of between 30,000 and 50,000 people. Within this population the committee envisaged a diversity in terms of occupation and wealth. To facilitate this, it recommended the building of a wide variety of housing and the transfer of employment from other areas. Essential to this was the concept of self-containment, with the provision of local job opportunities, and local facilities in the field of health, education and recreation.

It has been argued that a degree of paternalism crept into the report (Aldridge 1979 pp 32-34). Whilst emphasizing the need for the new towns to create their own cultural identity, the report also strongly indicated what that identity should be: each town, for example, should have two theatres, a concert hall and an art gallery. Cinemas, however, were frowned upon as 'the programmes shown in commercial cinema have a limited cultural range and American productions dominate'.

The problems of development in the South East led the Ministry of Town and Country Planning to postpone a comprehensive Town and Country Planning Bill in favour of a bill dealing with satellite towns (CAB 132/1: 1 Mar 1946). In December 1945 an Advisory Committee for London Regional Planning was established to co-ordinate the examination of Abercrombie's proposals for Greater London (HLG 71/126, 165-167). Leading up to the passing of the Bill, a London Planning Administration Committee was set up to advise the minister on the appropriate machinery for securing concerted action (HLG 71/168-174; HLG 104/1). A Bill incorporating the Reith Committee proposals was duly presented to the Commons on 17 April 1946. Under its terms, new towns were to be designated by the minister of town and country planning. They were to be administered initially by development corporations, with the question of who was to replace the 'temporary' corporations left open. The corporations were to be responsible for all planning and administration and would consist of not more than nine members, appointed by the minister. This was to cause problems later with accusations against the minister of political bias in appointments (CAB 124/226). Members of the corporation were unpaid, but pressure for the introduction of salaries led to the appointment of an official working party in 1948 (HLG 90/281).

The new corporations had the power to acquire, manage and dispose of land and other property, to carry out building and make provision for public services. This was to be financed by advances from the minister, with repayment made over a period of years out of income recovered from property. Ministerial influence was further secured through a standing conference of chairmen and vice-chairmen of the development corporations and the Ministry of Health (HLG 90/117-122).

The Bill was passed with only a limited degree of opposition. Within government departments, concern was expressed by the Ministry of Agriculture and Fisheries at the speed at which land was being acquired (CAB 134/323: 16 Apr 1946). Other departments, such as the Board of Education, were keen to secure some influence during the planning process (ED 31/619). Only a few minor amendments were made to the Bill, the most important being a provision for a public enquiry at the designation stage. Otherwise the Bill was passed unchanged on 5 July 1946. A Satellite and New Towns (Officials) Committee was established to overview the passing of the Bill (HLG 90/39, 350-351, 399).

The implementation of the Act, however, proved more difficult. A London Planning Administration Committee was set up to advise the Ministry of Town and Country Planning on the appropriate machinery for co-ordinating action on London's regional plan (HLG 104/1; HLG 71/168-172). This body recommended planning be carried out through the 12 local authorities involved. Boroughs became linked with new towns and transferred sections of their population to them (HLG 71/131-132). However this procedure took time and, while the new towns were being developed, it became apparent to the Ministry of Town and Country Planning that 'we are not continuing to prevent the growth of London. We are indeed at great risk of adding to it' (HLG 71/1341). Boroughs which had run out of space within their own boundaries were looking at other boroughs for available land on which to build (HLG 71/176-177).

The development corporations faced a number of problems in the building of new towns, particularly in relation to the old local authority in the area. The employment of private builders, for example, involved a complicated joint procedure with the existing local authority. Development corporations were free to allot up to one fifth of their programmes to houses built under licence. These licences, however, were issued by local authorities (outside their own quota). As with other licences, local authorities fixed the maximum selling price (HLG 104/31). In some cases this meant the selling price did not match the income group the development corporation wished to attract (HLG 104/31). This difficult relationship extended to finance (HLG 90/347), necessitating the appointment of a Working Party and a Joint Consultative Committee on the Financial Arrangements for New Towns (HLG 90/361-362, 485-486). Responsibility for the provision of public services caused further problems (HLG 90/346). Development corporations were also competing with other local authorities, and government departments, for building labour and materials. As shortages increased, the problems of meeting deadlines became more acute (HLG 90/110, 434; see chap 3.4.6). The biggest problem, however, was finance. The general halt in the building programme in 1947 (see chap 3.4.3) and the economic problems of 1949 meant there could be very little investment in new town building by the end of the decade (CAB 134/440: 9 Jan 1949). During the economic crises of 1947 and 1949 new town development was suspended (HLG 90/149). The remainder of the decade saw increasing Treasury concern at the cost of development, and gradual cuts in the programme (CAB 132/11: 9 Dec 1949).

The other aspect of the Abercrombie Plan, the expansion of existing small towns, did not achieve legislative status until 1952. The issue was looked at by the Interdepartmental Committee on the Greater London Plan (HLG 71/128) and in surveys covering England and Wales carried out by the Ministry of Town and Country Planning (HLG 90/66). Despite concern at the financial implications of the scheme (HLG 71/110, 1340), a Bill was approved in July 1951 (CAB 132/17: 20 July 1951) and passed by the new Conservative government as the Town Development Act 1952.

Records

The working papers of Professor Abercrombie for his Greater London Plan are at HLG 85. They include draft chapters, surveys of transport, housing, industry and decentralization, and correspondence with local authorities.

Files of the Lord President's Secretariat include CAB 124/878-879 on satellite towns; CAB 124/880-882 relating to the New Towns Bill; CAB 124/225-226 on the appointment of development corporations; CAB 124/228 on the remuneration of members; CAB 124/869 on the development of Stevenage; and CAB 124/885 on transport facilities. Prime Minister's Office files are at PREM 8/676 relating to the Bill, and PREM 8/900 on new towns in South Wales. PREM 8/1090, 1575 deal with development corporations membership. Cabinet Office papers relating to the New Towns Bill are at CAB 21/2296. Economic Section files relating to the new towns capital expenditure programme are at T 229/532.

The main Treasury papers on the new towns legislation are at T 227/323-325. Annual financial calculations are at T 227/661, with the issue of contacts at T 227/322. T 227/146 and T 233/762 deal with the accounts procedure for new town boards. General questions arising out of the development of East Kilbride are dealt with at T 227/662. Papers relating to grants to local authorities for the planned expansion of existing towns are at T 227/123. Later files on new towns are at T 227/681-688. Files of the Treasury Land and Building Division are at T 226. Files on the relationship between the Ministry of Town and Country Planning and the development corporations include T 222/233-235.

General correspondence and papers of the Ministry of Town and Country Planning are in HLG 71. Files of correspondence relating to new towns are in HLG 90, with papers on ministerial policy and correspondence at HLG 116. Files of correspondence with development corporations, listed by corporation, are in HLG 91, with further correspondence, reports by corporations and other memoranda at HLG 115. The bill papers of the New Towns Act 1946 are at HLG 29/288-289. Ministry files on London planning include HLG 71/116-204, 1341-1357, 2024-2061, 2180-2193, 2452-2453; correspondence on the Greater London Plan prior to publication is at HLG 71/116, with maps and plans at HLG 71/117; a file on the plan itself is at HLG 71/130; postwar policy files on Greater London satellite towns and development include HLG 71/119, HLG 90/352, HLG 116/20. Correspondence with local authorities on satellite towns is at HLG 71/129, 175.

The papers of the Reith Committee are at HLG 84, with further papers at HLG 90/471, 399 and DSIR 4/1919. Its reports are Cmd 7759, 6794, and 6876 (1946).

An Interdepartmental Committee on the Greater London Plan sat between 1946 and 1948 and attempted to secure co-ordination of policy upon any question relating to land use. Its papers are at LAB 8/866 and HLG 71/124-128.

Proposals for specifically named new towns are spread through HLG 90 but are mainly at HLG 90/181-220. Geographical reports are at HLG 71/1785-1794. Files relating to membership of corporations are at HLG 90/116. New town annual reports are included in HLG 90/53-56.

The provision of health facilities is dealt with at HLG 90/411, education at HLG 90/303, and various cultural, social and educational facilities at HLG 90/472. Housing rent policy is looked at in HLG 116/4-7. Investment programme reviews between 1947 and 1951 are at HLG 90/156-159. Labour requirements are at HLG 102/264. Publicity for the programme is at HLG 90/31-38.

Ministry of Works papers in relation to new towns include WORK 22/169. Liaison with the Ministry of Town and Country Planning on building licences is dealt with at HLG 90/100.

Ministry of Health files on London development include HLG 104/1-3. A social survey enquiry to obtain social data relevant to the establishment of new towns and to the re-planning of the borough of Willesden for the Ministry of Town and Country Planning is at RG 23/118. Local authority planning files are in HLG 79. Board of Trade papers relating to East Kilbride are at BT 177/1226. Ministry of Education papers on the Bill are at ED 31/619. Ministry of Transport files on road building are at MT 39/659, MT 95/74-83 and MT 119/63. Lord Chancellor's Office papers relating to the extension of Stevenage are at LCO 2/4285. Ministry of Agriculture and Fisheries files relating to specific new towns and land use considerations include MAF 144/25-26, 28-30, 33-36, 38-40, 46-53, 60-62, 78-81, 86-87, 118-119.

3.3.2.2 The Town and Country Planning Act 1947

After the controversy surrounding the recommendations of the Uthwatt Committee* (see chap 3.3.1) their translation into legislative form was postponed in favour of interim measures. The Town and Country Planning (Interim Development) Act 1943 and the Town and Country Planning Act 1944 extended planning control to the whole of the country and gave new powers of compulsory purchase to local authorities. In addition, following an investigation by the Subcommittee on the Wartime Contraventions of the Building Laws*, a Building Restrictions (Wartime Contraventions) Act 1946 was passed to deal with land which had been developed outside building regulations (CAB 124/363; HLG 71/367; HLG 102/31-38, 342-344, 367; HLG 52/976-983). Longer term measures were postponed until the passing of the New Towns Act 1946.

When further legislation was finally introduced as the Town and Country Planning Act 1947, it was not just a means of dealing with Uthwatt but a composite measure. It tackled the problems of compensation and betterment, the drafting of local development plans and the system of development control. The drafting of the plans and the system of control were linked, for the first time, under the same planning authority—in most cases a county or county borough. At one stroke this reduced the number of planning authorities from 1,441 to 145 in England and Wales. Joint committees were either abolished or replaced with Joint Planning Boards and Joint Advisory Committees (HLG 71/477-480). This created some opposition from smaller local authorities who resented their loss of power. In London, for example, the City of London protested to the prime minister over the loss of planning rights to the London County Council (PREM 8/674).

Under the terms of the Act, each planning authority was required to undertake a survey of its area and to submit it to the Ministry of Town and Country Planning by 1951, as a report on existing land use and a programme of future development. Land designated for compulsory purchase had to be acquired within twelve years or the designation lapsed. Unlike planning schemes under earlier acts, plans under the 1947 legislation did not confer any development rights and planning permission still had to be applied for. Notification of any plans was to be announced in the *London Gazette* and a local paper and any objection would be heard at a public enquiry or private hearing. Each authority was charged with revising the plan quinquennially and supervising development in accordance with it. All development therefore required planning permission and planning powers ceased to be merely regulatory.

The new powers allowed some of the errors identified by the Barlow Report to be corrected. New industry could now be sited on estates designed for the purpose; the layout of housing estates could be improved; public services could be planned ahead of development and checks could be made on urban sprawl by concentrating development in new towns or extensions to existing towns.

The legislation removed the landlord's right to develop his land by, for example, building on undeveloped land. If he decided to do so he had to pay a development charge, equal to the increase in value due to permission to develop: a 100% levy which was greater than that recommended by Uthwatt. If permission to develop was refused, the landlord had no general right to compensation. Landowners were, however, to be compensated for the loss of development rights by a one off payment fixed at 1948 values. A fund was established to cover compensation costs.

This settlement was strongly opposed by a number of interest groups. Representatives of the National Federation of Building Trade Employers argued that the development charge would stifle the market and that a development charge of less than 100% would encourage the sale of land by landlords as they would gain a share of the development value (HLG 71/488). Similar protests came from the Landowners' Association (HLG 71/495) and the Federation of British Industry (HLG 71/491).

Under the 1947 Act a Central Land Board was established under the direction of the Ministry of Town and Country Planning to assess and levy development charges and to administer the payment, from a central fund, of compensation to owners for the loss of development rights. It was also empowered, with ministerial approval, to acquire land by agreement or compulsory purchase for development. From 1950 a register of land acquired and disposed of by the Board was kept. An Official Committee on Development Charges was established in 1949 to look at the principles on which the Central Land Board determined the levels of charges (HLG 71/1502; CAB 21/2508).

Problems still remained, however. Under the Act, local authorities found themselves unable to control the restoration of any war-damaged buildings unless they had been totally destroyed, or to take action against an infringment of planning permission until four years had passed (CAB 132/14: 3 Nov 1950). An amending bill was subsequently introduced in 1950 to bring war-damaged buildings under planning control and to change the date from which the four-year rule started from the date of refusal, not development (CAB 134/336: 5 Dec 1950; HLG 71/1562).

Local authorities had no power to change existing land use, unless they paid the higher rates due to industrial and commercial property. This made the re-planning of older towns difficult. Problems were also created for other departments of government. Under the old system, local authorities had been able to stockpile land for educational use. Under the new regulations this could only be done in the short term, with any long-term developments becoming subject to the local planning authority's development plans (HLG 71/106). Educational needs, therefore, had to be anticipated well in advance (HLG 71/1329). The same applied to hospitals (HLG 71/1471).

In practice the betterment scheme was unsuccessful. In its first report the Central Land Board noted that land was still being offered for sale at prices which included full development value (CAB 132/9: 3 Dec 1948). Landowners were unwilling to sell at existing prices and hence private deals were being struck in which land changed hands for higher prices than officially allowed. The unpopularity of the measure with land-owners led to the terms of compensation and betterment being amended when the Conservatives came to power in 1951. Town and country planning powers passed to a Ministry of Housing and Local Government (HLG 124/8) and fresh legislation both abolished the development charge and raised the limits on claims for compensation when planning permission was refused.

The 1947 Act represented a significant shift towards greater state intervention, but failed to inaugurate the programme of land nationalization that had been called for in some quarters. The system of nationalizing development rights represented land planning and regulation rather than redistribution: 'the 1947 system probably represents the furthest a reformist political party can go in this field in giving the state a major interest and role without threatening existing structures and relationships in a fundamental way' (McKay and Cox 1979 p 79).

* for committee references see Appendix B

Records

The bill papers for the Town and Country Planning Act 1947 are at HLG 29/299-318. Prime Minister's Office papers relating to the drafting of the Bill are at PREM 8/901. Subsequent papers are at PREM 8/1293.

Papers of the Treasury's Land and Buildings Division are in T 226. These include T 226/6 which deals with discussions relating to the Bill and T 226/45-54 which contain miscellaneous papers on the Act. T 226/10, 105-109 deals with questions of acquisition and compensation, and T 226/111 with development charges. Treasury discussions on the machinery for the control of land use are at T 222/131, whilst the Lord President's Secretariat files on the same subject are at CAB 124/374. Treasury implementation files include T 227/33 and T 233/779. HLG 104/27 deals with the papers of the Treasury Committee on Land Transaction concerning the effect of the 1947 Act on the acquisition of land.

General policy files of the Ministry of Town and Country Planning are in HLG 71. Files relating to the Act include HLG 71/491-505 on proposals from various organizations, and HLG 71/1468 dealing with amendments to the Act. Administrative policy under the Act is at HLG 71/408-490, 1419-1465. Acquisition of land and compulsory purchase is dealt with at HLG 71/1507, 1543-1548. Ministry files on development charges are at HLG 71/1489-1503. Papers of the Ministry's Establishment Division are at HLG 124. Publicity material for the Appointed Day is at HLG 108/25-26.

The Ministry's policy files relating to the procedure for the submission of plans by local authorities are at HLG 71/205-226, 1358-1380, 2194-2210, 2445-2446, 2459. Survey work for the preparation and implementation of plans is at HLG 71/1518-1531. The main bulk of submissions, organized by local authority, are at HLG 79. Those for Wales are at BD 28 with consideration of some reports at BD 29. Papers relating to discussion and amendment of plans include HLG 71/398-407, 1262-1269, 1409-1418. Correspondence, mainly on technical details, with a number of authorities is at HLG 71/1283-1293. Ministry policy files relating to planning appeals are at HLG 71/273-282, 1389-1390. Files of the Ministry's Regional Development Office are at HLG 107.

The Ministry's files on the Central Land Board are at HLG 71/506-518, 1466, 1987-1993, 2461 with establishment files at HLG 124/26-28. The minutes of the Board are at IR 33/3-5. The Board's policy files are in HLG 98, with case files at HLG 99, appeal files in HLG 112, and the registry of dealings in land at HLG 106. A Treasury blue note on the Board is at T 165/95. T 226/103 deals with the organization and functions of the Central Land Board.

Central Statistical Office estimates on the cost of compensation are at CAB 139/120. Ministry of Health files relating to town and country planning issues are in HLG 104. In particular, files arising out of the 1947 legislation are at HLG 104/23-33. Ministry of Supply comments on the legislation are at AVIA 22/318. Home Office papers dealing with the effects of the legislation on the building of approved schools are at MH 102/1374-1376. Lord Chancellor's Office papers on the Act include LCO 2/4120. Ministry of Agriculture and Fisheries papers relating to the Act include MAF 142/246. MAF 144/37 deals with the implications of the Act for agricultural land and MAF 144/56-57 deals with development plans.

3.3.2.3 National Parks and Access to the Countryside Act 1949

Whilst the debates surrounding national parks are not directly related to housing and planning in strict welfare terms, the discussions on their formation affected, and were affected by, the wider debate taking place about town and country planning.

National parks were first considered by a National Parks Committee which reported in 1931 (HLG 52/713-723). This rejected parks on the American model but recommended national reserves and nature sanctuaries as well as improved access to the countryside. The subsequent lack of government action led the Council for the Protection of Rural England to establish an influential standing committee on national parks in 1936, which continued to press for the implementation of policy right up to the 1949 Act (HLG 92/51, 65). Its position was supported by the Scott Committee* on Land Utilization in Rural Areas 1942 whose report argued 'that the establishment of National Parks in Britain is long overdue'. The report, for the first time, placed access to the countryside and national parks in the wider context of the control of land use. The 1944 White Paper on *The control of land use* reinforced it by referring to the establishment of national parks.

In 1942 the Ministry of Works and Planning appointed one of its Planning Department research officers, John Dower, to survey the possible locations of national parks. His work was published in May 1945 as a personal report (*National parks in England and Wales*, Cmd 6628 1945) and defined national parks as 'an extensive area of beautiful and relatively wild country in which, for the nation's benefit and by appropriate national decision and action a) the characteristic landscape beauty is strictly preserved; b) access and facilities for public open air enjoyment are amply provided; c) wildlife and buildings and places of architectural and historic interest are strictly protected'.

Following a paper to the Reconstruction Committee*, Morrison sought to establish a Preparatory National Parks Commission. However the need to pass town and country planning and new town legislation overrode the importance of the national park proposals, and they were therefore passed on to a committee for further investigation.

The Hobhouse Committee on National Parks reported in 1947, proposing the formation of national parks with their designation, establishment and running costs the responsibility of central government. However, during the drafting of the 1949 legislation the government supported the alternative view that administration should rest with local planning authorities. Where parks spilled into the territory of more than one authority, the creation of joint boards was proposed. The overall scheme would be supervised by an advisory National Parks Commission, which was duly appointed in December 1949. As well as its responsibilities for preserving and enhancing the natural beauty of England and Wales, particularly in the National Parks, the Commission also had to report on long-distance routes, organize an information service, and establish codes of conduct for visitors. In the first few years it designated 10 national parks: the Brecon Beacons; Dartmoor; Exmoor; the Lake District; the Peak District; the Pembrokeshire Coast; Northumberland; the North Yorkshire Moors; Snowdonia; and the Yorkshire Dales.

Both the Dower and Hobhouse Reports had also envisaged the scheduling of areas of outstanding natural beauty which would not require the administration of a national park, but which still merited some degree of protection. Under the 1949 legislation no specific proposals were made, but the National Parks Commission was given powers to designate areas.

Whilst the 1949 Act was partly a product of the interwar lobby on access to the countryside, as indicated by postwar propaganda portraying the main enemy of national parks as the selfish landowners (HLG 108/7), the Act was also the final part of a trilogy which created the framework of peacetime town and country planning based around urban containment, the development of new towns and rural conservation.

* for committee references see Appendix B

Records

The bill papers of the National Parks and Access to the Countryside Act 1949 are at HLG 29/328-338.

Lord President's Committee Secretariat files on the Dower Report and other debates leading up to the Bill are at CAB 124/443-445. Treasury papers include T 227/41-46, and T 161/1183/S34705 which deals with issues up to 1942.

The main Ministry of Town and Country Planning files referring to the issue are in HLG 92. Wartime preparatory surveys are at HLG 92/46, with various proposals at HLG 125/1. Papers arising out of the 1949 legislation include HLG 92/69A-77, 84, with papers referring to the designation of national parks at HLG 92/88. Rights of way policy is at HLG 92/99-109, and Ministry files on the National Parks Commissions are at HLG 92/122-135. Correspondence with the Commission is at HLG 92/86-87.Specific area files include those on Scotland (HLG 92/50), the Peak District (HLG 92/48), and the Lake District (HLG 92/47). Ministry comments on the Dower Report are at HLG 92/49.

Minutes of the Hobhouse Committee on National Parks are at HLG 93/3-7. Further papers are at T 161/1183/S34705; HLG 93/1-57, and HLG 92/65. The Committee's report is Cmd 7121 1947. National Parks Commission correspondence and papers, divided into the 10 national parks, together with sections on areas of outstanding national beauty, long-distance footpaths, and publicity, are at COU 1. Minutes of the meetings of the Commission are at COU 2.

Ministry of Works papers leading up to the Act are at WORK 22/121-122. Home Office papers are at HO 45/25244. Ministry of Agriculture and Fisheries files include MAF 141/172-262 and MAF 144/2-3. Files relating to national parks in Wales include BD 28/473, 483-508.

A Footpaths and Access to the Countryside Special Committee under Sir Arthur Hobhouse looked specifically at issues surounding rights of way and long-distance footpaths. Its papers are at HLG 71/1703-1707, with its report Cmd 7207.

3.4   The postwar housing programme

3.4.1   General

The population of England and Wales in 1921 was 38 million. By 1951 this had increased to almost 44 million; these figures alone go some way to explaining the postwar crisis in housing. However, on top of this there had also been a significant change in the structure of society. People were marrying earlier and families were getting smaller. Consequently over the same period the number of households increased from 8.7 million to 13.1 million. Such trends were well documented. An investigation by the Ministry of Town and Country Planning into family structure thus found 20% of households did not contain a married couple, 6% of all households were old people living alone, and over half of all households had three persons or less (HLG 71/60-62).

Housing stock had been seriously reduced by the war. Almost half a million dwellings were destroyed or made uninhabitable, with over 3 million suffering lesser damage. In addition the transfer of labour to war work meant that as many as 1.75 million houses which would otherwise have been built were not. Thus a major postwar housing drive was essential if the population was to be adequately accommodated.

Housing was also important from an economic point of view. The need to provide accommodation for wartime workers had emphasized the importance houses played in industrial mobility. Existing companies such as Leyland Motors and Stewart-Lloyd Iron and Steel Production (AVIA 50/1-2) needed to attract workers as they sought to transfer from wartime to peacetime production. New projects, like the Atomic Energy Commission plant at Sellafield (AVIA 51/91), also needed to attract workers in large numbers. An Investment Programme Committee paper in 1949 concluded that 'investment in housing is necessary not only to maintain the efficiency and morale of industrial workers and to prevent excessive increase in house rents, but also to permit the industrial mobility which, during the next few years, will be a condition of making the structural adjustments that are required in Europe' (T 229/455).

3.4.2   Wartime planning

Wartime planning of a postwar housing programme was severely limited for a number of reasons. First, responsibility was divided between the Ministries of Works, Supply, Health, Town and Country Planning, and Reconstruction. A co-ordinated programme was therefore difficult to secure. Second, the direct problems of homelessness and war damage took up much of the departments' time. Finally, it was realised that any successful housing programme would have to be part of a wider scheme of town and country planning. Consequently the major reports at this time (Scott*, Uthwatt*, Barlow, Abercrombie) looked at issues with wider implications than simply housing.

Nevertheless, the loss of housing stock and the increased numbers of households meant the issue could not be wholly ignored. In 1941, the Ministry of Works and Buildings established a Postwar Building Study Division to look at the demand likely to be placed upon the postwar building industry (HLG 101/318). At this stage, planning took on board both the long-term and short-term approaches which were to be apparent after the war. Concern within the Ministry of Health at the prospect of 2.5 million people returning to London at the end of the war led to policy discussions in 1941 on requisitioning unoccupied property, billeting and carrying out repairs (HLG 101/317). These became important measures in the future short-term programme (see chap 3.4.3). From 1942 onwards, the Ministry began to formulate a longer term housing policy, with the assistance of the Official Committee on Postwar Internal Economic Problems*. Its estimate of housing shortfalls by the end of the war was 710,000. A subcommittee on Private Enterprise Housing was appointed in 1942 to consider the part to be played by the private sector in postwar house building (HLG 37/67-70).

In August 1942 the first of a series of interdepartmental conferences was held between officials of the Ministries of Health, and Works and Planning in an attempt to co-ordinate planning (HLG 101/345). During policy discussions it became increasingly clear that local authorities would have to be the main providers of housing under any scheme.

In building, they provided a closer control of standards and charged lower rents as they were non-profit making. They could also be controlled from the centre and therefore could be part of a planned strategy. Housing associations suffered from their inability to build on a large scale due to lack of finance, whilst private house builders tended to take a short-term outlook. Nevertheless, the latter did come to be seen as having an important contribution to make. It became clear that local authorities should concentrate on slum clearance and the provision of houses for the low paid, whilst the remainder should be left to private enterprise (HLG 101/383).

Cabinet concern at the need for a housing programme first became apparent in 1942. From this date housing policy was considered as one of the responsibilities of the Official Committee on Postwar Internal Economic Problems* (CAB 87/56: 5 Oct 1942, 25 Nov 1942; CAB 87/57: 22 Apr 1943, 15 May 1943). In turn, it took the issue to the Committee on Reconstruction Problems* (CAB 87/3: 25 May 1943) and later the Reconstruction Committee* (CAB 87/7: 6 Dec 1943, 22 Jan 1944, 24 Jan 1944; CAB 87/8: 13 Apr 1944, 22 Apr 1944, 13 June 1944, 17 June 1944, 20 June 1944). The latter appointed a subcommittee on the Control of Postwar Building (CAB 87/11; CAB 124/585) to calculate labour and financial costs of house building in the two years following the war, and a subcommittee on Housing to keep the housing position under review (CAB 87/35). From January 1945, a Housing Committee* supervised the progress of the programme.

The status of the building programme proved controversial. With Britain facing severe economic difficulties in the postwar period, many (especially within the Treasury and the Board of Trade) questioned the wisdom of embarking on the programme which could adversely affect the balance of payments (CAB 87/8: R(44)128). Correlli Barnett was to comment later that 'instead of starting with a new workshop so as to become rich enough to afford a new family villa, John Bull opted for the villa straight away— even though he happened to be bankrupt at the time' (C Barnett *The audit of war* 1986).

For Churchill, the priority was to allocate housing for servicemen to avoid the experience of the First World War when postwar housing provision failed to meet expectations. This contradicted local authority guide-lines on providing for the needy. The prime minister in turn argued that the families of servicemen without separate homes 'were outstanding cases of families living under unsatisfactory housing conditions' (CAB 78/28: 5 Dec 1944). However, by definition permanent house building was long-term; for Churchill what was needed were short-term measures which were extensive and highly visible. This meant, in particular, putting money into the prefabricated housing programme (see chap 3.4.3)

In 1945 a White Paper on housing was prepared by the minister of reconstruction. The coalition government outlined its objectives as providing a separate dwelling for every family that desired one (an estimated three-quarters of a million houses), completion of the slum clearance and overcrowding programme, and longer-term improvements to standards of accommodation and equipment. In the short term, therefore, the permanent house building programme would be restricted. The First World War had shown that an extensive programme meant a large number of starts but few finishes. Emphasis had therefore to be placed on prefabricated construction. The paper commented that whilst 'temporary houses are costly because of their short lives and they are sub-standard in terms of accommodation, though not in equipment', they were important in 'bridging the gap between the programme of permanent house construction in the first two years after the end of the German war and the housing needs of the country'. Other short-term measures included the repair of war damaged homes and the conversion of buildings (CAB 124/482).

Records

Files of the Lord President's Secretariat relevant to housing include CAB 124/446, CAB 124/630-634 and CAB 124/459. Parliamentary debates on the housing programme are covered in CAB 124/449. Papers relating to the Ministry of Health's role in the programme are at CAB 124/474, with those relating to the Ministry of Works at CAB 124/475. Papers dealing with the National Federation of Registered House Builders are at CAB 124/583. CAB 124/601 contains reactions to a booklet by the House Builders' Association of Great Britain, and CAB 124/395 contains correspondence with the British Industry National Council. Correspondence with the Town and Country Planning Association relating to housing is at CAB 124/604-605.

Reconstruction Secretariat papers on postwar building include CAB 117/26 dealing with the demarcation of duties between the Ministries of Health and Works. CAB 117/125 deals with Ministry of Labour proposals for a Housing Corporation.

Central Statistical Office reports on building figures and housing include CAB 108/37, 41 and CAB 139/144.

Prime Minister's Office papers relating to the administration of the housing programme are at PREM 4/93/4. Treasury papers on the postwar building industry include T 161/1136/S51920. Economic Section papers are at T 230/256.

Ministry of Health files include a number within HLG 68 on housing policy, and general policy files are contained in HLG 101. HLG 104 contains planning and redevelopment files. Ministry evidence to the Official Committee on Postwar Internal Economic Problems are at HLG 101/377. HLG 101/316 contains papers on postwar housing drafted by a Departmental Committee on Postwar Housing. Short-term plans are at HLG 68/86. A Central Housing Advisory Committee*, was set up under the Housing Act 1935 to give the Ministry advice on all matters. Its papers are at HLG 36 and HLG 37.

A social survey investigation into population change and housing requirements was carried out in early 1945, and its findings were presented by region (RG 23/74).

* for committee references see Appendix B

3.4.3 Short-term measures

In the short term there were three main options open to the new Labour government to provide accommodation: to repair existing houses, to requisition any houses which were empty, and to provide temporary prefabricated homes.

The number of houses damaged during the war was considerable and, from 1944 onwards, work began on carrying out repairs to make them habitable. However, the election of a new Labour government and the arrival of Aneurin Bevan at the Ministry of Health reduced the programme. Despite pressure from groups like the Parliamentary Labour Party's 'Blitzed Areas Group' which campaigned for the repair of badly bombed houses (HLG 101/516), the new minister of health wanted to provide new housing of good quality. Consequently resources available for repair were restricted. By 1946, however, it was becoming clear that a large body of people living in damaged houses were becoming increasingly discontented with the fact that their taxes were being spent on housing for others rather than on the repair of their own property. Consequently, from 1947, grants were made available to repair and upgrade old property. Whilst disliking the idea of giving funds to private owners, the government accepted the scheme could not work in any other way. Grants were paid through local authorities, which in turn were supported by a Treasury grant paid on the same ratio as new house builders (HLG 101/253). In areas of serious damage, work was carried out on a more organized basis. In London, for example, a London Repairs Executive co-ordinated policy (HLG 101/891). In 1949 the scheme was given legislative status in the form of the Housing Act. Local authorities were now empowered to provide generous grants for home improvement. By March 1950, 142,712 uninhabitable houses had been repaired, 76% by local authorities and, between 1945 and 1949, 775,000 occupied dwellings were repaired, through local authorities. The Act also allowed local authorities to provide up to 50% of the costs of converting houses into flats and of providing basic amenities to existing homes up to a ceiling of £800. Three-quarters of the local authorities' expenditure would be covered by a Treasury grant.

The requisitioning of houses for families who needed them most was agreed at the Lord President's Committee* meeting in July 1943 (CAB 71/11: 19 July 1943). At the end of the war proposals were passed making it easier for local authorities to requisition empty houses (CAB 65/53: 18 July 1945), accelerated in part by the outbreak of squatting in many parts of the country. However, such measures only scratched the surface of the problem. In 1946 the Ministry of Health tried to extend the scheme to hotels in London, only to be told that 'for the purposes of the export drive it was most important that buyers should be able to come freely to London' (CAB 128/6: 17 Sept 1946). By 1948 27,694 houses had been taken over.

By far the most popular short-term measure was the provision of temporary housing in prefabricated form. There were a number of reasons for this. First, during the Second World War both central and local government increasingly sought the advice of architects thereby introducing new ideas, including prefabricated construction. Second, industrial interests had a large stake in prefabs and pushed for their own interests: aluminium houses, for instance, despite their expense, were first brought into discussions by the Ministry of Aircraft Production under pressure from client industries. Third, prefabricated techniques were well known, having been used in steel houses before the war, and having been studied by the Burt Interdepartmental Committee on House Construction* from 1942. Fourth, the introduction of prefabs was championed by the Ministry of Works in the face of hostility from the Ministry of Health. The two departments were fighting a long running battle for the control of the building programme (see chap 3.4.4) and this encouraged the Ministry of Works to champion its own project. From 1943 onwards the Ministry of Works had in fact developed a prototype temporary house in order to provide accommodation at the end of the war; in 1944 the Portal House was established at the Tate Gallery site. This was seen by the Ministry as the basic model on which all others would be based. Finally, from a political point of view, the prefab programme provided excellent propaganda potential. One of the major grievances at the end of the First World War was the lack of 'homes fit for heroes'. The prefab programme allowed the government to reassure the nation about postwar reconstruction.

In an attempt to stop the programme, the Ministry of Health asked the Central Housing Advisory Committee* to evaluate prefabs. It appointed a subcommittee on temporary construction, which duly opposed temporary houses of fixed construction because they secured few savings in cost or labour, and had a shorter life than conventional housing (HLG 37/66). Despite this, the programme went ahead with official sanction being granted by the Reconstruction Committee* in June 1944. 100,000 prefabs were envisaged for the first year, with a further 100,000 the next. Local authorities were to pay the government ten shillings a week for each unit, with the rent the same as for ordinary houses. Each house would cost £550 and would have a ten-year life expectancy.

The Treasury expressed some concern at these costs, and shared the worries of the Minister of Health that the ten-year life expectancy meant simply postponing problems. In addition, concern was expressed that finance would be diverted away from permanent building (T 230/16). Nevertheless, it finally concluded that the housing shortage made the programme unavoidable and concentrated instead on limiting numbers (T 161/1244/S51518/01/1: 23 June 1944).

The 1944 Housing (Temporary Accommodation) Bill provided the programme with a legislative basis (HLG 29/276). Under the Act finance was provided for 200,000 to 300,000 houses, and the minister of health was empowered to enter into agreement with local authorities for the manufacture and erection of temporary houses by the Ministry of Works, on land belonging to local authorities (CAB 75/18: 18 July 1944). A further Act in 1945 allowed local authorities to use park space for up to two years (CAB 75/21: 1 May 1945). In September 1944 a Committee on Prefabricated Houses was appointed 'to make the best plan possible for the largest possible construction in the shortest time of prefabricated houses of all types'. Reporting after just two weeks, it concluded that the programme was inadequate for the needs of the population, but approved the Portal, Uniseco and Arcon houses for production. The Burt Committee, looking at permanent prefabs, opposed their construction, but concluded that the scheme was too far advanced to be modified. This was the view also taken by Bevan. Consequently, a Working Party on Prefabricated Houses was set up to review alternative systems of construction (HLG 101/54). In October 1945 a White Paper on the temporary programme committed the government to providing 158,000 houses. Further financial assistance was provided through the Housing (Building Materials and Housing) Act 1945.

Whilst 124,455 units had been provided by 1948, serious problems had been encountered. Costs had risen far beyond expectations with the 1945 estimate of £184.7m having reached £215.9m by 1948. To meet this overshoot the government was forced, in 1948, to pass a further Housing (Temporary Accommodation) Bill to increase the amount of Treasury subsidies available. The need for this increase was blamed on the cost of aluminium houses, the switch from timber to steel in constructing kitchens and bathrooms, and the delay in the preparation of sites by local authorities (CAB 134/327: 28 Oct 1947). Domestic political pressure had ensured that costly alternatives, like aluminium houses, were used in an attempt to bolster domestic employment and industry, whilst cheap foreign alternatives, like Swedish timber-built houses were avoided because of their adverse affect on the balance of payments (CAB 65/44: 18 Dec 1944).

The programme was wound down after 1948, yet costly problems continued to appear. The condition of many properties by the end of the 1940s was far from satisfactory. Many houses, and particularly those made from aluminium, suffered from severe condensation (WORK 22/314). In 1950 the Department of Health for Scotland concluded that 'many local authorities are becoming increasingly restive over the unsatisfactory conditions of these houses and the excessive maintenance costs which they are having to bear' (T 227/160: 30 May 1950).

The prefab programme was promoted by the Ministry of Works against the wishes of the Ministry of Health. The relative failure of the programme to solve the problems of postwar housing was, therefore, a major factor in accounting for the eclipse of the Ministry of Works by Bevan and the emergence of the Ministry of Health as the controlling ministry for housing.

* for committee references see Appendix B

Records

Significant memoranda to the Housing Committee can be found in CAB 87/37. Prime Minister's Office papers relating to wartime discussions on emergency housing are at PREM 4/93/3. Economic Section papers on the clash between permanent and temporary demand for resources are at T 230/16. Treasury papers referring to the 1944 temporary housing legislation are at T 161/1244/S51518/01/1-2, with policy and administration papers following the Act at T 161/1244/S51518/06/1. Borrowing by local authorities under the terms of the Act is dealt with at T 233/42. Ministry of Health papers relating to short term measures are at HLG 101/515-547, 851-891.

General correspondence files of the Lord President's Secretariat in relation to prefabricated housing are at CAB 124/291-292. Papers relating to government attempts to start the programme are at CAB 124/448. CAB 124/465-466 contain papers on factory-made housing; CAB 124/472 on prefabricated housing from the USA; CAB 124/835 on representations from the Timber Development Association; and CAB 124/476 on aluminium houses. CAB 124/480 deals with the use of parks and open spaces for accommodation. PREM 4/93/2 relates to the Committee on Prefabricated Housing. Prefabs from the USA are dealt with at PREM 4/93/6, and those from Sweden at PREM 4/93/7. Cabinet Office papers relating to temporary housing are at CAB 21/2023. T 227/272 contains papers on the financing of firms building prefabs. Timber requirements for the programme are at T 229/214. T 229/160 deals with aluminium house production and T 227/160 with the deterioration of temporary houses. Files relating to the Ministry of Work's Regional Building Committees are in WORK 49. Further Ministry of Works papers include WORK 22/346, relating to the temporary housing production programme, and WORK 22/319 on expenditure. Ministry of Supply inspectorate files on defects in aluminium houses include AVIA 56/13, 26-27. Papers dealing with employment conditions for employees working on prefabs are at AVIA 50/20. Ministry of Health papers relating to the Working Party on Prefabricated Houses are at HLG 101/54. Postwar temporary housing files include HLG 101/477-502, whilst papers relating to subsidy and grants are at HLG 101/228-229. Correspondence with various firms relating to the prefab programme is at HLG 102/12-29 and files on 'permanent' prefabs are at HLG 101/42-74, 556-561. HLG 101/477 contains correspondence with local authorities on the implementation of the programme. Files relating to the importing of prefabs are at HLG 101/49-52, 476, and to aluminium houses at HLG 101/43. Ministry of Health Files on homeless families include HLG 101/518-519, 522; HLG 68/33. HLG 101/341 contains a review of empty houses in London carried out between 1948 and 1952; HLG 101/539, 543 deal with the requisitioning of unoccupied housing; the maintenance and repair of requisitioned housing is dealt with at HLG 101/515. Files relating to the Housing (Temporary Accommodation) Bill 1944 include HLG 101/220-221, 478. Correspondence with the Ministry of Works in relation to the project is at HLG 101/357 and to various Ministry of Works bodies at HLG 101/356.

Files of the Welsh Board of Health, organized by local authority, with many dealing with short-term housing measures, are at BD 11.

Papers of the Central Progress Committee, which up to 1946 monitored reports on the repair of war-damaged houses, are at WORK 45/109 and HLG 108/10.

3.4.4 The postwar housing programme: the growth of the council sector

Overall responsibility for the national building programme rested with the Ministry of Works and, at the local level, its regional building committees were given responsibility for 'seeing that the programme of building and civil engineering work in the region proceeds in an orderly way and with due regard to priority and that more work is not started than can be completed in a reasonable time'. Its powers were, however, severely limited. Direct responsibility for the permanent housing programme rested with the Ministry of Health which had a tradition of work in this field. The building of new towns, and house planning in the wider context of town and country development, was the responsibility of the Ministry of Town and Country Planning. The Ministry of Supply also had responsibility for the supply of some raw materials, whilst the Ministry of Labour remained responsible for the supply and training of the workforce. House building in Scotland was the responsibility of the secretary of state for Scotland. This complicated administrative structure was the unfortunate legacy of the Second World War (CAB 21/1745; HLG 101/355).

The Cabinet Housing Committee, established in January 1945 to provide overall supervision of the housing programme, was wound up in December of that year, to be replaced by a stronger Standing Housing Committee which reviewed the progress of the programme and dealt with any major issues arising from it. However this too failed to provide a satisfactory level of co-ordination and was itself wound up in January 1947. Moves to reform the administration began after this date (T 222/46). An obvious move was to transfer the housing function of the Ministry of Health to the Ministry of Town and Country Planning, but this was resisted for fears of creating too powerful a planning ministry (T 222/621), and because of concern over increasing administrative costs (T 214/112). However, after 1949 a parallel concern over the excessive cost of the NHS began to reduce the time Bevan could devote to housing, and led to increased pressure to remove the housing portfolio from his ministry (T 273/190). In 1951, a Ministry of Local Government and Planning replaced the old Ministry of Town and Country Planning and took over responsibility for housing from the Ministry of Health (T 222/163-164, 727).

During the period of divided responsibility it was the minister of health who emerged *de facto* as the minister with overall responsibility for housing. This was in part due to the exclusion of the minister of works from the Cabinet and his Ministry's failures over the temporary housing programme (see chap 3.4.3), but also to the strength of character of Bevan himself, and to the traditional role in housing played by the Ministry of Health.

The emergence of Bevan as the main figure in the housing programme was significant. Whilst the Labour Party manifesto in 1945 had emphasized the importance which would be placed on house building, it did not commit itself to private or public sector building. Bevan, however, remained convinced that the best way to reach the Party's target of 240,000 houses a year was through a council-led programme funded by large Treasury subsidies, providing permanent houses of good quality. Local authorities were seen as best able to plan provision, build large-scale developments, and allocate to those most in need, although in practice this very much depended on the commitment of each individual local authority. Many, such as Cardiganshire, were in fact to reveal a distinct lack of commitment (BD 11/1427).

To emphasize the importance of central funding, the Local Loans Act 1945 required local authorities to do all their borrowing from the Public Works Loan Board, a quasi-autonomous government body established in 1917 (although it operated before the First World War under a different name) to lend money to local authorities at low rates. They were not allowed to borrow from the financial markets. The other source of finance was a system of subsidies established in 1946 under the terms of the Housing (Financial and Miscellaneous Provisions) Act. This increased the existing subsidy available from £8 5s per home payable for forty years, to £22 payable for sixty, on the condition that £5 10s of this came from local authorities. Additional grants were made available for high cost land, houses in rural areas, and the building of flats. These rates of subsidies were set with the aim of allowing local authorities to charge ten shillings a week rent, although the Treasury had wanted twelve shillings (HLG 101/322).

The ability of local authorities to secure land and build homes was eased by the passing of the Land Acquisitions Act 1946 (HLG 29/283). Authorities had been acquiring land since 1943, and by 1945 had enough for over 600,000 dwellings.

The quality of housing was considered essential by Bevan as he blamed the lack of quality in early housing for the number of slum dwellings in the 1930s. A Design of Flats and Houses Subcommittee of the Central Housing Advisory Committee* reported in 1944 (HLG 37/62-65), and its main recommendations were published in a housing manual the following year. The two major flaws in interwar housing were identified as the lack of variety in style, and the cramped living space: a minimum size of 900 square feet for a three-bedroomed house was recommended. Bevan adopted this standard. Of one and a half million dwellings built between 1945 and 1955, only half a million were maisonettes or flats whilst 85% of houses built between 1945 and 1950 had three bedrooms. Kitchens replaced the pre-war scullery, and in 1949 the Ministry introduced an awards scheme to reward local authorities for the best designed houses and estates (BD 11/1444-1448). From 1946, a Working Party on Building Research (HLG 1/672) carried on research into house design. Research was also carried out by private organizations such as the Housing Centre Trust (HLG 101/343, 599) and studies abroad continued to be made (HLG 101/332).

Despite the Labour pledge to build on average 240,000 houses a year, no specific targets were set for each year, and no balance sheet of needs and completions was established. Consequently it became difficult to gauge the success of the programme. Douglas Jay, Attlee's private secretary, and later MP for Battersea, was one of a growing number of Labour Party politicians who expressed concern at Bevan's inability to produce targets and his over-reliance on local authorities. He proposed a housing corporation to act in default of inefficient local authorities and wanted more direct building by the Ministry of Works. However, these moves were resisted, particularly after the failure to enlist the support of key organizations. The Treasury recorded: 'the Federation of Building Trades Employers were approached confidentially as to the names for the board and refused to play on the grounds that the corporation would certainly be a flop' (T 161/1249/S52616/01).

The house building programme in fact started extremely slowly. By January 1946 only 2,000 permanent houses had been built, despite 163,000 starts, and the growing crisis was highlighted in the autumn of 1946 by an outbreak of squatting. One case in particular, where 1,500 people took over a requisitioned building, attracted the attention of the Cabinet and added to the pressure on Bevan (CAB 128/6: 9 Sept 1946). As the programme settled down, however, Bevan experienced a change in fortune which coincided with the appointment of a Housing Production Executive, at Attlee's insistence, to promote greater programme co-ordination. By the end of 1946, 251,000 new homes had been approved of which 188,000 were under construction. In 1947, 139,000 houses were completed in England and Wales and, in 1948, 227,000. Of the latter 175,000 were council built. This proved to be the peak of the postwar building programme.

The housing programme aimed not just at building houses but also at targeting those who needed them most. Need was defined not just socially but also economically. Rural housing, for example, had been a problem for a number of years. The need to produce domestic food in order to reduce imports made it essential that accommodation be provided to agricultural workers. After the war, an extra subsidy was provided for rural house building under the Housing (Financial and Miscellaneous Provisions) Act 1946 (HLG 101/582). At a wider level, agricultural colleges were exempted from development charges under the Town and Country Planning Act 1947 (HLG 98/2, 4, 56-81; HLG 104/21; MAF 144/88). However the financial cuts from 1947 onwards necessitated financial savings and, after 1949, special priority for rural building was withdrawn in favour of assistance for specifically named projects (CAB 132/11: 15 July 1949).

The need to target housing applied to industrial priorities as well. The establishment of industrial development areas led to the need to build housing to accommodate key workers in these areas (T 161/1367/S52591/04; T 229/97; HLG 71/6; HLG 104/5-9B). This included the provision of temporary as well as permanent housing (HLG 101/43). Problems were particularly acute in the coalfields where, by 1947, problems of output were severe. This was in part because of difficulties of recruitment, which in turn were exacerbated by the lack of housing (PREM 8/531). Negotiations between the Ministry of Fuel and Power, the National Coal Board and the Ministry of Health led to a co-ordinated programme of mine expansion and house building (HLG 101/120, 132-135; BD 11/1440). Under the housing cutbacks of 1947, housing for miners was given the highest priority (CAB 132/6: 12 Aug 1947). A further extensive programme was developed after 1951, following criticism from the United States about Britain's failure to increase coal output (HLG 68/77; T 229/324).

The housing programme was curtailed by successive economic crises after 1947. Wartime inflation had increased the cost of construction; and the shortage of materials, notably timber, encouraged the use of new materials which were arguably quicker, but were definitely more expensive (see chap 3.4.6). In July 1947, the run on the pound led to strident calls for public expenditure cuts (see chap 1.3). In August the prime minister announced the curtailment of the original building programme which was confirmed by the Production Committee* in October (CAB 134/635: 13 Oct 1947). The Marshall Programme allowed local authorities to go ahead with house building in 1948, but only on the basis of finishing those houses already under construction. (CAB 134/438: 12 May 1948).

The export drive, however, increased existing problems. Attempts by Bevan to push his plans through in 1948 were resisted by Hugh Gaitskell who argued that 'the conflict between building and export is, unfortunately, apparent in many raw materials and there is no doubt whatever that the implementing of the new export programme will to some extent depend on whether or not we are prepared to cut building' (CAB 124/452). The devaluation crisis in the autumn of 1949 further threatened the building targets for the following year. At Cabinet, Bevan agreed to a possible 25,000 houses per year cut. However, on hearing that defence was only going to suffer administrative cut-backs, he wrote an angry letter to the prime minister arguing that 'a reduction in housing expenditure cannot be justified on the basis of the existing national emergency. Housing makes its own peculiar and essential contribution to economic revival'. Overall 12.5% was cut from the 1950 programme (CAB 134/440: 27 Oct 1949). The outbreak of war in Korea marked the climax of the cuts.

Concern continued to mount at the cost of housing, due to the high standards demanded. Surveys of costs found massive variations between various local authorities (HLG 101/410, 328). A Committee on House Building Costs sat between 1947 and 1952 to keep the problem under review (HLG 101/186-204). It estimated that the improved standards of building had put 35% onto the cost of each house. Consequently there was a significant shift away from quality to quantity. Changes to the standard were discussed by a subcommittee on the Revision of the Housing Manual (HLG 37/80-83). From 1951, the standards of house size and construction adopted after the Dudley Report were abandoned. The minimum space of 900 square feet for a three-bedroomed house was reduced; the requirement of two toilets per five persons reduced to one; and former minimum room sizes became maximums. There was a consequent move away from traditional semi-detached to terraced houses and four-storeyed blocks of maisonettes. By these measures the programme was kept at a reasonable level, minimizing political embarrassment (T 227/401; CAB 128/17: 17 Apr 1950). Nevertheless the number of completions fell away from the 1948 peak, to 197,000 in 1948, 198,000 in 1950 and 194,000 in 1951. The Treasury instituted still further cuts, arguing that even 'a housing programme of 175,000 houses in England and Wales to be completed by 1951 is inconsistent with housing making its full contribution to the deflationary policy' (T 229/474).

For the public the results of the cuts were serious. By 1949, one million people were on council waiting lists and 600,000 were living in accommodation which was too small (CAB 128/16: 20 Jan 1949; HLG 101/417). In Scotland a survey showed the problems to be severe (RG 23/153). In addition, those who had been placed in accommodation were facing increased rents due to the financial cuts (HLG 101/12-13).

Records

Lord President's Secretariat files on the postwar building programme are at CAB 124/632-634. CAB 124/630-631 deal with government control of the programme. CAB 124/485 deals with housing costs, and CAB 124/604-605 with the Town and Country Planning Association's views on housing policy. Files relating to the house building programme for each year are at CAB 124/450-454.

Central Statistical Office papers relating to housing include CAB 18/38, 102-103. Prime Minister's Office files include PREM 4/93/5 on methods of house construction and PREM 8/53 on the administration of the housing programme. Cabinet Office papers include CAB 21/2026. Economic Planning Section papers on cutbacks in the programme include T 229/233, 455, 473-474.

Treasury papers on housing expenditure include T 227/156. Papers relating to the Housing (Financial and Miscellaneous Provisions) Bill are at T 163/138/6. Papers on the cutbacks are at T 227/401. Investment Programme Committee papers relating to the cuts are at HLG 52/1574-1577. Papers relating to agricultural and mineworkers' houses are at T 227/159 and T 229/34. Papers of the Committee on the Control of Investment* referring to building are at T 229/237.

Policy files of the Ministry of Health are at HLG 101. Files covering a wide variety of its functions are at HLG 68. Memoranda on housing instructions issued by the Housing Department of the Ministry are at HLG 31, with instruments of consent at HLG 13/112-174. Bill papers for the Housing (Financial and Miscellaneous Provisions) Act 1946 are at HLG 29/286, with further papers at HLG 101/216-217. The Bill papers of the Housing Bill 1949 are at HLG 29/323-327. Information and publicity for the housing programme was co-ordinated by the Housing Publicity Committee. Its papers are at HLG 108/11. HLG 40 contains files relating to rural housing policy. A Rural Housing Subcommitteee of the Central Housing Advisory Committee* presented three reports on the problem (HLG 37/42-55). Other Ministry files on agricultural colleges include HLG 101/136, 152, 319. Files relating to rural housing in Wales are at BN 11/1411-1420. Debates on the rising cost of house building are at HLG 101/326. Relations with the International Federation for Housing and Town Planning, an international body set up to improve world-wide housing and planning problems are detailed at HLG 102/65. Papers highlighting Britain's contribution to European housing are at HLG 102/338.

Files of the Welsh Board of Health, organized by local authority, are at BD 11.

Files relating to the Ministry of Works Regional Building Committee are in WORK 49. Ministry of Agriculture Norwich Divisional Office records relating to agricultural housing are at MAF 147/1-27. Oxford Division files on the implementation of the housing programme are at MAF 169/136-145. Files of the Land Drainage, Water Supplies and Building Division are at MAF 234.

Minutes of the Public Works Loan Board are at PWLB 2. Account ledgers are at PWLB 5 with a register of applicants at PWLB 6. Annual reports are at PWLB 9. A social survey investigating public attitudes to the housing crisis in the 1950s is at RG 23/113.

A Social Needs and Problems of Families Living in Large Blocks of Flats Subcommittee was set up in 1950, anticipating problems which were to occur in later years. Its papers are in HLG 37/88-93.

A number of files exist relating to Scotland. CAB 124/460-461 contains the Lord President's Secretariat papers on postwar planning of housing in Scotland. T 229/344 contains correspondence between the Investment Programmes Committee and the Department of Health for Scotland on housing between 1947 and 1952. A Treasury blue note on housing in Scotland is at T 165/216.

The following Ministry of Health classes, which are organized by local authority, mainly cover the pre-war period but include some later files: HLG 47 deals with slum clearance, overcrowding and redevelopment of land; HLG 48 covers financial provisions to encourage the building of houses by local authorities; HLG 49 covers local authority proposals for programmes; HLG 67 deals with land acquisition and HLG 71/34 contains records of local authority conferences on planning technique.

* for committee references see Appendix B

3.4.5 The private sector: owner-occupied and rented accommodation

Owner occupiers

Wartime planners had envisaged an important role for private builders in the postwar plans for housing (see chap 3.4.2). Whilst council housing was to provide the main housing for the poor, private builders were to supply the rest. However, Treasury support for a financially independent private sector was resisted (T 161/1244/S51518/02). It was realised that some degree of central control would be required and the main debate centred on the subsidizing of private builders by local authorities as a means of controlling their building and selling prices. Legislation was prepared for this purpose (CAB 87/37: 2 June 1945). The expansion of the owner-occupied sector was not considered problematical. The building society structure remained in place, although its level of activity had been severely curtailed. Between 1940 and 1944 the societies had only made 220,000 loans, less than one year's lending in the 1930s.

These policies were, however, abandoned with the election of the Labour government. The keynote of Labour Party housing policy was the allocation of all available houses according to need, and this led to the granting of absolute priority to the council sector. The building of houses for owner-occupation was licenced by local authorities, and licences were only given when the ultimate owner of the house was known and the local authority was satisfied that the applicant was in need of accommodation. Moreover, the house could not be resold for four years and was then subject to price control. This in effect meant that speculative building, which had characterized the interwar years, was forbidden. Whilst individual councils granted licences, a ratio of one private house to five council built was established as a national target. Further restrictions were placed on private builders. Builders were registered along the lines of the voluntary National House Builders' Registration Council scheme (HLG 101/313-314). The Housing (Building Materials and Housing) Act 1945 contained provision to enforce conditions relating to the selling price of houses (T 227/158).

Whilst Labour Party policy represented a restriction of private building, it was not a direct attack upon it. Local authorities were allowed to use small builders on projects involving 2-6 houses (HLG 101/408), and the main support of the owner-occupied system, the building societies, remained unaffected. Despite the lord president's concern that Bevan's newly announced housing programme in 1945 failed to support the man buying his own home and offered no role for the building society (CAB 129/3: 6 Oct 1945), in the longer term this had beneficial consequences for the societies. No alteration was made to the basic building society structure because it was unnecessary for the successful implementation of the Labour Party's programme. Consequently building societies' assets continued to grow leaving them in a strong position for the change in political climate in 1951.

Indeed in many ways the government encouraged owner occupation through tax relief. In the 1920s, fiscal assistance had been made available on both owner-occupied and rented accommodation. The 1940s and 1950s saw a shift in emphasis favouring owner-occupiers. Before the war, tax relief had been allowed on mortgage interest, but liability to income tax began at so high a level of income that tax relief for owner-occupiers was irrelevant to all but the better-off households. After the war, both the lowering of the threshold for tax and the rise in incomes made tax relief much more important to an increasing proportion of owner-occupiers. However, more conscious moves to help this group, like mortgage credit schemes modelled on the USA, New

Zealand, and Canada and supported by, amongst others, Ernest Bevin, continued to be resisted (CAB 124/484).

The cutbacks in the housing budget after 1947 affected the ability of the private sector to build houses. In 1947 the minister of health decided no further licences should be issued to private builders (CAB 132/6: 12 Aug 1947), and this ban was extended in 1949 (CAB 134/440: 27 Oct 1949). The cutbacks also saw a clamp-down by local authorities on private builders, leading to complaints from the Law Society and other groups that local authorities were exceeding their powers in not allowing houses to be built without their permission (HLG 101/465).

Nevertheless, the private sector remained strong. Support from the central administration was apparent. Some Treasury officials argued that public housing discouraged saving as it required no deposit, and that it led to absenteeism from work as people were not committed to paying their mortgage (T 229/233). Private builders greatly benefited from the building of new towns, with development corporations allotting up to one fifth of their programmes to houses built under licence (HLG 104/31). The 1949 Housing Act recognized the inability of council housing to provide a complete solution to the housing problem and gave owner-occupiers recognition through grants for the repair and modernization of private homes.

Private rented housing

The private rented sector was the largest in the domestic housing market. The threat of war had led, in 1939, to the passing of the Rent and Mortgage Interest Restrictions Act which brought under control practically all privately owned houses let unfurnished (see chap 3.2). The workings of the Act and the implications for the postwar period were examined by an Interdepartmental Committee on Rent Control set up in 1943 under Viscount Ridley. Evidence taken by the committee showed that wartime inflation had eroded the value of rents, that the repairs were financially impossible, and that flat-rate increases in rent were needed. The Committee rejected the latter proposal in favour of recommending the formation of rent tribunals with powers to fix rents at a level at which repairs could be carried out. Local authorities would be required to register all rents actually being paid and these would be the rents legally recoverable unless the rent tribunal decided differently.

To deal with nearly six million rents in this way would have been expensive, time consuming and administratively difficult. In the event it was never tried. The Labour government after 1946 concentrated its efforts on bringing furnished lets into line with unfurnished. The Furnished Houses (Rent Control) Act 1946 and the Landlord and Tenant (Rent Control) Act 1949 extended existing regulations and allowed rent tribunals to determine a reasonable rent on request. Rent control was further reinforced by the system of building licences. Any private builder planning to rent out a house had to guarantee a rent before the licence was issued by the local authority. Nevertheless many landlords found ways of circumventing the legislation. Landlords converting houses into flats were able to escape the licensing laws (HLG 101/525). In many houses erected during the war for war workers the law was similarly evaded (HLG 101/25).

Rent control was the only area of the private rented sector tackled by the Labour government. Its policy to concentrate resources on the public sector meant that it virtually ignored the sector with most people in it. The private landlord was seen by many in the Party as the major reason for the poor housing conditions before the war and a major source of exploitation both during and after it. A long-term aim was, therefore, to achieve the gradual elimination of the private sector by starving it of resources, and allowing it to decline naturally. By 1950 the effects of government policy were beginning to be felt. Whilst income from rents remained at 1939 levels, the price of building maintenance work had nearly trebled, leading to the gradual sale of private rented accommodation to the owner-occupied sector. Pressure from individuals and organizations for change (HLG 41/90, 118) and the changing fortunes of the council-led housing programme, brought some relief in the form of the Housing Act 1949. This for the first time provided landlords with grants for house improvements and repairs (see chap 3.4.4).

Housing associations faired little better than private landlords. Towards the end of the war they were dismissed as too small to provide any real alternative to local authority building. In 1945 the most philanthropic of associations became eligible to receive grants, but it was accepted that their role could only be supplementary to local authorities (HLG 101/790). However, under Labour, attempts by the National Federation of Housing Societies to exempt housing associations from the provisions of the rent restrictions acts, as with local authorities, were resisted by the minister of health, who argued that there was no difference between the associations and private landlords (HLG 101/796).

Records

Records relating to postwar housing policy in general can be found in chap 3.4.4. The following records deal only with private housing.

Lord President's Secretariat files relating to the role of private enterprise in the house building programme are at CAB 124/464. CAB 124/468 deals with the selling price of houses. CAB 124/462-463 deal with the rent control legislation.

Treasury papers relating to subsidies for private enterprise are at T 161/1244/S51518/02, with papers on the Housing (Building Materials and Housing) Bill at T 161/1199/S52616/1 and fixing the selling price of homes at T 227/158.

Ministry of Health files on the 1945 Act are at HLG 101/3. Papers relating to private enterprise in the housing programme are at HLG 101/461, and on the selling price of houses at HLG 68/74. General correspondence with the National House Builders' Registration Council is at HLG 101/335. An enquiry into private enterprise housing, based on an enquiry by the Committee on House Building Costs into the costs of private homes, and who bought them, is at HLG 101/204. Bill papers for the Furnished Houses (Rent Control) Bill are at HLG 29/285. Files referring to rent control in unfurnished homes are in HLG 41; those for furnished houses are in HLG 101: 92011 series. Other files include HLG 101/103 referring to amendments to the rent control acts and HLG 101/99-101, 103-108, 562-568 on rent tribunals. Representative files (from Cornwall, Devon, and South Middlesex) of the rent tribunals themselves are at HLG 97.

Other miscellaneous files include: Ministry of Town and Country Planning papers on rent control legislation in new towns at HLG 90/173; Lord Chancellor's Office papers on the Landlord and Tenant (Rent Control) Bill at LCO 2/4480, with those for the Furnished Houses (Rent Control) Act 1945 at LCO 2/3100; Welsh Board of Health files referring to the postwar housing programme are at BD 11.

Papers of the Interdepartmental Committee on Rent Control are at HLG 41/69-85, CAB 124/462, T 161/1195/S51479. Its report is Cmd 6621 1945.

Annual returns from building societies during the period are at FS 14. Rules and amendments are at FS 13.

The selling price of houses was looked at by an interdepartmental committee between 1945 and 1953. Its papers include T 227/158 and HLG 101/552-555.

3.4.6 The supply of labour and raw materials

Labour

In 1939 over one million men were working in the construction industry. By 1945 this had decreased to 337,000. Conscription had depleted numbers severely, and yet the postwar housing programme required the service of more men than ever before.

The problem of co-ordinating the overall building programme rested with the Ministry of Works, which established regional building committees. Allocation of skilled labour was controlled through the Treasury's manpower budget and was implemented by the Ministry of Labour and National Service. Consequently the supply of labour for the housing programme was beyond the control of the minister of health.

From 1943 onwards it became clear that the programme of postwar reconstruction would be seriously hindered if an adequate supply of labour was not forthcoming (CAB 97/12: 28 Jan 1943, 30 July 1943, 21 Sept 1943). Shortages meant not only the slowing down of the programme but also increasing costs. A Treasury Subcommittee on Postwar Building pointed out that labour shortages would increase the bargaining power of workers and so increase industrial costs and unrest (T 161/1168/S56618).

In January 1944 construction workers were diverted from airfield construction to help local authorities prepare sites for housing estates (CAB 87/5: 31 Jan 1944). Early demobilization of construction workers was arranged with the services (AIR 19/419). Under the Labour government housing was given priority above other areas of social services. Nevertheless it was made clear that 'housing should not preclude the allocation of a reasonable amount of building labour for industrial purposes' (CAB 71/19: 13 July 1945). Subsequently, of the 953,000 men employed in the building industry in 1946, only 200,000 were building houses, whilst 229,000 were carrying out repairs and conversions. The lack of control of the workforce by the Ministry of Health made it difficult to keep the number of housing starts in line with available labour. Consequently the number of half-built houses continued to increase.

Part of the solution to the labour shortage was to provide better training for newcomers to the trade. An Education Committee of the Central Council for Works and Buildings considered the problem between 1941 and 1943 (LAB 8/518; WORK 45/19). After the war, improved apprenticeship schemes were offered to young trainees and refresher courses were offered to those with some knowledge of the trade (T 227/195; LAB 16/73; ED 46/670). The expansion of technological education after the war (see chap 5.4) increased the number of places available for the advanced study of building techniques and, from 1950 onwards, plans were made to introduce degree courses in building (T 227/97). At the local level, building trade advisory committees were established to provide guidance (LAB 18/284-286, 291-293, 297, 315-316, 320).

In February 1946 permanent housing was given essential works status in an attempt to alleviate the labour shortage (CAB 132/1: 15 Feb 1946, 22 Feb 1946) and attempts were made to increase the wages of building operatives by six pence an hour (HLG 68/110). The situation worsened during the economic crisis of 1947 and thereafter when export work was given priority. By 1950 the situation was so bad that the Production

Committee* was considering introducing incentives to encourage workers to work at night (CAB 134/644: 1 Nov 1950).

It was not only the shortage of construction workers which caused problems. Many skilled workers were required to work on the production of building components, and their numbers too had been depleted by war. In particular, the early postwar years saw a serious shortage of bricks which imports could not make good. Consequently men were made available on early release from the services and offered incentives, such as extra cheese rations and assisted travel schemes, to rejoin the industry (CAB 134/320; CAB 21/2021).

Building materials

As early as 1940 it had been recognized by the Official Committee on Housing Costs that, if the postwar building programme was to be effective, the building materials industry had to be reconstituted (CAB 87/103; LAB 8/912). The problem was looked at by the Official Committee on Postwar Internal Economic Problems*, along with that of labour supply, and calculations were made of likely postwar needs (CAB 89/57: 18 Jan 1943). It became apparent that there would be a shortage of certain key materials, in particular timber and bricks.

The shortage of building materials had become acute by 1944. In that year a Building Materials Co-ordinating Committee was established to co-ordinate and synchronize arrangements to ensure the production of adequate supplies of materials for the building programmes (HLG 102/134; BT 168/195-196).

Part of the solution to the problem lay in finding alternative methods of production and construction, and alternative raw materials. The prefab programme (see chap 3.4.3) was an illustration of this. Methods were also developed to use the same raw materials in different and better ways. The Committee on the Brick Industry (WORK 45/1-4; DSIR 4/1819; LAB 8/549), for example, from 1941 looked at production and quota methods, which led eventually to the formation of the National Building Brick Council. A 'simplified brick construction' was developed for the Interdepartmental Committee on Technical Methods of House Construction (PREM 4/93/5). Standardization of building components allowed products to be interchanged, reducing labour skills required, and allowing greater economies of scale in production.

The responsibility for the technical side of building lay with the Ministry of Works and, in particular, its Directorate of Postwar Building. The latter was established in 1941 to plan reconstruction work, particularly in the area of prefabs and the study of building techniques. The Ministry's work was carried out through an elaborate committee structure. In 1942 an Interdepartmental Committee on House Construction was established under Sir George Burt. Between 1942 and 1947 this provided information for the industry on the subject of materials and methods of construction. Further important research was carried out by the Department of Scientific and Industrial Research, established in 1921 as a small research station (DSIR 4). From 1944 the Ministry of Works had a chief scientific adviser who initiated and carried out research and experiments to improve the efficiency of builders and civil engineers. From April 1945, work was guided by a Scientific Advisory Committee which included leading scientists. A Building Industry Subcommittee and a Building Requirements Subcommittee carried out much research in this area and, in addition, the Ministry copied techniques used abroad (FO 371/34100: A7208, A7270, A7340, A7524).

Clauses 1 to 5 of the Housing (Building Materials and Housing) Act 1946 provided for the financing of the operations of the Ministry of Works by ensuring the adequate supply of building materials and components. The Ministry took over responsibility for the production and distribution of materials from the Ministry of Supply, establishing a Building Materials Priority Distribution Scheme (WORK 45/199) and working closely with trade organizations such as the National Council for Building Material Production (WORK 45/124). A Building Materials Distribution Committee looked at the organization and methods of distribution between 1946 and 1947 (WORK 45/200-201). From 1947 a Building Materials Prices Committee kept under constant review the price of materials (WORK 45/100, 105). After 1946 a Housing Production Executive was established to provide co-ordination between the various interested departments. It consisted of the Ministries of Health, Supply, Labour, and Works and reviewed the whole field of housing materials and component production (PREM 8/232; AVIA 49/74).

Nevertheless, the postwar period saw a persistent shortage of housing materials. In particular shortages of soft wood and other timbers caused serious problems (T 229/214) and the supply of materials from the United States proved erratic. Brick production caused further problems, with supplies having to be imported from abroad and reused from bomb sites (CAB 134/320; PREM 8/229). From 1947 onwards the economic crisis contributed to the decline in materials available, and increased the competition between departments for scarce resources. Pressure from the president of the Board of Trade to fix the supply of raw materials to the building industry succeeded in reducing the amounts available (CAB 131/10: 28 Mar 1947, 25 Apr 1947; CAB 21/1711). Ironically, the general running down of the building programme remained one step ahead of attempts to reduce material and labour supplies, and so led to short-term unemployment problems in the industry (LAB 8/1593).

Records

Ministerial meetings during 1950 and 1951 on the future policy towards the building industry are at CAB 130/59. Economic Section papers on housing investment for employment purposes are at T 230/22.

Lord President's Secretariat files on building components dealing mainly with standardization and bulk buying are at CAB 124/343-344. CAB 124/470 deals with timber supplies. Allocation of labour between government departments is dealt with at CAB 124/860, and general papers on labour requirements for the postwar building programme are at CAB 123/123.

Central Statistical Office files on building materials are at CAB 139/143-144, and on Ministry of Health manpower requirements at CAB 139/16.

Prime Minister's Office files include PREM 4/93/5 and PREM 8/229 on brick production, and PREM 8/232 on the 1947 Housing Programme.

Treasury files include T 161/1199/S52616/1 relating to the Building Materials and Housing Bill; and T 229/214 on timber requirements for the housing programme. T 161/1168/S56618 refers to wartime problems.

The main Ministry of Works papers on the construction industry and building matters are in WORK 45; most files deal with the production, supply and cost of building materials, although they also include files on training. Regional building committee papers are in WORK 49.

Ministry of Health files include HLG 68/116 which deals with the allocation of labour and HLG 51/997-1004 on the Housing Panel Subcommittee of the Local Government Manpower Committee*. HLG 101/3 deals with the Building Materials and Housing Act 1945.

Some Ministry of Supply files relating to raw materials are in SUPP 14. Files relating to timber supplies are in AVIA 46/481-494. Papers referring to the Ministry's responsibility for housing fitments are at HLG 68/132.

A Special Needs of Particular Areas for Postwar Building Subcommittee of the Reconstruction Committee* looked at regional problems at the end of the war and attempted to prioritize labour supply. Its papers are at LAB 8/1144. A Central Building Resources Subcommittee of the Local Government Manpower Committee sat from January 1950 to look at building resources (HLG 68/120; MH 102/1918).

Early Ministry of Labour policy files on labour supply for the industry are at LAB 8/647, 899. Relations with the Ministry of Works are chronicled at LAB 8/645. LAB 8/1144, 1200 deals with the special needs of particular areas. Ministry of Labour training files are in LAB 18. These include LAB 18/502 relating to the vocational training scheme as applied to the building industry, LAB 18/118 on wartime planning for the building trade training, and LAB 18/486 on training for the brick industry.

Lord Chancellor's Office papers on the Building Materials and Housing Act 1945 are at LCO 2/3080.

Papers of the Scientific Advisory Committee are at CAB 90/1-6, AVIA 22/178, HLG 71/1303-1307, and HLG 102/279. Those of its Subcommittee on the Building Industry are at HLG 71/1307 and DSIR 4/2136 and the Building Requirements Subcommittee at HLG 71/1303-1306 and DSIR 4/2129.

* for committee references see Appendix B

3.5   Bibliography

M Aldridge, *The British new towns* (1979)

J Burnett, *A short history of housing 1815-1970* (1978)

G Cherry, *The politics of town and country planning* (1982)

A Cox, *Adversary politics and land* (1984)

J B Cullingworth, *Town and country planning in England and Wales* (1970)

The political diary of Hugh Dalton, ed B Pimlott (1985)

P Hall, *Urban and regional planning* (1975)

A E Holmas, *Housing policy in Britain* (1987)

D H McKay and A W Cox, *The politics of urban change* (1979)

S Merrett, *Housing in Britain* (1979)

J R Short, *Housing in Britain—the postwar experience* (1982)

Chapter 4 – THE NATIONAL HEALTH SERVICE

4.1   Introduction

4.2   War and the emergency medical services

4.2.1   Introduction

4.2.2   The Emergency Medical Service

    4.2.2.1   General

    4.2.2.2   EMS: accommodation, equipment, staff

4.2.3   Wartime local authority health services

    4.2.3.1   ARP casualty services

    4.2.3.2   Antenatal and postnatal care, and child health

4.3   Planning a National Health Service

4.4   The National Health Service Act 1946

4.4.1   Policy proposals and discussions

4.4.2   Implementation of the Act

    4.4.2.1   General

    4.4.2.2   Central administration

    4.4.2.3   Hospital and specialist services

    4.4.2.4   Local health authority provision: health centres; maternity and child welfare; domiciliary and other services

    4.4.2.5   'Practitioner' services: GPs; dentists; chemists; opticians

    4.4.2.6   Mental health services

4.4.3   The financial crisis

4.5   Bibliography

4.1 Introduction

Whilst Michael Foot has called the National Health Service 'the greatest socialist achievement of the Labour Government' (Foot 1973), others have argued that 'the National Health Service Act of 1946 created no new hospitals, trained no new doctors, brought no new drugs or methods of treatment into being; these things were there already' (Watkin 1978). The creation of the NHS, therefore, not only promoted controversy at the time. It has continued to provoke it amongst historians.

In the interwar years, the health services in Britain consisted principally of provision available under the National Health Insurance Scheme (NHIS) (see chap 2.3.2), local authority health services, and services offered by voluntary hospitals. The NHIS approved societies were obliged to give medical care only to the subscriber, providing no coverage for families or dependants. The level of service offered varied greatly between societies, from a basic minimum up to a comprehensive service covering dental and optical care. It was often the case, however, that the greater the health risk to the individual concerned, the poorer the cover offered. This disparity was increased by the fact that general practitioners (GPs) tended to gravitate towards the wealthy regions where patients could afford to pay for private treatment, but where doctors were least needed. By 1938, plans were being revived to extend the scheme to dependants and to make other forms of health care available to the majority of people, in particular dental and ophthalmic services.

Local authorities had, over a period of time, acquired a variety of responsibilities. These included the provision of clinics for venereal disease sufferers, expectant mothers, new born babies and tubercular cases. They employed health visitors, certified midwives and district nurses. Following the abolition of the poor law guardians in 1929, they inherited responsibility for the poor law infirmaries which were generally filled to overflowing with chronic cases, the mentally deficient and geriatrics (see chap 6.3). Whilst care of the mentally deficient became a local authority responsibility, administration of mental hospitals remained with the Board of Control (see chap 4.2.2.6). Local authorities also ran general hospitals and specialist hospitals dealing with maternity, infectious diseases and so on. Here, notably in smaller authorities, provision overlapped with the voluntary sector. In less populated areas, local medical committees fulfilled their statutory obligations by paying a stipend to the local cottage hospital to guarantee treatment of their cases. In a similar fashion, approved societies, or at least those offering hospital treatment to their members, subscribed to voluntary hospitals for the same purpose. Those not insured could claim admittance to a public hospital on a means-tested basis.

Voluntary hospitals had expanded in the nineteenth century as a result of charitable endowments. In the twentieth century they remained funded by a mixture of charity, commercial insurance and patients' fees, and continued to play a prominent role in the provision of institutional care for the sick. However their continuing existence was becoming increasingly dependent on payments by patients and local authorities. By the end of the 1930s their financial viability was under question, and their geographical distribution a point of concern.

Preventative health care was a key feature of the public health services before the war. Local medical officers of health were charged with various responsibilities concerning the prevention of disease, including health education and the administration of the Public Health Acts, with their complex specifications concerning sanitary regulations and anti-pollution measures. The advent of war, however, was to shift the emphasis away from preventative to curative medicine.

Severe labour shortages threatened the war effort; and it became increasingly important to guarantee the good health of the whole population in the context of the national emergency. It was no accident, therefore, that wartime medical services, which initially were available only to those immediately concerned with the war effort, were gradually extended to cover nearly all the population. The trend towards curative medicine was reinforced by the National Health Service, with a consequent diminution in the role of public health authorities and a greater concentration of resources on the hospital service.

Records

C Webster *The health services since the war* and F Honigsbaum *Health, happiness and security* provide the most comprehensive account of wartime and postwar health service planning and make extensive use of PRO sources. However it should be noted that many of the references in the former refer to the old departmental numbers and not to the new references subsequently given to the records on their transfer to the PRO.

Early records of the Ministry of Health relating to the operation of the NHIS are in PIN 4; further material can be found in ACT 1, MH 49, MH 62, MH 65, MH 81, PIN 2, and PIN 19.

General files of the Ministry of Health relating to the public health services are at MH 55. Correspondence files are at MH 48 and MH 52. Files relating to public assistance welfare can be found in MH 57. Files of joint hospital boards are at MH 67.

Health services in Wales developed along semi-independent lines. A Welsh Board of Health was set up in 1919 and administered the service independently from the English Ministry of Health. Its records are at MH 96, BD 11 and BD 35.

4.2   War and the emergency medical services

4.2.1   Introduction

The majority of wartime health services, such as Air Raid Precautions (ARP) and casualty services, and the Emergency Medical Service (EMS), were set up as purely temporary wartime measures. However, their importance for the subsequent development of the National Health Service lies in their role in forming important precedents for the extension of services in the postwar period. The EMS established the idea of regional administration and a unified hospital service. Wartime circumstances also created new services which were to be incorporated into the NHS after the war, as was the case with the Emergency Blood Transfusion Service and the Ambulance Service.

4.2.2   The emergency medical service

4.2.2.1   General

The EMS came into operation on the outbreak of war in September 1939. It was a centralized organization, originally designed to provide treatment for the victims of air raids, but later it was opened up to a wider range of patients. It employed full and part-time doctors and other medical and nursing staff, organized the pooling of facilities in independent hospitals, built hutted hospital accommodation and organized medical supplies until 1941.

Preparation for an emergency wartime service stretched as far back as 1923 (MH 101/1). However it was the use of blitzkrieg bombing in the Spanish Civil War in 1936 which first emphasized the need to prepare full emergency services in case of war (MH 77/22). From 1937, preparations began to meet such an emergency. 200,000 casualties a week were anticipated, of which 66,000 would be killed—numbers in excess of the current capacity of the hospitals. In December 1937 the organization of base hospitals, situated away from likely air raid areas, was transferred from the Home Office to the Ministry of Health. At the beginning of 1938, the Ministry began a hospital survey to discover the level of existing accommodation and to plan for wartime needs. Completed in May 1938, it revealed a serious shortage in beds, as well as deficiencies in trained staff, facilities and equipment (MH 76/94-102). Simultaneously, an Advisory Committee on Casualty Organization in London looked at various proposals for a casualty hospital service in the capital (MH 76/348). As a result of the findings of the former, the Ministry of Health took over responsibility for all hospital provision and in June 1938 set up the Emergency Hospital Scheme (DT 16/204). In December 1938, it also took over responsibility for the ambulance service and the first aid posts which were to be administered through local authorities. An Administrative Division and Medical Section was created within the Ministry. Within the existing defence commissioners' regions, regional hospital officers of the Ministry of Health were appointed to co-ordinate public and voluntary sector hospitals, providing regional administration for the first time. Consultants were paid full-time salaries and distributed amongst the regions.

Regional hospital officers' surveys of accommodation in their areas (MH 76/129) showed the 1938 Hospital Survey to have been over-optimistic (Dunn 1952). In the ensuing panic the Ministry established the principle of bed clearing, particularly of the elderly and mentally ill, and 'crowding'. All existing hospital beds were pooled and 50,000 extra beds created. Some facilities were made available in non-civilian hospitals (MH 76/106) but, in the event, the relationship tended to be reversed with civilian places in EMS hospitals taken up by service casualties. The provision and distribution of medical supplies was a further problem. Between 1936 and 1939 the Ministry of Supply made calculations and prepared plans for the distribution of foodstuffs and drugs for the civil medical service (SUPP 14/622-623).

In 1939, a White Paper on the Emergency Medical Service was published. This laid out the financial basis for the hospital service. Local authorities were to provide three-tenths of the cost of hospital treatment up to the maximum of one-tenth of a penny rate. Voluntary hospitals were to pay the same percentage to a maximum of £1 per bed. The Exchequer agreed to fund the remainder.

On 1 September 1939, the process of the 'clearance' of hospital beds began. Admissions were restricted, discharges accelerated and many civilian patients transferred to convalescent accommodation. Assistance Board institutions, mental hospitals, and hospitals for the aged and the infirm were also seriously affected. The majority of patients were carried in specially converted ambulance trains to facilities away from the main areas of population. In London 3,600 patients were transferred from thirty-four hospitals in twenty-one ambulance trains on the first day alone. The use of these trains continued throughout the war (MH 76/249, 254-255, 267).

The failure of the expected air raids to materialize during the early months of the war, however, led to increasing pressure to readmit civilian sick to the hospitals (MH 76/138). From the end of September, therefore, hospitals were allowed to admit civilian cases at up to 75% of normal capacity (HLG 7/623). Subsequently all restrictions on admission were removed, provided one bed per 1,000 of population remained available for war casualties.

In the course of the clearance of hospitals, mental health services were severely cut back (MH 51/645-648). Most institutional buildings were in the form of large Victorian hospitals and as such provided excellent possibilities for conversion to casualty hospitals. During the early months of 1938 the Board of Control, at the request of the Ministry of Health, carried out a survey of accommodation in institutions and hospitals in England and Wales in order to see what capacity could be made available to the EMS. Initially the Board envisaged 16 out of the 101 hospitals being surrendered and 10 out of the 89 mental deficiency institutions. However it was later decided to clear sections of hospitals rather than resort to closure. In the event five hospitals were completely cleared with the remainder keeping a percentage of mentally ill patients. 36,000 beds were created for the EMS. Their return to the mental health services did not begin until the end of the war, and even then the process was slow (MH 76/605).

The first major users of EMS facilities were the armed forces. This was particularly true after Dunkirk (May 1940), when service hospitals found themselves over-stretched. However, from September 1940, the hospitals saw an influx of civilian casualties resulting from the heavy bombing of urban areas. After May 1941 these bombing raids became less intense. EMS facilities became available to those groups whose injuries could be ascribed to the war, and to those civilians involved in essential war work. From July 1943 a Ministry of Health departmental Committee on the 'Demobilization' of the Emergency Hospital Scheme prepared for the end of the EMS (MH 76/601-602, 613). The final large scale use of EMS facilities came in 1944 in the aftermath of the V1 and V2 rocket campaigns on London.

After the rocket attacks on the South East in 1944 the EMS was gradually wound down. In October 1944 all beds reserved for air raid casualties in voluntary hospitals were released, with the exception of three regions, and in December many voluntary hospitals were either suspended or withdrawn from the scheme. In February 1945 there was a similar release of some local authority hospitals. The pace increased with the defeat of Germany and the surrender of Japan. In June 1945 the EMS had 157,048 beds of which 118,205 were occupied. By the end of the year this was reduced to 137,176 beds occupied by 104,602 patients and by the end of 1946, 35,132 beds (McNalty 1968). The scheme operated in a reduced form until July 1948, when it became amalgamated with the National Health Service (MH 76/18).

The EMS set important precedents for the postwar health services. It introduced hospital staff to public work on a salaried basis and helped to break down the traditional distrust between voluntary and public medical staff as the two worked together (Webster 1988). It established regional networks of diagnostic and treatment centres and set performance standards for the medical and administrative services (Fox 1986). It established a blood transfusion service that was to be of lasting importance; and finally, through necessity, it created a major shift in emphasis away from the local preventative public health service, which had developed between the wars, towards a more central curative system based around a hospital structure, which was to become the basis of the National Health Service.

Records

The main files of the Ministry of Health relating to the setting up and running of the EMS are at MH 76. War diaries of the Ministry, consisting mainly of reports, circulars and diaries are at MH 101. Cabinet Office files relating to the official war history can be found at CAB 102/699-718, CAB 103/60, 265-266, 269-271, with similar Ministry of Health files at MH 76/14-15, 618-644. A large number of files relating to special wartime functions of the Ministry of Health in relation to the Emergency Hospital Scheme are at HLG 7/612-808.

Treasury files on the EMS include T 161/1435/S45159/1-6 and T 161/1421/S45149/7-8. Documents relating to the official war history of the Emergency Medical Service can be found at CAB 102/699-718 and MH 76/14-15, 618-644. Papers of the Cabinet Office Historical Section containing correspondence about the medical history of the Second World War are at CAB 103/60, with the preparation papers of the official history at CAB 103/265-266, 269-271.

Regional files on the operation of the scheme, listed by civil defence region, are at MH 76/409-486.

A number of file series exist documenting the armed forces medical services. AIR 49 deals with the history of the RAF medical service, with other files in AIR 2. War Office war diaries relating to the armed forces medical services are at WO 177, with the records of its Medical Branch at WO 165. Papers collected by its medical historian for the Second World War histories, relating to the army contributions to the UK medical service, are at WO 222.

A Committee on Emergency Hospital Organization sat from April 1939 and looked at the availability of accommodation (MH 76/130). An Advisory Committee on the Emergency Hospital Medical Service looked at the running of the EMS from October 1939 (MH 76/330).

4.2.2.2   EMS: accommodation, equipment, staff

One of the main purposes of the EMS was to provide enough beds to meet the expected demand. As has already been noted, this was done by a process of clearing. However, the Ministry of Health also provided extra beds through expanded accommodation. This was done by requisitioning non-medical buildings (HLG 7/615, 661), and through the provision of tents and huts attached to existing facilities (MH 76/242; HLG 7/674); the shortage of labour and building materials made it impossible to build new structures on a large scale. Over 40,000 beds were provided through the use of temporary accommodation. However conditions were often inappropriate to the uses to which it was put: a letter to the Minister of Health complained of tents 'leaking like sieves' and others 'quite unfit for the reception of patients' (MH 76/240-2; T 161/1038/S44471/1-3).

A major problem for the hospital services was bomb damage (HLG 7/713, 975; MH 76/167-175). The shortage of men and materials to carry out repairs meant that even minor damage could cause the closure of sections of hospitals. By the end of October 1944 the flying-bomb attacks on the South East had damaged 100 hospitals, of which 76 were in London, with the permanent loss of 2,600 beds and the temporary loss of 6,000. 8,000 civilian patients had to be evacuated (Dunn 1952).

The issue of medical supplies also provoked difficulties (MH 76/27-41). Before the war, the government had established several interdepartmental supply committees. The Ministry of Health was represented on the one which co-ordinated the requisitioning of drugs and medical equipment (CAB 60). During the early years of the war, responsibility was shared jointly between the Ministry of Health and the Home Office. As the service was new, it was funded entirely by the Exchequer. In competing with the armed services for supplies, the Ministry often found itself coming out second best. The situation became more difficult in November 1941 when the Ministry of Supply took over responsibility for medical supplies for both military and civilian hospital services; with no separate ministry to argue their case, civilian supplies received a low priority compared with those for the armed forces.

Staffing: doctors

The role of doctors within the service raised a number of difficult issues. In 1937 the Central Emergency Committee of the British Medical Association (BMA)(MH 76/330), which became the Central Medical War Committee in 1939, had begun to compile a register of GPs willing to offer their services during a national emergency, eventually covering 90% of the profession. In practice, the committee became the main recruiting agency for the supply of medical personnel to the services and to civilian hospitals. The role of doctors within the EMS was a matter of controversy. The Treasury were opposed to the employment of doctors by the state. They preferred to see the government functioning like an employment exchange, directing doctors where needed, but maintaining the hospitals as employers. The Treasury feared setting a postwar precedent (MH 76/207). Despite this, the Ministry of Health succeeded in employing doctors within the EMS on a full-time salaried basis (MH 76/21). By September 1939 some 2,500 doctors had enrolled for the EMS, although some, fearing the loss of private patients, were employed on a part-time basis.

Up to April 1940 the supply of doctors just about kept pace with demand, partly because the period of 'phoney war' resulted in fewer casualties than expected. However from April, the National Service (Armed Forces) Act 1939 became applicable to the medical profession. Doctors and GPs up to the age of 41 became liable to be called up; the Central Medical War Committee administered recruitment of qualified personnel into the armed services. Strong protests from the hospitals meant that a number of senior staff were kept by the EMS, but most doctors of junior rank were lost to the armed forces. The worst effects were felt by the new 'improvised' hospitals which were set up in temporary accommodation. These had not had the time to establish a permanent staff and their temporary nature made it difficult for them to attract new recruits. This was also true of the country-based hospitals which failed to lure significant numbers of doctors away from the cities.

As a result of these shortages, in December 1940 the minister of health appointed a Committee of Enquiry on Medical Personnel, under Sir Arthur Robinson, to look at the consequences for the civilian sector of the services' recruitment of doctors (MH 76/329; HLG 7/642, 803; LAB 14/321; ED 50/174). Whilst little could be done to improve the domestic supply, the committee did suggest important measures which were to ease the problem: posts per hospital were reduced in an attempt to spread supply more thinly over a wider area; it was made easier to employ doctors with overseas qualifications (HLG 7/699); newly qualified doctors had to practice six months in a civilian hospital or medical practice before joining the armed forces; final year students were employed. The employment of American doctors was legalized and by October 1941, fifty-seven Americans were employed. Finally a Medical Personnel (Priority) Committee (MH 58/775-843; HLG 7/642, 803) was established to keep the situation under constant review.

From 1942 onwards, debate focused on achieving a balance between the need for doctors in the armed forces and for the civilian population (CAB 71/13: LP(43)137; CAB 71/14: LP(43)257; CAB 71/16: LP(44)57; HLG 7/35, 720, 725; T 230/49-51). In the autumn of that year, the government set up a Reconstruction Secretariat and Interdepartmental Committee on the Machinery of Demobilization (LAB 6/202) to prepare a general scheme. Between November 1942 and November 1943 the Central Medical War Committee considered demobilization in relation to doctors. It was decided to increase the number of experienced doctors available to the civilian service by giving doctors over 44 priority status for demobilization. However the number of older doctors released could not exceed the number of young doctors recruited, and the service departments were given the power to veto any individual case.

Concern existed amongst service doctors that they would be disadvantaged in the postwar service because of the length of time they had been away from domestic health care. A partial solution was to offer refresher courses, mainly at postgraduate level, to medical staff before demobilization (MH 58/349-353). Further, the priority demobilization of older doctors and the call-up of younger ones meant vacancies were opened up which would otherwise have been taken by younger rivals. Brush-up courses were provided for GPs returning to practice and consultant trainees were provided with special six-month posts to complete their training. It was decided to continue the EMS for at least one year after the war to provide some degree of continuity. The minister of health would continue to pay all salaries (MH 79/547; T 230/48).

Staffing: nurses and midwives

Shortages of nursing staff proved to be as difficult as that of doctors (MH 55/1454-1470). Recruitment problems in the late thirties had led, in 1937, to the appointment of the Athlone Committee on Nursing Services to see how the situation could be improved. This was followed in October 1937 by the appointment of the MacNalty Committee on Nursing to prepare a scheme for the supply of nurses in wartime. The latter recommended the formation of a Central Emergency Committee for the Nursing Profession which was set up in December 1938. During the spring of 1939 this committee, in conjunction with local authorities, asked local nursing committees to compile a register of all trained nurses, assistant nurses and auxiliaries willing to come forward during a national emergency (MH 55/785). Nurses already in employment were ineligible. By June 1939, 7,500 trained nurses and 2,900 assistant nurses had enrolled along with 45,000 auxiliaries who were undergoing training. This formed the basis of the Civil Nursing Reserve (MH 55/2005-2029), providing nursing staff for the EMS and public health services (MH 55/785-791).

The major problem during the war was the supply and distribution of nursing staff as large groups of nurses became employed in the forces (LAB 8/793). Up to 1943 general policy within the Ministry of Health remained vague, with distribution carried out by the Ministry of Labour and National Service (LAB 8/521). One of the major obstacles to the recruitment of nurses was the profession's terms and conditions (MH 55/1984-1996). A 1943 investigation carried out by the Social Survey into the attitude of women towards nursing found a large pool of women attracted to the service, but put off by the long hours and poor pay (RG 23/45). Compared to alternative war work which was becoming available to women, wages and job security for nurses were low. A further investigation later that year found that the majority of recruits came from middle-class backgrounds and that expansion could be achieved only through attracting girls from lower educational and economic groups (RG 23/52). In August 1941, the Home Policy Committee* decided to make grants to voluntary hospitals conditional on the acceptance of an imposed nurses' salary structure. It also set up the Rushcliffe Committee on Nurses' Salaries to look at the establishment of a national pay structure (CAB 75/10: 1 Aug 1941). Policy discussions in 1942 (LAB 8/700, 1039) led, in 1943, to the publication of a Nurses Bill. This called for the establishment of a national pay system; the granting to assistant nurses of the recognized status they had previously lacked; the restricting of the term 'nurse' to suitably qualified persons; and the establishment of a central agency for the supply and distribution of nurses. This became law the same year (DT 2/8-14; DT 16/556; ED 31/498; LCO 2/2651; MH 51/602; MH 55/2540-2541; MH 80/22).

A National Advisory Council for the Recruitment and Distribution of Nurses and Midwives was set up under M M McCorquodale in 1943 to consider ways of relieving the nursing shortage. On the advice of the committee, a national register of nurses was created and an intensive publicity campaign started (LAB 8/1047, 1049). Fourteen to eighteen year olds were recruited as nursing cadets, a scheme designed to bridge the gap between leaving school and the minimum nursing age of 18 (LAB 8/796). Nurses disabled during the war were offered retraining and rehabilitation (LAB 8/1051). Nursing auxiliaries were offered free training courses based on first aid instruction and home nursing, followed by practical training within hospitals. Those qualified in nursing were directed to areas where they were most needed (LAB 8/932). Nurses were also recruited from abroad (MH 55/207-208). These provisions helped ease the problem, but up to the end of the EMS there continued to be a struggle between the civilian and services requirements in the supply of nurses (MH 79/521).

Staffing: opticians and dentists

The recruitment of other medical staff was carried out in much the same way as for doctors. Opticians were recruited for wartime services through a Central Emergency Committee for Opticians (England and Wales) (MH 58/375), set up in 1939 for the purposes of compiling a register of opticians prepared to offer their services in a national emergency. Likewise, at the request of the Ministry of Health the Pharmaceutical Society set up a Central Pharmaceutical Emergency Committee to compile and maintain a register of all pharmacists and dispensers willing to serve in the event of war. In 1942 the register was closed and a complete census was taken of all pharmaceutical undertakings, under the Pharmaceutical Undertakings Act 1942.

General dentistry remained outside the EMS structure with the exception of oral surgery and oral disease, although a division of qualified personnel between civilian and service needs was still introduced. In 1938 a Dental Emergency Committee was appointed (MH 76/342), to be superseded on the outbreak of war by the Dental War Committee. District committees were set up. Service departments notified the central committee of their requirements and local committees were called upon to fill their quota.

A major development arising directly from the demands of war was the formation of the Emergency Blood Transfusion Service. Before the war the service had been on a very small scale and almost exclusively concerned with the maintenance of lists of volunteer blood donors. In London a basic service had been established by July 1938. The Medical Research Council set up four depots around London for the collection, storage and supply of blood on behalf of the Ministry; and on the outbreak of war sufficient quantities of blood were made available to London hospitals. Outside London, however, no central provision existed before the latter half of 1940. What provision there was was local, voluntary, and unco-ordinated, and took the form of blood panels organized independently by local authorities, medical schools, and the Red Cross and St John Ambulance Association. In July 1940 a draft scheme was drawn up to form a regional blood transfusion service under the EMS. Centres were established in each civil defence region and staff recruited mainly from the voluntary sector. Donors were recruited from every section of the public by national campaigns in the form of broadcast appeals and posters, and locally organized meetings (INF 2/58; INF 2/131; INF 3/281). The service firmly established itself during the remainder of the war and continued thereafter as the National Blood Transfusion Service (MH 76/300-301).

* For committee references see Appendix B

Records

Cabinet war history papers relating to hutted hospital accommodation are at CAB 102/711-712. CAB 102/717 deals with medical supplies, while CAB 102/718 deals with the history of medical supplies between 1939 and 1949.

Files relating to the supply of hospital equipment and building records are sparse as few papers of the Ministry of Supply Medical Directorate have been traced. Regional files on the operation of the EMS, listed by civil defence area, are at MH 76/409-486. Ministry of Works files relating to the building of emergency hospitals at Bristol and Barnstaple are at WORK 12/122/4 and WORK 12/123/1-3.

Ministry of Labour and National Service files relating to the training and recruitment of medical staff are in LAB 8. Papers of the General Nursing Council for England and Wales, responsible for the training, examination and regulation of nurses, are at DT 1-DT 48. Lord Chancellor's Office papers on the Nurses Bill 1943 are at LCO 2/2651.

Papers of the Interdepartmental Committee on Nursing Services are at MH 71/31-49; MH 55/2003; ED 46/199; ED 50/203, 175; ED 136/649; T 161/1426/S44447/1. The Rushcliffe Committee on Nurses' Salaries papers are at MH 55/887, 890-893, 1991-1996; HLG 33/10; T 161/1426/S44447/1.

Papers of the National Advisory Council for the Recruitment and Distribution of Nurses and Midwives include LAB 8/735, 737, 932, 954, 998, 1001-1005, 1015, 1043,

1083, 1284-1299, 1452-1462, 1469; LAB 12/336; LAB 8/1463, 1467, 1773-1777, 1800-1807, 1821-1824, 1847-1850. Papers relating to Scotland are in LAB 8/1055. Papers on the Birmingham Local Advisory Committee are at LAB 8/1009, as are those for Coventry and Wolverhampton. Those for Kent and Sussex are at LAB 8/1008, and those for London are at LAB 8/1007.

Papers of the Central Medical War Committee of the BMA are at MH 76/330, MH 79/30-31, LAB 6/278, with papers of its support committee at MH 79/33-34. A Ministry of Health departmental Committee on the Conscription of Doctors in the Public Health Services sat from November 1940 (MH 79/38-39).

Papers of the Dental War Committee are in MH 79/42, 45-46, 48; MH 76/342; and MH 58/522.

Papers of the Central Emergency Committee for the Nursing Profession include those at PIN 15/3013.

War Office papers relating to the requirement of doctors and nurses for civil affairs in 1945 are in WO 32/11703.

4.2.3   Wartime local authority health services

4.2.3.1   ARP casualty services

A second consequence of the blitz bombings during the Spanish Civil War was the growth of Air Raid Precaution (ARP) schemes prepared by central government and local authorities. This was to be a key area of public health, providing short-term protection and basic first aid during air attack, and in the long term preventing epidemics and providing care for the homeless.

Between 1924 and 1939 air raid precautions were considered by a number of official committees (CAB 46). Until December 1938 all ARP services were under the control of the ARP department of the Home Office. After this date, control of first aid posts and the ambulance service passed to the Ministry of Health (HO 45/20225; HO 186/2248). The Air Raid Precautions Act 1937 (HO 45/17608-17609) made county councils and county boroughs responsible for the preparation of general ARP schemes including first aid posts, first aid points and an ambulance service. The Home Office kept charge of the training of staff. Responsibility for the overall co-ordination of the ARP services was vested in the newly created Ministry of Home Security.

Control of the bulk of the civil defence and ARP services rested with regional commissioners appointed to the various civil defence regions. These administrative areas created an obvious rival to local authorities, and after the war were considered as a serious alternative to them (see chap 6.2). Special commissioners were appointed to the London Region, and these were given the support of a London Regional Council (HO 207/8), providing contact between local authorities and commissioners, and a London Civil Defence Region Co-ordinating Committee (HO 207/7, 94).

The provision of air raid shelters was an important aspect of the work of the ARP services (MH 76/535-600; HLG 101/250). The provision of mass shelters in parks, public buildings, and on the London underground, however, also had serious implications for public health. The control of underground shelters rested with a Tube Shelter Committee, which was set up in late 1941 by the Ministries of Home Security and Health. It discovered serious outbreaks of disease (HO 200). On the underground, rats and mosquitoes were a major problem (MH 76/546) and in some shelters the use of germ masks was considered (MH 76/555). Health and disease in London shelters was monitored by an Advisory Committee of Medical Officers of Health (HO 207/162; HLG 7/626). On-site care was provided by a doctor/nurse service (HO 207/358). The problem of health was looked at by the Horder Committee on the Conditions of Air Raid Shelters (HO 207/428).

Under the Air Raid Precautions Act 1937, local authorities were obliged to make provision for emergency first aid. This involved the establishment of basic first aid posts and stretcher parties. Where possible, first aid posts were provided in hospitals, especially in areas most exposed to attack. Otherwise they were placed in protected buildings, with six posts per 100,000 of population. Their role was to deal with lightly injured and mentally disturbed persons who would otherwise flood the hospitals, to provide supervision and classification of casualties by a doctor, and to provide the necessary immediate treatment and shelter. Training in first aid was available on a number of temporary courses (HO 207/151).

Other facilities available included first aid points which provided basic cover in rural and semi-rural areas. They contained basic first aid equipment kept at a fixed location, such as a doctor's surgery, and were manned by part-time volunteers. Early in 1939 mobile first aid units were added to the ARP casualty services (HLG 7/659-660). These consisted of motor vehicles with first aid equipment. Their role was to attend specific incidents and set up first aid posts. In the event mobile units were rarely used. Heavy raids usually occurred in built-up areas, making it difficult to manoeuvre the large unit vehicles into position. Moreover, built-up areas usually had an adequate provision of fixed points. Stretcher parties were established by the Home Office and moved over to the ARP Casualty Service on the outbreak of war. Parties consisted of four men, with a car and driver. They provided emergency cover in case of large scale incidents at which the ambulance service could not cope. Special training courses were provided for new recruits (HO 207/201).

Other ARP services were provided by a number of emerging voluntary organizations. In particular the Women's Voluntary Service (WVS) was formed in 1938 to 'cope with the unimagined difficulties likely to arise in civil defence'. Services were provided only when required by local authorities, and the voluntary organizations became heavily involved in work in rest centres, communal feeding provision, and evacuation. Later they expanded to include special services for the elderly (see chap 6.3.1).

Before 1935 ambulances were maintained by local authorities. They were augmented by the St John Ambulance Association, the British Red Cross and other voluntary groups. However the system was not co-ordinated; procedure and equipment varied from area to area. In 1935 local authorities were asked to co-ordinate ambulance services for transporting air raid casualties, in addition to their peacetime duties. The Air Raid Precautions Act 1937 set up an emergency ambulance service under local authority control (MH 76/284).

The main priority for local authorities was to assemble a fleet of vehicles to meet wartime needs. Cars and vans were earmarked for the service. They included 6,000 trade vehicles considered non-essential for wartime needs. However, at the start of the war fewer vehicles than expected were available and, of those that were, the better quality ones were taken by other services; 'those obtained as ambulances were often in poor mechanical condition, unsuitable for the purpose and too heavy for women to drive' (Dunn 1952). In October 1939 the minister ordered local authorities to buy second-hand cars to convert in the absence of reliable trade vehicles. Problems occurred as the

 WITHDRAWN FROM STOCK LIBRARY SWANSEA

imposed £60 limit per car meant only older models could be secured. This greatly increased maintenance costs. Single decker buses were increasingly used as ambulances. These were usually converted to carry ten stretchers and proved more versatile than trade lorries. Improvised cars could usually carry between two and four stretchers. Numbers were boosted by the formation of a voluntary car pool for hospital services (MH 76/283). By the end of 1940 the service was operating 8,785 full-time and 6,078 part-time ambulances, compared with 6,900 and 5,350 before the war.

Recruitment of ambulance staff proved to be a major problem. The official war historian blamed 'apathy and the lack of uniforms and badges' as well as the high wage alternatives that were available elsewhere (Dunn 1952). However, by 1940 the service was employing 9,348 full-time men and 13,765 women with 23,519 men and 29,725 women part-time. Local authority provision was supplemented by a number of other ambulance services. Already mentioned were the St John Ambulance Association and the Red Cross which were well established at the outbreak of war. A significant newcomer was the organization American Ambulance (Great Britain). This was formed early in 1940 out of private donations in the United States and Britain. Initially it provided 50 ambulances, 50 cars and 50 mobile first aid posts staffed by women from the First Aid Nursing Yeomanry and the Mechanical Transport Corps. The number of vehicles was gradually expanded to over 260. Over 17% of stretcher cases in London were carried by the organization. At the end of the war it merged with the local authority service (MH 76/282).

Records

Cabinet files relating to civil defence services are in CAB 73. Reports to the War Cabinet by the minister of home security on the early operation of the ARP and casualty services are at CAB 68.

The main Ministry of Health files on ARP services are at MH 79/126-223. Other files can be found in HLG 7. Home Office files are in HO 45. Ministry of Home Security files relating to the planning and administration of air raid precautions and civil defence and the organization of civil defence regions under regional commissioners are at HO 186. Board of Education files on ARP are at ED 10/212-215, 314 and Ministry of Labour and National Service files at LAB 12/62-67. Ministry of Works files are at WORK 28. Files on research on air raid shelters carried out by the Department of Scientific and Industrial Research are at DSIR 4/746-842.

MH 101/1 contains the Ministry of Health 1939 war diaries which include a chapter on the formation of ARP services and air raid shelters, and the ambulance service. Air raid wardens operated outside the casualty services but acted as useful sources of information and provided local knowledge, essential in an emergency. Their main files are at MEPO 2/4922-4951.

Files on air raid shelter expenditure are at HO 45/18541-18547 and MH 76/490. Those on the authorization of local authority expenditure on the ambulance services are at HLG 7/666-667, and on first aid posts at HLG 7/662-665.

Files relating to the regional administration of the civil defence services are at HO 207. Ministry of Home Security research and development files relating to regional air raid damage reports are at HO 192; this class also contains analyses of the effects of bombing and the performance of the ARP services.

4.2.3.2 Antenatal and postnatal care, and child health

The health of pregnant women and of mothers and children was a major area of responsibility of the local health authorities before the war. The outbreak of war created new problems for the service.

A major factor which affected the shape of the wartime services was the evacuation of mothers and children from areas at risk from air attack to reception areas. The organization of the evacuation is dealt with elsewhere (see chap 5.3.1). The evacuation of expectant mothers created a number of problems for the health services. Large groups of women were moved from populated areas with general antenatal provisions to rural areas with hardly any. For those who remained, the antenatal clinics were often closed and taken over as first aid posts. Further, health visitors were either transferred to the reception areas or to other ARP services. The cost of the scheme caused some local authorities to charge mothers for their maintenance in homes and hostels (HLG 51/1042).

In the reception areas an improved structure of maternity homes had to be created. Dwelling houses were adapted, as were convalescent homes, hotels and boarding houses, and maternity units at semi-rural hospitals. However the majority of women were billeted and had to rely on the midwifery service (see below).

The staffing of the maternity service proved to be a major problem. The effect of the call-up of midwives to the military nursing service and to the Civil Nursing Reserve was worsened by the high number of midwives leaving the service of their own accord, attracted by growing job opportunities elsewhere (MH 58/378). At the same time, there was an increase in the number of home confinements due to the high demand for maternity beds in hospitals (see below). The training and distribution of midwives was controlled by the Central Midwives Board. This was a statutory body created in 1902 for the training and regulation of midwives, consisting of representatives of the Ministry of Health, the Royal College of Midwives and other professional bodies. The Ministry of Health attempted to ease the problem of shortages through its programme for the training of nurses (see chap 4.2.2.2) and in consultation with the Central Midwives Board (MH 55/788). As well as attempts to improve the image of the service (MH 58/378) shortages were tackled by the creation of a National Advisory Council for the recruitment and distribution of nurses and midwives to co-ordinate recruitment policy. This was supported by local advisory committees (LAB 8/1007-1009). The situation was slightly eased by the minister of labour, in 1943, requiring pupil midwives to practice midwifery for one year after the Central Midwives Board examination. However, complaints of shortage continued to occur (LAB 8/1045). The Ministry of Labour and National Service, from 1943, began an extensive publicity programme to aid recruitment (LAB 8/1047) and established various training and rehabilitation schemes (LAB 8/1051). However it was not until after the war that the service was properly reorganized.

These problems occurred despite a dramatic downturn in the demand for home confinement. Before the war two-thirds of births had taken place in the home. However as the war progressed this figure was reversed. Many wartime homes were overcrowded with evacuees and bombed-out relatives or friends and provided far from ideal conditions for childbirth. Many women also found themselves emotionally isolated because of the absence of husbands and close friends. In these circumstances, institutional confinement offered greater security.

Extensive home help schemes were set up to provide domestic assistance to women confined at home in an attempt to relieve the hospital services (LAB 8/901; MH 55/2361-2363). However the low pay and attractive alternatives available made it difficult to recruit women to the schemes. The situation was worsened by the start of the domestic help scheme for the elderly in December 1944 which provided a similar service to the home help scheme and competed for the same staff (see chap 6.3.1). At the end of the war, the government launched an extensive advertising campaign in an attempt to overcome the problem (LAB 12/342). Health visitors were another crucial part of the domiciliary childbirth services who proved difficult to recruit. Despite the establishment of a number of training centres (MH 53/121-122) they continued to leave the service for other work.

The shift in demand towards hospital and maternity unit confinement caused serious problems. Many maternity places had been lost to the EMS. In reception areas, provision was very makeshift and staff shortages severe (LAB 8/904). Even when hospital provision was extensive, maternity units did not exist on the scale required. The restrictions on building due to the shortage of labour and materials meant that no new maternity units could be built. Many hospitals found it necessary to restrict entry to first confinements and emergencies. By the end of 1943, hospitals had sufficient beds for just 50% of births. A consequence of this was the increasing use of private nursing homes for childbirth, as an alternative to hospitals.

To safeguard the nutrition of expectant mothers and young children a National Milk Scheme was introduced in 1940 by the minister of food. The scheme had been rejected by the Treasury in 1939 as financially impractical. However, with a new government and Attlee in the chair of the Food Policy Committee* the situation had changed. The scheme provided milk in liquid form, free or at low cost, to expectant mothers or those with young children. The scheme was used in part to alleviate public agitation at a fourpence in the gallon increase in the price of milk (CAB 74/2: 9 May 1940). In December 1940 provision was expanded when the Ministry of Food introduced the Welfare Food Scheme. This was designed to supplement the rations of various groups, the main recipients being expectant mothers and young children. The scheme provided cod-liver oil, concentrated orange juice and vitamin tablets. From 1942 children under 5 also received dried eggs. The success of the scheme, however, was mixed. The take-up rate was disappointing, especially in relation to vitamin supplements (McNalty 1953). Distribution centres were often inconvenient and the health value of the various products was not always appreciated (RG 23/59). In addition babies' general food rations were fairly generous and were considered sufficient by many parents.

At the same time the Board of Education decided that school meals should be generally available (see chap 5.3.5.1). The number of children benefiting from free or subsidized meals increased from 130,000 in July 1940 to 1,650,000 in 1945. The Milk in Schools Scheme (see chap 5.3.5.1) gave 50% of school children free or subsidized milk in 1940; 73% in 1945.

A further new development was the creation of an immunization and vaccination service (MH 55/1736-1761). Diphtheria and whooping cough had been two of the main causes of high infant mortality. Free vaccination against diphtheria was introduced to combat the epidemics feared as a result of the blitz and mass evacuation of children. This was accompanied between 1941 and 1943 by an extensive publicity campaign (HLG 7/750). Despite opposition from such groups as the National Anti-Vaccination League (MH 55/1901) by 1942 one-third of children under 15 had taken part in the programme

(RG 23/23). Over the next three years the service, working through the School Medical Service (see chap 5.3.5.2), established itself as a permanent feature of the preventative side of local authority work. By 1945 67% of children under 16 had been immunized and public awareness of disease and preventative measures had greatly increased (RG 23/77).

* for committee references see Appendix B

Records

Ministry of Health files relating to maternity and child welfare issues can be found in MH 55/1497-1578. War diaries of events referring to maternity and child welfare are at MH 101/39-40.

Records of the main evacuation scheme are referred to at the end of Chap 5.3.1.

Papers of the Central Midwives Board are at MH 55/1605-1619 and DV 1-DV 11. The main Ministry of Health files on the administration of the service are at MH 55/1579-1631. Papers of the National Advisory Council for the Recruitment and Distribution of Nurses and Midwives are referred to at the end of Chap 4.2.2.2.

Ministry of Food files on the Welfare Food Scheme can be found at MAF 101/451-548, with files on the National Milk Scheme at MAF 85/284. Corresponding files of the Ministry of Health are at MH 55/1548-1568, MH 56/413 and MH 55/639-649. Assistance Board files are at AST 7/500, 896, 899. Files of the Ministry of Health's Food Division on the child and mother milk scheme are at MH 56/526-530. MH 56/413, 535 refer to the provision of concentrated orange juice.

Minister of information papers relating to the campaign on diphtheria and immunization are at INF 1/344, INF 2/56, INF 3/280. Registrar general statistics on the programme are at RG 26/23.

4.3 Planning a National Health Service

From 1938 a small group of civil servants met to consider the future of the health services. Sir John Maude, deputy secretary at the Ministry of Health proposed either an expansion of national health insurance benefits to include further groups within the community or the development of local authority services. The Ministry of Health chief medical officer went further, putting forward 'the suggestion that the hospitals of England and Wales should be administered as a National Hospital Service by the Ministry' (MH 80/24). These plans were, however, overtaken by the outbreak of war when policy within the Ministry became concentrated on the Emergency Medical Service (see chap 4.2.2).

From 1940 onwards planning again became important. The formation of a coalition under Churchill brought many Labour Party politicians into government, providing a new impetus for reconstruction planning (see chap 1.2). Since 1934 the Labour Party had been pledged to a free and comprehensive health service, with a full-time salaried staff, administration under a reformed system of regional government, and the establishment of health centres to provide the majority of primary and preventative services.

The medical profession was also involved in debates about reform. The British Medical Association (BMA) was becoming increasingly pessimistic about the future of general practice, which doctors thought was being eroded by the expanding public health services and hospital contributory schemes. In 1938 the BMA published *A general medical service for the nation* which outlined its plans. In the early years of the war the BMA pressed for these policies to be considered.

Voluntary hospitals were also eager to see postwar reform. During the interwar period they had faced serious problems in recruiting staff because of low wages. Even more serious, in the long term, was their lack of financial viability. In the nineteenth century the hospitals had relied on charitable donations but they had come increasingly to rely on finance from patients, local authorities and approved societies. For many hospitals this income was insufficient to guarantee survival. Consequently the Nuffield Provincial Hospital Trust was set up in 1939 to offer some degree of regional and divisional control of services and thereby to secure better co-ordination and management of funds (MH 58/324). In terms of national planning the Trust was significant in two respects. It created the first regional administrative system for hospitals outside local authority control (MH 58/325-326; T 160/1158/F17988) and so acted as a precedent for future schemes. Indeed it was copied by the organization of the EMS and Civil Defence regions. Secondly, this regionalization was seen by local authorities as a major threat to their position and power. By the end of 1941, the Nuffield Trust had created three regional councils, a regional advisory council and eight divisional councils. Potential conflict between the two different administrative structures pushed the issue of hospital administration towards the front of the political agenda (CAB 71/2: 15 Oct 1941; CAB 117/211).

The government's first postwar hospital scheme was prepared by Malcolm Mac-Donald, the minister of health from May 1940 to February 1941 (MH 77/25; MH 80/24: 1 Dec 1940). Pressure from the Nuffield Trust succeeded in securing promises about the future co-existence of municipal and voluntary hospitals and their administration in regional bodies larger than local authorities. This scheme, however, remained within the confines of the Ministry of Health.

During 1941 the Ministry came under pressure to make public its intentions (MH 77/25), as discussions increasingly took place outside its control (CAB 117/211). In October 1941 the new minister of health, Ernest Brown, told the House of Commons that the government would provide a comprehensive service for all who needed medical care after the war. He hinted at local authority/voluntary hospital co-operation. He strongly emphasized, however, that the service was not to be free and that a hospital service should take priority over general health provision. To facilitate this he announced the setting up of hospital surveys to act as guides for future planning (MH 77/1-24).

The Beveridge Committee on Social Insurance and Allied Services* (see chap 2.2) sat from June 1941. Whilst its main role was to struggle with the problems of social insurance and workmen's compensation, Beveridge was determined to develop a blueprint for a comprehensive welfare service. By the time the Committee reported in 1942, he had received evidence from a wide variety of health service planners and was well ahead of the Ministry of Health in sounding out opinion and in formulating proposals. Assumption B of the report called for a 'comprehensive national health service [that] will ensure that for every citizen there is available whatever medical treatment he requires in whatever form he requires it, domiciliary or institutional, general, specialist or consultant, and will ensure also the provision of dental, ophthalmic and surgical appliances, nursing and midwifery and rehabilitation after accidents'. Beveridge proposed that health should take precedence over other uses of public and personal resources. He argued that the best system would be one free at the point of access (MH 80/31: 22 Feb 1942).

Many of the proposals in the report worried the Ministry of Health (MH 80/31: 2 Feb 1942, 6 Feb 1942) and made it essential for it to start developing its own concrete proposals. In November 1942 Maude laid down the basic principles of the service for presentation to ministers (MH 77/26; MH 80/24: Nov 1942). The scheme was to serve the whole population, to include a full-time salaried service for GPs, and the provision of non-competing health centres. Administration of the GP service was kept away from local authorities with a Central Medical Board acting as arbitrator. These proposals brought to the surface the concern of a number of ministers. Churchill warned his colleagues against giving people 'false hopes and airy visions of Utopia and Eldorado' (CAB 66/30: 14 Nov 1942), whilst Sir Kingsley Wood, the chancellor of the Exchequer, attacked 'Golden Age idealists' (PREM 4/89/2: 17 Nov 1942). The Treasury were concerned about the financial implications of any move away from the NHIS (ACT 1/708; MH 80/24: 8 Nov 1942). In the face of this opposition, the minister of health trod carefully.

However, his position became increasingly difficult as time passed. Both the Phillips Committee*, set up to look at the Beveridge Report, and the Reconstruction Priorities Committee* came out in favour of a comprehensive health service (CAB 143/45: 14 Jan 1943; CAB 87/13: 7 Feb 1943) and were eventually supported by the Cabinet (CAB 66/34: 12 Feb 1943) for a number of reasons. First, the Emergency Medical Service was gradually run down from 1943, making postwar planning essential. Secondly, the war had created a number of new services which needed co-ordination, in particular the blood transfusion service. Thirdly, the government from 1943 onward was committed to massive social security reform and health policy would be affected. Finally, the presence of Labour ministers was crucial in pushing the proposals through.

In January 1943 the minister of health prepared his first draft of a health services bill. In February this appeared as a confidential document, termed the 'Brown Plan' (MH 80/25: 26 Feb 1943). Whilst accepting the principle of public provision of a comprehensive health service available to all, it emphasized that no compulsion would be involved and patients would be free to use private medicine. Similarly there was to be no compulsion on the profession to take part. The service was to cover all provision with the exception of mental health. It was to be 'free', with payment through insurance contributions (although charging 'hotel' costs for in-patients was considered (T 161/1166/S50599: 7 Jan 1944)). Voluntary hospitals remained concerned about local authority control, despite concessions towards regional administration (MH 80/25: 11 Mar 1943, 3 May 1943, 26 Mar 1943; CAB 124/442). Local authorities initially welcomed the proposals (MH 80/25: 10 Mar 1943, 23 Mar 1943, 23 June 1943) but later became concerned at the role of the Central Medical Board and of unelected professionals (MH 77/27). It was the medical profession, however, which proved most hostile.

The remuneration of doctors was one of the key issues in the problem of setting up a national health service. Under the existing system doctors had the right to buy and sell practices and receive payment by capitation fees. For many within the BMA, and for many GPs, the issue at stake was the freedom of doctors and their relationship with the patient. 'We are fighting this bloodiest of all wars', wrote one GP, 'for freedom and this is not the time to put forward a scheme that will, in the short passage of time, take freedom away from the doctor and freedom and privacy away from the patient' (MH 77/84: 15 Mar 1944). The Treasury was hostile to salaries for both financial and ideological reasons. E Hale, principal assistant secretary at the Treasury, for example, argued that the sale of practices was 'a necessary ingredient in a doctor's practice, being in a competitive business. If that is scandalous—so is its sale; but if the competition isn't scandalous, neither is its sale' (T 161/1166/S50599). For others, the arguments of the BMA were simply in the interests of protectionism: 'their opposition', wrote another GP, 'is largely that of the consultants and those practitioners "farming" big practices with assistants, and is almost purely one of finance—however much this may be camouflaged by idealistic phrases' (MH 77/85: 8 Sept 1944).

From July 1943 a White Paper was prepared. Attlee's arrival on the Reconstruction Priorities Committee* as lord president greatly increased the pace of planning. The main arguments on the committee revolved around the issue of joint versus single authority control (CAB 87/12: 18 Aug 1943). This was mainly due to the presence of Herbert Morrison, whose background lay in local government. As head of the London County Council in the 1930s he had been keen to establish a free health service in the London area, and he was now determined to defend the position of local authorities as the main providers of health services. Disagreements also occurred about the government concessions in relation to a salaried profession and health centres. Whilst a commitment to health centres was confirmed, Brown's call for a gradualist approach sounded ominous to Labour leaders.

Henry Willink replaced Brown as minister of health in November 1943, and had prepared a draft White Paper by January 1944. This was passed to the Reconstruction Committee* for amendment (CAB 87/7: 3 Jan 1944, 31 Jan 1944) and then on to the War Cabinet (CAB 65/41: 15 Feb 1941). Whilst the White Paper proposed a service that was both comprehensive and free, administration was to be based upon existing structures. Industrial health provision and the school medical service remained unaffected. The balance of power between local and national government was maintained by giving planning responsibility to the Ministry but executive powers to local government. County and county borough councils became responsible for primary and preventative health services whilst joint authorities were to control municipal hospitals and make contractual agreements with voluntary hospitals. The latter were offered financial help if they joined the service. A Central Health Service Council and local equivalents made up of professionals were to be created to shadow public accountability. In the GP service, local insurance committees were to be abolished and a Central Medical Board with powers to refuse GPs work in overcrowded areas was to be set up. The issue of remuneration was left open, although it was hinted that salaries would form the basis of the scheme. The way was also left open for direct or indirect charges for appliances and hospital treatment.

Labour politicians felt that the Paper did not go far enough. This was particularly true of Attlee who found it 'tentative and unhelpful' (CAB 124/244). Labour MPs had wanted to see GPs, as part of a local authority service, working through a strong health centre structure and they felt this position had been eroded. Local government representatives remained dissatisfied with the influence of the medical profession in administration and with the proposed joint authorities (MH 77/30B, 81, 99). In many counties joint authorities would cut across county boundaries; the London County Council for example, would be split into four. In other areas local hostilities surfaced as towns attempted to avoid being dominated by a local rival, as with Bradford and Leeds (MH 77/76).

Once again, though, it was the doctors who provided the main opposition. Whilst reaction amongst the GPs seemed mixed (MH 77/84), the BMA took up a firm position of opposition to the proposals (MH 77/30B, 119). The 'Radio Doctor' and assistant secretary of the BMA, Charles Hill, portrayed the proposals on radio as creeping state control. The BMA called for the abandonment of the entire scheme and the postponement of policy-making until after the war, when a royal commission should be appointed to look at the issue (MH 80/27: April 1944). The Ministry, therefore, found itself caught between the demands of the Labour Party, local authorities and pressure groups like the Socialist Medical Association (MH 77/63) on the one hand, and those of the professional bodies and Conservative Party members on the other.

A major feature of wartime planning was the total failure of the approved societies to defend their position as the major providers of national health insurance. Beveridge himself had wanted to incorporate the friendly societies into the new scheme of health insurance whilst excluding the more commercially orientated industrial insurance companies. However, even this concession was ignored. Despite considerable protests (PIN 8/62; PIN 32/2), funding of the National Health Service was provided through national insurance payments. Approved societies failed to secure any role (see also chap 2.3.2).

During the early days of planning for a postwar health service, mental health was rarely discussed. The vast scale and distinctive identity of mental care institutions, and their independent development before the war made their integration into the overall system difficult. It was presumed the service would remain separate but develop in tandem with the other health services. It was, therefore, left out of the wartime hospital surveys and the first draft plans for reconstruction. The main resistance to change came from the Board of Control, the body charged with the overall administration of the service. It argued that no changes could take place without major revisions in the law, and that this was impossible without recourse to a royal commission (MH 77/25: 4 May 1944). This position was adopted as the Ministry of Health's policy.

Not until 1943 did the Board of Control come round to the idea of revision of the law without a royal commission. To secure its co-operation the Board's position as the main body in charge of mental health was guaranteed, although the Ministry of Health was to become more closely concerned. Consequently the mental health services were included in the 1944 White Paper.

A number of advantages existed in linking mental care with other health services. Hospital services could be spread more evenly to the benefit of the underfunded mental hospitals. This was also true of staff. The White Paper also called for the amalgamation of all services under local authority joint boards and it was hoped this would unite mental and mental deficiency services. Whilst there was some opposition to integration, for many others the advantages far outweighed the problems (MH 77/71, 30B).

The position of the dental service within the National Health Service remained in doubt for some time (MH 80/35). Postwar dental policy was considered by a committee chaired by Lord Teviot in 1942 (MH 77/124, 183). Under the Beveridge Scheme it was assumed that dental benefit would be universal. The Ministry of Health, however, was less convinced. The pre-war dental service had been greatly underdeveloped and contained few qualified dentists. Difficulties existed about the role of the school dental service in any scheme (MH 77/124; ED 50/197, 393). The possibility of providing a universal service of a satisfactory standard seemed difficult, and of low priority. The Ministry opted instead for a policy of gradual expansion of existing services for priority classes. This was supported by the British Dental Association (BDA) who feared that the only way of providing enough staff would be through dilution.

The impetus for the inclusion of dentistry within the National Health Service Act came from the Teviot Interdepartmental Committee on Dentistry*, set up to look at the stages necessary to make a comprehensive dental service available to the whole population, and the measures needed to secure the required number of dentists. An interim report in August 1944 proved sufficient to make the Ministry reconsider its position (MH 77/124).

Ophthalmic benefit was the most developed additional benefit under the NHIS. Members paid half the cost of treatment, with children treated under the school medical service. The Beveridge Report recommended the extension of provision to the whole population. The main difficulty in carrying this out was the relationship of the optician to the medical profession. The service was spread between specialist ophthalmic departments in hospitals, GPs involved in the National Ophthalmic Treatment Board (set up to get GPs into the field, using dispensing opticians as auxiliaries), dispensing opticians, and local authority eye clinics. Whilst it was agreed that a united service was desirable, it was accepted that the shortage of specialists made this impossible. Consequently it was agreed to continue with existing practice, with dispensing opticians doing the bulk of the work, but with the long-term aim of phasing them out and providing all ophthalmic care under the hospital service (MH 77/74, 120, 201; MH 80/35).

The plentiful supply of chemists' shops meant that pharmaceutical services were not prominent in early postwar planning. The service was divided between small establishments backed by the main professional body, the Pharmaceutical Society, and the shops owned by the large pharmaceutical companies. Their biggest worry was the possibility of pharmacies being established within local authority clinics. However, with the abandonment of plans for health centres by the Caretaker government this ceased to be an issue, until the arrival of the new Labour government. Pressure from the existing companies ensured minimal alteration in the proposed arrangements. Local professional committees were to be set up, based on joint authority areas rather than local authorities, with the rest of the service remaining in its pre-war form (MH 77/120; MH 80/35).

The defeat of Germany in May 1945 and the growing gulf between the two major parties (see chap 1.2), arising in part from the health debate, led to the Labour party National Executive Council's decision to withdraw from the coalition government in October 1945. On the 23 May Churchill resigned and became head of a Caretaker government until 5 July 1945. With the Labour ministers removed from office and a general election approaching, the minister of health came under increasing pressure to issue a statement on party policy in relation to health provision.

In *Progress with the proposals for a NHS* Willink announced changes to the scheme outlined in the White Paper. Under pressure from the medical profession, the Central Medical Board was dropped and the local insurance committees reinstated (MH 77/30A). The power to refuse GPs posts in over-subscribed areas was therefore removed, to be replaced by a system of inducements. The plans for health centres were dropped and replaced with a policy of experimentation only. Finally, the attempt to secure a full-time salaried service was abandoned in favour of the maintenance of capitation fees. The election of a Labour government in July 1945, however, meant these proposals were never implemented.

* for committee references see Appendix B.

Records

The main policy papers of the Ministry of Health can be found among the National Health Service Bill preliminary papers in MH 80/24-29; MH 80/31-32 refer specifically to doctors, MH 80/33 to local authorities issues, and MH 80/34 to hospital services. MH 77 contains the National Health Service postwar planning files of the Ministry of Health; about half the files deal with representations for and against the proposals. Treasury papers can be found in T 161/1166/S50599, T 161/1243/S50599/06/1, and T 161/1364/S42032/1-2. A Prime Minister's Office file on the White Paper is at PREM 4/36/3, with an Economic Section of the Cabinet file in T 230/102.

Papers of the Medical Advisory Committee, reconstituted in 1943 'to advise the Minister of Health on the medical aspects of problems relating to the health of the people' are at MH 71/97-106 and RG 47/13-15.

4.4   The National Health Service Act 1946

4.4.1   Policy proposals and discussions

During the war Labour Party policy on the health services remained unchanged; since 1934 it had been committed to a comprehensive, universal and free service. A consensus of sorts had been formed around the 1944 White Paper, which did not incorporate some long-term Labour Party demands, but this consensus had been shattered by Willink's concessions at the end of the war. The 1945 General Election brought the Labour Party to power and Aneurin Bevan to the Ministry of Health.

In framing his proposals Bevan had to balance the need for early legislation with a commitment to long-term party policy. The main themes of Bevan's proposals were worked out in August 1945. The new service was to be split into three, with overall administration charged to the minister of health. This took the move away from a unified service, which had developed during the war, to its logical conclusion. Whilst many of the wartime concessions remained, a number of Willink's compromises were abandoned: distribution controls over doctors were reintroduced; the sale and purchase of practices was to be prohibited; dental and eye services were to be available under executive committees in the short term, with the eventual aim of locating ophthalmic services within hospitals, and all dental services within health centres; health centres were to provide all primary health needs in the long term, their development being based on similar schemes in the Scandinavian countries (MH 79/576). Whilst these measures produced no real surprises, the proposals for hospital administration certainly did. All hospitals were to be nationalized and controlled through regional authorities. This marked a major shift away from wartime planning policy.

The establishment of a regional administration provoked widespread opposition from a number of quarters. Traditional supporters of local authorities, such as the lord president, Herbert Morrison, saw the loss of control of hospitals as part of a wider trend of reducing the power of local government. Such a move, he argued, would result in the inability of local authorities to attract good staff or good councillors, resulting in a weakening of democracy (CAB 129/3: 5 Oct 1945). For Treasury officials the establishment of regional bodies represented the breaking of the first rule of public finance: the body which spent the money should also have some role in raising money. Otherwise, argued Sir Bernard Gilbert, second secretary at the Treasury, they would become fiscally irresponsible and spend-thrift (T 161/1243/S50599/06/1). Within the Ministry of Health, a number of officials considered the measure was of insufficient importance to merit a course of action which would be violently resisted by the hospitals (MH 80/28: 7 Aug 1945; MH 80/34: 22 Sept 1945).

In the event, the reaction of hospitals was mixed and far from unified. Bevan considered that enough energy had been wasted during wartime negotiations, and that his policies should be shaped by parliament and not the medical profession. His decision, therefore, to consult but not negotiate with the professional bodies greatly reduced the direct access of the latter to policy making. However, concessions were made where they were considered appropriate. Local authority organizations, with the exception of the county councils, were placated by the offers of representation on the regional hospital boards, executive committees and the central advisory machinery and of control over a number of public health services (MH 80/30). Greater opposition came from the voluntary hospitals. They faced the loss of financial and administrative independence as well as an uncertain future (MH 77/76-80). Again, concessions were offered which won some support. Part-time contracts would allow private work within hospitals; private pay beds were retained, thus attracting to the new service the specialists who were essential to its success (CAB 134/698: 4 Mar 1946); and staff received guaranteed salaries and superannuation. Teaching hospitals were given special status, in that they were to be administered by boards of governors, independent of regional authorities.

From November 1945 Bevan experienced more difficulties in his relationship with the BMA, as its Negotiating Committee became increasingly suspicious of his motives (MH 77/119). At the top of its agenda was the freedom to buy and sell practices (CAB 124/245; MH 77/86-88). This right had been reintroduced into policy making by Willink in 1945, but was totally alien to Labour. The system could not function in a service in which doctors worked in publicly provided health centres, on a salaried basis. In order to avoid financial loss through the falling value of practices due to their uncertain future, Bevan announced in November 1945 that their sale would be stopped (CAB 134/697: 29 Nov 1945); compensation was to be paid upon the retirement or death of a GP. The Negotiating Committee, whilst accepting this as inevitable, held out for the best terms possible.

Doctors' pay was another key issue. This was considered by the Interdepartmental Committee on the Remuneration of General Practitioners*, under the chairmanship of Sir Will Spens, from March 1945 onwards. Although it reported in May 1946, its findings were very much linked to the policy of the Caretaker government. Its support for some degree of payment by capitation encouraged the BMA to fight for the principle and reinforced the division between it and Bevan. The report's significance lay in 'pushing the Government off course over salaried employment for general practitioners. It was even more significant in indicating the new superiority of the BMA in negotiations over the level of remuneration' (Webster 1988 p 93). Discussions broke down in March 1946 and heralded the start of a major battle between the two sides (see chap 4.4.2.5).

A summary of the scheme was placed before Cabinet in December 1945 (CAB 128/1: 20 Dec 1945). For the first time this introduced the separate administrative divisions which were to be the basis of the new health service: central administration; hospital and specialist services; local authority services; and the family practitioner service. The hospital services were to be run by regional hospital boards, supported by local hospital management committees. About twenty regions were envisaged, centred around existing teaching hospitals. Teaching hospitals themselves came under the administration of boards of governors, although under overall public control. As part of the concessions given to local authorities, local clinics, domiciliary and child welfare services, and the ambulance services were detached from hospitals and given over to them. Control of the GP and other practitioner services was taken away from the local insurance committees and given to the newly created executive councils. These proposals were accepted by the Cabinet.

The National Health Service Bill was published in March 1946. The House of Commons stage of the Bill proved reasonably uneventful. Whilst the Conservatives voted against the Bill, the bulk of arguments were restricted to the nationalization of the voluntary hospitals and the move towards doctors' salaries. On the Labour side criticism centred on pay beds in hospitals and the failure to force through a full salaried service for doctors. However the Bill was easily carried in May 1946.

The main provisions of the Act were the nationalization of hospitals; the setting up of regional boards of administration; the redistribution of doctors to under-supplied areas; a new salary structure; the permitting of some pay beds; and the opening of health centres.

* for committee references see Appendix B

Records

The Bill papers of the National Health Service Act 1946 are at MH 80/24-41, and refer also to problems relating to doctors (MH 80/31-32), local authorities (MH 80/33), hospitals (MH 80/34), and opticians, chemists and dentists (MH 80/35). The main Ministry of Health file series on the postwar planning of the NHS Act are at MH 77. Cabinet Office files of papers leading up to the Act are at CAB 21/2019-2020. Treasury papers are at T 161/1243/S50599/06/1. PREM 8/288 contains a Prime Minister's Office file on the Bill relating mainly to Cabinet discussions. Ministry of National Insurance files include PIN 8/25, PIN 18/25, and PIN 32/30, 43. Papers relating to the Scottish Health Service Bill are in MH 77/158. Treasury papers leading to the passing of the Scottish Bill are in T 161/1300/S54359.

4.4.2 Implementation of the National Health Service Act

4.4.2.1 General

The structure and role of the general practitioner (GP) service presented the most problems during implementation of the Act. The battle with the BMA (see chap 4.4.1) continued after the passing of the 1946 legislation and centred around the issues of the sale and distribution of practices and the remuneration of doctors. The publication of the report of the Interdepartmental Committee on the Remuneration of General Practitioners* undermined the Labour government's arguments for a full-time salaried GP service and created a rallying point for opposition to the scheme. On top of this, one of the major aims of the Act was to correct the distribution of GPs which had caused an imbalance in the level of service between different areas of the country. The end of the right to sell and purchase practices was a key element in this policy. The BMA's refusal to accept these terms, and Bevan's threat to impose them (MH 77/177: 17 June

1946, 22 July 1946—8 Aug 1946), soured the relationship between the two sides. Bevan became increasingly depicted as a dictator, his proposals as creeping state control and doctrinaire socialism. This led in December 1946 to a plebiscite of BMA members to decide whether to discuss the new regulations with the government. On an 81% poll, 54% were against continuing discussions.

After the intervention of Lord Moran, and the agreement of Bevan to accept a degree of capitation and negotiate on the subject, the BMA returned to the negotiating table. Between March and November 1947 the Negotiating Committee of the BMA and six subcommittees went through the legislation in fine detail with the Ministry of Health. Once again, however, the problems of the GP services proved insurmountable and negotiations ground to a halt.

The arguments arising out of a year's negotiations came to Cabinet in January 1948. Bevan argued that no more concessions should be given to the Negotiating Committee which was clearly holding out for all it could get. The Cabinet agreed, although it called for more measures aimed at winning over young doctors (CAB 128/12: 22 Jan 1948). In February, Bevan used a motion in the House of Commons welcoming the new service to attack the BMA. In March, the BMA held a further plebiscite. This time 46,814 doctors voted against the NHS, with 4,735 in favour. The minister and the Cabinet were now faced with the serious possibility that doctors would refuse to join the service (CAB 128/12: 29 April 1948). The deadlock between the two sides was broken once again by Lord Moran, who pushed through a resolution calling for an amending act to preclude a full-time salaried service (MH 77/119: 24 Mar 1948). For Bevan this required little compromise, as he had already accepted this in principle, and legislative backing made little difference. However, for the BMA membership this proved to be the guarantee they had been looking for.

In April 1948 the BMA and the Ministry of Health reviewed their differences at a joint conference and agreed amending legislation. By May the terms of the legislation had been agreed and included limitations on the payment of full-time salaries and a special Spens Committee to look at the remuneration of consultants and specialists (UGC 7/753; Cmd 7420 1948). A further plebiscite by the BMA found a majority still against joining the new service but with too small a number of GPs to mount an effective boycott. The BMA was therefore forced to back down. At the end of May it decided on a policy of 'strength and unity in order to mould the service'. In May 1948 26% of English and 36% of Scottish and Welsh GPs had joined the service. By July the lists were almost fully subscribed.

* for committee references see Appendix B

Records

A Prime Minister's Office file on the confrontation between Bevan and the BMA is at PREM 8/844. For relevant files in general series see the following section.

4.4.2.2 Central administration

The provisions of the Act were due to come in on the Appointed Day, 5 July 1948. In the meantime the government was faced with the job of persuading the public and profession alike of the merits of the new service. Publicity for the Appointed Day was co-ordinated by the lord president, Herbert Morrison, through the Central Office of

Information and the Ministry of Health (see chap 1.3). Discussions concerning publicity for the National Health Service began in October 1946. A final plan was not agreed, however, until December 1947 (MH 55/962; CAB 124/1015). The scheme aimed at securing the early enrolment of the public and encouraging the middle classes to forsake private health care. The campaign was, however, very low key. Only after the battle between the BMA and Bevan had become public, and it seemed that the NHS might face a doctors' boycott, did the government begin to see the benefit of publicity.

From February 1948, ministers met to consider publicity for the Appointed Day (CAB 124/1015-1016). Morrison was very keen to use the overall welfare scheme as part of wider publicity on the merits of postwar reorganization. Bevan, on the other hand, had wanted publicity specific to the NHS. A leaflet on the service was released in April (MH 55/962-963) and distributed from house to house. More extensive booklets were made available for sale (MH 55/961). Films were used in an attempt to reach a wider audience. The service was formally launched with a broadcast by Attlee on 4 July 1948 and by advertisements in the newspapers headed 'This Day Makes History'.

Overall responsibility for the NHS in England and Wales rested with the minister of health (although in Wales the existence of a Welsh Board of Health complicated the issue). Between 1946 and 1948 it was charged with securing the implementation of the 1946 legislation and, after the Appointed Day, with the efficient running and future planning of the service. Up to January 1951 the minister of health remained Aneurin Bevan, but after that date he was replaced by Hilary Marquand. In the same year the Ministry lost its housing functions to the new Ministry of Housing and Local Government, and its place in Cabinet as well. At a time when the debate on NHS finance and the introduction of charges was crucial, this had the effect of weakening the position of the Ministry in relation to the Treasury and other departments (see chap 4.4.3).

Prominence was given in the 1946 NHS legislation to a Central Health Services Council (CHSC) 'to advise the Minister on general matters relating to the service provided under the Act, or any service provided by local health authorities in their capacity as such authorities'. This began life on 27 July 1948. It consisted of forty-one members of whom a small majority were medically qualified. Members were selected by the minister from lists provided by appropriate organizations. The importance of the Council lay in its role as the first real central advisory body to exist within the Ministry of Health, a factor held responsible in part for the lengthy negotiations needed to secure legislation in comparison with other departments. In addition it was viewed by voluntary hospitals as part compensation for power lost through the nationalization of the hospitals.

Underneath this structure, standing advisory committees were developed on specific issues, such as nursing, mental health, and dentistry. At this level, the system failed to perform satisfactorily. Meetings tended to be poorly co-ordinated and too infrequent. It also proved difficult to secure satisfactory representation on the committees. Members tended to argue for their own interests. Because of these flaws in the nature of the advisory committees, the minister and department officials tended to look elsewhere for advice.

Records

The main Ministry of Health public health files are at MH 55. MH 137 contains Ministry files relating to legislation, regulation, administration and financial questions following the Act. The papers of the Central Health Services Council are at MH 133. Standing

Advisory Committees were set up to look at Nursing (MH 133/303-345), Pharmacy (MH 133/366-382), Ophthalmic Policy (MH 133/383-394), Midwifery (MH 133/395-414), Mental Health (MH 133/495-521), and Dentistry (MH 133/275-302).

Papers relating to propaganda on the NHS are at MH 55/901-995. Publicity leaflets and booklets are at BN 10/32.

Treasury blue notes on the Department of Health for Scotland, and on the National Health Service in Scotland are at T 165/135, 300.

4.4.2.3   Hospital and specialist services

The 1946 legislation called for all existing hospital services to be united under the Ministry of Health. Local administration of the hospital service was to be the responsibility of regional hospital boards (RHBs) centred on an existing teaching hospital. Members were to be appointed by the minister of health after consultation with representatives of the medical profession, local health authorities and other interested organizations. Members were appointed for three years, with a third of places falling vacant each year. The Boards in turn appointed hospital management committees (HMCs) to control the day to day administration of individual hospitals. By June 1947 most RHBs had been appointed. Key hospital staff were appointed between August and October 1947. By spring 1948, 370 HMCs had been formed. Bevan was particularly careful to avoid controversy in his appointments. Among the initial batch of fourteen chairmen of RHBs only three had Labour Party or TUC connections. Despite this, accusations of political bias were made (CAB 21/2034).

Teaching hospitals were administered along different lines as one of the concessions offered to voluntary hospitals during the pre-1946 negotiations. The administration of the thirty-six teaching hospitals was entrusted to boards of governors who combined the functions of RHB and HMC. These were directly responsible to the minister of health and were required to submit annual forecasts of expenditure. This system was to lead to a lack of co-ordination between teaching hospitals and the RHBs, particularly in relation to hospital planning and staff development.

In the interim period between the passing of the Act and the Appointed Day, a number of problems of administration and maintenance of the hospital services emerged. Funding for the Emergency Medical Service was run down from 1944 onwards and yet money needed to be found for higher salaries and the move from wartime to civilian services. Voluntary hospitals were therefore offered *ad hoc* grants to carry them over into the post 1948 period (MH 77/217), and given help with the purchase of equipment and repairs (MH 58/672-682). The organization of the transfer of hospital staff and premises to the new service began in 1946. The dissolution of existing joint hospital boards and committees took place in 1947 and 1948 (MH 77/219-240). However the winding up of accounts and the transfer of assets of old institutions was not fully complete until 1949. Schemes and institutions left behind moved into other areas of health provision. The British Hospital Contributory Scheme Association, for example, which had formerly provided payment for treatment in voluntary hospitals to subscribers, now became involved in the supply of surgical and optical appliances, domestic help, cash benefits and financial support (MH 99/18). A departmental Committee on Hospital Problems during the Transitional Period looked at these problems (MH 76/614).

Staffing: hospital doctors

The difficulties experienced in wartime over the recruitment of staff continued after the war. These difficulties were increased by the need to persuade existing doctors and specialists to join the new service (see chap 4.4.2.5). The involvement of the consultants in the hospital service was essential to its success and significant concessions were therefore given by the minister of health. Consultants, for example, were permitted to opt for part-time or full-time contracts. This offered a high degree of financial security and succeeded in luring consultants away from the traditionally prestigious hospitals and practices. The recruitment at junior level was based upon automatic access to consultant ranks. These numbers were swollen by demobilized doctors, creating pressure for the expansion of consultant posts towards the end of the 1940s. Occurring at a time when Bevan was under pressure to make cutbacks in establishments, this situation created tension between the Ministry and the profession. Bevan resorted in the end to a drastic cutback in the number of trainees (CAB 134/518: 21 Nov 1950). In the 1950s, this in turn was to lead to problems of recruitment in many areas and to inflated salaries as regions competed to attract personnel.

The greatest professional 'perk' offered as an inducement to join the service was the merit payments system. The profession regarded this as compensation for the loss of private practice (where it was lost). The system was shaped by Lord Moran, who presided over the awards committee. Consultants employed by the London teaching hospitals received the largest share of awards, those working for provincial regional boards the least. This tended to reinforce the recruitment difficulties of the provincial hospitals.

The existence of part-time consultants within the service was a move away from Labour Party policies. Ministers were keen, therefore, to ensure that only the small number retaining an interest in the private sector would be allowed to stay part-time. However, after pressure from the profession, this option was opened up to all. Indeed the terms of part-time employment were so favourable that there was little inducement for consultants to go full-time. The recruitment of doctors into the service is discussed elsewhere (see chap 4.4.2.5).

Staffing: nurses

The recruitment of nursing staff raised an equal number of problems. A Working Party on the Recruitment and Training of Nurses had surveyed the whole area in 1945 (MH 55/2059-2076; LAB 8/1387). However, the general expansion of the nursing services as a result of the NHS legislation, both within the hospital service structure and in other areas (MH 55/1949-2099), meant recruitment failed to keep up with demand. Recruitment remained the responsibility of the Ministry of Labour and National Service (LAB 8/1308) and from 1945 onwards it mounted a General Nursing Recruitment Campaign in order to attract recruits to the service (LAB 12/390, 1302; MH 79/609; INF 2/107), with mixed success (RG 23/150A). In addition, training courses were realigned to emphasize domestic rather than wartime needs (ED 46/431-436).

The main difficulty, as in wartime (see chap 4.2.2.2), was attracting nurses to a profession where terms and conditions were less favourable than in other areas. The setting up of a Whitley Council to fix wages and conditions (LAB 10/740; MH 78/205-219) provided greater co-ordination but failed to overcome the problem. The establishment of

117

nursing posts and the rising costs of salaries made the hospital service a major target of financial cutbacks during the expenditure crisis of the late forties (see chap 4.4.3); from November 1948 the Ministry of Health was locked in battle with the Treasury over hospital staff numbers. The imposition of a ceiling on expenditure in 1950 made an adequate expansion of nursing services impossible (LAB 8/1470).

Attempts to circumvent these problems included efforts by the Ministry of Labour to attract nurses and other staff from outside Great Britain (LAB 8/1305, 1786), in particular from the colonies (LAB 8/968, 1306) and Ireland (LAB 8/1221, 1805; LAB 12/284). Other places were filled by young people on the 'bridging the gap' schemes, designed for people who wanted to be nurses but had not reached the minimum entry age of 18 (DT 16/232). This led to concern that trainees were being used before they were qualified (LAB 8/1779). Finally, attempts were made at achieving a more equal distribution of staff by offering grants and allowances to transferred nurses and midwives (LAB 8/1097).

The Nurses Act 1949 passed responsibility for the training and enrolment of assistant nurses to the General Nursing Council, which since 1919 had been responsible for the regulation and training of nurses. It also established fourteen area nurse training committees. These were to oversee the manner in which nurses were trained in each area, to promote improvements in training, to advise and assist hospital management committees and boards of governors of teaching hospitals on recruitment, and to assist the General Nursing Council in the approval of hospitals for teaching purposes (DT 17). In addition the Act allowed the General Nursing Council to register any nurse whose training was considered satisfactory (DT 18).

Staffing: other hospital staff

Wages and conditions of hospital domestic staff were controlled by the National Joint Council for Staff of Hospitals and Allied Institutions (LAB 10/559). As with nursing services, it proved difficult to recruit staff to the service. From 1945 a Ministry of Labour and National Service Consultative Committee on the Recruitment of Domestic Workers for Hospitals dealt with all problems which arose and planned future policy (LAB 8/1386).

The increasing link between hospital staff costs and the growing NHS budget was a major problem for the hospital services, particularly in the provinces where hospitals needed attractive terms and conditions to overcome their lack of prestige. Increasing attention was given by the Ministry of Health to the issues of terms and conditions (MH 123/1-63). From 1950 onwards local autonomy in setting a budget was increasingly undermined. In 1950 the Committee on the National Health Service* decided that HMCs should prepare monthly financial reports which should then be reviewed by RHBs and submitted to the Ministry (CAB 134/518: 6 May 1950).

Hospital beds, equipment and drugs

At the start of the new service the hospital services had access to 90,000 beds in 1,143 former voluntary hospitals, and 390,000 in 1,545 municipal hospitals. In order to meet likely demand it was necessary to adapt existing provision and to increase hospital capacity. In new urban developments, and especially in the new towns developed after the war, hospital provision was negligible and so the building of new services there was a priority (HLG 90/411). Overall control of the hospital building programme lay with the minister of health. RHBs wanting to build or use compulsory purchase powers had to go through him (MH 77/230; MH 90/30). In practice, however, power rested more with the Investment Programmes Committee*, set up to restrict capital investment except where it contributed to the export drive. It decided in May 1948 that money should only be allocated to maintenance and repair. This decision was made not only in the light of rising NHS costs but also of Labour Party pledges on housing expansion and the consequent shortage of building supplies and labour (see chap 3.4.6). Only mental hospitals were allowed to carry out some small extension schemes (CAB 134/438: 27 May 1948). At the end of 1948 further restrictions were imposed when Cripps, the chancellor of the Exchequer, persuaded Bevan to make £50m cuts in hospital capital expenditure (T 227/185: 4 Jan 1949). Whilst 1949 to 1950 saw some expansion in the capital investment programme (CAB 134/440: 22 May 1949) this was curtailed at the end of 1950 with cutbacks on hospital building and repairs as part of the general economy drive (T 229/456; MH 123/219). Attempts by the Ministry of Health to borrow funds for capital expenditure were received with hostility by the Treasury (T 227/62) although, under the 1947 Town and Country Planning Act, development of land for hospital purposes had to be included in local planning authorities' development plans (HLG 71/1471).

The consequence of this policy, coupled with the unexpectedly high demand for NHS services and the setting aside of pay beds for private patients (MH 99/33, 35), was lengthening hospital waiting lists. London, in particular, found difficulty in coping. In an attempt to solve the problem the Emergency Bed Scheme was set up; however this too became congested (MH 99/29, 115). The chronic sick and the elderly found themselves being passed over in favour of more 'needy' cases (MH 99/41).

Equipment and drugs were also in short supply. The balance of payments crisis from 1947 onwards meant that the import of drugs had to be severely restricted and so shortages occurred (MH 136/53). The monitoring of drugs required, and of drugs available, was carried out by the Drugs Requirement Advisory Committee (MH 136/33-34; MH 58/687).

The waiting lists problem extended to the treatment of outpatients too. Under the old system, outpatient clinics tended to be used by those individuals not covered by health insurance. Under the new Act, access to GPs and outpatient facilities were equally available and so more GPs referred patients. The problems caused by the increase in patients were also made worse by the lack of adequate outpatient accommodation and the problem of providing sufficient consultant supervision (MH 99/61).

The Emergency Blood Transfusion Service had developed during the war as a part of the Emergency Medical Service (see chap 4.2.2). The NHS legislation created a National Blood Transfusion Service which continued where the old service left off. Its organization was based on the RHBs which became responsible for the administration of the service (MH 76/297-309). A Blood Donors Advisory Committee provided advice to the minister on the welfare of blood donors (MH 77/138). In the early fifties, the regional structure was confirmed and a national supervisory body set up to give the scheme a national perspective (T 222/280). Through publicity campaigns the service achieved increased public awareness (MH 55/950-958) and increased its donors from 437,000 in 1949 to 803,000 in 1956 (MH 123/182-188).

* for committee references see Appendix B

Records

MH 137 contains the Ministry of Health files dealing with legislation, regulations, administration, and financial questions relating to hospitals. Files relating to the setting up and administration of regional hospital boards are in MH 90. They include the appointment of board members, improvements and alterations in policy and procedure, building and hospital supplies, and circulars. MH 88 contains Ministry of Health head-quarters files relating to Newcastle upon Tyne, and Southwest Metropolitan RHBs. These cover board constitutions, building plans, land acquisition, accommodation, staff, expenditure and estimates, and supplies, and have been selected as being representative. Individual files also exist for Leeds, Sheffield, East Anglian, North West, North East, South East, South West, Oxford, Manchester, Liverpool, and Wessex RHBs. Files on other RHBs have been destroyed. MH 92 contains files relating to the constitution, composition and business of hospital management committees. Correspondence between the Ministry and a number of selected HMCs is at MH 87. Ministry of Health files relating to the designation of teaching hospitals, annual statistical and financial reports, provision of facilities and general correspondence with the boards of governors of teaching hospitals are at MH 93. Ministry files relating to two particular boards of governors (St Thomas's, London and Newcastle upon Tyne), selected as representative, are at MH 89. Other case files of boards of governors which contain papers on major policy and development of particular hospitals are also included. The remaining files have been destroyed. Correspondence of regional officers of the Ministry of Health with various local committees and boards is at MH 112.

Files from the Ministry of Health covering general aspects of the hospital services such as medical and surgical treatment, medicine, ambulances and maternity are at MH 99. Files referring to more specialized services such as blood transfusion, occupational therapy and mass radiography are at MH 123. The papers of Sir William Maycock, consultant adviser on blood transfusion to the Ministry of Health, 1946-1978, are at BN 13/1-142. Equipment and supply files are in MH 136.

Treasury papers relating to hospital accounts are in T 227/589-590, with papers on RHBs in T 227/595. T 227/667 deals with contracts with non-NHS hospitals and T 227/668 with the transfer of local authority hospitals. Files on the control and prescribing of drugs are at T 227/734-738.

Standing advisory committees set up by the Central Health Services Council to look at issues relating to the hospital service include the Standing Medical Advisory Committee and the Standing Nursing Advisory Committee. Their papers are in MH 133.

Papers of the General Nursing Council for England and Wales are at DT 1-DT 48. DT 1-DT 9 deal with the constitution of the Council and its committees; DT 10-DT 14 with the registration of nurses; DT 15-DT 21 contain the correspondence and papers of the registrar; DT 22-DT 32 deal with examinations; DT 33-DT 38 with the education and training of nurses; and DT 35 contains correspondence organized by region. Postwar Ministry of Health files on the Council are at MH 55/2103-2151. The Council also dealt with midwives and health visitors.

Ministry of Labour booklets relating to nurse recruitment are at LAB 44/4,18. Others relating to careers in hospital administration are at LAB 44/6. Papers of the Office of Population Censuses and Surveys inquiry into hospital records systems are at RG 26/83-87. Papers relating to a social survey investigation into the blood transfusion service are at RG 40/7-10. Minutes of meetings between regional transfusion offices after 1945 are at BN 13/30-31.

A National Joint Council for Staff of Hospital and Allied Institutions sat from November 1945 and was responsible for the regulation of wages and conditions of employment of domestic and other such employees. Its papers are in LAB 10/559.

4.4.2.4   Local health authority provison: health centres; maternity and child welfare, domiciliary and other services

Local health authority services and responsibilities had expanded to such a degree that by the outbreak of the Second World War they were the main providers of health care in the country. The National Health Service Act 1946 marked a reversal of this trend. Under the Act, local health authorities lost control of all the general and most of the specialist hospitals to the new regional boards. With the postwar shift towards curative medicine this represented a major loss of power. Local authorities, were, in fact, left with six areas of responsibility under the Act: mother and child welfare services; health centres; domiciliary welfare; preventative health care; the ambulance service; and the care of the mentally deficient (see chap 4.4.2.6). Under the terms of the Act they were required to submit plans for these services to the minister before the Appointed Day. By the end of 1947, 1,200 schemes had been submitted. Scrutiny and revision of the schemes were completed by July 1948 (MH 77/194-201).

Health centres

The introduction of health centres and their control by local authorities was an important feature of the 1946 legislation, and one of the few proposals which represented a radical departure from the past. It was the major concession given to local authorities for the loss of hospital services and their best chance of retaining some influence in health provision.

Since 1933, health centres had been a major feature of the policy statements of the Labour Party and the Socialist Medical Association. Between 1943 and 1946, a Medical Advisory Committee Subcommittee on Health Centres looked at the layout and medical functions of health centres (MH 71/103) and, despite growing hostility from the medical profession, they were included as an important feature of the 1946 Act. They were to provide the main focal point for primary and preventative health care, bringing together general medical and dental services and the clinic services of local authorities. They were also to be the focus of health education, an indication that their main role was preventative, rather than reactive. In 1948 a Health Centre Committee (MH 133/63-70; MH 134/48) was appointed by the Central Health Services Council to look at the implementation of the Act in relation to health centres.

Yet the progress of the health centre programme was disappointing. There were a number of reasons for this. First, their planning occurred at a time between 1947 and 1948 when Bevan's fight with the BMA was at its peak. Health centres were perceived by the BMA as a potential source of local authority control. Its intransigence made implementation difficult. Second, many schemes prepared by local authorities exceeded the Treasury's financial targets. Finally, as pressure on the NHS budget increased, all capital development was restricted and thus the health centre programme reduced. In particular, this seriously affected new town and large estate developments which had previously experienced expanded provision (HLG 71/1564; MH 134/54).

At the local level, it had proved difficult to gather together medical staff who could agree on policy and functions. In Birmingham, health centre plans were dropped after GPs refused to participate because of the prohibiting of private patients in the centres. In Sheffield, the entire health centre team withdrew amid mounting rivalry amongst practitioners (Webster 1988 p 384). From 1950 onwards, the Ministry of Health began to accept that the position of health centres had been fatally undermined. The Committee on the National Health Service* began to discuss the possibility of forming small informal groups of doctors and dentists and using existing buildings, like schools out of hours (CAB 134/518). The Ministry of Health, in a circular in December 1950, advised local health authorities to give priority to conventional GP accommodation and surgeries in new housing developments over health centres. Health centres, therefore, became an experimental, rather than an essential, part of the overall scheme.

Maternity and child welfare

At first Ministry of Health policy for mother and child welfare centred on the encourage-ment of home care. Hospital beds and maternity units were in short supply, a situation worsened by the postwar baby boom which peaked at the time of the inauguration of the NHS. Institutional confinements were to be offered only in priority cases on social or medical grounds, with a target of 50% home confinements. This policy went against current trends in childbirth. Throughout the war there had been a constant increase in demand for institutional confinement (see chap 4.2.3). This trend was accelerated with the introduction of a universal, free, hospital service. Despite Ministry efforts, by 1957 two-thirds of all births were taking place in hospitals compared with only one-third before the war.

The failure to recruit and train sufficient midwives to provide a home service was a major reason for the growth in hospital provision. The problems of recruiting and keeping midwives continued in the postwar period (MH 55/1582; see chap 4.2.3). An extensive publicity campaign was launched to recruit nurses and midwives (LAB 8/1302) and attempts were made to recruit staff from abroad (LAB 8/1470; MH 55/1583; see also chap 4.4.3). In 1946, a special appeal was made for new recruits to come forward (MH 55/1584).

Hospital authorities therefore came to dominate childbirth services, heralding the start of the erosion of local mother and child welfare services in general. Local authority provision shifted away from confinement towards postnatal services such as clinics and day nurseries (MH 77/194-195; see chap 6.4.2).

The Welfare Foods Scheme introduced by the Ministry of Food in December 1941 (see chap 4.2.3.2) to supplement wartime rations for children and expectant mothers, mainly in the form of milk, cod-liver oil, concentrated orange juice and vitamin tablets continued after the war (MH 110). However its continuation was to cause serious disagreement between the Ministry of Health and the Treasury. The former wanted to incorporate the scheme into permanent postwar arrangements. The Treasury, however, argued that the provision of subsidized milk to homes, in times of increased supplies, would only reduce domestic bills and not increase consumption. Orange juice provision, they argued, necessitated imports from the USA which adversely affected the balance of payments. In the event the service was maintained, although means-tested free milk to homes was abolished (T 223/15). Provision of milk in schools continued until the early 1970s (see chap 5.3.5.1).

Domiciliary and other services

The development of domiciliary welfare proved to be unco-ordinated and varied from area to area. In theory the provision of health visitors, home helps, and home nurses was a vital part of postwar policy. Health visitors played an important part in the care of infants; and their recruitment and training was thus crucial to a domiciliary based child welfare service (MH 53/169-179). These services often overlapped with voluntary provision (see chap 6.3.2). After the war home helps and home nurses were concerned more with the elderly (MH 130/274; see chap 6.3.2). Policy discussions at the end of the war indicated that the elderly should be cared for primarily in their own homes (MH 77/30B, 121); this was confirmed by the Labour Government. In practice, however, services were often inadequate in scope to cater for the expanding elderly population. This was caused in part by the inability to recruit staff, despite extensive campaigns (LAB 12/342), and in part by local authority priorities.

One of the key roles of local authorities before the war was the prevention of disease and health education. In the postwar period, local authorities were given virtually total control of this area. The hospital services were unashamedly curative. In 1927 local authorities had established and funded the Central Council for Health Education (CCHE) to act as a co-ordinating body for health propaganda. After the war, this played important roles in publicizing immunization programmes and in raising public awareness of the physical fitness and youth service movements (ED 121/40-49; see chap 5.5). However, the postwar shift towards curative medicine, and the unwillingness of the CCHE to tackle major issues like alcohol abuse and family planning led to a decline in its role and a growing lack of belief in the principle of preventative health care.

Immunization and vaccination were included as part of the 1946 legislation and catered for in local authority plans (MH 77/197). They were to have priority in preventative policy for a number of years, but again suffered from the lack of drive in the propaganda services and from the failure of health centres to provide a co-ordinated community health service (MH 55/1904-1913).

The ambulance service had developed out of the war emergency but it had tended to be patchy and unco-ordinated (see chap 4.2.3.1). Postwar planning for the service tended to be vague (MH 55/1081). The 1946 legislation gave local health authorities the role of administering the service as a concession for the loss of hospital services. However, the transition from war to peace proved difficult. One town, for example, reported that 'at least half the vehicles need replacement almost immediately and the other half within the next two years. Repair work is continuous and often vehicles have been kept off all the roads for long periods due to delay in the delivery of parts' (MH 77/198). Reports such as these were numerous. Not until the EMS was fully incorporated into the NHS did the service regain some stability (MH 76/54). After this date the proper training and registration of ambulancemen was instituted (MH 55/1082) and a Committee on the Training of Ambulance Staff formed (MH 134/177-179).

* for committee references see Appendix B

Records

Ministry of Health local health authority service files are in MH 134. The main policy papers following the Act are in MH 134/1-11. Policy discussions relating to health centres are at MH 134/48-64; policy on the care of mothers and babies is at MH 134/65-84; on midwifery at MH 134/136-150; and on the ambulance service at MH 134/157-180. MH 134/151 deals with evacuation and MH 134/188 with payments for domestic helps.

Ministry of Health files relating to the administration of the public health services are at MH 55. MH 53 contains files dealing with specific groups of local authority employees. MH 137 contains Ministry papers dealing with legislation, regulation, administration, and financial questions in connection with local authority health service.

MH 52 contains Ministry of Health files arranged by local health authority relating to public health services. Local authority implementation plans are at MH 77/194-201. Correspondence between regional officers of the Ministry of Health and local health authorities and committees is at MH 112. A Ministry of Health Health Panel subcommittee of the Local Government Manpower Committee* looked at the problems of local government administration and in particular the recruitment of staff. Its papers are in HLG 51/1005-1008.

Papers of the General Nursing Council are at DT 1-DT 48. These include papers relating to domiciliary nurses and midwives. The main regulation of midwives was, however, carried out by the Central Midwives Board. Its papers are at DV 1-DV 11. Ministry of Health files on the General Nursing Council are at MH 55/2103-2151. The recruitment and training of midwives was looked at between 1947 and 1949 by a subcommittee of the National Advisory Council on the Recruitment and Training of Nurses and Midwives (Inquiry into Midwives); its papers are in MH 55/1593-1600. A Standing Maternity and Midwifery Advisory Committee co-ordinated policy at the highest level (MH 133/395-414). Papers resulting from the Ministry of Health's working party on midwifery are at DV 6/7.

The papers of the Central Council for Health Education are at MH 82. Ministry of Health files on the Council are at MH 55/920-929.

Ministry of Food Statistics and Intelligence Division files on the uptake of vitamin products are at MAF 156/714-724.

* for committee references see Appendix B

4.4.2.5 'Practictioner' services: GPs; dentists; opticians; chemists

Part IV of the National Health Service Act 1946 established executive councils as the means of securing the local administration of the practitioner services. These replaced the old insurance committees which had had similar roles. They were established between May and November 1947, 138 councils being set up in all. They were appointed by the minister of health, local authorities and the local professional committees. In this way old vested interests secured some say in postwar local health provision.

GPs

The Medical Practices Committee was set up in 1948 to ensure an adequate distribution of GPs throughout England and Wales (MH 128/1-23, 36-63). Together with the abolition of the right to sell practices, this was the main measure aimed at ensuring a GP service existed in poorer areas. It exercised control by reviewing the need to fill vacancies as they occurred and by considering all applications from GPs wishing to be included in the medical lists of practitioners. It appointed doctors directly to single-handed practice vacancies. The power of the Committee, however, was severely curtailed during the protracted negotiations with the BMA. Six of the eight committee members were appointed after consultation with the profession. In practice, therefore, the Committee became more a referee than an interventionist body.

In 1949 a National Health Service (Amendment) Act was passed, in line with Bevan's promise to the medical profession (MH 80/57). This guaranteed the status of GPs as independent practitioners with rights to take private patients and receive part payment by capitation. For the BMA the Act was of symbolic importance because it represented the only concrete success from two years hard campaigning.

The executive council machinery tended to follow a 'hands off' policy in relation to GPs and allowed the profession to continue as it saw fit. This trend was reinforced by the new system of remuneration. Doctors with large patient lists received greater income than those with small ones, so encouraging short consultation times and rapid turnover. This further weakened the health centre structure (see chap 4.4.2.4).

Dentists

Under the Act, the dentistry service was split between the hospital service (MH 123/64-72) and the practitioner services. The latter provided most dental care. The proposed structure was acceptable to both the British Dental Association (BDA) and the Ministry of Health. Dentists were to be based in health centres with local control exercised by the executive councils. Local dental committees would act as the profession's representatives in liaising with the councils (MH 77/125).

The method of payment of dentists had been considered by a Committee of Enquiry into the Remuneration of General Dental Practitioners in 1946 (MH 77/163-171). Whilst Bevan hoped to introduce a salaried service into the dentistry profession, with the exception of a few local authority officials, this proved impossible. Instead payment was based on the type of service provided. The 1946 Act established a Dental Estimates Board consisting of a chairman qualified in dentistry, six other qualified members and two lay members, all of whom were appointed by the secretary of state. The Board had the duty of examining and approving estimates for dental treatment and authorising payment of fees for completed courses of dental treatment. In addition the Board's duties included the detection, and the bringing to the attention of the executive councils, of any apparent failure by a dentist to comply with their terms of service. In Scotland, a Scottish Dental Estimates Board did the same work. In 1949, Treasury concern about its size and work, led to an investigation into it by the Treasury's Organizations and Methods Division (T 222/281).

The failure of the government to implement its pledges in relation to health centres meant that dentists remained in individual practices outside health centre control. Because of this, they enjoyed a high degree of independence and financial flexibility.

Dentists were able to supplement their income by working longer than the recommended thirty-three hours a week, and by exploiting more lucrative work. Dentures, for example, were a particularly good source of income because many patients were eager to replace ill-fitting pre-war dentures with free NHS ones. The cost of the dental service, therefore, rose from £1m under the NHIS to £41m in 1949. In 1949 and 1950 the remuneration of dentists was reduced amid concern at the rising cost of the service, the high income of many dentists, and the need for economy in general (CAB 134/518: 6 May 1950). From 1951 charges were made for dentures, leading to a 66% fall in demand between 1950 and 1953.

Moves to improve the provision of dentists were not implemented. The Teviot Committee on Dentistry* which reported in 1946, estimated a comprehensive dental service would require 20,000 dentists. It called for a separate central dental council, the expansion of dental schools, and postgraduate refresher courses. These proposals were accepted by the Lord President's Committee* in 1946, but were excluded from the Act because of lack of time (CAB 132/1: 20 Sept 1946). The long delayed Dentists Bill was revised in 1950 (CAB 132/14: 3 Nov 1950) but was abandoned after its first reading in 1952.

Opticians

In the long term, ophthalmic services were to be provided through the hospitals under the provisions of the 1946 legislation. However, in the short term, it was accepted that this was impossible and so 'temporary supplementary arrangements' were made available under the executive councils. Authorized sight testing opticians were able to prescribe glasses to patients with GP certificates. Because this was a short-term measure the profession was excluded from representation on the Central Health Services Council or on the executive councils (MH 80/35: Feb 1946). An Eye Service Committee was set up in order to organize the entry of opticians into the service (MH 55/2167-2170).

In the first few months the service operated along the lines of the old NHI scheme, except with a wider base. Ten types of free spectacles were available with charges made for smarter frames and for repairs (MH 77/202). Any eye defects not catered for by GPs were dealt with in the ophthalmic units set up within hospitals. As with other areas of the new service, the main concern in the early years was cost. £3.5m was allocated to the service for the first year, but the first nine months alone cost £15m.

In part the problem again was 'excessive demand'. Before the war, many people outside the insurance schemes had bought spectacles by trial and error at local shops and stores. Under a free service they now demanded better provision. In 1950 plastic frames were removed from the list of free spectacles (CAB 134/518: 6 May 1950) but demand remained strong. As part of the NHS cutbacks, from 1951 ten shillings was charged per lens, plus the full cost of the frame. This led to a massive drop in demand.

The 'temporary' supplementary eye service under the executive councils became permanent in the early fifties. The hospital service, faced with high capital costs and shortages of consultants and auxiliary staff, had failed to expand ophthalmic services to a level at which they could take over from dispensing opticians. An Interdepartmental Committee on Statutory Registration of Opticians, from 1949 onwards, supervised the registration of all opticians (MH 135/646-688).

Chemists

The plentiful supply of pharmacists, and their long-established organization, meant that they were omitted from much health service planning. They remained, therefore, as before the war, working in locally owned shops and national chains. By July 1948, 14,000 pharmacists had joined the service.

The main difficulties which arose centred on remuneration. The NHS scheme was basically an update of the old NHIS. Under the NHS pharmacists received the wholesale cost of ingredients, an on-cost allowance of 33% to cover overheads, an average dispensing fee of one shilling, and a counter allowance of twopence per prescription. Under the expenditure cutbacks these rates were cut. In particular the on-cost allowance was reduced from 33% to 16% (CAB 134/518: 6 May 1950). Problems also existed about prescription payments, with the high demand for GPs services greatly boosting the income of pharmacists (T 222/528). This problem was solved with the introduction of a prescription charge in 1952 (see chap 4.4.3).

* for committee references see Appendix B

Records

Ministry of Health files on general medical, pharmaceutical, dental, and supplementary ophthalmic services are in MH 135. Ministry files on executive councils are at MH 135/1-60. Files relating to the supply of drugs and appliances are at MH 135/61-84. MH 135/116-302 relates to medical practitioners, MH 135/430-543 to dentistry. MH 135/576-598 covers the pharmaceutical services and MH 135/599-641 the supplementary ophthalmic services. Ministry of Health files on the financial, administrative, and regulatory side of the services are in MH 137. Papers of the Interdepartmental Committee on Medical Certificates, appointed in 1947 to look at ways of simplifying the procedure for issuing certificates, are in PIN 21/87, HO 45/23493, LAB 12/706, MH 51/619, and MH 135/712-751.

Treasury papers relating to the pay of GPs are at T 227/754-771. T 227/772-773 deal with the sale and purchase of practices. T 227/779-783 contain papers on the dental service, whilst T 227/885-886 deal with fees for dispensing chemists. T 227/734-738 deal with the controlling and prescribing of drugs.

The standing advisory committees of the Central Health Services Council included committees making policy recommendations on pharmaceutical (MH 133/366-382), ophthalmic (MH 133/383-394), and dental services (MH 133/275-302). Records of seven Executive Councils (Merioneth, Newcastle upon Tyne, Birmingham, Kingston upon Hull, Salford, Bedfordshire and Luton, Middlesex), and the national insurance committees which preceded them are at MH 69. Correspondence of regional officers of the Ministry of Health with various local committees and boards is at MH 112.

A Practices Compensation Committee looked at claims for compensation for the loss of the right to sell medical practices. Its papers are at MH 135/166-169.

Representative files of complaints against doctors made to the Medical Service Committees and Executive Councils, and appeals to the minister of health are at MH 111. Similar files for dental services are at MH 105. Appeals by doctors against the decisions of the Medical Practices Committee are at MH 116. A selection of files on the prescribing of drugs by GPs is at MH 117.

Papers of the Dental Estimates Board are at MH 129, with policy files relating to the Board in MH 135. Central Statistical Office papers relating to chemists' accounts in England and Wales are at CAB 141/70. Negotiations between the Ministry of Health and a liaison committee representing the Joint Emergency Committee for the Optical Profession and the Guild of British Dispensing Opticians are at MH 136/56.

4.4.2.6 Mental health services

The Mental Deficiency Act 1913 merged the Commissioners in Lunacy into a new Board of Control, with enlarged powers including the supervision of the mental deficiency service established by the Act and run by local authorities. Following the Royal Commission Report on Lunacy and Mental Disorder in 1926, the Mental Treatment Act 1930 gave the Board central duties concerning the reception, care, and treatment of patients in mental hospitals and other facilities for the treatment of such cases.

Although it was decided to include mental health services as part of the postwar legislation (see chap 4.3), the 1946 Act failed to unify the service. Instead the local health authorities were made responsible for after-care, and the Regional Health Boards (RHBs) for hospitals and institutions.

At the end of the war, there were 147,000 mental patients and 53,000 mentally deficient patients in institutional care, with another 47,000 believed to be in the community. These figures were increased by the incidence of mental instability associated with the effects of war (MH 76/115; T 161/1421/S45172/02/2) and by the closure of many mental institutions during the war to create accommodation for the Emergency Medical Service (see chap 4.2.2.1). Difficulties were often experienced in regaining control of hospitals after the war (MH 90/54: 19 Nov 1948; 21 Dec 1948).

The main problem for the postwar mental health service was, therefore, one of accommodation. When buildings were available they were often nineteenth-century institutions, more like remand than medical centres. Replacing these buildings and expanding local authority services proved difficult. Not only did they face the problems of labour shortages and competition for resources shared by all other services, but also the 'not in my backyard' attitude of many local authorities and local residents. 'It is no use', wrote one official, 'blinding ourselves to the fact that the usual first reaction will be for objectors to say that although appropriate provision has got to be made for those unfortunates it should not be made near the objectors' (HLG 71/524). In 1947 Bevan urged the chairman of the RHB to unify the mental and general hospital services as a means of sharing accommodation and provision. This was resisted because of fears that the mental health service would come out the loser in any battle for resources with the hospital service (MH 90/52: 23 July 1947).

A severe shortage of staff was another major problem. The poor working conditions and the nature of the work itself proved to be major disincentives (HLG 71/524), especially when the level of pay was no higher than in other areas of nursing. Attempts to increase wage levels were resisted for fear of setting precedents in other areas. This problem had been foreseen at the end of the war (LAB 8/954) and had been studied by the Mental Nursing and the Nursing of the Mentally Defective Subcommittee (MH 55/2003). However, concentration on the hospital services meant the situation remained unchanged. An investigation by RHB chairmen in 1952 found 2,819 mental health beds and 2,145 mental deficiency beds closed for want of nursing staff (MH 90/559: May 1952; LAB 8/1787). There consequently developed a reliance on untrained nursing assistants and part-time staff.

Local authority after-care tended to focus on institutional rather than domiciliary provision (MH 77/204). Residential homes (halfway houses) acted as overflows for mental hospitals, but failed to provide the levels of care required. Community based services were slow to develop and were often neglected. Adult training centres, for example, were restricted because of the cuts in capital expenditure.

Responsibility for the detention and care of the criminally insane originally fell to the home secretary and the administration of his duties was carried out by the Board of Control. Ministerial responsibility for their care passed to the minister of health in 1921, but the home secretary remained responsible for the detention of the criminally insane and for the administration of Broadmoor. Rampton and Moss Side institutions were, however, transferred to the direct control of the Board. This direct control continued after 1948, even though the Board of Control had lost many of its other functions under the 1946 National Health Services Act. The management of Broadmoor was transferred to the Board under the Criminal Justice Act 1948.

Records

Ministry of Health postwar financial, administrative, and regulatory files on the mental health services are at MH 137/374-415. Ministry of Health local health authority service papers on mentally defectives and discharged mental patients are in MH 134/182-183.

A statutory Mental Health Committee acted as the main central advisory body in this area. Its papers are at MH 133/415-437.

Papers of the Standing Mental Health Advisory Committee of the Central Health Service Council are at MH 133/495-521. Minutes of the meetings of the Board of Control are at MH 50. Files of correspondence relating to all aspects of the running of the service are at MH 51, with monthly conference papers at MH 100.

A correspondence file of the Board relating to the NHS is at MH 51/598, with a corresponding file of the Ministry of Health at MH 77/229. The transfer of hospitals under the new act are dealt with at MH 123/296. Lord Chancellor's Office papers relating to the mental health services and the drafting of the 1946 Act are at LCO 2/3644.

Patient case papers and files, closed for 75 years, are in MH 85-MH 86. Registers of admissions of patients are at MH 94, with reports of statutory visits of commissioners to institutions at MH 95.

Board of Control files relating to special hospitals (ie Broadmoor, Rampton, Moss Side) are in MH 118. Home Office records relating to criminal lunatics can be found in HO 13, HO 136, and HO 145. MH 51/49 contains reports and correspondence on Broadmoor, and MH 51/799 contains the papers of the chairman of the Board of Control in relation to Broadmoor. Selected case files of patients are in MH 103. Board of Control statistics are at RG 26/75.

4.4.3 The financial crisis

During the planning of the National Health Service the main debates had centred around the terms and conditions of staff and the power structure within the service. There was a general consensus on the need for a universal service and from 1944 general agreement that it should be 'free'. The cost of the new service, whilst of some concern to the Treasury, never threatened to halt its development. Beveridge and subsequent policy-makers presumed that health service costs would decrease as the nation became healthier, eventually becoming essentially a low-cost preventative service. There was a general failure to anticipate the fact that the new service would generate its own demand, or to make the connection between unrestricted demand and finite resources. NHS finance, therefore, made demands on tax revenue which were not foreseen. Under the Act it was envisaged that one-fifth of NHS finance would be covered by national insurance contributions. However the increasing cost of pensions and other benefits, and the massive growth in NHS expenditure, meant that by 1957 only one-seventeenth of NHS funds was provided through NI contributions (PREM 11/1805).

The first indication of these problems appeared at the end of 1948, when it became increasingly clear that expenditure was running ahead of the estimated £176m for 1948-49 by something like £225m. Bevan blamed a high level of demand representing a backlog from earlier times and the difficulty of estimating accurately the cost of a new service (CAB 129/131: 13 Dec 1948).

The major cause of 'excessive' expenditure was the hospital service, where there had been an urgent need to appoint large numbers of staff and to increase wages. The Ministry faced a problem in that salaries could not be affected without tampering with the Whitley Council system. Therefore the main area targeted for cutbacks was establishments. This in turn highlighted a debate which was to occur again and again over the coming years: the professionals' desire for perfection at any cost, and the administrators' need to balance the books.

In March 1949, the Treasury intervened for the first time in an attempt to move control over staff numbers away from HMCs to the more controllable RHBs. Pressure to set up joint working parties to control staff levels was, however, resisted. Pressure from the chancellor of the Exchequer, Cripps, to find savings of £100m ended in £50m in cuts, mainly from the hospital capital expenditure programme. Bevan also approached the Whitley Council in an attempt to secure lower wage increases.

Hospitals, whilst being the single most expensive service, only accounted for half of the NHS expenditure. The other services, grouped under executive councils, were supported by all parties in their right to exercise clinical freedom, ie the right to prescribe any drug and refer a patient to hospital at any time. This made expenditure 'uncontrollable' from the centre. In response, the Treasury proposed the introduction of charges on certain items: 'In principle I think a charge is right', argued Hale. 'I have never been able to see why people should get dentures and spectacles for nothing any more than houses, food and clothing' (T 227/185: 11 Jan 1949). The Treasury argued that the main reason for the supplementary estimates was excessive public demand. Whilst a Ministry of Health publicity campaign from 1948 encouraged the more responsible use of the NHS (MH 55/965) the main solution for the Treasury remained the introduction of charges. This was resisted by the Cabinet on the basis of the political damage any such move would cause (CAB 128/15: 23 May 1949).

The summer of 1949 saw the financial problems increase. During preparations for the 1949-50 budget, Cripps argued that the limits of taxation had been reached and announced the need for a thorough review of the social services expenditure (T 171/399). The devaluation crisis in the summer of 1949 increased the need for economy (CAB 124/1187; see chap 1.3). During discussions in the autumn of 1949, the chancellor proposed a one shilling increase in national insurance contributions to help towards health service finance. This was opposed by Bevan who maintained that control could be achieved by 'tighten[ing] up the administration of the health service and check[ing] any abuse of the facilities which it provided' (CAB 134/220: 14 Oct 1949). Bevan was willing to accept that abuse, particularly of the GP and pharmaceutical services, existed— hence his famous comment that 'I shudder to think of the ceaseless cascade of medicine which is pouring down British throats at this present time' (Webster 1988 p 145). Under pressure from the Economic Policy Committee* and the Treasury, Bevan was willing to bow to an alternative proposal, that a one shilling prescription charge be introduced (CAB 134/220: 14 Oct 1948). He was simultaneously facing pressure on his housing programme and consequently finding it difficult to fight a battle on 'two fronts' (see chap 3.4).

After agreement was reached in principle to a charge, problems arose about its administration. The granting of exemptions for old age pensioners and the war disabled gained the support of the minister of pensions (PIN 15/3525) but was opposed by Bevan who wanted the Ministry of Health to have nothing to do with adjudication. He preferred any concessions to be paid via the National Assistance Board (CAB 132/11: 4 Nov 1949). Difficulties over the administration of the scheme continued into the Conservative government (T 222/279).

Although entering the statute books in 1949, the implementation of prescription charges did not occur until 1952. In part this was because of the falling potential revenue of the charge. The exemption of old people reduced potential revenue from £10m to £6m, and the agreement to charge per script rather than per item reduced it further. However, the main reason was that the mounting cost of the service demanded more immediate and drastic measures.

In March 1950 supplementary estimates totalling £89m were published. Bevan argued that this was inevitable in any new and expanding organization. Cripps, on the other hand, argued that to pay supplementary estimates would weaken the government's credibility and proposed a ceiling for the year 1950-51. Other members of the Cabinet expressed resentment at the fact that they had limits whilst the NHS did not, and called for the introduction of widespread charges (CAB 128/17: 13 Mar 1950). Whilst willing to compromise on prescription charges in 1949, Bevan was unwilling to make further concessions. He argued that 'the abandonment of a free and comprehensive health service would be a shock to their supporters and a grave disappointment to socialist opinion throughout the world' (CAB 128/17: 3 April 1950). Bevan's close relationship with Cripps meant he successfully avoided the implementation of charges. However it was agreed that there would be no increase in funding whatsoever and any expansion in one area would have to be matched by a contraction in another. In addition, a Committee on the National Health Service* was set up under the prime minister to monitor NHS expenditure continually (CAB 128/17: 6 April 1950).

The Committee on the NHS* began work in April 1950 with the knowledge that expenditure was already £10m above the budget for the whole financial year. Hugh Gaitskell, who was appointed to a junior post in the Treasury after the 1950 General Election, became a member and immediately began to call for the introduction of charges (T 171/400: 22 Feb 1950). The existence of the Committee was resented by Bevan and contributed to his increasing anger and isolation over the handling of NHS finance. The mounting mistrust between Bevan and other ministers on the committee is illustrated by Cabinet Office evidence of ministerial disagreements over NHS expenditure and, in particular, the belief amongst some ministers that Bevan was withholding important information (CAB 21/1733).

Bevan's own inquiry into the NHS under Sir Cyril Jones concluded in July 1950 that well over half the increase in costs was inflationary and nothing to do with bad management (MH 137/26). He agreed, however, that greater control could be achieved by the Ministry of Health administering HMCs directly (T 227/94; CAB 134/518: NH(50)17). This was Bevan's main defence, arguing hospital expenditure was under control and that HMC expenditure was being carefully scrutinized by RHBs (CAB 134/518: 6 May 1951).

However, pressure to implement charges continued to build up. The outbreak of war in Korea led to an escalating defence programme, while exacerbating existing economic problems arising from inflation and the balance of payments. In June 1950 Gaitskell proposed to the Committee on the NHS* the idea of 'hotel charges' for hospital patients (CAB 134/518: 23 June 1950). By late 1950 Gaitskell was chancellor, whilst Bevan had been transferred to the Ministry of Labour. Attlee used his departure to split the Ministry of Health, passing its housing function to the Ministry of Town and Country Planning. The Ministry of Health became a non-Cabinet post.

One of Gaitskell's first proposals in November 1950 was to reduce the pay scales of consultants (CAB 134/518: 21 Nov 1950). In January 1951 he spoke of the massive problem of diverting men and resources to defence, and even hinted at the need to direct labour compulsorily (CAB 131/10). Along with social security, health was the biggest area of expenditure and the most likely to face cuts. At a special Cabinet *ad hoc* Committee on the Expenditure on the Social Services in March 1951, therefore, the chancellor proposed the Health Service be singled out as the area in which savings could be made. He proposed keeping estimates for the coming year at the current level of £393m. With the support of the Committee on the NHS* (CAB 134/519: 14 Mar 1951) he proposed a half scale fee for dentures, £1 per pair of spectacles and a one shilling prescription charge (CAB 130/66: GEN 357).

The issue moved to Cabinet at the end of March when the financial ceiling was raised slightly to allow prescription charges to be dropped. Bevan, with the support of Harold Wilson, called for decreased defence spending and threatened to resign (CAB 121/19: 22 Mar 1951; T 171/403). Gaitskell's budget speech in April 1951 announced the above charges as well as a six pence increase in income tax and the raising of purchase tax from 33% to 66%. On the 27 April Bevan resigned, joined the following day by Wilson.

The National Health Service Amendment Act 1951 introduced charges for dental services and supplementary ophthalmic services, allowing the chemist and optician to keep the charge and reducing the Exchequer contribution accordingly (MH 80/58; T 227/92).

In 1956 the Guillebaud Committee, looking at the cost of the NHS, supported the findings of the Sir Cyril Jones enquiry that the rises in expenditure in the NHS in the late forties were mainly due to price inflation. It concluded that 'the rising cost of the services in real terms during the years 1948-1954 was less than people imagined' (MH 137/225-253; Cmd 9663 1955-1956).

* for committee references see Appendix B

Records

Prime Minister's Office papers on the introduction of prescription charges are at PREM 8/1239. The main file on NHS finance is at PREM 8/1486. Treasury Social Services Division files are at T 227. T 227/185 details the economy drive within the NHS. Hospital accounts are at T 227/589 and details of financial estimates at T 227/153 and T 233/544. T 227/955 covers policy on the control of capital expenditure. T 222/528 refers to the pricing of prescriptions. Bridges' personal papers on NHS expenditure are at T 273/329. Treasury budget papers are in T 171. Those for 1951 are particularly relevant and are at T 171/403-407.

Ministry of Health financial files can be found in MH 137. Hospital and local health authority services investment programme reviews are at MH 137/129-131.

Lord President's Secretariat files on NHS finance are at CAB 124/1187. National Assistance Board files on charges are at AST 21/11.

4.5 Bibliography

A Bevan, *In place of fear* (1952)

C L Dunn, *The Emergency Medical Service* vol II (1952)

H Eckstein, *The English National Health Service* (1952)

M Foot, *Aneurin Bevan* vol II (1973)

D M Fox, *Health policies, health politics* (1986)

The diary of Hugh Gaitskell 1945-1956, ed P M Williams (1983)

F Honigsbaum, *Health, happiness and security: the creation of the National Health Service* (1989)

R Klein, *The politics of the National Health Service* (1983)

A S MacNalty, *The civilian health and medical services* (1953)

A S MacNalty and W Franklin Mellor, *Medical services in war* (1968)

J E Pater, *The making of the National Health Service* (1981)

B Watkin, *The National Health Service, the first phase* (1978)

C Webster, *The health services since the war* (1988)

P M Williams, *Hugh Gaitskell* (1979)

Chapter 5 – EDUCATION

5.1   **Introduction**

5.2   **Wartime policy and the shaping of the 1944 Education Act**

5.3   **Primary and secondary education**

     5.3.1   Wartime problems

     5.3.2   Implementation of the principles of the 1944 Act

     5.3.3   School building programme

     5.3.4   Supply of teachers

     5.3.5   Special services

          5.3.5.1   School meals and milk

          5.3.5.2   School medical service

          5.3.5.3   Special educational treatment

5.4   **Further and higher education**

     5.4.1   Technical, further and adult education

          5.4.1.1   General

          5.4.1.2   Technical education

          5.4.1.3   Day continuation schools

          5.4.1.4   Further education

     5.4.2   The universities

5.5   **Youth service**

5.6   **Bibliography**

5.1   Introduction

Despite the degree of public attention and popular acclaim that greeted the Beveridge Report on Social Insurance and Allied Services, reform of the education system—which had found no place in Beveridge's scheme—was the first major measure of postwar reconstruction to reach the statute book. There are a number of reasons for this.

The issue of education had commanded much public attention in the interwar years. In 1926, the Hadow Report had recommended the raising of the school leaving age from 14 to 15 and the introduction of a system of universal secondary schools for all pupils over the age of 11—proposals that had long been central to Labour Party policy. As a result of opposition from the churches, the 1931 Labour administration had failed to implement these recommendations. The issue, however, had been reopened by the report of the consultative committee chaired by Sir Will Spens in 1938, which had also stressed the importance of 'equality of opportunity' and advocated both the raising of the school leaving age and the establishment of secondary education for older children. On this occasion, steps were taken to implement Spens' proposals, but the outbreak of war in 1939 forced the suspension of the initiative. Even so, the main elements for future reform—which were eventually included in the 1944 Education Act—had been well established before Butler turned his attention to the question in 1942.

Wartime evacuation helped expose existing weaknesses in state education and brought home to the middle classes the poor educational attainment of many inner city school-children. The slump had forced local education authorities in the depressed areas to cut their services to the bone. Hence children of similar ages were offered very different standards of education and displayed equally different standards of intellectual development. The wastage of human potential was highlighted by the war itself. Shortages of skilled labour were acute at a time when new technologies were being developed to prosecute the war-technologies which were vital for Britain's industrial future. In contrast to other countries, particularly Nazi Germany, the British government was failing to provide sufficient technical and further education and this posed a threat to the nation's future prosperity (see, in particular, Barnett 1986).

The existing state education service was not particularly popular. An official survey in 1945 revealed that two out of every three adults questioned had been dissatisfied with their own education: a proportion that rose distinctly among those who had only attended local elementary schools (RG 23/71). The Treasury, moreover, was more willing to fund an education programme than it was to spend money on the Beveridge Plan. The former initiative could be seen as a valuable investment in the nation's future, while the latter appeared to be an unlimited drain on the Exchequer, for no possible return. The Treasury tended, however, to view education reform as a matter of the reorganization—not the extension—of the existing system and came to oppose the raising of the school leaving age when this was incorporated in the 1944 Education Act. Finally, credit for the comparatively swift introduction of new legislation should also go to the president of the Board of Education, R A Butler. He proved adept at handling the opposition from interested pressure groups, notably the churches, and at overcoming resistance from within the Cabinet, from Churchill and other ministers, to the passage of wartime legislation.

While the Board of Education remained the centre for discussion of reforms, responsibility for their implementation remained with the local education authorities (LEAs). These consisted mostly of county and county borough councils, with supplementary Part III authorities in the larger urban districts and non-county boroughs controlling elementary schools. The war initiated a change in the relationship between central and local authority. Decision making became more centralized as wartime measures like the extension of the school meals service and evacuation required greater national co-ordination and extra finance. These changes were rendered permanent under the 1944 Act; the Board became the Ministry of Education, with greater powers to enforce the execution of a central policy through the LEAs. Section 68 of the Act allowed the minister to enforce co-operation when necessary.

These changes, however, were more apparent than real. The Ministry proved reluctant to use its new powers. Both postwar Labour ministers, Ellen Wilkinson and George Tomlinson, were eager to avoid confrontation. Further, the drafting of section 68 had been contentious and any attempt to use it was likely to provoke dissent. LEAs like Cardiff, therefore, were able to ignore ministry directives to reorganize their elementary schools (Green 1981). At the same time, the Ministry was willing to use its powers over financial resources to discourage expenditure. When a number of LEAs submitted plans for the building of multilateral schools in the postwar period, the Ministry was able to use financial constraints to limit the initiative to an experimental basis. In adopting this strategy, the civil servants were operating in a manner traditional to the pre-war Board: adopting a 'hands off' attitude when it came to enforcing policy, but maintaining central government's normal response to anything requiring additional financial resources.

Records

The PRO *Current Guide* part 1 describes extensively the structure and branches of the Board and the Ministry of Education and lists the majority of the appropriate classes.

Policy files are listed at the beginning of each records section and usually contain central government or Board of Education papers. Implementation files follow and frequently contain correspondence files, usually with LEAs. These are organized by local authority and give detailed information on specific areas.

A large amount of secondary material is available on the topic, particularly for the war years. P H J Gosdon, *Education in the Second World War* (1976) provides a comprehensive survey of both local and national issues, and uses PRO sources extensively. Chuter-Ede was parliamentary secretary at the Board of Education and his diaries have been edited by K Jefferies. A copy of the war diaries exists at CAB 102/249-260. For information on R A Butler, president of the Board of Education during the drafting of the Act, see his autobiography and Howard's biography. A fuller bibliography is provided at the end of this chapter.

5.2 Wartime policy and the shaping of the 1944 Education Act

The failure of the Board of Education to implement the recommendations of the 1938 Spens Report meant that there was already pressure for reform before 1939. The changing circumstances of the war added to it. For the first time the Board had to plan and control rather than just advise. Weaknesses in the existing system became more visible. Pressure for change from the press, interested organizations and individuals increased, whilst the reputation of the Board declined (ED 11/254; ED 136/295).

The setting up of a committee of senior officials on postwar education in November 1940 was the Board's reply to this pressure (ED 136/212; ED 46/155). Consisting of senior civil servants, it was to gather information on, and discuss the future of, education informally. It has, though, been suggested that its main purpose was to act as a safety valve. In the summer of 1941 the Green Book *Education after the war* was circulated, looking forward to the raising of the school leaving age, the establishment of day continuation schools and the expansion of the secondary school system to cover all children. Circulation was restricted to local authority organizations, churches, and teachers' unions. In a reforming climate this only increased general suspicion of the Board (ED 136/215).

R A Butler became president of the Board of Education in July 1941. The protests surrounding the circulation of the Green Book made him eager to press ahead with reform. In September he wrote to Churchill outlining his proposals for an education bill (ED 136/215). Churchill, however, wanted all reforms to be postponed until the end of the war. Preparations for a bill continued but were more discreet.

One of Churchill's main concerns was the possible adverse response of the churches. In 1902 the Conservatives had experienced a massive backlash from the churches over the abolition of school boards and the introduction of LEAs. In 1941 the Church of England issued a public statement calling for, amongst other things, religious education for all and the starting of each school day with a religious assembly; the so-called Five Points. However, the place of religion in schools was never really questioned by the Board (ED 31/533-534). The real issue was once again the question of church control. The 1902 settlement had allowed the co-existence of church and local authority schools, the so-called Dual System. However, any move to introduce a primary and secondary school system, as was proposed in the Green Book, would inevitably lead to a diminishing of church power. The division of elementary schooling at 11 years would necessitate the building of secondary schools to house the 12 to 15-year-olds as well as the employment of more administrative and teaching staff. The churches did not have the resources to finance this expansion and so would lose control and influence over the older age group. Meetings between the Board of Education, the Church of England (ED 136/228) and the Free Church Federal Council (ED 136/239) throughout 1941 failed to find a satisfactory solution. The Roman Catholic Church was totally opposed to any loss of control over its schools (ED 136/226).

In April 1942 William Temple succeeded Lang as archbishop of Canterbury. The Board hoped that a new face would create a new opportunity for a settlement and so between February and March it re-drafted existing proposals in the form of a White Memorandum (ED 136/219). It offered the churches the choice of 'aided status', the church putting up 50% of the cost of necessary improvements (essential in most church schools which had been badly neglected) and keeping control of the administration of the school; or 'controlled status' with the local authority taking control of and responsibility for the school, but with a guaranteed religious content in the curriculum. Temple, as president of the Workers' Educational Association, already had a good deal of sympathy with the general educational reform proposals. Butler, at what he termed the 'hot interview' on 5 June, was able to persuade him of the impending financial crisis facing church schools and the need for swift action (ED 138/20). The Free Churches fell into line.

Roman Catholic opposition, however, remained. Church leaders had not even had the opportunity to present their case to the minister until September 1942, long after Temple's support had been won. Butler was able to present them with a virtual *fait accompli* (ED 136/226). The reforms were particularly difficult for the Church to accept because of the centrality of the church schools in the daily life of the Catholic community. Matters were made even more difficult for Butler by the disjointed nature of the Catholic leadership and the vociferous opposition of the Catholic press. Whilst Butler continued to believe that their opposition was based on a misunderstanding of the proposals (CAB 71/11: 67th Meeting), it was clear that Roman Catholic support for the reform plans would not be forthcoming (ED 136/379: LP(43)254). Preparations for a White Paper went ahead without them.

Church of England and Free Church worries remained, in particular over the future of village and denominational schools in single school areas (ED 136/223). However, with the approval of loans to help churches to implement the reforms (CAB 65/36) and the favourable settlement in terms of religious education in the school curriculum, the minister felt able to proceed with the drafting of a bill. Problems were to continue in the postwar years, particularly at the local level (see chap 5.3.2). However, the 1944 Act proved very favourable to the churches. Most of their schools remained intact and were better financed, and the churches had gained a strong foothold in the new curriculum.

Further problems were created by the need to alter the local administrative structure in order to implement reform. Local educational control rested with counties and county boroughs. However the 1902 Education Act had also set up Part III authorities. These administered elementary schools in non-county boroughs with a minimum population of 10,500 and urban districts with at least 20,000 inhabitants. Secondary school and all other provision was made by the appropriate county council. The system was over-complicated and, with the proposed expansion of the school system, it seemed likely that the authorities would be unable to cope with the extra responsibility. Whilst many local authority organizations accepted this, others, such as the Federation of Part III Education Committees (ED 136/243), had a vested interest in maintaining the *status quo*. The Association of Education Committees stood to lose half its members and most of its political influence (ED 136/215). Fears also existed about the increasing centralization of power and Board control over educational standards and provision. In part these problems were eased by the setting up of the divisional administration scheme after the war, creating smaller administrative units within county authorities to provide greater local influence (ED 151). Worries about the cost of reform led to the awarding of special grants to help local authorities implement new measures (CAB 71/11: 58th meeting; CAB 71/15: 15th meeting). The Treasury also expressed concern that the larger authorities would prove more expensive and so increase local rates (T 161/1127/S48249/01).

This opposition, however, started to be eclipsed as postwar reconstruction began to take on a wider dimension. The foundation of the Conference of Allied Ministers (later to become UNESCO) gave an international context to educational planning. By 1943 Churchill was beginning to bow to pressure and look forward to the postwar period. The publication of the Beveridge Report (see chap 2.2) created a climate in which reconstruction plans could flourish. Sir Kingsley Wood, chancellor of the Exchequer, indicated that he would consider backing reform, possibly in the education field (ED 136/215). Butler's plans seemed cheap in comparison with Beveridge's and involved less sweeping measures. Indeed Wood told Chuter-Ede that 'he would rather give money for education than throw it down the sink with Sir William Beveridge' (CAB 102/254: 16 Sept 1942; ED 136/229).

In July 1943 a White Paper was considered by the Lord President's Committee* and the War Cabinet (ED 136/405) and approved for publication later that month. On the whole the public and parliamentary response was favourable. Treasury concern only began to develop as the full cost became known (T 161/1193/S48249/2), in particular after the White Paper failed to allow for the expense of raising the school leaving age or increasing teachers' salaries. However opposition tended to focus on particular measures like the school meals and medical service (see chap 5.3.5) rather than against the Bill as a whole, which was published in December 1943. A major political storm developed during the second reading when Clause 82 of the Bill on pay was defeated in favour of an amendment establishing equal pay for women. This was the first parliamentary defeat for Churchill's government. A second vote was treated by the prime minister as a vote of confidence in the government and the amendment was consequently defeated. Apart from this incident, the passage of the Bill proved to be non-contentious. Protests from outside parliament, particularly in relation to the Dual System, continued but had little effect on the proceedings. In May 1944 the Bill passed through the House of Lords and received royal assent on 3 August 1944.

The main features of the Act were the acceptance of the principle of secondary education; the transformation of the Board of Education into the Ministry of Education; the concentration of administrative powers on counties and county boroughs; the planned raising of the school leaving age to 15 and eventually to 16; the expansion of part-time education and the compulsory attendance of school leavers between 14 and 18 at day continuation schools; the extension of the school medical service and the development of the school meals and milk schemes; and the abolition of secondary school fees.

* for committee references see Appendix B

Records

Board of Education private office papers relating to all aspects of education are at ED 136. Records relating to general educational questions are at ED 10. Departmental files relating to the Green Book discussions include ED 136/243-291 containing negotiations with outside organizations, and ED 136/212-218 containing the drafting papers. Board of Education bill papers are at ED 31/500-537. In particular ED 31/526-532 relate to local authority administration, whilst ED 31/502-523, 533-534 refer to negotiations over the Dual System. ED 31/544 contains bill papers of the Education (Scotland) Bill. Treasury papers on the Scottish Bill are at T 161/1247/S51941. ED 136/449-455, 475-494, 496-501 deal with matters arising from the passing of the Bill.

Treasury files on the postwar reorganization of education include T 161/1193/S48249/1-4. T 161/1193/S48249/04 deals with discussions on the grant formula with LEAs, as does ED 136/393.

Reconstruction Secretariat files on postwar reorganization are at CAB 117/109-113. Lord President's Secretariat files on the Bill include CAB 123/219-220. Prime Minister's

Office papers relating to the Education Bill 1944 are at PREM 4/11/3. Files relating to the Dual System are at PREM 4/11/2 with general educational issues covered in PREM 4/11/6.

Other departmental files on the 1944 Act include papers of the Admiralty at ADM 1/16578, General Register Office at RG 26/63, Home Office in HO 45/20669-20670, Lord Chancellor's Office in LC 2/2657, 5821. Correspondence with the Ministry of Labour on the Bill is at LAB 19/129,132 with further papers at LAB 9/92. Registrar general estimates in relation to the Act are at RG 26/63. Nuffield College Social Surveys on education are at CAB 117/160 and ED 10/272.

Dr Weitzman's official history of education in the Second World War is at CAB 102/238-241, with notes at ED 138/1-6. It deals extensively with postwar planning. The official history of the Green Book discussions is at ED 138/18, 22. A 1945 interview with R A Butler by Dr Weitzman on the subject of the negotiations with the churches is at ED 138/20.

External relations files on educational research and information at national and international level are at ED 121. Papers relating to the Conference of Allied Ministers of Education are at ED 42 and ED 121/263-269. Postwar UNESCO files are at ED 157.

5.3   Primary and secondary education

5.3.1   Wartime problems

By far the biggest impact on the education service during the early years of the war came from the evacuation of children from the major cities. Following the report of the Anderson Committee on Evacuation* in 1938, the Ministry of Health, responsible as it was for the planning and administration of any scheme, established an evacuation division staffed jointly by Ministry of Health and Board of Education officials (HLG 7/284). Plans were developed for the evacuation of schoolchildren and mothers with young children. These plans (HLG 7/101-102) were put into operation on 31 August 1939 when over three million people were successfully moved in only three days. The evacuation of pupils was organized through the schools, with teachers taking a central 'parental' role and moving with the pupils. All day schools in evacuation and reception areas were closed and children found billeting places. Local authorities within reception areas surveyed the available accommodation and arranged for the billeting of the majority of the evacuees in private households (LAB 12/301-304). Billeting allowances were paid to the householder and recovered as far as was possible from the parent (CAB 65/1: 4 Oct 1939). Local authorities became responsible for the overall administration of the scheme. In addition a number of children were sent abroad, particularly to Canada and the United States, with guardianship arranged for each child (HLG 7/320), and to Eire (HLG 900/5). Other parents made private arrangements with friends or relatives. These arrangements were considered independent of the official scheme and were initially ineligible for a billeting allowance (HLG 900/27). Many private clinics made their own arrangements for the evacuation of infants (HLG 900/4).

Success, however, was short-lived. Not least were the dramatic social consequences of the large-scale uprooting of large sections of the population. Social differences were never more contrasted. Children became disorientated and people living in reception

142

areas came to find their new guests increasingly unacceptable. A number of children, indeed, were considered unsuitable for billeting and were placed in hostels (HLG 7/172). Further, the Ministry of Health's administration of the scheme began to draw criticism as features of the old Poor Law began to creep in. In October the Cabinet introduced charges to parents to meet the cost of billeting (CAB 65/1), with a means-tested allowance for those who could not afford to pay (AST 11/14). At a local level administration often became confused. Health officials had given responsibility for administering the scheme to local housing authorities, many of which were too small to cope. LEAs often duplicated their work. Many authorities faced serious financial problems coping with the scheme but found the Treasury unhelpful and banks often their only source of funds (CAB 65/8).

It proved very difficult to provide a reasonable level of schooling in many reception areas. Evacuated schools often found their pupils spread over several villages because of a lack of accommodation and billeting places. The need to acquire village halls and other buildings led to conflicts with the Treasury over the cost of compensation (ED 10/246; T 161/1077/S45384). Roman Catholic leaders were worried that some of their children had been placed in non-Catholic schools (ED 138/50; HLG 7/323). Camps were a possible solution and were used to house a number of evacuees, but proved to be unpopular with both teachers and pupils. The lack of family life or sense of community only increased homesickness amongst the children, whilst the lack of teaching space and adequate accommodation made teaching very difficult (ED 10/238; HLG 900/8).

The biggest problem, however, was caused by the return of children to the evacuated areas. By January 1940 45% of children had returned home, swelling the ranks of those who had never left. Extensive publicity campaigns failed to stem the tide (HLG 108/18). In the evacuated areas the Ministry of Health introduced a Nursery Centre Scheme to ease some of the burden of child care from mothers (see chap 6.4). This had limited impact. The extended summer holidays delighted the children but created serious problems for local authorities and, indeed, the law enforcement agencies. Many authorities introduced part-time schooling in private homes and in schools, where available. The Board of Education maintained its position on the closure of schools in evacuation areas, fearful of the collapse of the whole scheme. A circular at the end of September 1939 (ED 142/55) suggested a home education service as a possible solution to the problem. It soon became apparent that this was not enough and on 1 November 1939 schools were allowed to reopen. The need to provide air raid provisions and the requisitioning of buildings meant this was not instantaneous. Not until March 1940 was compulsory education for children over 11 restored to London, and not until April for all over 8. By the summer term, 50 of 68 evacuation areas had reintroduced compulsory attendance for 5 to 14-year-olds.

For London and the South East, the official evacuation policy was continued until 1945. Evacuation plans for 1940 were restricted to unaccompanied schoolchildren; this was put into operation between June and July 1940. As the bombing increased, however, this was expanded to include homeless mothers and children (HLG 7/306), then to all mothers and children (HLG 7/305-306), and finally to expectant mothers (HLG 7/234-259). Nevertheless, a conference of representatives of the Board of Education and the Ministry of Health in June 1942 decided to take no positive action to prevent the return of evacuees (ED 10/249). As the war progressed, therefore, the mass evacuation of the early years gave way to a more 'do-it-yourself' scheme. Free travel vouchers and billeting allowances were provided to mothers and children making their own arrangements for accommodation in the reception areas. This, along with the decline of bombing raids, saw a gradual decrease in the numbers of evacuees between 1942 and 1944. Early in 1943 a committee on the closing down of the evacuation scheme reported on the problem of responsibility for those children left behind at the end of the scheme (see chap 6.4). With the arrival of the flying bombs in June 1944, the decline in the number of evacuated children was temporarily halted and between July and September 1944 118,000 children were moved from London. However the Allied advance into the Low Countries in the autumn eased the pressure and the scheme was officially suspended in September 1944. Co-ordination of the winding down of the scheme was carried out by a Civil Defence Committee Subcommittee on the Government Evacuation Scheme (CAB 73/21).

When schools were able to re-open they faced serious shortages in a number of areas. Most important of all was the shortage of teaching staff, often conscripted or employed on war work (see chap 5.3.4), and accommodation shortages caused by requisitioning and war damage (see chap 5.3.3). The provision of equipment also proved to be a serious problem. By 1940 the supply of paper was down to half its pre-war levels (ED 10/292) and the supply of books was poor (ED 77/173). The shortage of wood made it difficult to acquire desks and chairs. Subjects like music and domestic science which required specific materials suffered badly (ED 10/289-306). These shortages, however, also produced unexpected gains. Because of the lack of basic equipment teachers had to improvise. This often resulted in more challenging and interesting classes and in the development of new teaching methods based around practical demonstration and discussion rather than reading, writing and examinations. After the war teachers' organizations fought hard to keep examinations out of the new secondary modern schools because they threatened to restrict teachers' new found freedom.

Rural hostility to education was long-standing. With the outbreak of war, the shortage of casual farming labour led to growing pressure from farmers to relax the school attendance and child employment legislation to allow children to work in agriculture. This pressure was resisted by the Board of Education and the Home Office (ED 11/230; CAB 75/5). Not until 1941 did the shortage of labour become acute, adding weight to the Ministry of Agriculture's claims for the easing of restrictions. A Board of Education circular in February 1941 suggested LEAs could co-operate in the moving of holidays to meet the needs of agriculture (ED 142/53), despite opposition from the TUC and other groups (ED 11/229). In 1942 new defence regulations allowed children over 12 to be employed on urgent seasonal work under the strict controls requested by the Board (CAB 75/13: 12 May 1948). These controls, however, proved difficult to enforce and a serious decline in attendance became apparent in a number of areas (ED 11/229). The danger to children also increased. The issue of insurance became important after an incident at Mobberly Boys School when a boy lost his leg in a threshing machine (HO 45/19328). Harvest camps proved easier to regulate (MAF 47/105, 109, 142, 146, 153), but the need for more mobile labour remained. This need continued long after the war due to the serious world food crisis (ED 142/1, 3, 4, 56).

* for committee references see Appendix B

Records

A number of files relating to general wartime issues exist. ED 134 contains LEA files for the wartime period covering such issues as ARP in schools, refugees, timber supplies, evacuation, camp schools and war damage. ED 10-ED 12 contain general files on elementary, secondary and general education up to 1946 and give a good indication of the impact of the war upon schools. ED 35 contains individual school files on secondary education establishments up to 1946, with LEA files on the same subject at ED 53. Individual elementary school files are at ED 21 and LEA files at ED 16. School attendance files are at ED 18. ED 136/163-172 relate to the closure of schools due to wartime conditions. ED 138 contains the papers of Dr S Weitzman, official war historian, on education during the war. Board of Education circulars and memoranda are at ED 142.

Ministry of Home Security papers relating to the effect of bombing on schools in Birmingham, including attendance figures and evacuation, are at HO 192/1248. Similar files on Hull are at HO 192/1293. Board of Education papers on damage to schools include ED 10/308 and ED 13/9A-9B.

A number of records exist relating to evacuation. An Advisory Committee on the Evacuation of School Children was established under Sir George Chrystal. Its papers are at ED 136/113-114, 118 and HLG 7/310-317. Papers on the Committee on the Government Evacuation Scheme are in ED 136/128. Ministry of Health files are at HLG 7/59-337 and at HLG 900; the latter includes material on billeting arrangements, transport, and medical provision but are only representative files of a destroyed series which contained mainly local material. HLG 102/78 deals with progress reports on the winding up of the scheme in 1944 and HLG 102/79-82 with the requisitioning of premises, coastal evacuation, and other issues. HLG 108/3 illustrates the attempts by government to stop reporting of the evacuation scheme by the media whilst HLG 108/18-24 deals with propaganda for the scheme in general. MH 101/1 deals with the formation of the Emergency Medical Scheme and includes a chapter on evacuation. Further files relating to health provision on the scheme are at MH 101/3, 14-19. Ministry of Health Building and Housing section papers relating to the scheme are at HLG 68/5. Statistics for 1939 are at RG 26/76. A report was prepared by Dr E Roy Bronsby on the extent and causes of poverty among families in London containing elementary and secondary schoolchildren in order to estimate charges for billeting (MH 57/394). Ministry of Education Private Office papers are at ED 136/110-128. Treasury files include T 161/1435/S45159/1-6 and T 161/1421/S45159/7-8 whilst a Prime Minister's Office file can be found at PREM 4/99/1. Official war history papers specifically on evacuation are at ED 138/48-54. ED 10/235-251 refers to evacuation areas and camps. Records on health and dental arrangements for evacuees are at ED 50/208 along with provision of clothing and footwear at ED 50/212. Assistance Board records are at AST 11/29-64. Ministry of Supply files relating to the scheme are at AVIA 22/35. Ministry of Labour and National Service papers include LAB 25/9. ED 147/374 deals with problems faced after the war. Evacuation was frequently discussed as a civil defence measure and consequently was discussed on such committees as the Civil Defence Committee. Its papers are in CAB 73/1-80. Cabinet papers relating to civil defence are at CAB 73. Further papers are listed elsewhere (see chap 4.2.2.2).

Private Office Papers on child employment in agriculture are at ED 136/199-200. The official history, *The employment of children in agriculture* by E K Ferguson, is at CAB 102/246 and ED 138/62. Ministry of Food policy on the issue is at MAF 47/94, 101, 158. Ministry of Agriculture papers include MAF 186/16, 31, 35, 40. Papers of the Harvest Camps Advisory Committee are at MAF 47/105, 109, 121.

5.3.2 Implementation of the general principles of the 1944 Act

The 1944 Education Act aimed to abolish 'all-age' elementary schools; children over 11 would henceforward be educated within a new system of specialist secondary schools. Both the Labour and the Conservative parties supported the implementation of this scheme during the general election campaign of 1945. The incoming Labour government, however, was not fully committed to the principle of selectivity implied by a specialist system. As early as 1944, the London County Council had drawn up a scheme involving partial multilateral reorganization and many within the Labour Party remained convinced of the merits of this approach (Benn 1980).

The 1943 Norwood Report, produced by the Committee on Curriculum and Examinations, had advanced the principle of a tripartite system of secondary education as the best way to progress. Schools were to be divided into grammar, secondary modern and technical. Grammar schools were to cater for the children most academically gifted and selection was made via the 11-plus examination. Technical schools were aimed at those children who were more 'practical', whilst secondary moderns were to provide a general education to those who remained—the vast majority of children.

Despite criticisms within the profession and the Labour Party, it was this structure which Labour put forward in its pre-election manifesto *The nation's schools* and in the post-election *Organisation of secondary education*. For many in the party, and not least for the new minister of education, Ellen Wilkinson (herself a product of the system), grammar schools represented the best way for working-class children to progress in society. Despite a revolt at the 1946 party conference, pressure from the NUT, local councils and some backbenchers, Wilkinson and her successor George Tomlinson kept faith with this system. Rather than revolutionizing the old system through the abolition of the grammar schools and the integration of the independent and public schools, government policy concentrated on the opening up of the existing system through raising the school leaving age, building more schools, and providing both better access to higher education and aided places to independent schools.

The 1944 Act sought to secure implementation of its proposals through development plans. All LEAs were required to produce plans to indicate how they proposed to meet the needs of their area under the new legislation. However, postwar staff shortages and existing workloads meant that the plans were often late in being produced and approved. Warwickshire County Council, for example, blamed 'an unusual number of retirements and breakdowns' for their delay (ED 152/169). The deadline for submission was 1 April 1946 but by 1948 only twenty plans had been approved. The complicated procedure and building regulations slowed down the submission of plans still further.

The vast majority of authorities reflected national policy and implemented a tripartite secondary system. There were, however, notable exceptions. London County Council's 1944 multilateral proposals were translated into the 1947 London Plan proposing 103 multilateral schools for the area. Middlesex envisaged a large number of small comprehensive schools (ED 152/111-114), whilst Bradford proposed eleven comprehensives on the outskirts of the city to provide extensive playing fields (ED 152/235-237). In the West Riding the Ministry reported that 'the majority of the County Council, led by the chairman of the education committee, adopted a dogmatic attitude in favour of multilateral and bilateral schools' (ED 152/194). Similar proposals came from Coventry, Southend, Oldham, Bolton, and others. Whilst these authorities were within their rights to propose such schemes (the Education Act did not lay down what system of secondary education should be provided) the Ministry of Education did all it could to block them. In contrast, authorities like Cardiff were allowed to avoid any sort of implementation and maintained an elementary school structure until 1950 (Geen 1981). The difference in treatment illustrates the fact that whilst LEAs had a degree of control in implementation, the Ministry was able to use financial constraint to enforce its own wishes. The need for large building programmes for multilateral schemes placed the authorities in question very much at the mercy of the Ministry of Education. Middlesex was allowed to experiment with three multilaterals from 1946, and London with eight between 1946 and 1949. Only in rural areas were such schemes not strongly resisted, as the dispersed population often made multilateral schools cheaper and more flexible to run. Anglesey became the only area to implement a complete multilateral system.

The extensive demands of the 1944 Act placed a number of rural local authorities in difficult financial positions. This was particularly true in Wales where, for example, the county councils of Brecon, Cardigan, Merioneth, Montgomery, and Radnor reported on their 'inability to carry out the provisions of the Act, without considerable additional grant, except by the imposition of an intolerable burden on the rate-payers'. Additional money was subsequently granted (BD 11/1362).

Demand had also been increasing for the reform of the independent school system. As early as 1942, R A Butler had been in negotiation with the Public Schools Governing Bodies Association about the future of the schools. The public schools themselves were anxious for change after facing severe financial difficulties in the late thirties. The Fleming Committee on Public Schools was appointed in 1942 to look at ways of developing the association between the public schools and the state system. Its report in 1943 recommended reserving 25% of places in independent schools for children from grant-aided primary schools supported by public funds. All private schools were to be registered and inspected. However the scheme allowed for the non-participation of local authorities and the schools themselves. Local authorities in the postwar period were hard pressed financially and were not necessarily eager to take on an extra burden. Further, the postwar period provided a real financial boost for private education which meant private schools did not need to become involved in government schemes. The poor conditions of state primary schools (see below) contrasted with the spacious accommodation, small classes and wider curriculum enjoyed by some of the preparatory schools. The same was true of many secondary schools. Employment patterns meant that more people could afford to pay for private education. By the end of the decade the majority of private schools were not operating the aided places scheme.

The main effort of the Labour administration in the education field came in its attempts to raise the school leaving age to 15. The Education Act 1936 had planned to do this but had been stopped by the outbreak of the Second World War (CAB 75/1: HPC(39)28). The 1944 Act restored these plans and announced the eventual intention to raise the leaving age to 16. Wartime pressures, predictions of postwar financial problems, and concern from industry over the effects on production costs (LAB 10/265; ED 46/234) meant the plans were delayed until 1945 and then postponed, in the face of strong opposition (ED 11/232), by the 1945 coalition government (ED 136/589).

At a Cabinet meeting in August 1945 Ellen Wilkinson restated the case for the raising of the school leaving age to 15 and received general support (CAB 128/1: 23 Aug 1945). An *ad hoc* Committee on the Raising of the School Leaving Age concluded that Labour had no political choice but to implement a Raising of the School Leaving Age Scheme (ROSLA) (CAB 78/36) and its decision was accepted by Cabinet in September (CAB

129/1). The supply of teachers and the provision of adequate accommodation to meet this deadline became the top educational priority (see chap 5.3.3 and 5.3.4).

1946 saw severe fuel and food shortages aggravated by the cold weather. The end of lend lease by the Americans worsened the economic crisis and led to growing concern about the implementation of ROSLA. The secretary of state for Scotland warned that implementation in Scotland would lead to part-time study in schools by 1948. Treasury concern grew throughout 1946 and 1947, culminating in an attempt in January and February 1947 to delay ROSLA (ED 136/727). At Cabinet in January, the Committee on Economic Planning attempted to get the plan postponed (CAB 128/9: 17 Jan 1947). In February, however, opposition from the chancellor of the Exchequer was overcome by Ellen Wilkinson in Cabinet when she successfully argued that the economic merits of delay would be overshadowed by the political damage caused. On top of this were the moderate successes of the Emergency Teacher Training Scheme (see chap 5.3.4) and the HORSA prefab building programme (see chap 5.3.3) which had at least made ROSLA practicable. The school leaving age was raised to 15 on 1 April 1947.

The raising of the school leaving age to 16, as the 1944 Act had suggested, proved impossible. The growing class sizes, increasing child population, and the general building crises at the end of the decade made a further rise in school rolls unthinkable. A report by George Tomlinson in 1949 called for indefinite postponement. He considered it more realistic to accept 15 as the norm and concentrate instead on part-time education for 16 to 17-year-olds (CAB 132/11: 11 Feb 1949). Not until 1973 was the leaving age to be raised to 16.

The 1943 Norwood Report also recommended major changes in the curriculum. It saw the need for a common 11 to 13 curriculum to facilitate the movement of pupils between different schools, condemned the specialization of many schools and recommended examinations at 11-plus and 16. However opposition to these ideas from the Secondary Schools Examination Council (SSEC) led to something of a stalemate. In February 1946 the SSEC was reconstituted, with a reduction in the influence of university examining boards who had been the main obstacle to change. Two groups were set up to look at examinations at 16 and at 18. The '18' report came out in January 1947 and its recommendations eventually led to the 'A' level examination system. The '16' enquiry split between those wanting no examinations at 16 and those favouring the introduction of subject-based examinations. Fears about universities creating their own examination structure led to the acceptance of the latter proposals by George Tomlinson in 1948. The first General Certificate of Education ordinary level examinations were held in 1951.

Primary school education found it very difficult to develop as planned in the postwar era. The large progressive movement behind child-centred primary education failed to secure any major advances. The acute shortage of buildings and teachers hit primary schools badly. The postwar baby boom began to feed itself into the system in the late forties producing a crisis in available places. In 1951 1,700 classes still contained fifty or more children, 37,000 forty or more, and 106,000 thirty or more (Lowe 1988). The concentration by the Labour administration on secondary school issues like ROSLA and the debate over structure meant little political or financial attention was paid to the primary service. Consequently it proved difficult to improve teaching techniques and conditions in the old elementary schools . Local authorities eager to bring about change often found their way blocked by opposition from church organizations which, especially in rural areas, proved vociferous in their attempts to defend the *status quo*.

Such battles proved to be a major feature in the development plan discussions (for example ED 152/85; ED 152/172).

The new secondary schools faced their own problems. Technical schools, despite attempts to prove otherwise (ED 147/195), were never established satisfactorily. It has been argued that as early as the Norwood Committee enquiry, with its bias towards liberal education, technical schools were never seriously considered as a part of the education system and so their successful integration into it was impossible (Barnett 1986). Certainly it is true that local education authorities found it difficult to define their role. Difficulty was found in providing a satisfactory curriculum and many schools based their classes around grammar school patterns. Many simply created technical streams within secondary moderns or grammar schools. This lack of identity made it even more difficult to attract pupils. Not surprisingly they became seen as inferior grammar schools. By 1949 only 310 technical schools had been set up, compared with 3,064 secondary moderns and 1,229 grammar schools.

Secondary moderns faced similar problems. Whilst many established courses and examinations equal to those in grammar schools, it proved difficult to dispel the notion that they were merely a dumping ground for the majority of children who had failed the eleven plus examination. Provision was often different from that in grammar schools and so was perceived as inferior. The wartime success of improvised teaching led many teachers to resist examination-dictated curricula and teaching methods. A 1948 government survey found that whilst 98% of grammar school children had homework, only 25% of modern or technical school children did (RG 23/47). The situation was made worse by the fact that many secondary modern schools took over old elementary school buildings, which had been expanded by the erection of prefab huts. This made teaching difficult and subjects like science virtually impossible. They also received the bulk of newly-qualified teachers from the Emergency Training Scheme (see chap 5.3.4), whilst university-trained teachers tended to teach in the grammar schools.

Records

The papers of the Committee on Curriculum and Examinations are at ED 12/478-480, with other files at ED 23/758, ED 138/16, ED 136/681, and CAB 117/109.

General Ministry of Education files on postwar primary and secondary education are at ED 147 and include minutes of the Secondary Schools Examination Council and of its subcommittees and panels. Primary and secondary school development plans can be found at ED 152 and procedure papers at ED 147/415. Development plans from Welsh county councils and boroughs are at BD 7. Inspectorate reports on primary schools are at ED 156. ED 161 contains files on individual primary schools from their establishment to 1966. Individual secondary school files are at ED 162. ED 53 contains LEA files on secondary education, a number dealing with the reorganization after the 1944 Act. Technical school files are at ED 82. General files on primary and secondary education for various LEAs are at ED 147/448-508.

ED 151 contains papers on the divisional administration scheme, set up in county areas to provide local influence after the replacement of Part III authorities (see chap 5.2).

Inspectorate reports on independent and public schools can be found at ED 172. A Private Office file on independent schools is at ED 136/129 with general files at ED 147/142, 176-177. Returns of private schools not recognized for grants up to 1944 are at ED 15, whilst those on recognized schools are at ED 33. Papers of the Fleming Committee on Public Schools are at ED 136/599-607, ED 12/518, ED 23/696, ED 138/17.

A social survey investigation into public attitudes towards education and the Education Act in 1945 is at RG 23/71. Ministry of Town and Country Planning papers on rural schools are at HLG 125/12. HLG 51/867-868 refer to financial arrangements following the restructuring of local administration under the Act.

Teachers' salaries were set by the Burnham Committee. Its papers are at ED 108/113-194 and ED 138/77. A London Area Special Subcommittee looked at the issue of additional payment for specified regions between 1946 and 1947.

5.3.3   The school building programme

The commitment in the 1936 Education Act to increase the school leaving age necessitated the expansion of school building, but the cost of fighting a war and the disruption of the education service (chap 5.3.1) led conversely to cutbacks in the school building programme. In the early years of the war the Treasury tried to gain significant savings (T 161/996/S45280; ED 11/283) and encouraged the initial move towards prefabricated construction (ED 10/293). Yet the need for school accommodation was greater than ever. The loss of buildings through requisitioning for war service (ED 10/281; ED 100/44; WORK 22/129) and war damage (ED 10/308; ED 147/387) had created a serious problem by 1941. By the end of the war 20% of schools had been destroyed and 12% damaged.

This shortage was intensified in the short term by the return of children from evacuation areas. In the longer term, the shortage was all the more serious because of the commitment to expand. The Board (later the Ministry) of Education became increasingly vociferous in its requests for a share in building resources (CAB 87/7: 30 March 1944; ED 136/336). Cabinet support was first obtained during the debate in 1944 on school building on the new estates for war workers (ED 11/293; ED 136/558). For the first time it was recognized that school provision was an essential feature of new housing estates. At a wider level the development of town and country planning towards the end of the war (see chap 3) made it imperative that the Board should be represented in the planning process (ED 31/493) and enjoy the benefits of compulsory purchase powers in order to secure proper educational provision (ED 136/541; CAB 75/13: 1 Sept 1942).

Following the work of the Building Regulations Committee (ED 23/697), the 1944 Education Act laid down for the first time uniform building regulations for all educational establishments. Previously LEA building schemes had been considered on their own merits. The 1945 building regulations imposed statutory minima on school sites and classroom sizes. This was later to become a burden as local authorities tried to find ways of saving money by cutting corners.

Three major factors convinced ministers of the need to expand school building: the decision to increase the school leaving age; the growth of new towns and new housing estates; and the post-war baby boom.

The main stimulus to school building came with the agreement of the Cabinet to raise the school leaving age to 15 from 1 April 1947 (see chap 5.3.2). To implement the proposals, school accommodation needed to be expanded by a significant amount. Classrooms were already overcrowded. The provision of permanent buildings was impossible in the short time available, and with the shortage of men and material. The Hutting Operation for the Raising of the School Leaving Age (HORSA) provided cheap, easily constructed buildings, built mainly onto existing schools. The prefabricated units were built and provided by the Ministry of Works with LEAs paying 8% per annum of the total cost. At the end of 1946 Ellen Wilkinson was able to announce an increased capital expenditure of £17m, mainly to be spent on the HORSA programme. Hertfordshire Council, one of the leaders in the field, had expanded thirty primary schools using prefabricated units by 1948. So successful were they that their representatives were brought in to the Ministry's architectural development group to offer advice.

However, the scheme also faced a number of difficulties. Some local authorities, such as Northumberland, refused to co-operate with the scheme. Building contractors took on average twice as long as expected to erect the buildings. The quality of the buildings was often questionable. The Royal Institute of British Architects described them as 'inconvenient to use, sub-standard in accommodation, uneconomical to heat, erected on playing spaces and unnecessarily costly' (Lowe 1988). Usually they were attached to the old elementary school buildings and contrasted badly with the newer schools built in the suburbs. Despite this, the scheme enabled the Ministry to push ahead with its plans for the raising of the school leaving age. Of 263,000 additional places provided between 1945 and 1949, 153,000 were provided through the HORSA scheme.

The raising of the school leaving age also placed an additional demand upon the supply of teachers, which in turn led to a need for more training places. Consequently extra building was needed to provide accommodation at existing colleges as well as on the Emergency Training Scheme (see chap 5.3.4).

The postwar period saw a large increase in the number of new housing estates (see chap 3). Since the development of estates for war workers the Ministry had been keen to ensure that education was given adequate resources (HLG 101/406). At the local level, education authorities increasingly co-operated with the Ministry of Town and Country Planning in planning future housing developments (ED 152/82-83) and the Ministry tried hard to gain representation on New Town Planning Committees (ED 31/619). Within new town plans, sites for educational purposes were set aside (HLG 90/303; HLG 90/472). The new estates tended to get the new permanent structures as opposed to prefabricated units. It was also necessary to attract teachers to the new estates, and at least one union expressed concern that housing should be set aside for this purpose (HLG 90/93).

The postwar period saw an explosion in the birth rate which began to feed in to the primary schools towards the end of the decade. The 1950 school building programme envisaged an extra one million pupils. Coming on top of the decision to raise the school leaving age, this meant that expenditure on school building had to rise simply to keep classroom sizes at their existing level. In the postwar financial climate this did not always prove to be possible.

In its 1945 election manifesto the Labour Party had paid a good deal of attention to its proposed housing programme. This placed a large demand on both financial resources and on the supply of workmen and materials (see chap 3). Education was left to fight with other government departments for what remained (CAB 132/1: 20 Dec 1946). This became true at the local level as well. In Newcastle upon Tyne, for example, the education authority fought a battle with the Housing Committee over land taken for housing (ED 152/334).

Land for the building of schools was acquired by LEAs through the provisions of the wartime Town and Country Planning Acts. They could do this either through agreement or compulsory purchase (ED 147/415; T 227/292). Local authorities therefore tended to stockpile land for future development. Under the Town and Country Planning Act 1947 this was no longer possible. Long-term development now had to be included in development plans submitted by local planning authorities (HLG 71/106; chap 3).

Along with other social services the school building programme faced serious cutbacks in the second half of the Labour government. The 1947 balance of payments crisis led to pressure from the Treasury and the Central Economic Planning Staff (T 229/492-493) to implement cuts in the programme as part of wider economy measures (T 227/150). This coincided with growing concern at the Ministry over the rising cost of school building (ED 147/54). From December 1947, it required local authorities to submit annual building programmes for approval by the Ministry before any schemes could begin. Eleven regional priority officers were appointed to allocate labour and resources. In October 1949 a departmental Committee on Building Costs was appointed to look at the cost of primary and secondary schools built since the war, and to recommend economies (ED 150/131). Concern was expressed at a meeting of the Lord President's Committee* in 1949 at the disparity in building costs between various LEAs, and the introduction of cash limits was discussed (CAB 132/11: 11 Feb 1949). These were implemented later in the year. Cost ceilings of £170 per place for primary schools and £270 for secondary schools were set. Building regulations were eased and the need for some auxiliary facilities, like cloakrooms, withdrawn. The Architects and Building Branch of the Ministry of Education was expanded to investigate ways of using cheaper building methods and design.

The devaluation crisis of 1949 led to even more dramatic cuts. School building was maintained at a minimum level but at the expense of associated services, in particular the school meals service (ED 142/3). In October 1949 all canteen building was indefinitely postponed (see chap 5.3.5). In Scotland, the cuts were even more severe (T 229/463). The outbreak of the Korean War in 1950 deepened the crisis still further. Steel and building components were in short supply and the Treasury demanded further cutbacks (T 229/456). Cost ceilings were reduced to £140 per primary place and the minimum area per place cut (ED 142/4: 5 June 1950). In December 1951 the new Conservative government placed a three-month ban on all new building projects.

* for committee references see Appendix B

Records

ED 150 contains the papers of the Architects and Building Branch of the Ministry of Education. General education files which include postwar building files are at ED 147. ED 10-ED 12, which deal with general educational issues, include a number of files on building. Investment Programme Committee papers on cuts in the building programme are at CAB 134/438-440. ED 147/412 deals with the application of building regulations. Details of LEA building programmes are at ED 154. ED 16 deals with the provision of accommodation up to 1944 by LEAs and includes files on wartime housing estates, war damage, and evacuation. ED 99 contains elementary education premises surveys carried out by HM Inspectorate up to 1942. LEA development plans, many referring to postwar building are at ED 152. For individual elementary and secondary school files see chap 5.3.1. Papers of the Committee on School Planning, which looked into standardized construction and layout in schools during the war, are in ED 23/693.

Ministry of Town and Country Planning Statistics Section papers on school population estimates in relation to buildings are at HLG 71/1329.

ED 138/63-64 contains papers of the official historian relating to wartime accommodation.

5.3.4 Supply of teachers

Evacuation (see chap 5.3.1) meant not only the movement of children but also of their teachers. The scheme was organized through the schools and so teachers took a central part, often assuming the role of parent, and sometimes suffering financially as a consequence (HLG 900/29). The return of many children to the cities in late 1939 led to serious difficulties with the distribution of teaching staff. The second wave of evacuation in the summer of 1940 deepened the crisis and whilst pre-war staff-pupil ratios were maintained, regional inequality was marked. Added to this, the conscription of many male staff into the services left many schools depleted and subjects like physical education and science, which were traditionally taught by men, in disarray.

A partial solution to the problem was to increase the supply of teachers. Former teachers who had retired or left the profession were brought back in and those about to retire had their retirement date postponed. Women who had left the profession upon marriage, a compulsory pre-war requirement, were also brought back. Not all LEAs co-operated and the Board found it necessary to issue a circular asking them to allow married women back, at least until the end of the war (ED 142/54: June 1942). The Ministry of Labour and National Service was approached in an attempt to gain priority status for the supply of teaching staff (ED 10/268). Major publicity campaigns were mounted to attract women to the profession (INF 2/144).

The supply of teachers coming out of teacher training colleges was severely disrupted. Whilst some colleges in evacuation areas had closed at the beginning of the war, by 1940 the majority were open again, subject to requisitioning. However, many were finding it increasingly difficult to attract enough entrants. In November 1939 the male entrance age was reduced from 18 to 17 and conscription delayed for five terms in an attempt to improve supply. Despite this, a number of male colleges were forced to close at the end of 1940. The situation worsened when increasing numbers of school-leavers were attracted to the new opportunities provided by industry.

This situation continued up to 1944 when there was a slight relaxation of the National Service conditions. From October 1944, men under 18 were allowed to complete six terms of study, and from spring 1945, age restrictions on women were completely lifted. However, many buildings remained requisitioned and a quick expansion of training proved impossible. Sixteen colleges were sequestered in 1944 and attempts to secure their release failed (ED 10/281). The issue was raised at the Lord President's Committee* in February 1945 (CAB 71/19: 16 Feb 1945), and at Cabinet (CAB 65/51); in May the Ministry of Works promised to release seven colleges by November.

The main attempt to solve the problem of teacher distribution was through a quota system introduced in 1942. LEAs were required to provide details of staff requirements for the coming year and staff were allocated according to the greatest need (ED 142/54: 5 June 1942). Authorities did not receive grants for any teachers employed above the quota. Students were required to stay in post for at least twelve months and lost their teaching status if they left before. Problems arose within less attractive areas, such as Birmingham, Manchester, Hull and Essex, which had problems finding teachers to fill their quota. However, on the whole, the system helped to ease the problem. Grammar schools became part of the scheme in 1945, to ensure that they did not poach staff from the new secondary modern schools.

In the longer term, consideration of the future of teacher training followed the critical remarks made in the Green Book about existing practices. About eighty colleges existed, fifty run by the voluntary sector and thirty by local authorities. They were small (usually training between 100 and 200 students) and culturally and academically isolated. Their influence and importance in the educational world was negligible.

Discussions following the publication of the Green Book led, in March 1942, to the appointment of a committee on the Recruitment and Training of Teachers*, chaired by Arnold McNair, the vice-chancellor of Liverpool University. Its role was 'to investigate the present sources of supply and the methods of recruitment and training of teachers and youth leaders and to report what priorities should guide the Board in these matters in the future'. A subcommittee was established under A P M Fleming to look specifically at the training of technical teachers (ED 86/95). The Committee as a whole was eager that the system should be overhauled and rejected piecemeal changes. However disagreement occurred over the form this overhaul should take. S H Wood, principal assistant secretary at the Board, saw future teacher training centred around university schools of education, thus raising the status of the teaching profession and giving to the universities a greater role in the shaping of the students they would receive at 18 (scheme A) (ED 86/94: 12 Mar 1943). A number of committee members, including the chairman, totally opposed this scheme. In particular, they feared the numbers of students involved would swamp the universities and believed it was not their role to provide such training. McNair proposed an alternative scheme involving a regional training council for each university area with representatives from universities, LEAs, teachers' organizations and religious bodies (scheme B). The Committee's report was published in May 1944 with the issue unresolved.

An early meeting with university vice-chancellors in August 1943 showed neither scheme to be very popular (ED 136/422). However, a number of teachers' associations and many at the Board of Education, including Butler, began to favour scheme A (ED 86/109: 16 Sept 1944). In September a committee under Sir Hector Hetherington, chairman of the committee of vice-chancellors, attempted to solve the problem by proposing a scheme C: the formation of institutes of education, administratively independent but staffed jointly by university and college staff. A letter from the Ministry to universities in November 1944 attempted to assess their positions in relation to the three schemes (ED 86/109: 29 Nov 1944). Manchester, Birmingham, Nottingham, Exeter and Southampton came out in favour of proposals along the lines of scheme A; Cambridge, scheme B; and Durham, Bristol, Leeds, Liverpool, Reading, and Sheffield, scheme C (ED 86/109: May 1945).

Ellen Wilkinson brought to the Ministry a strong preference for scheme A, but under pressure from Ministry officials, was forced to concede a degree of flexibility. Universities were given the right to choose (ED 142/56: 11 June 1945). Most universities in the end followed schemes along the lines of A, usually after internal battles. Only Reading, Liverpool and Cambridge refused financial and constitutional responsibility and here institutes were set up funded directly by the Ministry.

On the general issue of recruitment, the McNair Committee* had recommended that a Central Training Council be formed to review recruitment, supply and training. Despite early opposition, Wilkinson came increasingly to accept the need for some permanent machinery to overview the process and bring together colleges, teachers and the Ministry. Whilst the idea was developed, an interim committee for teachers was established in 1947 under D R Hardman to deal with urgent matters (ED 86/174, 265, 267, 269). Wales had its own committee (ED 86/268). Its success led the new minister, George Tomlinson, to inaugurate a new permanent body, the National Advisory Council on Training and Supply of Teachers (NACTST) in 1949. This in turn established subcommittees in technical teacher training (ED 46/639; ED 86/452-453), on the recruitment, training, and conditions of service of youth leaders (ED 124/129), on the training of teachers of handicapped children (ED 50/307-315), and two standing committees (ED 86/276-277, 449-450).

Whilst the long-term organization of training was important, it was the immediate shortfall in staff which caused the greatest concern towards the end of the war. This problem was looked at in 1943 by a departmental Committee on the Postwar Supply and Training of Teachers* under the chairmanship of Sir Robert Wood (ED 143/1). Two main solutions to the problem were pursued: early demobilization of trained teachers and the formation of an Emergency Training Scheme (ETS) for those wishing to train for the profession. There were also a number of minor schemes such as the attempt to recruit British prisoners of war whilst they were still being held in Germany (ED 86/99).

From early in the war the Board attempted to gain recognition of teachers as an occupational group for demobilization purposes (ED 136/313) but government moves towards a policy based on age and length of service made its task difficult (ED 136/308). The War Office's intention to keep teachers to provide staff for their further education programmes caused additional worries. Even by 1944 when the minister of labour, Ernest Bevin, was developing a scheme for the release of those workers taking part in the reconstruction programme (class B workers) (ED 136/315) teachers were still excluded as a profession. Butler approached Bevin in late 1944. He was able to use Bevin's support of the 1944 Education Act to make him change his mind over the inclusion of teachers in class B (ED 136/314). By November 1945, 4,000 teachers had been released under class B and an unknown number as part of the on-going demobilization programme.

Demobilization alone, however, could not provide sufficient teachers. In 1943, S H Wood had reviewed the existing system of teacher training colleges and proposed a number of emergency colleges to supplement them (ED 136/542). Sir Robert Wood's Committee recommended the opening of around fifty emergency training colleges each offering one-year courses to about 200 students (ED 143/1). This was to be financed by the Treasury and operated by the LEAs.

Union reactions to the scheme were mixed. The National Union of Women Teachers feared dilution of the profession and so opposed the scheme (ED 143/1). The NUT accepted the need for emergency courses, but favoured further courses of training after four years. Union fears were eased by the introduction of a two-year probationary period for teachers, rather than one, and by the ending of a long-standing area of dispute: the uncertified teacher. A Committee on Uncertified Teachers under W C Cleary looked into the problem and concluded that the grade should be abolished and qualified status given to those who had been teaching for more than 20 years (ED 143/8). Special one-year courses were offered to those with five years' teaching experience (ED 143/8).

The first group of ex-servicemen took a pilot course organized by Goldsmith's College in London in September 1944 (ED 143/22). After its success fifty-four emergency colleges opened up to all ex-servicemen and women. No formal academic qualifications were required. Individuals were selected on the basis of interview and a combination of personal qualifications, war experience and enthusiasm.

In a number of ways the scheme became a victim of its own success. After the end of the war in the Far East, the scheme became inundated with applications and by 1946 was receiving 5,000 a month. The problem was particularly acute in male colleges. This was worsened by the fact that the postwar baby boom was first felt in primary schools where the majority of teachers were women. In a reverse of the wartime trend it became clear that schools were facing a male surplus and a female deficit. From 1947 applications to male colleges were closed (ED 142/1: 9 April 1947). As ETS colleges were phased out towards the end of the decade every effort was made to convert them into permanent women's colleges (ED 86/119). Applications were further boosted in 1947 with the agreement of the Ministry to pay incidental expenses to individuals in the form of a grant. LEAs were able to offer supplementary aid in the hope that 'no suitable student should be debarred from training because his parents are unable to pay the necessary fee' (ED 142/1: 17 June 1947). Shortage of buildings and staff reinforced the problem and contributed to waiting lists of between twelve and eighteen months. Despite these problems, and criticisms that it reinforced divisions between grammar and secondary modern schools by providing staff mainly for the latter, the scheme was essential to the realization of the Ministry's policy of raising the school leaving age. By 1951 it had provided more than 23,000 men and 12,000 women teachers.

Records

ED 86 contains general files on issues arising out of the training of teachers. Files on the setting up and running of the Emergency Training Scheme are at ED 143, with details of the change over to permanent colleges at ED 86/174. Papers arising out of the conclusions of the McNair Committee are at ED 86/109, 189-192 and ED 136/608. ED 10/264-270 refer to the demobilization of teachers. Files relating to terms and conditions policy include ED 147/83, T 161/1258/S7651/06/2, 4 and T 161/1259/S7651/06/3, with files relating to teachers' salaries at ED 108. ED 143/1 and ED 136/687 contain the papers of a departmental Committee on the Postwar Supply and Training of Teachers.

ED 105 contains the papers of the Joint Examination Board set up to provide examinations for prospective teachers. Details of in-service training courses are at ED 86/222 and ED 143/19. ED 161 deals with the provision of short courses for teachers at further education colleges etc.

ED 78 contains files on teacher training colleges maintained by voluntary bodies, LEAs and universities. ED 81 contains files on university training departments. Inspectorate reports on teacher training colleges are at ED 115. LEA provisions for the preliminary training of teachers are detailed at ED 67. University files on the setting up of institutes of education are at ED 119, with university deliberations over various schemes at ED 159. Papers of the Committee on Scales of Salaries for Teaching Staff of Training Colleges, set up in 1945, are at ED 108/118-119, 160, 195-197. Papers of the National Advisory Council on the Training and Supply of Teachers are at ED 86/270-285, T 214/85, and ED 86/448-459.

Official war history papers on teacher training are at ED 138/69. ED 60 contains wartime staffing and attendance returns and illustrates the problem of staffing caused by evacuation and the quota system. ED 10/234 deals with evacuation allowances, ED 86/113-115 with the quota system.

A social survey investigation in 1944 into the attitude of parents and teachers to the profession, and the implications of this for recruitment, are in RG 23/63 and ED 121/103.

The papers of the Education Subcommittee of the Local Government Manpower Committee* are at ED 46/751 and HLG 51/1017.

* for committee references see Appendix B

5.3.5   Special services

5.3.5.1   School meals and milk

The provision of school meals was first authorized by the Education (Provision of Meals) Act 1906 and continued to gain acceptance in many areas up to the start of the Second World War. At its outbreak 110,000 children were receiving free meals and 50,000 paid for them. The former were mainly the urban poor, affected by poverty, unemployment and industrial disputes. The latter were often rural children who lived too far away to travel home at lunch-time. The Board of Education aided LEA expenditure on the service with a 50% grant. School milk was first provided at low cost in 1934. It had the advantage of providing free or cheap milk to as many children as possible whilst at the same time helping farmers to reduce the increasing milk surplus. Before the war, 2,500,000 children received milk, 440,000 paying for it. The immediate consequence of the outbreak of war was to reduce dramatically the number of children receiving either service. As schools in evacuated areas closed, milk provision dropped by 40% and free meals by 50%. An extension of the service, particularly in the reception areas, became essential (ED 136/175).

The Board increased the pressure on LEAs to provide school meals and milk in some form, both as a means of helping the evacuation programme and as a way of solving the problem of malnutrition amongst the young; a 1939 nutritional survey of Margate by the Board's Medical Section found one in ten children suffering from sub-normal nutrition (ED 123/79). Initially, however, 95 LEAs refused to co-operate and 12 failed to reply to the Board's proposals.

The real drive at ministerial level for a full school meals service came from Clement Attlee after he became lord privy seal in 1940. He saw the issue as one of providing cheap food to the poorer classes in wartime. He received strong support at the Food Policy Committee* and from the minister of food, Lord Woolton (CAB 74/2). The Board of Education, however, felt demands for a full school meals service were impractical. It argued that problems over the supply of equipment and buildings would prove insurmountable and proposed instead the targeting of needy groups, like the children of war workers and the undernourished, a position Woolton hesitantly accepted. Circular 1520, issued in 1940, called on LEAs to provide school meals at cost price to the children of parents who required the service (ED 142/53).

Many parents were hesitant to take advantage of the new service, associating it with the stigma of the old Poor Law (CAB 74/2: FP(M)(40)74, 77, 80). Progress was also hampered by difficulties in the supply of equipment and the effects of war damage. Leyton Council, for example, complained of the problems of implementing Circular 1520 'because of the intensification of air attack and its effect on organization' (ED 123/50).

In October 1941 the Board attempted to push more intransigent LEAs into providing meals by increasing the rate of grant to them, despite Treasury concerns (T 161/1239/S46977/1). In 1942 school dinner provision was extended to include school holidays after concern that children with parents working or in the services were not properly supervised (ED 142/54: 30 June 1942). Nevertheless provision remained mixed. A government survey carried out in 1942 found only 47.5% of parents questioned were given the opportunity of sending their children for school meals, and of these only 29.5% took advantage of it (RG 23/15).

By 1943 the national food situation was critical. Woolton increasingly came to see school meals and milk as an excellent way of supplementing the general ration (CAB 71/11: 19 Mar 1943; ED 50/190). Professor Drummond, scientific adviser at the Ministry of Food, urged the Board to regard school feeding as an emergency service and to expand it accordingly (ED 50/233). Butler accepted the need for expansion. The Board successfully negotiated with the Ministry of Works to provide prefabricated buildings as a matter of priority (ED 50/239). Difficulty was experienced, however, in gaining Treasury co-operation. Attempts to secure a 100% grant to expand the service were resisted, mainly because of Treasury concerns at being given financial responsibility for a service which would clearly continue after the war. In the end it agreed only to finance capital expenditure on premises and equipment with local authorities providing the daily running costs (CAB 71/11-12: 22 April 1943, 8 May 1943; T 161/1239/S46977/2; ED 50/233). The accelerated proposals were implemented in May 1943, with LEAs advised to aim for 75% provision (ED 142/54; ED 50/241).

The expansion of the service was only a partial success. Dinners continued to be unpopular with many parents and children. A social survey on the subject in August 1943 found complaints from a number of children about school meal provision both in terms of quality of food ('sometimes the meat hash has a very unpleasant and peculiar taste rather like Brasso, but we can never make up our mind what is the cause'—girl 14) and the environment ('the boy opposite is filthy and grabs the bread. You find proper table manners and conduct at home'—girl 13) (RG 23/47). The quality of provision varied from area to area. In Bradford, for example, the inspector was critical of the nutritional value of the food (ED 123/216). Expansion proposals were often delayed in the planning stage as a result of the new Town and Country Planning (Interim Development) Act 1943; and by January 1944 the rate of approval of planning applications was down by 75% (ED 50/221). In March 1944 reductions in the building programme meant that proposals costing more than £5,000 could not be considered. In April the restrictions were further tightened. Throughout 1944 the president of the Board remained concerned that progress was being jeopardized (CAB 87/6: 20 Oct 1944; CAB 87/9: 18 Oct 1944) and in early 1945 it was considered necessary to call on LEAs to make real efforts to improve the service (ED 142/55: 4 Jan 1945). By 1945 1,782,000 children were receiving school meals. The Milk in Schools Scheme continued to expand and by 1943 75% of children regularly received some sort of provision (RG 23/33).

The 1944 Education Act laid on LEAs a statutory duty to provide meals and milk to all children who required it, but left it to future regulations to decide if the service should be free (ED 136/611). Initially the Board believed that free provision would become part of the family allowances scheme (see chap 2.5). The Green Book (see chap 5.2) had originally proposed this and received some support from the Treasury (ED 38/60); and with the publication of the Beveridge Report (see chap 2.2) it became increasingly apparent that the government saw child welfare measures as supplements to family allowance cash payments. Butler took this to mean the inevitability of free meals and milk and began to plan for such a scheme (ED 50/233). However, the Treasury successfully argued that meals at cost price could be considered part of the scheme as no profit was made. When the service came into operation in 1945 meals were indeed charged at cost price, with concessions for those on low income. This led to protests from parents receiving national assistance whose income still exceeded LEA scales for receiving free meals, who argued that they were receiving allowances in one hand and paying them out with the other (AST 7/796). Charges for milk continued until August 1946, when it became free on the introduction of family allowances (T 161/1239/S46977/2; CAB 128/5: 28 Feb 1946). Administration of both schemes remained with the Ministry of Education (PIN 18/12; CAB 132/1: LP(46)36; ED 50/402; MAF 101/530).

A number of problems remained during the postwar period. Concern amongst teachers about their role in the School Meals Service and, in particular, in the supervision of children led to problems in certain areas and necessitated a circular from the ministry reinforcing the requirements of staff (ED 142/56; ED 86/118). Problems over equipment and building supplies continued to affect the service. The West Riding County Council, for example, complained that 'the conditions under which these [meals] are prepared and served are deplorable and in some cases even dangerous' (ED 152/192). Authorities were refused permission to buy equipment on the open market for fear of reducing supply still further (ED 123/329). A Canteen Equipment Committee was created to look at the problem of supply (ED 50/452-458).

The devaluation crisis of 1949 led to an immediate halt to any expansion of the service (see chap 5.3.3). In October, the prime minister announced that 'there will be a slowing down in our advance. We shall maintain the progress of school and technical buildings, securing the necessary savings by reducing costs and postponing the expansion of the school meals service'. All new building was indefinitely postponed. The service did not regain its momentum until well into the 1950s (ED 142/3). The provision of free milk was unaffected as it was distributed within the class rooms. The service continued until 1972.

* for committee references see Appendix B

Records

ED 50 contains the papers of the Medical and, from 1945, Special Services Section of the Board and Ministry of Education, which was responsible for the School Meals Service and the Milk in Schools Scheme. Private Office papers are at ED 136/662.

Files from other departments include Assistance Board files on the postwar service at AST 7/796, 896, 899. Treasury files on the Milk in Schools Scheme are at T 161/1108/S39098/013/1-4. Treasury O&M reports are at ED 23/929. Treasury Agriculture and Food Division papers relating to the Milk in School Scheme and family allowances are at T 223/15.

Ministry of Food files on the Milk in Schools Scheme are at MAF 101/457, and school meals policy files at MAF 99/1652-1653. Details of early co-operation between the

Ministry of Food and the president of the Board of Education are at ED 136/83 and MAF 99/1650-1651. Ministry of Food Supply Division papers on the extension of the Milk in Schools Scheme during the war are at MAF 85/284.

LEA files on the School Meals Service are at ED 123. Ministry of Food information files for LEAs are at MAF 102/51-52 and an LEA sample file on school meal provision is at MAF 900/103.

E K Ferguson's wartime history, *The nutrition of the school child*, is at CAB 102/245 with notes on the school meals and milk service at ED 138/59-60.

5.3.5.2 School medical service

At the start of the Second World War the School Medical Service had developed to a point at which LEAs were providing medical inspections at least three times during a child's school life. Skin diseases, dental and eyesight problems were all treated, and many schools also provided advice on infections, heart disease and rheumatism.

The outbreak of war, and evacuation in particular, highlighted the failings of the existing system. The low standards of health and hygiene of many city children led to an outcry from many host families during the first wave of evacuation in 1939. To avoid similar protests during the second wave in 1940, the Board laid plans to examine all registered evacuees at least three times during the evacuation process. Unfortunately most children failed to register properly and so were only examined once. Children were accordingly labelled 'suitable for ordinary billeting', 'suitable for hostels', or 'requiring special attention' (ED 50/206). The biggest problem, and the cause of the loudest outcry, was lice (MH 55/880-881). At the outbreak of the war the medical service had estimated that about 10% of children were affected. However, the high level of complaints suggested the real number was much higher. An investigation organized by the Board and the Ministry of Health in 1940 found that 50% of girls up to the age of 14 in industrial centres were affected as were a large number of boys (ED 50/196).

In attempting to tackle these problems the service suffered from that wartime affliction: a shortage of staff. As well as losing staff through conscription, the medical service also faced demands from other areas particularly during the heavy bombing of 1940 and 1941 (see chap 4.2.2.2). In a number of cities it became impossible to maintain the service (ED 50/174). Worst affected in terms of staff was the School Dental Service which had a high percentage of young male staff eligible for national service. Early in the war no emergency service was available in a number of areas (ED 50/208). The Board and the British Dental Association in June 1940 decided on a policy of treating only those children (labelled 'appreciative patients') who had good dental and regular attendance records. A Consultative Committee of School Medical Officers was appointed to consider all these problems and to look at the future of the service (ED 50/192).

The war did, however, lead to a number of innovations which were to continue into the postwar period. Fear of the spread of infectious disease, with large groups of children from different backgrounds mixing freely, led to moves for an immunization drive in 1941 (see chap 4.2.3). This was offered free. By 1942 one third of children under 15 had taken part in the programme (RG 23/23). This was followed by a further drive in 1942 and thereafter became a regular feature of the preventative side of the service's work. By 1945, 67% of children under 16 had been immunized and public awareness of disease and preventative measures had risen (RG 23/77).

A large number of maladjusted children considered unsuitable for billeting were placed in specially built hostels. Although initially simply an evacuation measure, they increasingly came to be seen as treatment-based institutions. By 1943, 225 were offering psychiatric treatment of some kind for over 3,400 children. Their increasing success led the Mental Health Emergency Committee (MH 58/573; ED 50/273-274; ED 102/28-29) to ask for the extension of the facilities to local children as well as evacuees. At the end of the war a number of LEAs, under guidance from the Board, took over hostels as permanent peacetime institutions (ED 50/274; see chap 5.3.5.3).

Growing demands for an extensive postwar service raised the question of who would be responsible for it. The assumption in the Beveridge Report of a free national health service questioned the need for a school medical service at all. In terms of treatment, the work of the two services would overlap and in a number of cases it was unclear what class of people would use which scheme. The Board's desire to cater for 14 to 15-year-olds who had left school clearly infringed on the Ministry of Health's responsibilities (ED 50/196). Agreement was reached at meetings in February 1943 on a workable structure whereby a school medical service would exist alongside a national health service but with the latter carrying out all treatment. The School Medical Service was to develop as a preventative and screening operation for children. Only the school dental and speech therapy services remained independent of the Ministry of Health, with LEAs being responsible for carrying out treatment (ED 50/351). Representations to the Interdepartmental Committee on Dentistry* (MH 77/124) had secured a degree of independence for the School Dental Service.

The 1944 Education Act imposed on LEAs a statutory duty to provide medical and dental inspections in all maintained primary and secondary schools and to ensure the provision of treatment without cost to the parent (ED 142/55: 12 Mar 1945). The appropriate section of the Act was due to come into force in April 1945 but this coincided with negotiations which were taking place between the Ministry of Health and the medical profession over the inauguration of the NHS. Any separate negotiations on the implementation of the School Medical Service could have undermined the minister of health (ED 50/287; MH 77/137). In the interim period, therefore, LEAs made arrangements with voluntary and local authority hospitals to secure provision for their children. However, once Labour came to power and it became clear that a national health service would be created, the treatment side of the service was run down. The service now developed its preventative role. Detailed arrangements for the relationship between the NHS and the School Medical Service were laid down in 1948 (ED 142/2: 4 Aug 1948).

* for committee references see Appendix B

Records

ED 50 contains the papers of the Medical, and from 1945, the Special Services Section of the Board and Ministry of Education which was responsible for the School Medical Service. LEA files on the service are at ED 137.

E K Ferguson's war history of the School Medical Service is at CAB 102/244 with notes at ED 138/56, 58. A Private Office file is at ED 136/664.

Ministry of Health papers on the position of handicapped children under the School Medical Service are at MH 134/194. Files relating to the postwar School Dental Service include MH 135/435, 440, with files on the school eye service at MH 135/600-601, 639.

5.3.5.3. Special educational treatment

The statutory foundation of special education provision for disabled children was laid down in the last decade of the nineteenth century, and remained largely unchanged until the 1944 Education Act. The Elementary Education (Blind and Deaf Children) Act 1892 laid upon every school authority the duty of providing education for such children in a special school certified by the Education Department. In 1899 these powers were extended to cover training of the physically and mentally defective and epileptic children. In 1921 attendance at such schools was made compulsory up to the age of 16.

The education of the disabled was the responsibility of the Board of Education and the LEAs. This was, however, changed with the passing of the 1944 Disabled Persons (Employment) Act which gave responsibility for the training and employment of the disabled to the Ministry of Labour and National Service (see chap 6.5). However the Ministry of Education kept responsibility for children of school age. It also provided some general education for young recruits to the Ministry of Labour and National Service's scheme (ED 50/265, 648-650; ED 142/56: 12 Nov 1945).

The identification of 'exceptional children' (blind, deaf, physically defective, mentally defective, and epileptic) was the responsibility of the school medical officers of the LEAs. These duties, however, were never completely fulfilled. Many areas failed to make special provision for the mentally defective and so avoided identifying the children involved. The 609 special schools provided by LEAs and voluntary bodies were well short of the required numbers.

The Second World War exacerbated these problems. Evacuation of special schools was a major problem, as pupils could not normally be billeted. Special camps, hostels, and large homes were therefore established and schools were moved as complete units. Whilst the arrangements proved satisfactory in 1939, the shortage of accommodation proved a major problem thereafter (HLG 7/283).

The need for evacuation, and the need to exercise care in choice of site, was highlighted in a controversy in West Sussex when a camp for the physically disabled was bombed, after an attack on a nearby searchlight by a German plane. Three people were killed (ED 50/258).

General war conditions led to a reduction in the number attending special schools. By the summer of 1941 the number of mentally defective London children attending school had been halved. The decrease in physically handicapped children attending schools in London was 55%, in Birmingham 25% and in Manchester 44%. This was due to a number of factors: there was a shortage of suitable premises with many buildings requisitioned or being used as ordinary schools; transport difficulties; the disorganization of the School Medical Service which meant new cases were not always spotted and the lower number of special schools in reception areas compared to the towns (Webster 1988 pp 177-179).

The 1944 Education Act laid upon local authorities the duty to secure that 'provision is made for pupils who suffer from any disability of mind or body by providing, either in special schools or otherwise, special educational treatment, that is to say education by special methods appropriate for persons suffering from that disability'. The Act extended the classification of disabled from five to eleven categories: blind (ED 50/571); partially sighted; deaf (ED 50/577-580); partially deaf; delicate; diabetic; educationally sub-normal; epileptic; maladjusted; physically handicapped (ED 50/629); and children suffering from speech defects (ED 50/641-642). It abolished the need for a medical certificate prior to the enrolling of a child into a special school, except where parents questioned the choice of institution. Under the Act, provision could range from adaptation of the curriculum within an ordinary school to the provision of special schools for whole groups of children. An Advisory Committee on Handicapped Children was set up to advise the minister (ED 50/598).

The classification 'educationally sub-normal' was new and an advance on the previous categorization of such children as mentally defective. The new category covered those needing help within an ordinary school to those who would benefit from a special school. Emphasis therefore shifted from certification of the mentally defective to assessing the needs of each individual child. In practice, however, the provision of special schools for the mentally defective was the worst of any of the categories and so assessment was difficult to maintain (ED 50/590-592).

The category of diabetic was also new. This had arisen specifically out of the circumstances of war. The problem of billeted children suffering severe forms of diabetes led to the establishment of special hostels by the London County Council. This illustrated the need for facilities for children unable to cope with the condition because of either its unstable nature or home circumstances. In 1948, 1,200 children were diagnosed as having diabetes, of whom 150 were recommended for hostels. These were provided by voluntary agencies.

By 1949 there were 47,119 pupils in special schools, taught by 3,266 teachers. However the number of schools was lower than before the war (601), and it was estimated that at least 22,000 children were awaiting places. This excluded those who should have been diagnosed but were not, because of shortage of places. Once again the problems with the school building programme (see chap 5.3.3) and the concentration of funds on primary and secondary education (see chap 5.3.2) accounted for this shortfall.

Records

Papers of the Special Services Division of the Ministry of Education, which was responsible for special educational treatment are at ED 50.

ED 133 contains files dealing with the provision of special schools and associated problems in particular LEAs. Files on individual schools are in ED 32. ED 62 deals with training establishments providing further education for disabled children. LEA development plans, which deal in part with special school provision are in ED 152. Papers on boarding homes for maladjusted, educationally sub-normal and diabetic children are at ED 122.

The papers of the Home Office's Children's Department on educationally sub-normal and mentally deficient children include MH 102/2264-2288, 2349-2374.

The official war history notes on disabled pupils and special schools are at ED 138/57.

Between 1950 and 1955 the Underwood Committee on Maladjusted Children looked at their medical, educational and social problems and at their treatment in the education system (ED 50/316-345).

5.4 Further and higher education

5.4.1 Technical, further and adult education

5.4.1.1 General

At the outbreak of war the Technical Branch of the Board of Education was responsible for policy on technical training and further education, which included technical and art colleges, evening institutes, day continuation schools and junior technical schools. The majority of students were part-time. Recommendations in the 1938 Spens Report for the expansion of the service had to be abandoned on the outbreak of the war.

As with school reform, implementation of the clauses in the 1944 Act on further education was to be ensured through development plans, which LEAs were to present by 1948. Again, as with the school plans (see chap 5.3.2), the vast majority were late (ED 155/14, 22, 51). By the end of 1948 just over one-third had been received, swelling to two-thirds by 1949.

The diversity of further education meant that the qualifications and experience of those teaching were also diverse. The McNair Committee on the Training of Teachers* concluded in 1943 that training could not be made compulsory because of the impossibility of finding a general standard. Indeed, it found it desirable that a large part of formal training should take place after the start of teaching. Generally, therefore, the majority of staff teaching in further, technical and adult education had professional experience rather than a teaching qualification. However, in order to meet the immediate postwar shortage of staff, four training colleges were established on a temporary basis at Huddersfield, Bolton, Wolverhampton and London. These were later to become permanent. From March 1946, the minister extended the thirty-day grant for training to six months to encourage teachers to gain wider experience of industry and commerce.

* for committee references see Appendix B

Records

Further education general files of the Ministry of Education are at ED 46. Postwar LEA development plans are at ED 155. Building files arising out of the plans are at ED 160 and ED 46/695, 697. Establishment files of further education colleges including the approval of courses, provision of equipment and general building matters are at ED 51. Inspectorate reports on individual colleges are at ED 114. Provision of equipment and general building matters are at ED 168. A Further Education Schemes Committee helped LEAs in submitting their schemes. Its papers are at ED 46/396.

5.4.1.2 Technical education

During 1939 technical schools and colleges suffered in much the same way as ordinary schools (see chap 5.3.1). Those in evacuation areas were closed and whole schools, where possible, transferred to the reception areas. Many buildings were requisitioned for war services. However it soon became apparent that the specialist nature of technical teaching, with its dependence on specialist equipment, made it virtually impossible to transfer a school without affecting the quality of its education. Further, the expansion of war industries meant there was a great demand for technically trained personnel. On 9 September 1939 technical institutions were allowed to reopen where they were training students for war industries. Agreement was reached with the Ministry of Works that no more buildings would be requisitioned without consultation with the Board (ED 10/281). Junior technical schools were allowed to reopen in line with other elementary and secondary schools (see chap 5.3.1). By the end of 1939 many courses were back in full operation.

From this date, pressure from industry began to increase for improved training programmes, particularly for the unskilled and unemployed (ED 46/237). As a result the Board was able to increase greatly the amount of day-time teaching in colleges and introduced six-month courses to teach specific skills. Negotiations with the Ministry of Labour and National Service led to scheme M, designed to train entrants specifically for the engineering industry. It offered short-term training at colleges paid for by the Ministry of Labour and National Service and in 1940 provided 4,000 places.

Provision, however, remained mixed. Whilst many local authorities actively promoted technical education, a number used war conditions to cut back. Also the response from industry was often disappointing with few firms taking full advantage of courses offered. The traditional suspicion between British industry and the Board of Education continued.

The wartime initiatives were only short-term solutions to the problems of technical training, and belatedly it was recognized that more sweeping proposals were needed if technical education was to meet the demands of a modern industrial society. In 1935 a survey of accommodation for technical and art education in England and Wales had found provision poor compared with western Europe and the United States. In March 1939 the president of the Board of Education, De La Warr, had circulated a memorandum to Cabinet on the problems facing the service, calling for new buildings, better technical training facilities and the expansion of day continuation schools (ED 46/226). The outbreak of war, however, meant that little could be done. When postwar planning began in 1940 further education was rarely discussed. Within the Technical Branch of the Board a number of proposals for the expansion of the service were debated (ED 136/296) but in the Board as a whole the emphasis was mainly on primary and secondary education (see chap 5.2). The Green Book simply reviewed existing provision and offered few new ideas, with the exception of day continuation schools (see chap 5.4.1.3). Junior technical schools were discussed as part of the secondary school reorganization but their role was limited (see chaps 5.2 and 5.3.2). A small group under R S Wood was created by the Board to hold informal discussions on the development of technical education but it failed to find a way of linking the needs of industry to the provision of college courses (ED 136/669).

When the Education White Paper appeared in 1943 the section dealing with further and technical education was far from revolutionary. It proposed placing a statutory duty on LEAs to provide adequate facilities for technical, commercial and art education. Its only radical proposal was for the compulsory attendance for school leavers at day continuation schools (see chap 5.4.1.3). The limited scope of the proposals and the small amount of money set aside to finance them led to a number of protests. These included complaints from Technical Branch inspectors and the Board's Consultative Committee on Engineering (ED 136/427). When the Education Bill appeared later in the year the level of finance had been greatly increased.

To placate its critics further, the Board appointed a Committee on Higher Technological Education* under Lord Eustace Percy in 1944 to look at the relationship between universities and technical education. It consisted of representatives of universities, technical colleges and industry. In its report, published in August 1945, it recommended the formation of regional advisory councils to co-ordinate the work of universities, colleges, LEAs and industry, as well as regional academic boards to bring together the teaching staff of various institutions. A National Council of Technology would overview the whole structure. A limited number of colleges were to be given a greater measure of academic freedom to develop degree level work. It also recommended that individual colleges should conduct, as part of their activities, national schools in particular branches of technological study and receive special financial assistance for so doing. This latter recommendation was accepted by the minister in April 1946. It was suggested that courses might be developed within existing colleges by the industries concerned (see, for example, ED 46/502). Industries would support the schools, assist in their direction and release employees for full-time study and accept students for employment on completion of courses. These institutions were named national colleges. The regional advisory councils came into existence in February 1946. Ten were set up in England and Wales and, despite problems over representation, their inauguration went ahead fairly smoothly (ED 46/760). In 1948 the minister set up a National Advisory Council on Education for Industry and Commerce to advise on national policy. The attempt to free a number of colleges in order to develop their higher level work did not, however, succeed. A number of organizations like the Federation of British Industry tried to encourage research within technical colleges but found the structure of the system a hindrance (ED 46/464-465). Not until 1951 did the government begin to discuss ways of achieving technological education of a university standard outside the universities (CAB 132/17: 27 July 1951).

Agricultural education was administered by the Ministry of Agriculture and Fisheries, and local authorities outside the LEA structure. In 1943 a committee under Lord Justice Luxmoore reported on the future developments of the service and recommended the formation of a National Council for Agricultural Education to administer the system (ED 136/679; Cmd 6433 1943). Concern expressed by the Board of Education at its lack of involvement led to a compromise offering it a share in the administration of the scheme. This, however, was opposed by the Treasury (ED 136/554-555). A final compromise passed local control over to the LEAs, whilst overall control remained with the Ministry of Agriculture. The postwar development of the service was jointly co-ordinated by the two ministries under a Joint Advisory Committee on Agricultural Education under the chairmanship of Dr Loveday, vice-chancellor of Bristol University.

* for committee reference see Appendix B

Records

Postwar technical education files on training for specific industries are at ED 46/562-637. Wartime files on the same include ED 46/9, 121-129, 254-286 and ED 136/669. Lord President's Committee files on postwar higher technological education are at CAB 124/558-559.

MAF 115 contains the papers of the Education Advisory Service, the Ministry of Agriculture division responsible for agricultural education. ED 174 and MAF 33 contain

Ministry of Agriculture files on rural education. Ministry of Education files are at ED 46/297-307. The papers of the Joint Advisory Committee on Agricultural Education are at ED 46/685-688, with others at ED 46/256 and ED 136/555, 753. Files on individual technical schools and technical colleges up to 1944 are at ED 82 and ED 90. Later papers can be found in ED 166. Individual junior technical school files up to 1946 are at ED 98. National College files are at ED 165, with minutes of the regional advisory council at ED 46/763-793.

The official wartime history of technical education is at CAB 102/242 and CAB 102/858 with notes on training for wartime industries at ED 138/81-84.

The papers of the National Advisory Council on Education for Industry and Commerce are at ED 46/699-755, ED 121/403, and ED 136/813.

5.4.1.3 Day continuation schools

The proposal in the 1944 Act to establish day continuation schools was one of the first casualties of the postwar period. Originally, compulsory attendance for 14 to 16-year-olds at day continuation schools became law under the 1921 Education Act but it had never been fully implemented. The Green Book sought once again to make attendance at day continuation schools compulsory. The schools were aimed at 14 to 18-year-olds. They required attendance one day a week for 40 weeks a year, on a day release basis from work. Support for such a measure came from a number of local authorities (ED 46/155). In October 1942 the Board set up a Day Continuation School Committee under W Elliott (chief inspector of the Technical Branch) to look at the issue. In its report the following September, it recommended high priority be given to the scheme in terms of planning and building but that any scheme should be administered as part of a wider provision of further education. Vocational work was not to occupy more than five-eighths of school life; physical education was to be compulsory; and recreational and cultural facilities were to be provided. Whilst concern was expressed that such a scheme would lead to a heavy financial burden on employers (ED 46/234; LAB 10/265), an enquiry by the Board of Trade and Ministry of Labour found that, on the contrary, costs would rise by less than 1% over four years. Further, the minister of labour, Ernest Bevin, was known to support the scheme. He had earlier called for full-time boarding places for school-leavers to provide vocational education (ED 136/292) and, in response to concern from the unions, expressed the opinion that wages would be unaffected as payments moved away from hourly pay towards salaries (ED 136/547). The ideas, therefore, were incorporated into the 1944 Education Act and became its most significant further education proposal. A Central Advisory Council for Education was set up in February 1945 to monitor the education of 14 to 16-year-olds who had left school (ED 146/1-28, 592-593).

After the war, however, the Labour government's commitment to the raising of the school leaving age and the problems of building and staff supply meant the provision was never enacted. However, day release did expand both in the 14 to 16 year group and for older employees, as industry began to see the benefits of training (ED 46/508). A number of companies, such as the John Lewis Partnership, offered their own schemes and noted that 'the old brittle type of business structure, built out of single track minds held together by managerial rivets, is giving place to something more like group organism, flourishing by a kind of symbiosis and demanding from its members not merely the mechanical fulfilment of functions but the powers of adaptation that belongs to intelligent life' (ED 80/26). Throughout the period the Ministry tried to provide a co-ordinated policy (ED 46/380), but on the whole it failed. Nevertheless by 1949 240,000 people were attending day release courses.

Records

Files on day continuation schools up to 1947 can be found in ED 75. Subsequent papers are in ED 166. Papers of the Day Continuation School Committee can be found in ED 21/127, 472-492, ED 46/155, ED 135/2, and ED 136/683.

5.4.1.4   Further education

The expansion of further education after 1945 was in part boosted by a number of demobilization schemes. Throughout the war, the forces education service provided facilities for a wide range of courses; and, at the end of the war, the War Office continued with this policy in order to prepare service personnel for civilian life. By far the greatest impact, however, came from the Further Education and Training Scheme. This offered financial support and places at colleges to demobilized service personnel to train for postwar vocations. It therefore gave a number of colleges the resources to expand and offer higher level courses. By 1949, 9,000 full-time places had been created. This number was further boosted by the inclusion of civilian war service personnel in the scheme.

Refugees were another source of expansion. Manpower shortage at the end of the war led the Labour government to introduce official immigration schemes bringing a quarter of a million Poles into the country. The Polish Resettlement Act led to the formation of a Committee for the Education of Poles in 1947 and the setting up of language courses run by LEAs through technical and further education colleges.

The provision of adult education up to 1944 was vested in the hands of a number of bodies. LEAs provided classes in evening institutes and colleges. Universities and voluntary bodies like the Workers' Educational Association (WEA) provided tutorial classes and evening courses. Universities ran vacation courses. Generally their aim was to provide a liberal education of general use to the individual. It was clear, however, that existing provision would be insufficient to meet the postwar demands of the popul-ation. In particular the Board expected a large increase in demand from demobilized men and women (ED 142/55: 9 July 1945). This reinforced the pressure for reform which had been applied by a number of organizations like Ruskin College and the WEA during the general educational planning in the early forties (ED 80/44). The 1944 Act noted the need for 'leisure time occupation in cultural training and recreational activity' and imposed an obligation on local education authorities to satisfy this need. Grants to local authorities were simplified and by 1947 approximately half a million people were attending LEA run classes.

The postwar period also saw a growth in the number of university extra-mural classes. In 1947-48, 138,000 students were attending 6,000 classes compared with 60,000 in 3,000 classes before the war. The residential schools which had been conducting courses in liberal studies were closed down during the war, but in 1945 the Catholic Workers, Ruskin and Hillcroft colleges reopened followed by Fircroft and Harlech. Eleven new centres were created providing short courses lasting a weekend or a week.

Records

ED 80 contains general adult education files. ED 76 deals with adult education vacation school files and ED 73 with tutorial classes. Residential college files are at ED 68. Evening institute files are at ED 41 and Private Office papers at ED 136/678. An historical survey of adult education from 1800 is at ED 138/7. Correspondence courses are discussed at ED 46/382.

ED 128 contains files relating to the Polish Resettlement Act 1947.

For further information on the demobilization schemes, see the Hankey Committee on Further Education and Training* and the Barlow Committee on the Further Education of Demobilized Soldiers (CAB 87/3; LAB 8/519-520, 744, 773; ED 136/546; ED 54/74; T 161/1125/S47945/2-5). LAB 12/679 contains documents on resettlement and LAB 8 on the Further Education and Training Scheme.

LEA fees and scholarship files are at ED 55 and aid to pupil files at ED 63. ED 37 contains endowment files up to 1944.

Papers relating to the Royal Air Force educational service are at AIR 2.

* for committee references see Appendix B

5.4.2   The universities

The universities presented a unique problem for the Board of Education. They were essential in the consideration of any scheme of educational reconstruction and yet were outside the Board's control. The responsibility for allocating funds and influencing the course of their academic development rested with the Treasury. However, since 1922 a University Grants Committee had advised the Treasury and had, in effect, become the day to day administrator of the system.

For these administrative reasons, discussions of postwar reform often excluded the universities; and yet their expansion was essential. The war severely retarded the position of many universities. Most members of staff up to the age of 40 had been conscripted, as were male students not training for qualifications relevant to war work (LAB 6/219). Students who avoided conscription were often used as agricultural labourers or on war damage work (ED 136/198). Many university premises were requisitioned.

Because of the improvement in secondary education and the demobilization of men and women eager to prepare for their new lives, postwar demand for university places was expected to be exceptional. This belief was reinforced by the reports from a number of committees. The McNair Committee on the Training of Teachers had estimated that 15,000 newly trained teachers would be required at the end of the war and that the universities would play a major role in this (see chap 5.3.4). The Hankey Committee on Further Education and Training* report in spring 1944 predicted a 50% increase in the demand for university education from war service personnel. The Percy Committee on Higher Technological Education* report pointed towards a developing relationship with technical schools. Finally, in the longer term, the Barlow report on Scientific Manpower in 1946 anticipated a doubling of the number of science graduates over a ten year period and called for the building of new universities.

After 1942 the Board debated the idea of pressing for a royal commission to look at the role of universities, but this option was never taken up. The Board then tried to bring about change by securing closer links with the universities, but meetings with the Treasury in 1943 proved unproductive. E Hale, principal assistant secretary at the Treasury, commented that 'the universities themselves would regard subordination to the Board of Education with horror, and my own opinion is the same. It seems to me that the independence of the universities from political control...is the very essence of what we are fighting for. Unified planning is all very well but the other side of the coin (totalitarianism) is not so pretty' (T 161/1412/S50774/1: 29 Jan 1943). In September 1943 a meeting between the Board and thirteen vice-chancellors showed Hale to be right (ED 136/422). In the end, the Board of Education had to make do with increased representation on the UGC as a way of influencing the universities (ED 136/560, 643). After the war Ellen Wilkinson, the new minister of education, attempted to control the universities but failed in the face of opposition from the Treasury (ED 136/716; T 222/516). Debates on the issue continued throughout the decade (T 227/72).

The return to normality began with the call by the UGC for a return to pre-war conditions by October 1944 irrespective of the state of the war. By VE day this process was well under way. Some controversy arose over the early release of arts students. Deferment had been granted to about 3,000 science and engineering students each year. In 1945, 600 arts students were added to the list. At Cabinet Butler (now minister of labour) pointed out that 30,000 arts graduates had been lost because of conscription and as a result the professions were suffering. The Cabinet approved the early release of 3,000 arts students (CAB 65/53: CP(45)80, CM(45)15).

In November 1944 the UGC prepared a memorandum for the Treasury on the postwar needs of the universities. It recommended that the Treasury provide three-quarters of the additional funds needed (UGC 2/25). The Treasury responded favourably and the grant for 1945/1946 increased from £2m to £6m. More than half of university funding now came from the Treasury, compared with one-third before the war. It is ironic that the only area of direct Treasury control was increasingly better financed, whilst other areas of the social services were facing pressure from the Treasury for cutbacks. In July 1946 the terms of reference of the UGC were widened to include the development of the universities. In 1947 a ministerial Committee on Universities was appointed to keep under review government policy on universities and their relation to the rest of the education system (CAB 134/704-705; CAB 21/2491).

By the end of the war awards to students had changed little, with the exception of those to ex-servicemen. About 300 state scholarships were awarded on the basis of Higher School Certificate results, while LEAs ran their own scheme. Undergraduates were, on the whole, expected to live with their parents and so awards usually covered fees only. LEA awards were usually only part grant, with up to 50% consisting of loans. Some universities and colleges offered scholarships. In 1946 the government brought in supplementary awards to enable scholarships to be brought up to state level and met fees and residential costs. Under pressure from the minister, LEAs reformed their grant system from 1946. From then on much fuller provision was given (ED 142/56). By 1951 four-fifths of LEA awards were calculated on a full maintenance basis (ED 147/142).

Despite building problems and staff shortages, the number of full-time students in British universities had increased from 50,000 in 1939 to 85,000 by 1950. The universities were involved in teacher training on a large scale for the first time (see chap 5.3.4) and their part-time role in the community was extended with the growth of extra-mural departments (see chap 5.4.1.4). In the early fifties they were seen increasingly as models for higher technological education (see chap 5.4.1.2).

Records

Papers of the Board and Ministry of Education's University Branch are at ED 119. Further papers can be found in ED 46.

The minutes and papers of the University Grants Committee are at UGC 1-UGC 2, with its subcommittee papers at UGC 8-UGC 9. Committee reports are at UGC 6. UGC 5/14-17 deals with the operation of universities during the war.

Treasury files on university policy are at T 161/1412/S50774/1. Files on universities during the war are at T 161/1426/S44863/1-2. The postwar issue of building licences is discussed at T 227/23. Investment Programme Committee* files on the university building programme are at T 229/821. Files on grants for higher education include T 161/1219/S21051/4. T 161/1202/S1824/6 deals with grants to universities through the UGC.

Returns from universities showing details of staff, students, organization, courses and other general information are at UGC 3. Postwar blue notes on universities in Britain are at T 165/430.

ED 54 contains awards and scholarship files of the technical, university and awards bodies of the Board and Ministry of Education. ED 153 refers to LEA awards for higher education. Higher education endowment files up to 1944 are at ED 39. Student award personal files used as precedents up to 1961 are at ED 94.

An official university and technical wartime history file is at CAB 102/858. Papers relating to the suggested writing of an official war history on the role of universities during the war are at CAB 103/207.

* for committee references see Appendix B

5.5   Youth service

The Board of Education took over responsibility for youth welfare in October 1939. There were already organizations in the field such as the scouts, guides, the YMCA and the YWCA, which had all started before the First World War. The growth of state youth movements in Europe in the thirties contributed to a growing desire amongst many in Britain for similar organizations. The Physical Training and Recreation Acts of 1937 gave LEAs powers to provide physical training and recreational facilities for the 14-20 age group and set up a National Fitness Council to oversee the process. However the success of the Act was limited and on the outbreak of the war its provisions were suspended.

Wartime conditions led to a growing concern from the government, organizations and individuals about the welfare of young people, seeing them both as potential delinquents and future conscripts. A National Youth Committee was created to administer grants and develop facilities aimed at young people outside full-time education. Ministry of Labour representatives attended the meetings and stressed employment conditions were a major part of youth welfare (see below). LEAs and voluntary organizations were encouraged to set up their own local committees to facilitate co-operation between the two groups. The level of co-operation varied from area to area. However, by March 1940 nearly half of the Part II authorities had submitted schemes whilst the majority had taken moves towards setting up committees. Early discussions in the National Youth Committee revealed a distinctive Welsh point of view. A Welsh Youth Committee was therefore constituted (ED 136/183).

Calls for further measures increased with the growing awareness of juvenile delinquency, particularly amongst those under 17 (ED 136/92; HO 45/19064-19066). The absence of fathers, the taking up of war work by mothers, and the blackout were all blamed. The main problem, however, was identified as the absence of recreational facilities (ED 124/8). In the spring of 1940 the Board issued a circular entitled *The challenge to youth* which outlined the aims and purposes of the youth service (ED 142/53). Concern from existing organizations that their position and memberships would be undermined led to an assurance from the president of the Board that any new schemes would be based upon existing structures (ED 124/58-112).

Co-operation with the Ministry of Labour developed early in the war. The Board of Education became an agent of the Ministry in the supervision of the welfare of industrial employees aged between 14 and 20 in their leisure time. The duties were passed to the National Youth Committee and local committees. Welfare officers of the Ministry of Labour worked closely with the committees at the local level (ED 124/24, 30, 42). The Juvenile Employment Service was a further area of co-operation. Since 1927, the Ministry of Labour had been responsible for the service providing help and advice to young people leaving school, but a number of LEAs had played a role in the service as well. During the Second World War these arrangements continued. However, it became clear that, if the service was to operate successfully in the wider context of youth welfare and manpower management, it would need to be restructured and expanded. Whilst Treasury approval was obtained to expand the service (LAB 12/211) the main problem was its structure. Between 1943 and 1944 inconclusive discussions were held between the Ministry of Labour, the Board of Education and the Scottish Education Department (ED 46/233).

In November 1944 an interdepartmental meeting with LEA representatives finally decided to appoint a Committee on the Juvenile Employment Service under Sir Geoffrey Ince to look into the problem (LAB 19/112). It recommended the formation of a Central Youth Employment Executive (CYEE) consisting of officials from the Ministries of Labour and Education and the Scottish Education Department. The proposals were transformed into the Employment and Training Act 1948 (LAB 19/215-216). The CYEE handled all questions of policy and supervised the enforcement of standards by local youth employment committees. However, LEAs could decide to keep local control and many continued to do so (LAB 19/205). An advisory role was taken up by a National Juvenile Employment Council (LAB 19/249-261, 219). A youth employment service subcommittee of the Local Government Manpower Committee* looked at problems concerning the supply of staff at the end of the decade (HLG 51/1025).

Co-operation with the War Office led in late 1940 to greater emphasis being placed on physical recreation. This was seen as an ideal way of boosting the work of the youth service and preparing young people for national service. A Directorate of Physical Recreation was formed in August 1940 to secure an expansion in facilities; and in November the Board issued a circular outlining the role of physical recreation in the youth service (ED 142/53).

The Dunkirk crisis brought further developments. Many young people sought to contribute to the war effort. Youth Service Squads began to spring up, initially in East Anglia, for people too young to join the army. Whilst youth committees were not the instigators of the movement, they were very quick to respond and had soon set up county youth service corps in a number of areas (ED 124/31). Badge schemes were offered as incentives (ED 124/10) and work included ARP work, assisting the police in various duties, digging trenches, and numerous other tasks. Agricultural work was a particularly vital area of service (ED 124/22) and was later to include schoolchildren as well (see chap 5.3.1). The Board, however, were very keen to keep these corps as a local initiative and no model scheme was offered (ED 124/10, 15; ED 142/53).

The issue of youth conscription was aired early in the war but was not considered a serious option until late in 1941, when Churchill proposed the training of young people as cadets. An interdepartmental conference on the training of boys in November 1941 decided against the compulsory conscription of young people into cadet units but favoured registration of those aged between 16 and 19 (ED 136/174; CAB 64/24). The Board of Education particularly opposed a compulsory scheme which would jeopardize chances of creating a permanent youth service. Registration, on the other hand, proved to be an ideal opportunity to reinforce the service. Whilst the process was carried out under the Ministry of Labour, the registration cards were then passed on to LEAs who arranged for interviews to be held between individuals and the youth committees. At the interviews those who were not already part of some youth organization were encouraged to join one (ED 138/90-96; ED 136/316-326; ED 124/46-47).

In the summer of 1942 moves were made to abolish the National Youth Committee. It was felt by some that the committee failed to represent all the departments involved in youth work and that, as the service had passed its infancy, it should be treated like any other section of the Board of Education (ED 124/8). However, concern was expressed about the ability of the service to stand on its own feet. Finally the National Youth Committee was abolished and the youth service integrated into the Board of Education structure. A Youth Advisory Council was appointed to look at longer term policy. It published two pamphlets, *The youth service after the war* (September 1943) and *The purpose and content of the youth service* (July 1945), which were to play an important role in postwar planning.

The large expansion of the youth service in the war years led to an acute shortage of trained leaders. A conference in April 1941 on this issue led, via the deliberations of a committee under S H Wood (ED 124/16), to government proposals for a training scheme in July 1942. Recognition for grant purposes was offered for full-time courses up to one year and two-year part-time courses submitted by training colleges. Short in-service courses were offered towards the end of the war (ED 142/54). In the longer term, the training of youth workers was considered by the 1943 McNair Committee* (see below and chap 5.3.4) and a Ministry of Education Committee on the Recruitment, Training and Conditions of Service of Youth Leaders and Community Centre Wardens.

The Board (and later Ministry) of Education was determined that the expansion of the youth service that had taken place during the war should not be reversed after 1945. The end of registration in August 1945 made the problem all the more urgent. However postwar circumstances were unfavourable. Plans to take over responsibility for youth employment work were successfully resisted by the Ministry of Labour (see above) and this meant that an important area of youth guidance remained outside the main structure of youth work. Further, postwar plans as required from LEAs under the 1944 Education Act were slow to materialize (see chap 5.3.2). By the time many schemes were submitted, the resources required were simply not available.

The creation of a Central Advisory Council to advise on all aspects of education saw the end of the Youth Advisory Council and the full integration of youth service policy into educational planning as a whole. The timing was unfortunate as other educational expenditure was rising and general economic restraint urged. Relatively little in the way of resources was made available to the postwar youth service.

Part of the problem remained the diversified organization of the service. Within government, aspects of youth policy lay with the Ministries of Education and Labour, and the Home Office. Outside, a vast number of local authority and voluntary organization schemes existed. Employees of voluntary bodies proved hesitant in joining national professional organizations and the organizations themselves were not represented by any single national body. Measures to develop the service, therefore, proved particularly difficult to co-ordinate.

One way of providing a unified structure was to give youth work a professional status. The McNair Committee on the Training of Teachers* (see chap 5.3.4) had included recommendations about the future of youth worker training. It had recommended a single qualification for workers within the service giving them professional status. However, this had been rejected as impractical (ED 124/16-21). In June 1945 grants did become available for one-year courses (ED 142/55) but these continued to lack co-ordination, being offered in a variety of voluntary, university and local authority institutions (ED 124/127). In 1948 the Ministry of Education's Committee on the Recruitment, Training and Conditions of Service of Youth Leaders and Community Centre Wardens reached similar conclusions. By 1950, however, the service had declined from its wartime peak. The Ministry diverted resources towards providing school places and vocational further education. Non-vocational education in general suffered.

* for committee references see Appendix B

Records

Ministry of Education files on youth welfare are at ED 124, with inspectorate reports at ED 149. Files relating to the Juvenile Employment Scheme are at ED 45, with further papers at ED 46/420-426.

Minutes of the National Youth Committee are at ED 136/176. Further papers can be found in ED 124/7-9, ED 136/173, 177, 179-182, and MH 102/1262. Papers of the Youth Advisory Council are at ED 23/695, ED 124/11A-14, LAB 19/99, and MH 102/1263.

Ministry of Labour files on the Juvenile Employment Service include LAB 12/215, 380, 469-475, 492-493, 714 and LAB 19/223, 239, 279, 292-322. Regional office files can be found at LAB 21/34-46. Ministry of Labour publications relating to careers in youth leadership are at LAB 44/17. War book papers relating to juveniles are at LAB 25/32.

A Prime Minister's Office file on the youth service is at PREM 4/36/1. Central Office of Information social surveys on the Employment of Adolescents (1950) and on youth leisure time (1948, 1950) are at RG 23/128, 158, 160.

Papers of the Committee on the Juvenile Employment Service are at LAB 19/141-142, 195-196, 215, 239, LAB 12/380, LAB 25/176-178, LAB 9/120, and ED 46/420-427.

Papers of the Committee on the Recruitment, Training, and Conditions of Service of Youth Leaders and Community Centre Wardens are at ED 121/408, ED 124/126, 129, 132-133, and ED 54/83.

LEA development plans, which include the youth services, are at ED 155. LEA youth welfare files are at ED 126. The minutes of local youth committees are at ED 136/173-183. ED 101 contains files relating to social and physical training, with HLG 104/29 highlighting the problem of providing recreational facilities during the war.

Postwar correspondence between the Ministry of Education and voluntary organizations is at ED 124/137-178.

The official wartime history of the service, *Young people and the problems of leisure*, by E K Ferguson is at CAB 102/247 with notes at ED 138/90-96. War history notes on the registration of young people can also be found at ED 138/90-96 with files on registration at ED 136/316-326 and ED 124/46-47.

Ministry of Health files relating to the provision of facilities for physical training for young people, and its link with health include HLG 109/1-2. The records of the National Fitness Council are in ED 113. Treasury papers on grant-in-aid for physical fitness are at T 161/1279/S41627/5. ED 56 contains LEA files on the administration of physical training and recreation up to 1940.

5.6　Bibliography

C Barnett, *The audit of war* (1986)

C Benn, 'Comprehensive school reform and the 1945 Labour government', *History Workshop*, 10 (1980)

R A Butler, *The art of the possible* (1971)

A G Geen, 'Educational policy making in Cardiff 1944-70', *Public Administration*, 59 (1981)

P H J H Gosden, *Education in the Second World War* (1976)

P H J H Gosden, *The education system since 1944* (1983)

A Howard, *Rab—The life of R A Butler* (1987)

B Hughes and D Rubenstein, 'In defence of Ellen Wilkinson' and 'Ellen Wilkinson reconsidered', *History Workshop*, 7 (1979)

C Jackson, *Who will take our children—The story of evacuation in Britain* (1985)

K Jeffreys, 'R A Butler, the Board of Education and the 1944 Education Act', *History*, 1984

M Kogan, *The politics of educational change* (1978)

Roy Lowe, *Education in the postwar years* (1988)

D Thom, 'The Education Act' in H L Smith, *War and social change* (1986)

B D Vernon, *Ellen Wilkinson* (1982)

R G Wallace, 'The origins and authorship of the 1944 Education Act', *History of Education*, 10 (1981)

Chapter 6 – OTHER LOCAL GOVERNMENT SERVICES

6.1 Introduction

6.2 Local government reform

6.3 The elderly

6.3.1 Wartime services

6.3.2 Wartime planning and the National Assistance Act 1948

6.4 Children

6.4.1 Pre-war service and the war emergency

6.4.2 Nursery provision

6.4.2.1 Day nurseries
6.4.2.2 Residential nurseries

6.4.3 Child care reform proposals and the Curtis Committee

6.4.4 The Children Act 1948 and its implementation

6.5 The physically disabled

6.6 Bibliography

6.1 Introduction

Local authorities had traditionally played an important role in the development of policy in each area of welfare. During the interwar period, however, doubts had begun to arise over their ability to provide services at a nationally uniform level, and such doubts were intensified during the war. In particular, the establishment of regional administrative bodies for civil defence raised questions as to whether local government was capable of implementing the far-reaching programmes of postwar reconstruction.

The supporters of local authorities were many and varied. They included Labour MPs who had risen through the political ranks of local government, such as Herbert Morrison. He was secretary of the London Labour Party from 1915 to 1947 and leader of the London County Council from 1934 to 1940. Throughout the 1940s he argued forcefully that local authorities were an essential part of a healthy democracy. Amongst the other supporters were many civil servants who maintained that traditional local government would be financially more responsible than any possible alternative. In particular, Treasury officials argued that those who spent public revenue should also be responsible, at least in part, for raising it. They feared, in addition, that any new regional bodies might provide an effective challenge to central government control as well as being spendthrift. Against these arguments, however, others maintained that traditional local government was antiquated and poorly equipped to deliver modern, national welfare services.

The implications of these debates about local authority services have already been covered in earlier chapters. The role played by local authorities in the postwar housing programme has been dealt with in chapter 3, as has their role in the town planning process. The loss of control of the hospital services, and the administration of the remaining local health services was examined in chapter 4. Education provision was covered in chapter 5. This chapter looks at the remaining services covered by the Children Act 1948, the Disabled Persons (Employment) Act 1944, and the National Assistance Act 1948. It starts with a summary of the debate over the restructuring of local authorities after the Second World War.

6.2 Local government reform

Local government continued to play an important role in the provision of welfare services after the Second World War. Whilst it lost some functions, such as the control of hospitals and residual responsibilities for the relief of the poor, it remained central to the provision of education, housing, and the personal social services. However, during the war local government had faced a crisis in terms of functions, structure and finance.

Part of the problem lay in the way the economic and social structure of Britain had changed in the first fifty years of the twentieth century. The situation was highlighted by the Barlow Commission on the Distribution of the Industrial Population (see chap 3.3.1) which made clear that the population movements over the period had made older boundaries obsolete: 'the network of local government areas has...retained the main outlines of the structure established in the last century in conditions vastly different from those today. With but rare exceptions the important industrial towns have long outgrown their boundaries as local government units' (Cmd 6153 1939). In many areas the distinction between rural and urban authorities was obsolete, and the largest county had a population eighty times that of the smallest.

The responsibilities of local authorities had also expanded to include such welfare services as education, housing, the care of the elderly, child care, care of the disabled, hospitals and health. In the area of public assistance, many new duties were gained after the Local Government Act 1929 had abolished the separately elected poor law guardians.

A major issue in postwar reconstruction was the ability of local authorities to carry on delivering these services. The war illustrated the weaknesses of the system and highlighted possible alternatives. On the outbreak of war, the Ministry of Home Security had appointed regional commissioners to ten regions of the country with responsibility for the co-ordination of civil defence work. In May 1940 these powers were extended to allow direction of local authorities in the civil defence field. They were further extended in 1941 along with the strengthening of the regional administrative structure (see chap 4.2.2.1). The success of these regional bodies frequently contrasted with the inefficiency of many local councils, and their retention at the end of the war was given serious consideration.

The war also placed under question the financial viability of many authorities. Emergency measures increased costs but also destabilized the local population and so disrupted the raising of local revenue. Despite attempts by the Treasury to restrict the levels of local authority capital expenditure and their ability to borrow funds (T 160/1095/F16352/1-3), local authority overspending continued to be a problem (T 161/1228/S33386/5). Many were forced to take out large bank loans to solve their immediate problems (T 161/1191/S47312). Short-term Treasury grants were made available (T 161/1115/S42351/05) and the Public Works Loan Board played an important role in financing capital spending at low rates of interest. It was accepted, however, that in the longer term the problem had to be looked at in the wider context of local government reform.

In 1941, the minister without portfolio invited Sir William Jowitt to undertake a review of local government problems, and in particular to consider whether the regional arrangements for civil defence could be used to solve some of the problems of local authority structure. Whilst no report was ever produced, many leading local authority figures were consulted and local government reform was placed firmly on the agenda. In 1942 Nuffield College carried out a survey on local government reorganization (CAB 117/174), and in the same year the problems of local government finance were looked at by the Official Committee on Postwar Internal Economic Problems* (CAB 87/56: 1 Sept 1942).

Not all local authorities agreed that the situation required change. Both the Association of Municipal Corporations, representing the interests of the county boroughs, and the County Councils Association fought for the preservation of the *status quo*. Consequently, when a White Paper did finally appear on local government reorganization in 1945 (Cmd 6579 1945) restructuring was not considered an option. The paper argued that local authorities had shown 'no general desire to disrupt the existing structure of local government or to abandon in favour of some form of regional government the main features of the county and county borough system'. The alternative was change within the existing framework by reshaping boundaries and reallocating responsibilities.

A Boundary Commission was duly established by the Local Government (Boundary Commission) Act 1945, but it was given no powers over the functions of local authorities. However, after studying the problem for two years, the Commission concluded that boundary changes would not be enough by themselves. Consequently its final proposals included large scale restructuring. The seventeen largest cities with populations over 200,000 were to be retained as single-tier authorities. The remainder would be administered on a two-tier basis with a minimum county population of 200,000, subdivided into borough, urban, and rural districts.

Not surprisingly the proposals met with strong resistance. The minimum population restrictions meant that counties like Herefordshire and Worcestershire faced merger, whilst counties like Rutland would be abolished. Further, the restriction on the number of county boroughs meant many would lose their status. With many of these councils Labour-controlled, and with a general election approaching in 1950, a battle with local authorities was the last thing the government wanted. Consequently the Commission's proposals were ignored and, in 1949, it was abolished.

The bulk of changes to the responsibilities of local authorities, therefore, came indirectly through the passing of the welfare reform acts. The first of these was the Education Act 1944. After lengthy and sometimes hostile discussions with local authorities, educational powers were removed from non-county borough and urban district councils and placed with the larger county and county borough authorities (see chap 5.2). Following the war the National Health Service Act 1946 removed hospital services from local authority control and established, under the Ministry of Health, a regional organization of health authorities to run them (see chap 4.4.2.2). The Act also removed the miscellany of personal health service functions from non-county boroughs and passed them to counties and county boroughs. The larger local authority units, therefore, took responsibility for mother and child welfare, health centres, domiciliary welfare, preventative health care, and the ambulance service. The Town and Country Planning Act 1947 also gave local planning powers to county and county borough councils (see chap 3.3.2.2). Finally the National Assistance Act 1948 transferred the remains of the poor law structure from local authorities to the National Assistance Board. Some responsibility was left with local authorities for providing care for the elderly and infirm. The Act gave local authorities powers to arrange services for the disabled and, at the minister's direction, this could become a duty. The services provided included instruction for disabled people in their own homes and the provision of workshops and hostels. Finally the Act gave local authorities the power to give grants to voluntary organizations providing social services. The Children Act 1948 also established local children's committees and thereby changed the role of local authorities (see chap 6.4.4).

* for committee references see Appendix B

Records

Reconstruction Secretariat papers relating to local government reorganization and the enquiries into regional organizations are at CAB 117/213-221. Prime Minister's Office papers on the 1945 White Paper are at PREM 4/88/3.

Treasury files relating to local authorities during the war include T 161/1228/S33386/5-6, T 160/1095/F16352/1-3, T 161/1191/S47312, and T 161/1115/S42351/05. Home Finance Division papers are at T 233/37. Postwar files include T 161/1236/S42351/06/1, T 161/1237/S42351/06/2, T 227/289, and T 161/1370/S53555/03.

Local government financial statistics for the period 1937-48 are at HLG 32. Papers of the Public Works Loan Board, which advanced funds to local authorities for capital projects, are at PWLB 2, PWLB 5, PWLB 6, PWLB 9.

6.3 The elderly

This section deals with local authority welfare services for the elderly during and after the Second World War. However a discussion of benefits for the elderly, such as supplementary pensions and retirement pensions, will be found elsewhere (see chap 2.3.4 and chap 2.4).

6.3.1 Wartime services

In 1939 services for the elderly were underdeveloped and poorly administered. Contributory pensions were available for those aged 65 to 70 whose earnings had been below a certain income, and non-contributory for those aged over 70. Many, however, were not covered or the payments failed to meet daily requirements. Many had to turn to the public assistance committees for help, and their number expanded as prices rose in the early stages of the war. Most welfare services were administered through the old poor law structure. The Local Government Act 1929 had transferred the functions of the 625 poor law unions to the public assistance committees of county and county borough councils. The old poor law atmosphere remained, with the result that many old people were afraid to ask for help, fearing placement in large institutions.

The declaration of war had an immediate impact on the elderly. In the first two days of war 140,000 elderly patients were discharged from hospitals to make way for the Emergency Medical Service (see chap 4.2.2), resulting in many deaths. Public assistance institutions, however, remained outside the EMS structure and therefore became badly overcrowded as the sick or elderly destitute, many former hospital patients, were given their statutory right to accommodation.

Problems were also experienced by the elderly living at home. The presence of elderly people in air raid areas was seen as a serious liability by the authorities. Not only were many restricted to their homes or immobile to varying degrees, making it difficult for them to follow civil defence procedures, but those who could reach the air raid shelters often found conditions unsuited to their needs. A committee under Lord Horder, set up to look at the conditions within air raid shelters, concluded that the elderly were clogging up the system and should be evacuated. The same problem was experienced in rest centres. These had been designed to provide a resting point for people made homeless before they could find permanent accommodation. However, government plans had overestimated the number of deaths due to bombing and underestimated the amount of homelessness. A large number of those in rest centres were the elderly who were often considered 'unbilletable' and so stayed in the centres on a semi-permanent basis.

Consequently evacuation of the elderly from areas of likely air raids became regarded as essential. Responsibility for this rested with the Ministry of Health, although the bulk of policy decisions was significantly made in its Public Assistance Division rather than its Evacuation Division. The first scheme was organized in June 1940. Circular 2060 authorized local authorities to pay travelling expenses and billeting allowances for elderly people. Processing of applicants was carried out through the Education Department of the London County Council. As numbers increased, EMS beds were once more opened up to the elderly in reception areas and, by December 1940, 4,000 had left London. After this date, however, the programme was halted as air raids extended to other urban areas and pressure was again placed on EMS beds.

Emphasis now shifted away from the provision of beds to hostels. In November 1940 an Evacuation of the Aged Committee was formed to 'supplement the arrangements for the evacuation of old people from London' in which 'the purpose was to mobilize voluntary effort, to discover premises that might be suitable for hostels, and to assist the local authority to start such hostels' (HLG 7/395). The first hostels for victims of bomb damage were established by Quaker relief organizations without government support. However, by January 1941 local authorities were running twenty-five hostels for elderly people who were unable to find billets in the London area. This proved to be the majority. By November 1941, 285 elderly people had been placed in billets whilst 1,158 were in hostels.

Two major problems emerged during the programme. First, arguments took place over who had financial responsibility for each person. Whilst there did eventually emerge a general consensus that the home authority should be responsible, the procedure for payment was cumbersome. A removal order had to be served by the reception authority, then suspended on the grounds that the individual would be in danger. Only through a suspended order could finance be obtained from the home authority. This inevitably led to disputes and poor relations between authorities. Secondly, most hostels were outside urban areas and it proved difficult to persuade people to leave London (MH 76/365: 9 April 1941). As a solution, the London Hostels Association Ltd was established as a non-profit making firm financed by the Exchequer to provide London-based residential hostels. Eventually forty-six hostels were opened in London for the elderly providing 1,856 beds (HLG 7/332).

The fact that these measures were instituted as part of civil defence measures, and not explicitly for the welfare of the elderly, is illustrated by the plans to evacuate the south-east coastal towns. In April 1941 plans to move elderly infirm people from the area in case of invasion were stopped on the grounds that the aim of the scheme was to stop people flooding onto and blocking the roads. As these elderly people were bedridden they would be unable to do so. (HLG 7/84).

After the main bombing raids ceased, hostel provision decreased and occupancy rates dropped. Pressure on the public assistance institutions was eased by the opening up of some EMS beds to elderly people (HLG 7/332). However, in June 1944, the flying bomb attacks revived interest in evacuation. Over 500 old people were placed in regional hostels by July, with 6,224 placed in private billets (HLG 7/333: 19 July 1944). Hostel places were allocated by a selection panel established by the Evacuation Division of the Ministry of Health, and not the London County Council. The scheme was open only to those who were homeless. Those in air raid shelters, or in their own homes, were initially excluded. Only after protests from voluntary organizations did the Ministry allocate 740 further hostel places to such people.

By February 1945 the Ministry of Health estimated that 50,000 old people were still in reception areas, of whom 3,000 were in voluntary or local authority hostels (HLG 7/535) providing a serious dilemma for the government and local authorities. Both realized that passing them over to the public assistance authorities would lead to a massive public outcry, but local authorities were concerned at the financial implications for themselves. In August 1945 an official meeting decided that the evacuated elderly should remain part of the Government Evacuation Scheme and should not be passed over to the Poor Law (HLG 7/30/8/45). In October 1946, circular 195/46 clarified who should be responsible for the evacuated elderly: voluntary organizations would be encouraged to take over hostels, and those run by district councils would be handed over to county councils. Any empty spaces could be filled by public assistance cases, to keep them a viable proposition.

The passing of new regulations saw the gradual ending of the scheme. Elderly evacuees living with relatives in reception areas no longer got billeting allowances but were allowed to claim an increased supplementary pension from the Assistance Board. Voluntary hostels were no longer to receive money, but residents would be allowed to claim maintenance costs from the Assistance Board. Local authority hostels would continue to get financial support, but voluntary organizations would be encouraged to take them over. The problem of returning the homeless elderly to London was tackled by permitting the LCC to build a rest home for 250 (HLG 7/535). These arrangements ended with the passing of the National Assistance Act 1948 (HLG 7/118).

Many other welfare services developed for the elderly during the war. A major feature of these services was the role played by a number of voluntary agencies. A committee on old people's welfare was established at the time of the mass bombing raids, which was called by a seemingly endless variety of names (August 1939-January 1941 Committee for the Welfare of Old People; January 1941-May 1944 Old People's Welfare Committee; May 1944-July 1955 National Old People's Welfare Committee; July 1955-December 1970 National Old People's Welfare Council; January 1971 onwards Age Concern). The organization originated in the work carried out by the Assistance Board under the Old Age and Widows' Pension Act 1940. Under the Act, the Assistance Board had been given responsibility for all supplementary pensioners (see chap 2.4). Consequently the loneliness of some elderly people became apparent and the formation of an organization to deal with the problem was recommended by the National Council of Social Service. Later, the Committee became involved in support for the evacuated elderly, the supervision of conditions in rest centres and air raid shelters, and campaigned for increased provision for the elderly infirm. It provided information on private billeting, private homes and voluntary homes, and established a local organization which, by 1944, had set up seventy local committees.

The Women's Voluntary Service (WVS) was formed in 1938 as 'a new women's organization sufficiently flexible to cope with unimagined difficulties likely to arise in civil defence' (see chap 4.2.3.1). Services were provided only when requested by local authorities and all costs were paid by the Home Office. However, in practice the work extended beyond civil defence and the WVS became heavily involved in the evacuation programme, rest centres and communal feeding. Indeed, they were given the major responsibility for the evacuation of the elderly during the 1944 flying bomb attacks.

The first statutory powers to allow home helps had been provided under the Maternity and Child Welfare Act 1918 and the Public Health Act 1936. These provisions were not extended to the elderly until December 1944, when they were used by the Ministry of Health to encourage old people to stay at home and keep out of residential accommodation. The new scheme differed in a number of ways from that offered to mothers. To differentiate between the two, the new service was called 'Domestic Help'. Expenses were paid by the government as opposed to the local authority and local authorities were given the responsibility of maintaining a register of domestic help available, establishing

184

a priority list of the most urgent applicants, and assessing what costs could be recovered from individual households. The Ministry of Labour allocated extra staff to local authorities to run the scheme.

Many areas were slow to take advantage of the scheme. Consequently in June 1946 the home help and domestic help schemes were combined to form the Home Helps Service, with helpers available to either group. New emphasis was placed on the role of the voluntary sector and in particular the WVS. Provision was further reinforced by the passing of the National Health Service Act 1946. Section 29 gave local authorities power to provide domestic help 'for households when such help is required owing to the presence of any person who is ill, lying in, an expectant mother, mentally defective, aged, or a child not over compulsory school age'. The service was now, therefore, grant-aided on the same basis as other local authority health services.

As in all other welfare services, shortage of staff proved to be a major impediment to growth. In 1945 a National Institute of Houseworkers was formed to encourage recruitment and training. Particular emphasis was placed on the training of regional organizers who would be able to recruit and organize other members of staff. Courses established by the WVS were funded by the Ministry of Health, the first of which began in February 1948 (MH 130/274).

Another important development was the growth of the meals on wheels service. This was based on much work carried out by voluntary organizations, and the WVS in particular. From the beginning of the war it had been involved in food cooking and distribution, mainly for evacuated children, and for the Emergency Canteen Service. As bombing decreased, however, the WVS looked for new outlets. They consequently became involved in the British Restaurants which, although the responsibility of the Ministry of Food, used 17,000 WVS volunteers. This in turn led on to the meals on wheels service.

Whilst the new service was a great success in London, elsewhere the provision was patchy. By August 1947 only twenty-three schemes had been established in the regions. Often the problem was one of facilities, with attempts by LEAs to expand the scheme by using school canteens being resisted by the Ministry of Education (ED 50/411). Enthusiasm for the scheme was mixed within the Ministry of Health. The early drafts of the National Assistance Act 1948 made no mention of the service. However after criticisms about the impact of rationing on old people, a clause was included that 'a local authority may make a contribution to the funds of any voluntary organization whose activities consist of or include the provision of recreation or meals for old people' (AST 7/851).

Records

Papers of the Ministry of Health's Public Assistance Division can be found in MH 57. Evacuation Division files are at HLG 7/59-367. Ministry of Health social welfare files relating to the elderly are at MH 130/251-277. Attempts to co-ordinate the work of voluntary organizations are detailed at MH 76/363.

Assistance Board papers on their involvement with the elderly are at AST 7. In particular AST 7/479 contains general policy papers; AST 7/664 deals with visitations to old people; AST 7/756, 801 with charges for home helps; AST 7/627, 794 with housing; AST 7/710 with provisions for old people living on their own, and AST 7/610 with the home help scheme.

Papers dealing with the National Institute of Houseworkers can be found in LAB 20/249 and LAB 8/976, 1258, 1263, 1395-1399, 1758, 1772, 1870.

For further information on evacuation see chap 5.3.1.

6.3.2 Wartime planning and the National Assistance Act 1948

The Beveridge Committee on Social Insurance and Allied Services* concentrated mainly on national insurance, but it also covered the wider area of welfare provision. In relation to the care of the elderly its report argued that responsibility for assistance should be transferred to a Ministry of Social Security, whilst responsibility for institutional care should remain with local authorities. However the Phillips Committee*, amongst others considering the implementation of the Beveridge Report, concentrated on the social insurance issues and ignored the care of the elderly.

Not until October 1943 did the Cabinet Committee on Reconstruction Priorities* conclude that the Poor Law should be abolished and 'local authorities should continue to undertake the duty of providing accommodation for the aged, either as a public health function, or as a housing function' (MH 80/47). Following this, the Ministry of Health prepared a paper on the breakup of the Poor Law and the care of children and old people, which was presented in February 1944. The paper made clear that whilst any legislation would have to await the passing of the social insurance legislation, the position was urgent because of the large number of evacuees. Discussions in 1944, therefore, concentrated on simplicity and speed. However, as pressure for reform increased, the Ministry became conscious of the need to treat the subject in greater depth (MH 80/47). In 1945 child care planning within the government was separated from provision for the elderly and a separate child care committee appointed (see chap 6.4.3).

Under the new Labour government it was made clear that any legislative change would have to await the passing of the national health service and social insurance legislation (CAB 134/698: 12 July 1946). In the meantime, a Committee on the Breakup of the Poor Law* was appointed in April 1946 under Arthur Rucker. The report assumed the repeal of the Poor Law and the establishment of an entirely new structure on the same day as the NHS, the national insurance scheme and the Children Act came into force. The Assistance Board would be made responsible for any persons living at home whose needs were not fully met by national insurance. In addition, local authorities would be responsible for providing institutional care for those who needed it. It recommended that, in providing this service, local government should move away from large institutions and start using smaller homes. It also proposed that pensions continued to be paid to the elderly in homes, which had not been the case under the old system, and that 'hotel' charges be made. The report also called for local authority powers to remove elderly people to institutions by force if they were living in self-inflicted bad conditions, or were clearly 'eccentric'. Finally it called for the registration and inspection of private and voluntary residential homes.

The report received a favourable response from central government (CAB 134/697: 18 July 1946) but local authority associations were less happy. Many felt that a service which was compulsory should receive a direct government grant. This had not been recommended by the Rucker Report, and was opposed by the Treasury on the grounds that local authority provision for the elderly was long-standing. However, after direct grants were made available under the Children Act 1948, it became more difficult to resist the pressure. Therefore, despite Treasury opposition, the final Act included provision for a subsidy for new residential care (MH 80/49).

Whilst the Children Act 1948 emphasized the need to move away from institutional care, the provisions for the elderly within the National Assistance Act did not. It did not establish old people's committees, equivalent to the children's committees under the Children Act, nor did it stimulate an emergency training programme, as in child care. Local authorities had a duty to provide residential accommodation, but only the option to offer certain domiciliary facilities. Institutional care, therefore, remained the main form of care available to the elderly. However, the use of large institutions was in decline. During the war, public assistance institutions (PAIs) had begun to fall into disrepute. A letter placed in *The Manchester Guardian* in March 1943 illustrated the problem, 'on each chair sat an old woman in workhouse dress, upright, unoccupied. No library books or wireless. Central heating but no open fire. No easy chairs. No pictures on the wall…There were three exceptions to the upright old women. None was allowed to be on her bed at any time throughout the day, although breakfast is at 7 am but these three, unable any longer to endure their physical and mental weariness, had crashed forward, face downwards onto their immaculate bedspreads and were asleep' (Means & Smith p 80). The following year a Nuffield Foundation survey on the problem of ageing and the care of the elderly considered that PAIs needed to be replaced by smaller houses of 30-35 residents. As an interim measure, homes for 200 were proposed.

This pressure led to a gradual change in attitude at the Ministry of Health. Pending legislation in 1947, public assistance committees were instructed to improve conditions and increase freedom within institutions (MH 130/252, 254-264). By 1948 PAIs had become an embarrassment, part of the old world and out of step with the mood of postwar reconstruction. The 1948 Act, therefore, proposed the building of small homes for between 30-35 residents. Pressure on accommodation and building resources made this change a slow process. New towns were amongst the first to provide the new facilities (HLG 91/53) but not until the 1950s did the change to smaller institutions really begin.

The postwar period saw the continuation of the important role played by voluntary organizations during the war (see chap 6.3.1). The 1948 Act had provided them with direct local and national government funding and opened them to inspection and regulation. They were also used increasingly within existing schemes, like the meals on wheels service, and by the Assistance Board in their visiting schemes (AST 7/664). The financial position of voluntary organizations had also been strengthened by outside contributions. South Africa, Canada, Australia and the USA often provided funds which in turn were passed to voluntary organizations for 'reconstruction work' (MH 130/253).

The expansion of the voluntary sector took place despite the election of a Labour government committed to the public provision of services. Most voluntary groups were independent of government control and were therefore free to develop their own policies. However even where organizations were tied to government departments, as was the case with the WVS, they had by the mid-1940s established so important a role that they could not easily be dismissed. Whilst the WVS lost its position as the only voluntary body totally funded by central government, it was secure. Local authorities were encouraged to use them, and after 1949 with the slow increase in state welfare funding, their old preferential position in government funding was restored.

Unlike other welfare legislation at the time, the National Assistance Act failed to allocate responsibility clearly for a number of services. Particular difficulty was experienced in deciding who should be responsible for geriatric cases: the hospital service or local authorities. The Act had stated that people too frail to look after themselves should be provided with residential accommodation by local authorities, whilst those needing medical attention should be placed in hospitals. In practice, however, it was not always easy to distinguish between the two. The problem was intensified by the lack of accommodation and staff in both sectors, which meant that each was keen to pass clients on to the other. The division of responsibility between the National Assistance Board and local authorities was also imprecise. The Act required the NAB to 'increase their functions in such a manner as shall best promote the welfare of the person concerned'. This often meant infringing on the welfare responsibilities of local authorities.

* for committee references see Appendix B

Records

Ministry of Health social welfare files are at MH 130. These include MH 130/251-277 referring specifically to the care of the aged and infirm. MH 57 contains the papers of the Public Assistance Division of the Ministry which includes correspondence on homes at MH 57/564, papers relating to standards in homes at MH 57/553-554, and MH 57/463 on the National Old People Welfare Committee. Interim measures after the war are discussed at MH 55/2100. Discussions between voluntary organizations and local authorities are at MH 132/272. Further papers can be found in MH 122.

The main Assistance Board files relating to the care of the elderly are at AST 7. These include AST 7/794 relating to the housing of the aged, AST 7/758 on hostels and special homes, AST 7/634 on local authority homes, and AST 7/710 on people living at home.

Papers relating to the National Assistance Bill are referred to in chap 2.4.

6.4   Children

6.4.1   Pre-war service and the war emergency

Before the war, responsibility for children had been divided between a number of agencies. Central powers rested with the Board of Education, the Ministry of Health and the Home Office which were responsible respectively for school children, infant welfare, and juvenile delinquents and criminals. Residual powers remained, however, with the Ministry of Pensions, the Admiralty, and the War Office, following their assumption of responsibility for children who lost parents during the First World War. The Ministry of Pensions' role was extended in 1942 to cover the orphans of wartime servicemen. A separate administration existed under the Scottish Office.

Protection of children under the law was consolidated in England and Wales by legislation passed in the 1930s. The Children and Young Persons Act 1933 protected children from harmful conditions of employment, and from cruelty and moral corruption, and regulated their treatment by courts of law, and whilst they were in the care of public authorities and voluntary bodies. The Public Health Act 1936 included provision for the protection of children and ensured regular visits by the health visitor to advise foster parents.

Children were taken into care for a number of reasons. Many were without an alternative home, either because of the death of parents or because they had been abandoned. Others were taken from existing family units for their own safety or well-being. Others were placed in care because of misdemeanours or non-attendance at school. Borstals (for older children) and approved schools provided a place for habitual delinquents.

The type of care provided varied greatly. Institutional care was still widespread and had its roots in the expansion of voluntary homes in the nineteenth century, and in the institutional confinement of children under the Poor Law. However, the fostering of children was becoming increasingly popular. Since the mid nineteenth century, the poor law guardians had experimented with boarding out, as had many of the voluntary foundations. Under the 1933 Children and Young Persons Act, education authorities were required to board out any child committed to their care by a juvenile court. Adoption became legal in 1926 and was followed by the widespread growth of adoption societies. However, their work was unsupervised and consequently standards were mixed. The whole area of adoption was studied by a committee of enquiry under Florence Horsbrugh in 1936. This in turn led to the Adoption of Children (Regulations) Act 1939, which empowered the secretary of state to make regulations about the way societies conducted their work, allowed for compulsory registration, and required the approval of societies by local authorities. The running of children's homes and the administration of the boarding-out scheme remained the responsibility of local authorities; but the voluntary sector continued to play an important role, particularly in the provision of residential homes.

The war proved a catalyst for the child care services. First, the decision to evacuate children from areas at risk of air raids revealed many new problems (see below and chap 5.3.1). Second, the high level of civilian deaths because of air raids greatly increased the number of orphans requiring official help. Under previous legislation the Ministry of Pensions was only responsible for the children of service casualties; but a Home Office Committee in December 1941 decided to extend benefits to children orphaned by air raids (CAB 75/10: 2 Dec 1941). This became law under the War Orphans Act 1942. Third, the high degree of illegitimacy increased the number of babies placed in local authority care. The Ministry of Health, for example, found a large increase in the number of mixed race children requiring homes, mainly arising from the arrival of black American GIs (MH 55/1656). Finally, the rise in juvenile delinquency necessitated a major reconsideration of the youth provision and custodial services (see chap 5.5).

The problems experienced by children's homes during the war were similar to those in schools (see chap 5.3.1). Homes located in evacuation areas were often moved which, in turn, created difficulties in finding alternative forms of accommodation and appropriate facilities (HLG 7/268-282; HLG 900/37). Homes also experienced severe difficulties in recruiting and keeping staff. The recruitment of women into war work and the services, and the calling up of men into the armed forces, as well as the expansion of alternative welfare facilities, made it difficult for children's homes to compete. Despite the creation of courses to train staff (ED 46/652) problems were experienced both during and after the war. The London County Council, for example, complained in 1945 that they had been unable to get staff for the previous four years and that the situation was getting worse. 'I am concerned', wrote the chairman of its Education Department, 'that at any moment the council may find itself unable solely by reason of lack of staff to provide for the care of children to whom it is *in loco parentis*' (MH 102/1314).

189

Some children evacuated under the Government Evacuation Scheme never returned to their parents. Whilst they were far fewer than had been anticipated—probably no more than 1,500—the question still arose as to who was responsible for their welfare. In the short term this was accepted by central government, which took care of board and lodging costs; but in the longer term responsibility devolved to the counties and county boroughs (ED 142/56: 31 Dec 1945). Public assistance committees were specifically excluded from this process as it was decided that no fault lay with the parent or child (MH 122/1-2).

The National Assistance Act and the Children Act brought the last vestiges of the government evacuation scheme to an end in July 1948. Central responsibility for evacuated unaccompanied children passed from the Ministry of Health to the Home Office, whilst local responsibility passed to the local authority in which the child was living. The latter also had the responsibility for deciding on the long-term situation for each child (MH 102/1692). Owing to the number of children involved many evacuation hostels and homes were simply converted into children's homes (MH 102/1639, 1693). Consequently wartime evacuation had a direct impact on the organization of the postwar child care services.

The progress of adoption was initially halted by the outbreak of war; the implementation of the Adoption of Children Act 1939 was postponed. Only in 1943, as the number of needy children continued to increase, and the consideration of postwar reconstruction was gaining momentum, did the Lord President's Committee* decide to approve implementation (CAB 71/11: 25 Jan 1943). Registration of adoption societies was then carried out, advertising prohibited except by local authorities, and health visitors allocated to supervise the scheme (HO 45/19299-19300).

Approved schools and remand homes faced an increasing number of referrals, due mainly to increases in juvenile delinquency. In 1941 the Incorporated Clerks' Society told the Home Office that 'there is a pressing need that many additional Approved Schools and remand Homes should be provided and strict discipline enforced therein'. In response, the Home Office blamed the local authorities for their failure to carry out their obligations to provide care or protection for children and young persons (MH 102/1119). However, the problem was exacerbated by divided responsibilies for child care services. Attempts by the Board of Education to take over the child care responsibilities of the Home Office (ED 10/216) were resisted, and discussions on the reorganization of the service had to await the end of the war.

* for committee references see Appendix B

Records

Home Office files relating to children can be found in HO 45. Papers of the Children's Department are at MH 102.

Files on the adoption of children include MH 102/1362-1373B, 2259 and HO 45/19299-19300. Lord Chancellor's Office papers relating to regulations passed under the Adoption of Children Act 1939 are at LCO 2/3020-3021, 2642.

Files on the inspection of approved schools are at MH 102/916-919, with files on absconding at MH 102/889-904. Appointments of welfare officers to approved schools are dealt with at MH 102/1347-1354. Correspondence is at HO 45/18799.

Files relating to the evacuation of children's homes are in HLG 7/268-282. For the main files on evacuation see chap 5.3.1.

6.4.2 Nursery provision

6.4.2.1 Day nurseries

Although official nurseries were not unknown in the early twentieth century, it was the First World War that witnessed their initial expansion. The need for women to work in factories in unprecedented numbers demanded radical measures including the provision of nurseries for mothers with young children. By 1919, 174 officially sponsored nurseries had been established with grants from the Board of Education.

After the war the nursery service was divided in two. Day nurseries took the children of working mothers at any age under 5. They were staffed by nurses and their primary role was to care for the health of the child. They consequently became the responsibility of the Ministry of Health. The second group were nursery schools and the nursery classes in the public elementary schools. These took children between 2 and 5 and they became the responsibility of the Board of Education, since their aim was broadly educational. The interwar period, however, saw a decline in nursery services. By 1938 only 104 day nurseries were in operation, with 118 nursery schools. Of 1,750,000 children under 5 in England and Wales, only 180,000 attended publicly funded nurseries.

On the outbreak of war a number of day nurseries and nursery schools were evacuated to the country as residential units (see below). Nursery classes were abandoned. However, the majority of children under five were unaffected by these changes, as those in the evacuation areas were either evacuated with their mothers and found billets, or remained at home. For those billeted, life was—to say the least—problematic. Young children found it difficult to adapt to the new environment, whilst mothers found themselves not only unable to go to work but also unable to manage their own household. For the people receiving their new 'guests' the new circumstances were often intolerable. Not surprisingly, the trek home began almost immediately (see chap 5.3.1).

To prevent this trickle from becoming a flood, the Nursery Centres Scheme was developed. In November 1939 a joint committee of the Ministry of Health and the Board of Education had worked out a plan to relieve mothers of their young children (ED 102/22). It proposed the establishment of nursery centres to be staffed by voluntary workers and organized into groups under the supervision of a nursery school teacher. Children between 2 and 5 years old would be given both instruction and play facilities, and would return to their billets for meals. However, Treasury fears that the scheme would provide a dangerous precedent for a permanent nursery service delayed implementation for three months, by which time the majority of mothers had returned to the evacuation areas.

The second wave of evacuation in the mid-1940s saw the scheme revived with more success. The need now was less to encourage evacuation, than to release women into the workforce, and nursery policy therefore began to change. This change saw an increasingly important role for the Ministry of Labour. Before May 1940 the Ministry had taken a reactive rather than proactive role, only acting on direct complaints from employers about a lack of married women workers (MH 26/57). This position changed when Bevin became minister of labour in May 1940, as he argued for nursery provision in advance of the recruitment of women into war work. However, an overall policy strategy was limited by the complicated administrative structure. The Ministry of Health retained over-all control of nursery policy, with the Ministry of Labour merely making recommendations as to where provision was necessary to ease labour shortages. Further, it was the appropriate local authority which had actually to set up the nursery and contribute to the running costs.

In June 1940 the Ministry of Health submitted proposals to the Treasury for the provision of nurseries, but initially finance was made available only in areas where the Ministry of Labour reported a shortage of women workers. The Exchequer was to provide the entire capital cost for each new nursery, and pay one shilling a day for each child in attendance. Each nursery was to be run by an experienced matron with the aid of a trained helper, and an additional helper where there were more than forty children.

The response of local authorities was mixed. A number of local authorities had already developed nursery services. Others had been impaired by financial factors and were now able to expand their provision. Many, however, and particularly rural authorities, were strongly opposed to nursery provision. Consequently the number of nurseries remained low. Six months into the scheme only fifteen had been opened, seven of which were in Birmingham.

The picture was complicated by the fact that many new nurseries found themselves half empty, especially in areas such as Lancashire and Cheshire where there was a strong tradition of child-minding. Under the existing minding system, neighbours were paid one shilling a day to look after a child of a woman employed in work of national importance; the minister of labour eventually began to expand this scheme through government contributions towards the cost of employing minders and the registration of minders (CAB 75/10: 26 Feb 1941). However the scheme proved an inadequate substitute and nurseries came to be accepted as more and more women took work. Nursery waiting lists then became the norm.

Part of the problem of poor provision lay in the division of responsibility for the nursery service. The arguments between day nursery and nursery school, or Ministry of Health and the Board of Education, were heated. However it became increasingly clear that LEAs were ill-equipped to deal with children under 2 years old and the Board was forced to accept that day nurseries would provide better facilities. Consequently, in May 1941, the Ministry of Health was given the main responsibility for the wartime service.

Two distinct types of nursery began to develop under the Ministry. Full-time nurseries, run by a matron, provided day-time care for children up to school age and were aimed at children of women in full-time employment. Part-time nurseries run by a teacher, and open during school hours, catered for children from 2 to 5 years old. They catered for evacuated children and children whose mothers had part-time jobs. Mothers paid one shilling a day for the whole-time, and sixpence a day for the part-time nursery.

By November 1941, 194 wartime nurseries had opened, 209 were approved but not ready, and another 284 were being prepared. The scheme was further extended in December 1941 when nursery classes in public elementary schools were brought into the scheme. Hours were extended, and eating and washing facilities provided. The peak of nursery development was reached in the summer and early autumn of 1944. In September of that year more than 106,000 children in England and Wales were attending nurseries whilst 102,940 children under 5 years old were attending reception classes at public elementary schools.

In a few cases, individual firms established on-site nurseries. This avoided a special journey for the mother, and meant that she was at hand should any problems arise. The Ministry of Health, however, disliked the idea. Standards were difficult to supervise, and the risk of air attack on the plant made it dangerous. The Treasury, however, liked such schemes, as employers covered many of the major costs such as the provision of premises. Therefore, whilst not encouraging large scale development, the Ministry of Health did provide some grants-in-aid for work place nurseries.

A major problem faced by expanding war nurseries was the securing of premises. Stringent building standards requiring 25 square feet of space per child were not matched by adequate funding, with the consequence that a number of towns supporting ordnance factories could not provide new nurseries. Under pressure from the Ministry of Labour these conditions were later relaxed, and indeed the Ministry of Health began providing some prefabricated huts. Nevertheless these remained in short supply (LAB 26/58).

A further problem faced by the new service was that of finding staff. The problem was compounded by the insistence of the Ministry of Labour on maintaining its pre-war staffing ratios. Trained and qualified nurses were required, therefore, in particular to care for the younger children, whilst teachers were needed for the older children. Nursery assistants were also required, as were domestic staff.

The shortage of teaching and nursing staff was in part alleviated by recruitment of untrained people and the provision of short training courses. Proposals for such courses had been put forward in May 1940 by the National Council for Maternity and Child Welfare and a Child Care Reserve was eventually established whose members would be trained in nursery work. Courses were to be run by LEAs and at the end of each course the student would be qualified to work in nursery and child care work. By June 1941, seventeen such courses had been established. With the advent of the Wartime Nurseries Scheme in May 1941 the courses were expanded and instruction became more specialized. By September 1942, 173 courses had been held and 4,017 students trained. When the scheme was wound up in 1945, a total of 399 courses had been completed and 9,954 students trained.

As part of longer-term planning, nursery provision was considered during the framing of the 1944 Education Act. This was opposed in some quarters. The feelings of one Treasury official were typical, 'day nurseries etc may be very necessary in wartime but is it old fashioned to hope that after the war family life may begin again? It may be that many mothers are incompetent as mothers, but universal nursery schools are a confession of defeat' (T 161/193/S48249/2: E Hale, 1 June 1943). A similar response was received from some local authorities in their development plans. Warwickshire, for example, were 'unconvinced that the mother of a child of two with good home conditions should normally be encouraged to send him to school' (ED 152/169-172). The Ministry of Education itself came out in favour of a limited degree of provision, but as always was careful to distinguish between nursery schools and wartime nurseries (ED 34/7). It had no desire to be burdened with the Ministry of Health's 'temporary' nurseries. On the conversion of wartime nurseries to nursery schools the Ministry was clear, 'war nurseries have never been considered as a welfare activity except so far as the care of mothers and children could be served incidentally to their main purpose of freeing additional woman power' (ED 102/32: minister of health brief, 1945).

The end of the war, therefore, saw attitudes to nurseries begin to change. After 1944, the Ministry of Health began the process of closing the day nurseries, arguing that their existence was merely a temporary war measure. The new Labour government was at first ambivalent to nursery education, and later restrictive. After 1945 the Exchequer's grant to local authorities was halved and responsibility for the running of nurseries passed from central government to local authorities. With little central direction, the continuation of nursery provision rested upon the commitment of the local authority involved. Nurseries were now competing for finance with other areas of local welfare provision. The Ministry of Education's commitment to nursery schools, always rather half hearted, also began to flag. The 1947 economy measures introduced by the education minister, George Tomlinson, meant that no new nursery schools or classes could be opened, except to help mothers enter industry.

The closing down of nurseries seemed to go against the need for women workers to offset postwar labour shortages. This was, however, a misreading of the situation. The return of servicemen to peacetime jobs meant that many women were forced out of their wartime employment. The postwar recruitment drive for women workers sought not women in general, but only those for certain industries. The textile industries of Lancashire, for example, were traditionally female dominated and were told by the Labour (Textile Industry) Committee that they would have to provide on-site nursery provision if they were going to recruit staff. However the production drive of 1947 reinforced the view of nurseries as an adjunct to production rather than a welfare measure, and so did little to improve care provision over the country as a whole (Riley 1981). 'The government's opinion,' wrote John Edwards, parliamentary secretary to the minister of health, 'was that the proper place for a child under two was at home with his mother... mothers of children of two ought to be positively discouraged from going out to work' (Lowe 1988). By the end of 1947, there were 879 local authority maintained day nurseries—a drop of 700 from the wartime peak.

Records

see chap 6.4.2.2, *Records*

6.4.2.2 Residential nurseries

The wartime residential nursery first appeared as part of the government evacuation scheme. Whilst children under 5 were to be evacuated only with their mothers, exceptions were made for those children already attending day nurseries or nursery schools, and for children in the public assistance nurseries. Where these nurseries were willing to be evacuated as a unit and the staff were willing to take complete charge, then the children could go without their mothers.

Much of the preparation had been carried out after the Munich crisis of 1938. Road transport had been prepared and country houses set aside. In September 1939, 150 nurseries were evacuated; 4,600 children in all. Initially the nurseries found it hard to adapt. Financially they survived on billeting allowances and incurring debts. The Ministry of Health had placed responsibility on the receiving authorities, but in practice many were rural and district authorities which lacked either the experience of running welfare services or sufficient finances to cope. The new accommodation was also often cramped and the risk of infection was considerably increased. By December, however, many of these problems had been ironed out. Most of the groups had been properly accommodated, more equipment and staff had been provided, and better standards had been laid down to combat infection. Furthermore, financial responsibility was placed on either the London County Council, whence most nurseries had come, or the welfare authority, usually the county council, in the district to which the nursery had been sent.

As the war developed, the demand for residential nursery places increased. A number of young children found themselves temporarily without parents. With the call-up of men to the armed forces and the need of many women to work in order to supplement the meagre service allowance, many families found themselves in a precarious position. Illness, confinement, or an accident could easily cause a family breakup. The newly created Citizens Advice Bureaux (AST 7/789; HLG 102/312, 316-321; T 161/1221/S25035/01/1-3) found themselves inundated with requests for help.

The Ministry of Health did not wish to assume responsibility for the growing number of such cases and expected either the assistance authorities or the voluntary organizations to deal with them. The Ministry was prepared to pay a billeting allowance for individual children; but it would only help establish residential nurseries if places were restricted to public assistance cases, and then only on the understanding that the assistance authorities would be responsible for maintenance. The main assistance authority involved, the London County Council, was reluctant to agree. It argued that many of the children did not come from destitute families but were victims of the war and so were not its responsibility.

In an attempt to solve these problems an Under-Fives Panel was formed in March 1940 at the insistence of the Ministry of Health. It consisted of representatives of the Standing Joint Committee of Metropolitan Borough Councils, senior officials of the London County Council's Social Welfare Department and a representative of the Evacuation Department of the Women's Voluntary Service (WVS). Its task was to consider applications for evacuation on behalf of under-fives from the metropolitan area, to prioritize cases and to find places for them in residential nurseries or billets.

The new panel soon found itself facing an ever-rising tide of applicants. In March they received 264 applications for help, in April, 358; in May, 777; and in June, 1,644. By September the situation was reaching crisis point, and the Ministry of Health became actively involved. With local authorities already overstretched, it was the voluntary sector to which the Ministry had to turn for help.

In September 1940 the American Red Cross became involved in the plight of the permanently and temporarily motherless under-fives. They guaranteed sufficient finance to open 100 nurseries with the Ministry of Health helping to provide equipment and premises. Problems continued to arise, however. By the end of 1940 accommodation was again becoming short and the service ministries usually had priority. By January 1941 the waiting lists for places had become so long that the minister of health was forced to approach the secretary of state for war personally to secure a compromise. Supplies of equipment were also getting increasingly scarce. Of five factories manufacturing cots, for example, four had suffered war damage.

An aim to provide 10,000 nursery places was set for the end of 1941. Such a figure was beyond the capacity of the voluntary sector alone, so the London County Council, with the Treasury refunding its costs, agreed to help. By September 1941, 313 nurseries were operating, with places for 9,544. 163 were new, of which 76 were provided by American funds.

Despite this expansion, demand still outstripped supply. Between 1940 and 1941, 20,372 applications were made in London to the Under-Fives Panel. Of these only 53% were accepted. Furthermore, those applications reaching the Panel had been screened by social workers and other recommending bodies. Those unlikely to succeed had already been rejected.

The entry of the United States into the war in December 1941 necessitated a major reassessment of the nursery services because American finance was now diverted back to the United States. As nurseries had demonstrated their important role in the Evacuation Scheme, the Treasury was forced to cover this loss of funds. In addition, it guaranteed to fund the total expenses of nurseries, less any income received from parents, local authorities, voluntary organizations, or fund raising. The target for places was now revised to 15,000 by the end of 1942, a total lowered to 13,500 places when demand began to fall with the easing of air attacks.

The slackening of air attacks made it possible to widen the functions of the residential nurseries which, up to then, had been a part of the general evacuation scheme. They could now begin to play a wider welfare role. In April 1942 it was decided to accept children whose mothers wanted to take up nursing or join one of the women's services. In August 1942 places were opened to children outside evacuation areas, which might be liable to sporadic attack, or to those children in neutral or reception areas who had been deprived of parental care as a result of bombing. In March 1943 children of servicemen living anywhere in the country also became eligible for admission.

The final major wartime test for the service occurred in June 1944 with the advent of the flying bomb attacks. In July 1,600 additional places were created by increasing the capacity of certain nurseries by 20%. A number of nurseries lay directly along the path of the flying bombs and were evacuated. The crisis, however, was short lived.

Early in 1946, 12,276 children remained in 384 nurseries; but the conclusion of the war against Japan and the early demobilization of many servicemen meant that parents could bring their children home earlier than had been expected. By October 1946 the nursery population was below 2,000, and by the end of the year only 28 nurseries with 521 children remained. Decisions about those children which remained, as with other children left in reception areas after the closing of the evacuation scheme, passed to the Curtis Committee on the Care of Children* (see chap 6.4.3).

* for committee references see Appendix B

Records

The main Ministry of Health files relating to day nurseries and nursery schools are at MH 55/883-884, 1642, 1665-1711. The main Board and Ministry of Education papers on nursery education are in ED 102. Treasury papers on the provision of day nurseries are at T 161/1190/S46901/1-2. Lord President's Secretariat papers are at CAB 124/340.

Board of Education Private Office papers on wartime nurseries are at ED 136/674. Official war history papers relating to the under-fives include ED 138/11-13. The official history by E K Ferguson is at CAB 102/243, with notes at CAB 102/776. MH 55/1696 contains the papers resulting from an investigation by the Select Committee on National Expenditure into the number of wartime nurseries built, the cost of building, the number of children accommodated, and the average attendance. ED 66 contains reports on individual nurseries provided for the children of women war workers. ED 69 contains individual nursery school files between 1919 and 1966. LEA development plans, which included proposals for nursery provision after the war, are at ED 152. A special report on nursery classes in the borough of Coventry in 1945 is at ED 77/183.

Ministry of Health files on war factory nurseries include MH 55/1670-1671 on the establishment of day nurseries in factories, and MH 55/1673 on the recruitment of women in industry. Additional information on nurseries in war factories is provided in MH 58/362. Ministry of Labour and National Service papers relating to the wartime provision of nurseries for the children of war workers are at LAB 26/57-59; postwar papers are at LAB 26/286. A Ministry of Supply wartime file on the provision of creches and nurseries to encourage the recruitment of women to industry is at AVIA 22/1302.

Ministry of Health papers on the training of nursery nurses include MH 55/1505, 1507, 1682-1690. Ministry of Health Public Assistance Division files on the training of nursery nurses are at MH 57/268-280. ED 46 contains the papers of the Further Education Division of the Board of Education which covered the training of staff for nurseries. In particular ED 46/200 deals with the establishment of the child care reserve and ED 46/516-526, 539-542 with the establishment of courses within technical colleges. Other files on the training of nursery teachers include ED 86/98 and ED 143/21. Ministry of Labour and National Service papers on the training of nursery nurses include LAB 8/1140 and LAB 9/155.

Wartime services files relating to the evacuation of nursery schools are at HLG 7/285-304. An example of a report file on evacuated day nurseries (Rotherhithe) is at HLG 900/41.

6.4.3 Child care reform proposals and the Curtis Committee

During the wartime reconstruction debates, the care of children was considered within the wider context of the breakup of the Poor Law. It was envisaged that the relevant work and powers of the public assistance committees would be transferred to the counties and county boroughs, with a children's committee established in each. These committees were to include persons of specialist knowledge of whom at least one quarter would be women. They were to have responsibility for all children under 18 subject to public care, except in regard to education, housing or medical treatment. Their main areas of provision would be the boarding out of children with foster parents; the establishment of receiving homes prior to adopting or boarding out; residential nurseries for infants or children under three; and residential homes for older children. At this stage the Ministry of Health was considered the likely central authority, much to the concern of the Home Office (MH 102/1378).

The failings of the child care system, revealed by the war, led to a number of private campaigns to improve the situation. Outstanding amongst these was that of Lady Allen of Hurtwood who, after a long-standing correspondence with the ministries involved, carried out an investigation into the provisions for children in homes (CAB 124/780; MH 102/1289, 1293). This campaign was carried out very much in the public eye and, in particular, through the pages of the press. A famous letter to *The Times* in 1944 highlighting the conditions within homes greatly increased newspaper coverage of the issue and thus the pressure on central government to act (MH 102/1160).

Whilst the Lady Allen campaign drew attention to the problems of children's homes, an infamous case the following year illustrated the dangers of fostering. Denis O'Neill died at the hands of his foster parents after having been removed from his own home. A subsequent inquiry, under Sir Walter Monckton, revealed a whole line of administrative failures and a lack of effective supervision. It concluded that divided responsibility, in this case between the home local authority and the local authority where the child was placed, had been largely responsible.

As the debate surrounding child care grew more heated, it became clear that it would have to be separated from the reform of the Poor Law, if the latter were not to be delayed. Consequently the issue was independently examined by the Curtis Committee on the Care of Children* which was appointed in March 1945 to calm public pressure and to provide a new direction for child care services. In Scotland the Committee on Homeless Children under J L Clyde carried out a similar investigation (CAB 124/781). The Committee's terms of reference, it should be noted, covered only those children in need of care and did not require the committee to look at why care was needed. In the longer term this meant that, following the Children Act 1948, local authorities found themselves accepting children freely into homes without any legal power to investigate the causes of the problem, or to take preventative action.

During the course of its proceedings the Committee visited 451 institutions and interviewed members of 58 local authorities. Its members also visited children in foster homes and discovered a high degree of neglect. In its conclusions the Committee stated that standards were variable and often very poor. Failure was blamed on the lack of co-ordinated administration and the poor training facilities for staff. Remedies, therefore, concentrated on these areas.

Since the turn of the century social science training at university had been recognized as a preparation for social work. However, specialist courses had evolved to train workers in the mental health, probation, and hospital services and the report called for similar courses in child care. A central training council was proposed to promote the establishment of courses. The first priority was the training of staff for children's homes. Two-year courses were proposed which would be run at universities, technical colleges, teacher training colleges, or based on voluntary bodies like Dr Barnado's which had already developed its own training scheme.

The Committee also made important recommendations about the administration of the service. Many of the problems at local level were blamed on a lack of co-ordination between various departments, and the unimaginative and insensitive approaches taken by many local authorities. It therefore suggested the appointment of children's officers and children's committees to be based at each authority which would provide a co-ordinating role and bring a human touch to the services.

The Committee's findings reflected policy in the other areas of welfare in recommending a move away from institutional care. Adoption was seen as the ideal substitute for the family home. However it was largely restricted to orphans and to the very young, as these were most readily acceptable to the adopters. It could never be, therefore, more than a marginal solution. Of far greater significance was fostering. This provided a useful halfway stage between institutional care and adoption. Evacuation had not only created homeless children, but had also introduced many people to the benefits and problems of fostering. Contemporary thinking at the time was also greatly influenced by Dr J Bowlby's work *Maternal care and mental health*, later published by Penguin Books as *Child care and the growth of love*, which emphasized the importance of family life and which became standard reading in the profession. For the government, the major advantage of fostering was cost. The nineteenth-century problems of baby farming had illustrated the dangers of fostering for profit. Future foster parents would, therefore, be expected to be largely unpaid, and would provide a cheap alternative to residential care. The Curtis Committee recommended the use of fostering in preference to institutional care.

The Curtis Committee was specifically debarred from considering the problem of responsibility for the central administration of the services. The debate over this had been long-standing and often heated. The Home Office, with its tradition of institutional care of children and youth custody together with its large Children's Department and Inspectorate, argued that it was best placed to administer any children's legislation. The Ministry of Education argued responsibility for children was an educational issue and so its concern (ED 10/216). The Ministry of Health, at least in terms of numbers, had been the main department for the administration of child care before the war, and as a result of its involvement in the evacuation scheme and the wartime nursery programme, its role had increased. The first committee to look at the problem had been the official Interdepartmental Committee on the Breakup of the Poor Law*, which had established a specialist subcommittee. In its report the subcommittee stated that 'there was a cleavage of opinion between the departments represented on the subcommittee and it was consequently impossible to do more in the report than state and examine the various possibilities in order that decisions may be taken by the Minister' (MH 102/1390). When the issue was raised on the Curtis Committee, a similar stalemate was reached (CAB 130/15: 6 Dec 1946). The issue, therefore, remained unresolved until after the publication of the report.

* for committee references see Appendix B

Records

Papers of the Home Office Children's Department are in MH 102. Home Office correspondence files can be found in HO 45.

Ministry of Health papers relating to the Curtis Report, the Children Act and its implementation include MH 55/1632-1664. Further papers can be found in MH 122. Wartime policy papers are at MH 102/1378 with papers leading up to the appointment of Curtis at MH 102/1161. MH 102/2256 and MH 102/2261 deal with adoption. MH 102/1379-1398 chronicle the disagreement over departmental responsibility. Board of Education wartime policy papers include ED 10/216.

Lord President's Secretariat files relating to the Curtis Committee are at CAB 124/781. Ministry of Education Private Office papers relating to Curtis are at ED 136/583-584, 718. Papers dealing with the Curtis Report and responses to it are at ED 147/392, 414. Ministry of Health papers relating to the Curtis Committee are at MH 55/1662-1663. Policy papers on the care of homeless children are at MH 55/1664. Board of Education files on the training of staff for children's homes are at ED 46/652-654.

6.4.4   The Children Act 1948 and its implementation

The report of the Curtis Committee on the Care of Children* was put into legislative form in the Children Act 1948. The Act attempted to bring together under one service responsibility for all homeless children. Local authorities now had a statutory duty to receive into care children whose parents were temporarily or permanently unfit or unable to care for them. In addition they retained the duties imposed on them by earlier legislation which was not repealed. These included supervising children maintained for reward; the registration of adoption societies; the supervision of third party placings for adoption; and responsibility for the care of children sent to remand homes. The age at which children could be received into care was raised to 17 from 16, and children could remain in care until they were 18 years old. Regulations applying to adoption were extended to incorporate children up to school leaving age—the limit had previously been 9 years old—and fostering could continue up to 18.

The Act transformed the approach to child care from one of provision for the abandoned, wanton, or destitute to one of care for the needy. Whereas the Poor Law Act 1930 had placed a duty on local authorities to 'set to work and put out as apprentices all children whose parents are not, in the opinion of the council, able to keep and maintain their children', the 1948 Children Act made it the 'duty of the authority to exercise their powers with respect to him [the child] so as to further his best interests and to afford him opportunities for the proper development of his character and abilities'. Standards were no longer set at the minimum.

Administration of the service was streamlined by the Act. The child care responsibilities of the Ministries of Health, Education and Pensions and the Home Office were amalgamated, and the Home Office given sole responsibility. An Advisory Council on Child Care was established to advise the secretary of state. At the local level the child care responsibilities of the health, education and public assistance committees were taken over by new children's committees. Each committee had its own children's officer who was a specialist in the needs of deprived children, and was approved by the Home Office.

The finance of the new service was shared between the Exchequer and local authorities. The Treasury accepted Curtis's conclusion that an extra Treasury grant should be made available to assist local authorities (MH 102/1505). Each authority was, therefore, to receive grants of up to 50% of total expenditure.

An indication of the change in attitude towards child care was the new emphasis placed on the return of children to their own homes wherever possible. The new Act encouraged local authorities to identify problems and to resolve them. The importance of maintaining contact with parents while children were in care was stressed, and parents had a duty to maintain contact with the local authority. Parental control was further increased by giving them the right to appeal to a court of law for the resumption of parental rights.

The various ways in which local authorities could provide for children were laid out in Part III of the Act. The basis of the new policy was individual care. To make an assessment of each child at the point of entry into the system, reception centres were to be provided where each child could be judged and appropriate action taken. Special emphasis was laid on boarding out in foster homes.

Whereas fostering had previously been entered into on a long-term basis, the use of foster parents as an alternative to homes saw an increase in the number of short-term placements, with children eventually returning to their own homes. However, there remained a serious shortage of foster homes, with the consequence that the rate of boarding out remained at around 40%. The shortage of foster places led to the offering of incentives by local authorities in some areas and the consequent suspicion that some foster parents were taking in children in order to gain priority for council housing (HLG 101/329).

Following the recommendations of the Curtis Committee, the first Central Training Council courses, initially of fourteen months duration, were introduced at the Universities of Birmingham, Leeds, Liverpool, Nottingham, Cardiff, and at the LSE. They ensured that a small pool of boarding-out officers were available when the Act became effective. Nevertheless, staff shortages remained. Problems were often exacerbated by the unwillingness of some local authorities to take on newly qualified recruits, preferring experienced people to young graduates.

Despite the emphasis placed by the Act on the placement of children in foster homes, the numbers in residential care continued to increase. In 1946, 46,000 children were in homes; in November 1949, 55,000; and in 1953, 65,309. The reason for this was, in part, the widening of the criteria for providing care from destitution to need. The increased numbers placed a severe strain on accommodation. For some time local authorities were obliged to rely on old public assistance institutions for residential accommodation. Children's committees therefore tended to place priority on the building of new accommodation and to ignore the training of staff or the development of new services. The problem of the shortage of foster families also restricted growth in that area.

By 1951 the number of old poor law residences still in use had been halved, but capital investment in them came under challenge. The 1950 budget required cuts in the local authority and voluntary programmes (MH 102/2408-2410). The building of reception centres, on which much of the policy depended, was therefore slow to start. The economic difficulties also hit the centres because they were designed to study the needs of each individual child and were therefore both labour intensive and expensive. By 1951 only fifteen had been provided.

Similar problems were experienced with hostels for older children who had been brought up by local authorities and had started work. The general shortage of staff and buildings meant they received a low priority and by 1951 only six hostels had opened.

As well as its new responsibilities in child care, the Home Office maintained its role in administering approved schools and remand homes. The main problem experienced was again a shortage of staff, exacerbated by a lack of adequate training courses. This was addressed by the Central Training Council. However the service also offered poor terms and conditions when compared with other areas of employment, making it difficult to keep and attract staff (MH 102/1688).

As the numbers in residential care increased, and financial cuts bit, pressure began to build up for the reduction of the numbers in care. The late 1940s, therefore, saw an increase in the number of small family group homes located mainly on the housing estates. Indistinguishable from other local homes, they accommodated eight or fewer children who were in the care of a married house mother paid for by the local authority.

One important area the 1948 Act did not cover was the problem of children ill-treated or neglected in their own home. Whilst it was possible to prosecute parents for cruelty under the 1933 legislation, this required an individual or an organization to undertake legal action. However, the 1948 Act dealt only with the circumstances in which children might come into public care on a voluntary basis and with how they should be treated once there. Concern over this lack of protection for neglected children led to pressure in the House of Commons, in particular from Barbara Ayrton Gould MP who put forward a number of motions (MH 102/1961, 1964). This lead eventually to the appointment of a working party of officials from the Ministries of Health and Education, and the Home Office. It concluded that the problem was not lack of adequate powers but administrative (MH 102/1966). A joint circular to local authorities in 1950 therefore advised that 'if effective help is to be given at an early stage it is essential that there should be co-ordinated use of the statutory and voluntary services'. Consequently by 1960, 90% of authorities had made such arrangements, in particular with the National Society for the Prevention of Cruelty to Children (NSPCC).

* for committee references see Appendix B

Records

Home Office files relating to the drafting and passing of the Act are at MH 102/1504-1547, with submissions from individuals and groups at MH 102/1595-1637. MH 102/1394 deals with discussions on the central administration of the service. The Ministry of Health's Public Assistance Division papers on the Act are at MH 57/436-437. Ministry of Education papers on the Act are at ED 31/761. Prime Minister's Office papers relating to the central administration of the service are at PREM 8/665, whilst Treasury papers on the subject are at T 222/12-13. A Treasury blue note relating to child care is at T 165/10. Board of Control papers relating to the Act are at MH 51/609. Lord Chancellor's Office papers include LCO 2/4473, 4119 on the Act and LCO 2/4483, 4456-4459 on adoption. Assistance Board papers relating to the Act are at AST 7/947.

Policy files of the Children's Department of the Home Office are at MH 102. In particular, MH 102/1699-1717 deal with the implementation of the Children Act 1948. Files after 1949 are in BN 29. Representative case files are at BN 28. Correspondence files of the Home Office are at HO 45.

Papers relating to capital investment in children's homes are at MH 102/2408-2410. Papers relating to the Cabinet's Investment Programmes Committee* are at MH 102/2515. Voluntary home expenditure for 1948 is dealt with at MH 102/2587 with a further review in 1951 at MH 102/2413. Papers arising out of the Local Government Manpower Committee in relation to children's homes are at MH 102/1920 with papers of its Home Office Subcommittee at MH 102/1098. Correspondence concerning adoption includes MH 102/1801-1805, MH 102/1833-1875 and MH 102/2111-2133. Registration of adoption societies is at MH 102/1988-1991. Files relating to individual cases are at MH 102/1998-2008. Adoption statistics and trends are at MH 102/2021, 2024, with further papers at HO 45/25303. MH 102/1961-1987 deal with the cruelty to and neglect of children. Files on remand homes can be found at MH 102/920, 1347-1354, 2517 and in BN 62. Files on individual children's homes include MH 102/841-877. Berkshire County Council files are at MH 102/1638-1643; those for the East Riding of Yorkshire are at MH 102/1654-1659; and those for Manchester at MH 102/1660-1667. Files for other areas are at MH 102/1644-1653. MH 102/1721 contains papers dealing with the effects of the Act on residual evacuees, with further issues at MH 102/1695.

Ministry of Health Social Welfare files are at MH 130. Ministry papers following the Act include MH 55/1661. MH 57/436 deals with the central administration of the service.

Ministry of Education papers relating to the neglect of children include ED 147/434. Files of selected poor law schools are at ED 132.

Minutes of the Central Training Council in Child Care are at MH 102/1577-1590. Further files relating to its work are at BN 29/98-248 and MH 102/1829-1832.

Papers of the Advisory Council on Child Care are in MH 102/1501-1503, 1761-1797 and ED 147/428.

6.5 The physically disabled

Welfare services for the physically disabled were often provided under the auspices of the health services (for records dealing with mental health, see chap 4.4.2.6). Responsibility for the education of the younger disabled rested with the Special School Service of the Board of Education (see chap 5.3.5.3). The remaining services had been available under the Poor Law and were administered by the Assistance Board and the local public assistance committees. Finally, the Ministry of Labour was becoming increasingly involved in the training of the disabled. Disabled policy, therefore, developed in two main areas outside the health and education fields. Training policy was developed by the Ministry of Labour and was administered through its organization at national and local level. Welfare services were also considered as part of the National Assistance reforms (see chap 2.4 and chap 6.3.2) and remained a part of local authority provision.

The first retraining centre for disabled persons had been introduced during the Boer War, and new ones were opened during the First World War. The numbers of people injured during the war and the widespread public belief that they deserved the help of the nation were the major stimulants behind reform. In 1920 the retraining centres were opened to the civilian blind.

The Second World War had an even greater impact, with a higher level of civilian casualties compared with military ones. In 1941 the Home Policy Committee* approved a proposal that one service should cover all military personnel and civilians injured as a result of enemy action (CAB 75/10: 26 Feb 1941). In the same year, an Interdepartmental Committee on the Rehabilitation and Resettlement of Disabled Persons was established to make specific proposals. Its recommendations were accepted in principle by the Lord President's Committee and were put into legislative form as the Disabled Persons (Employment) Act 1944 (CAB 71/11: 29 Sept 1943).

The Act established a scheme to be administered by the Ministry of Labour and National Service. It included the assessment of individual needs, the provision of residential care, vocational training with maintenance grants, help in securing employment, and the obligation on the part of employers to accept a quota of disabled people. Under the Act, a National Advisory Council on the Employment of the Disabled was created to advise the Minister.

Training policy had been a long standing source of friction between the Board of Education and the Ministry of Labour. Whilst the responsibility for most aspects of training rested with the Board of Education, the Ministry of Labour throughout the 1930s had been in charge of training schemes for the unemployed. Administration was, therefore, divided. As a compromise, responsibility for the training of the disabled passed to the Ministry of Labour, but Education kept responsibility for the training of the blind, and of those attending special schools (LAB 19/194; LAB 20/153; ED 50/265; T 161/1163/S48249/02). In 1946, however, the Ministry of Labour took over responsibility for the training of blind persons over 21 (LAB 12/908). To oversee the administration of the scheme locally, a regional administrative structure was established (LAB 12/38-39). Regional medical advisers were appointed to Ministry of Labour regional offices to give advice and carry out research (LAB 12/359). To assist in the expansion of employment opportunities for disabled people, a number of ventures were also funded by the Ministry of Labour, including some voluntary undertakings (LAB 9/100, 109-110). In particular, in November 1946 a financial agreement was drawn up between the

Ministry of Labour and the Disabled Persons Employment Corporation, which had been established in April 1945 as a limited company with the prime purpose of providing sheltered employment for severely disabled persons. In July 1946 it was renamed Remploy and in July 1949 became Remploy Ltd (BM 1-BM 12; LAB 16/82-84).

Provision for the physically disabled was further extended under the National Assistance Act 1948, when it became a statutory duty for local authorities to provide services for the disabled. They were able to do this either directly or through the funding of voluntary organizations acting as their agents. Services included the provision of home visitors, the organization of recreational activities, the provision of hostels, and the supervision of training. Overseeing the whole structure was an Advisory Council for the Welfare of Handicapped Persons which was established under the National Assistance Act 1948 (MH 57/479-514).

* for committee references see Appendix B

Records

The Bill papers of the 1944 Disabled Persons (Employment) Act are in LAB 12/559-560 and LAB 16/476-477. Ministry of Pensions papers relating to the Act are in PIN 15/2863. Lord Chancellor's Office papers are at LCO 2/3038.

Papers of the National Advisory Council on the Employment of the Disabled are at LAB 20/157-158, 165-169, 352-367, 403-409, 488-490, 544-547.

Ministry of Labour files relating to the training of the disabled following the 1944 Act are in LAB 18. The papers of the Employment Division of the Ministry are at LAB 8 and those of the Finance Division at LAB 9. Files of particular relevance here include LAB 9/228-237, 131. Papers of the Establishment Division are at LAB 12, and include LAB 12/123, 347 on the quota system, LAB 12/362 on the employment of blind persons, LAB 12/391 on the employment of the disabled in government departments, LAB 12/450 on the implementation of the Act, and LAB 12/453 on publicity. Files relating to Remploy Ltd are at BM 1-BM 12. Ministry of Labour files on the finance of the company include LAB 9/122, 142. Policy papers are at LAB 16/82-84. Other records can be found in LAB 16 and LAB 20.

Papers of the Special Services Division of the Ministry of Education are in ED 50. ED 50/652 relates to the further education and training of disabled pupils and ED 50/648-650 to the effects of the National Assistance Act 1948 on the training of the blind. Further education files are at ED 46; these include ED 46/552-553 relating to the training of the disabled and ED 46/667 on relations with the Ministry of Labour.

Ministry of Health Public Assistance Division papers relating to the physically disabled are in MH 57. They include MH 57/532-550 on the blind, MH 57/574 on the partially sighted, and MH 57/285-286 relating to epileptics. Ministry papers relating to homes for the blind include HLG 102/82 whilst other files on blind welfare are at MH 55/1083-1101. Papers relating to the rehabilitation and resettlement of disabled persons are at MH 55/2158-2166. Further social welfare papers can be found in MH 130.

Treasury papers relating to the training of the blind are at T 161/1163/S48249/02. Papers on the rehabilitation and employment of the disabled are at T 161/1165/S49326/1 and T 161/1166/S49326/2. Papers relating to vocational training of war casualties are at T 161/1190/S47285/2.

Assistance Board files relating to duties imposed under the National Assistance Act in relation to retraining are at AST 10.

6.6 Bibliography

S M Ferguson and H Fitzgerald, *Studies in the social services* (1954)

Roy Lowe, *Education in the postwar years* (1988)

R Means and R Smith, *The development of welfare service for elderly people* (1985)

J Parker, *Local health and welfare services* (1965)

R A Parker, 'The gestation of reform: the Children Act 1948' in P Bean and S MacPherson, *Approaches to welfare* (1983)

R A Parker, *Away from home: a short history of provision for separated children* (1991)

D Riley, 'War in the Nursery', *Feminist Review* 2 (1979)

K Slack, *Councils, committees, and concern for the old* (1960)

P Summerfield, *Women workers in the Second World War* (1969)

R M Titmuss, *Problems of social policy* (1950)

B Watkin, *Documents on health and social services* (1975)

E Younghusband, *Social work in Britain 1950-75* (1978)

Rationing of food, clothing and domestic fuel

This appendix contains a list of the main classes of records at the Public Record Office relating to the rationing of food, clothing and domestic fuel in the period covered by this handbook. While it is acknowledged that rationing was always designed to be temporary—and therefore did not form part of the welfare state in the longer term—it cannot be denied that it formed an essential part of government policy designed to further the well-being of the population in a period of reduced circumstances.

The appendix is divided into three sections: the first examines records of the Prime Minister's Office and the Cabinet, which provide an overview of aspects of rationing policy at central level. The section on food rationing identifies the main classes of records created by the Ministry of Food, together with relevant files from the Treasury and other departments. The final section is concerned with Treasury and departmental records relating to clothing and domestic fuel. Unlike the rest of this handbook, the records are presented in class, rather than subject, order and the editors would therefore advise searchers interested in rationing to read the whole appendix. Although some individual files of particular significance have been identified, this appendix is designed to indicate the classes where relevant material may be found and does not provide the detailed guidance found elsewhere in this handbook.

1. Central direction

CAB 102	Official War Histories (1939-1945): Civil. These are a confidential set of the official histories with references to original sources (not in the form of PRO references), drafts, revisions, critical commentaries, unpublished papers etc.	
	CAB 102/15-17	*Food* by R J Hammond
	CAB 102/102	*Consumer rationing* an unpublished draft by A Jenkin used in the compilation of the official histories *British war economy* and *Civil industry and trade*
	CAB 102/245	*The nutrition of the school child* unpublished drafts by E K and S M Ferguson
	CAB 102/300-321	Drafts, correspondence and comments on *Food*, 1941-1972.
	CAB 102/324	*Food production campaign in the United Kingdom* an unpublished draft by E Whetham used in the compilation of *British war economy* and *Food*
	CAB 102/325-327	*Agricultural policy and food production* unpublished draft by E Whetham, with correspondence and comments, 1942-1950
	CAB 102/328-329	*The legal aspects of food control* unpublished draft by P W Millard, 1947-1948
CAB 140	Official Historians' Correspondence	
	CAB 140/6-16	R J Hammond's files on the preparation of the official history *Food*, 1942-1954.

The following classes of records of the **Prime Minister's Office** include correspondence and papers on rationing:

PREM 1	Prime Minister's Office: Correspondence and Papers, 1916-1940	
	PREM 1/295	Food rationing proposals, 1939
PREM 4	Confidential Papers, 1939-1946	
	PREM 4/2/1-18	Agriculture and food supply
	PREM 4/9/8-10	Fuel rationing, 1942-1943
	PREM 4/95/9	Clothing policy, 1943-1945
PREM 8	Prime Minister's Office: Correspondence and Papers, 1945-1951	
	PREM 8/15	Possibility of easing rationing of clothing
	PREM 8/199-209	Food supplies, 1946
	PREM 8/502-510	Food supplies, 1946-1947
	PREM 8/981	Cheese ration, 1946-1949
	PREM 8/1194-1199	Food supplies, 1947-1950
	PREM 8/1420-1425	Food supplies, 1949-1951
PREM 11	Prime Minister's Office: Correspondence and Papers, 1951-1964 (the later files in this class cover the end of food rationing).	
	PREM 11/143	Christmas bonuses, and increase in bacon ration, 1951
	PREM 11/661	End of butter rationing, 1952-1954
	PREM 11/663	End of meat rationing, 1951-1955

The following classes of records of the **Cabinet Office** include discussions, memoranda and reports on rationing:

CAB 65	War Cabinet Minutes
CAB 66-CAB 68	War Cabinet Memoranda
CAB 128	Cabinet Minutes from 1945
CAB 129	Cabinet Memoranda from 1945

The following CAB classes and files are also relevant:

CAB 63	Hankey Papers	
	CAB 63/134-139	Food and nutrition, 1939-1941
CAB 74	War Cabinet Ministerial Committee on Food Policy	
CAB 75	War Cabinet Home Policy Committee	
	CAB 75/27	Sub-committee on rationing, 1939
CAB 89	War Cabinet Survey of Economic and Financial Plans Committee	
	CAB 89/13	Wartime diets of working class families. A study by E R and N B Bransby, 1940-1941
CAB 103	Historical Section: Registered Files. These are files of the Historical Section of the Cabinet Office, containing progress reports, estimates, correspondence, and information about sources used by official historians.	
CAB 118	Various Ministers: Files.	
	This class consists of papers collected by Attlee when he was Deputy Prime Minister.	
	CAB 118/12	Attlee's personal file on food and agriculture, 1940-1945
	CAB 118/43-46	Correspondence with the Ministry of Food, 1940-1943

CAB 123	Lord President of the Council: Secretariat Files.
	These are files of the Lord President's Committee established in 1940 to co-ordinate the work of other ministerial committees concerned with home and economic affairs.
CAB 130	Ad Hoc Committees: Gen and Misc Series
	CAB 130/10	Extra rations for underground miners, 1946
	CAB 130/37	Food policy, 1948
CAB 134	Cabinet Committees: General Series from 1945
	CAB 134/276	Food Distribution Committee, 1948
	CAB 134/729-731	Food Supplies Committee, 1946

2. Food

The history of food rationing is described in great detail in R J Hammond, *Food*, History of the Second World War, United Kingdom Civil Series (3 vols, 1951-1962). (See CAB 140/6-16 above). The 1984 reissue of this work includes comprehensive references to sources used.

Records of the **Ministry of Food**, which was responsible for food rationing, are in the following classes:

MAF 67	Food Control Committees Selected Minutes
MAF 72	Board of Trade Food (Defence Plans) Department (1936-1939). This class includes later papers of the Ministry of Food.
MAF 74	Ministry of Food Central Registry: Correspondence and Papers. Some files concern rationing procedure, registration etc. The class is closed for 50 years.
MAF 75	Ministry of Food Permanent Record of Operations (1939-1954)
MAF 79	Animal Feeding Stuffs Correspondence and Papers. This class contains many files concerning rations for livestock, etc.
MAF 83	Ministry of Food: Supply Department: Supply Secretariat
MAF 84	Ministry of Food: Supply Department: Cereals Group
MAF 85	Ministry of Food: Supply Department: Dairy Produce and Fats Group
MAF 86	Ministry of Food: Supply Department: Fish and Vegetables Group
MAF 87	Ministry of Food: Supply Department: Groceries and Sundries Group
MAF 88	Ministry of Food: Supply Department: Meat and Livestock Group
MAF 98	Ministry of Food: Scientific Advisers Division
MAF 99	Ministry of Food: Services Department: Distribution Group
MAF 100	Ministry of Food: Services Department: Regional Administration Group
MAF 101	Ministry of Food: Services Department: Food Standards Group
MAF 102	Ministry of Food: Services Department: Public Relations Group
MAF 103	Ministry of Food: Services Department: Services Secretariat
MAF 127	Ministry of Food: Establishment Department
MAF 128	Ministry of Food: Senior Officers' Papers
MAF 129	Ministry of Food: Finance Secretariat
MAF 138	Ministry of Food: Finance Department
MAF 150	Ministry of Food: Legal Department Registered Files (L Series)
MAF 151	Ministry of Food: Committees
MAF 152	Ministry of Food: War History Papers
MAF 154	Ministry of Food: Orders Committee
MAF 156	Ministry of Food and Ministry of Agriculture, Fisheries and Food: Statistics and Intelligence Division: Correspondence and Reports
MAF 223	Ministry of Food: Publications
MAF 286	Ministry of Food: Ministers' Office Papers

A number of other departments exercised responsibilities connected with food rationing. Some material will be found among the following classes:

Board of Education (later **Ministry of Education**)
ED 50   Special Services, General Files

Ministry of Home Security
HO 192   Research and Experiments Department Registered Papers
                 HO 192/1230   Effect of air raids on food supplies in Birmingham,
                                        1941-1942

Ministry of Information (later **Central Office of Information**)
INF 13   Posters and Publications
RG 23   Social Survey: Reports and Papers

Ministry of Health
MH 56   Foods
MH 79   100,000 Series Files. This class includes files on diet and nutrition
MH 96   Welsh Board of Health: Registered Files
                 MH 96/280   Rations for hospital patients, 1940-1943

Ministry of Transport/Ministry of War Transport
MT 55   Emergency Road Transport Organization

General Register Office
RG 28   National Registration: Correspondence and Papers. This class includes a number
                 of files concerning the issue of rationing documents by local National Registration
                 Offices.

Treasury
T 161   Supply Files.
                 There are a number of relevant files under the heading Materials: Food General,
                 including:
                 T 161/948/S45375/1   Food rationing scheme, 1939
                 T 161/1014/S21959/04   Food rationing in Northern Ireland, 1939-1941
T 165   Blue Notes
                 T 165/255   Ministry of Food, 1948-1952
T 171   Chancellor of the Exchequer's Office: Budget and Finance Bill Papers
                 T 171/349   Keynes's plan to manage the war, includes com-
                                           ments on rationing of goods and services, 1940
T 172   Chancellor of the Exchequer's Office: Miscellaneous Papers
                 T 172/1929   Publicity given to Lord Stamp's press conference on
                                           rationing, etc, 1940
                 T 172/1980-1981   Notes by Lord Keynes on schemes for complete
                                           rationing, 1942
T 222   Organisation and Methods Division: Files
                 T 222/60   Food policy, 1948
                 T 222/244, 527, 625, 629 Future of Ministry of Food, 1944-1954
T 223   Agriculture and Food Division: Files
T 229   Central Economic Planning Section: Files
                 T 229/280-281   National food policy review, 1950-1951

T 230	Economic Advisory Section: Files	
	T 230/12	Note by Miss M E W Joseph on the principles of rationing, 1940
	T 230/13	Note on food rationing by Professor Robbins, 1941
	T 230/118-120	Rations and rationing: general policy, 1940-1942

3. Clothing and domestic fuel rationing

The clothes rationing scheme was administered by the Industries and Manufactures Department of the **Board of Trade**. Fuel rationing was the responsibility of the Board's Mines Department until June 1942 when that Department was absorbed in the newly created Ministry of Fuel and Power.

BT 131	War Histories (1939-1945) Files	
	BT 131/35-47	Clothing and clothes rationing, 1939-1948

Relevant records are in the following classes:

BT 64	Industries and Manufactures Department: Correspondence and Papers (See also BT 258 below)
BT 70	Statistical Department, etc, Correspondence and Papers
BT 96	Industrial Supplies Department
BT 204	Wool Control Papers
BT 258	Industry and Manufactures Department: Policy, General and Record Files (P,G & R)

Ministry of Fuel and Power, 1941-1945

POWE 3	Solid Fuel Control and Rationing (1939-1958) Representative Papers. These files illustrate the working of the various systems of control and rationing, and have been drawn from the London, Northern and Wales Regions.
POWE 16	Coal Division, Early Correspondence and Papers
POWE 17	Coal Division: Emergency Services: Correspondence and Papers
POWE 18	Coal Division, Fuel and Lighting Correspondence and Papers
POWE 19	Coal Division: House Coal: Correspondence and Papers
POWE 21	Coal Division, Mines Department War Book and Associated Matters, Correspondence and Papers
POWE 26	'A' Files. These include signed copies of statutory rules and orders concerning restrictions etc of coal supplies.

Supplementary material will be found among records of the following departments:

Ministry of Information (later **Central Office of Information**)

INF 13	Posters and Publications. This class contains material used with the 'make do and mend' and fuel economy campaigns.	
RG 23	Social Survey: Reports and Papers	
	RG 23/20A	Concerns a survey of public attitudes towards fuel rationing, 1942-1943. There are also a number of pieces in this class concerning fuel distribution schemes and clothes rationing.

Ministry of Transport/Ministry of War Transport

MT 55	Emergency Road Transport Organization

General Register Office

RG 28   National Registration: Correspondence and Papers

      RG 28/43   Contains correspondence between the General Register Office and the Board of Trade about the issue and surrender of clothing cards, 1941-1942

Treasury

T 161   Supply Files

      T 161/1414/S53992/01/1-2,   Stabilization of clothing prices: rationing scheme,
      T 161/1409/S53992/01/3-6   1941-1945

      T 161/1117/S44226/1   Rationing of consumption of coal, gas and electricity for domestic and quasi-domestic purposes in wartime, 1939-1943

T 165   Blue Notes. These include notes on the functions etc of the Board of Trade and the Ministry of Fuel and Power prepared in connection with the annual estimates

T 228   Trade and Industry Division: Files

      T 228/87   Fuel Allocations Committee papers, 1947

      T 228/88   Stabilization of clothing prices; clothes rationing scheme, 1945-1948

T 229   Central Economic Planning Section: Files

      T 229/260-261   Coal rations and rationing: allocations to home and export markets, 1948-1951

T 230   Economic Advisory Section: Files

      T 230/152   Proposals for increasing and subsequently removing the clothing ration, 1946-1949

T 273   Bridges Papers

      T 273/305   Includes papers concerning proposals for domestic fuel rationing, 1947

Details of committees referred to in more than one section

Beveridge Report, Official Committee on the

Chairman	Sir Thomas Phillips
Secretary	Mr Hendrie; Mr Lester
Terms	'to examine the major questions of policy arising out of the report on social insurance and allied services... and to report for the consideration of ministers, not later than January 9th, on the issues involved...'
First met	10 Dec 1942
Papers	ACT 1/692-708; AST 7/607; ED 136/373; LAB 12/6-8; PIN 8/115, 116; T 161/1129/S48497/02

Care of Children Committee

Chairman	Myra Curtis
Secretary	D M D Rosling, G T Milne
Terms	'to inquire into existing methods of providing for children who from loss of parents or from any cause whatever are deprived of a normal home life with their parents or a relative, and to consider what further measures should be taken to ensure that these children are brought up under conditions best calculated to compensate them for the lack of parental care'
First met	1945
Papers	CAB 124/781; CAB 130/15; ED 135/5; ED 136/583-584; ED 147/392; MH 55/1661-1664; MH 102/1163, 1165, 1296, 1412-1451E, 1490, 2256; PIN 32/5
Report	Cmd 6760, Cmd 6922 1945-46

Compensation and Betterment, Expert Committee on

Chairman	Mr Justice Uthwatt
Secretary	H E Williams
Terms	'to make an objective analysis of the subject of the payment of compensation and recovery of betterment in respect of public control of the use of land; to advise, as a matter of urgency, what steps should be taken now or before the end of the war to prevent the work of reconstruction thereafter being prejudiced; to consider (a) possible means of stabilising the value of land required for development or re-development, and (b) any extension or modification of powers to enable such land to be acquired by the public on an equitable basis...'
First met	7 Feb 1941
Papers	CAB 117/128-130; CAB 123/44; ED 136/330; F 18/256; HLG 68/67; HLG 71/877; HLG 81
Report	Cmd 6291 1940-41

Dentistry, Interdepartmental Committee on

Chairman Lord Teviot
Secretary H F Summers
Terms 'to consider (1) the progressive stages by which... provision for an adequate and satisfactory dental service should be made available for the population (2) the measures to be taken to secure an adequate number of entrants into the dental profession (3) existing legislation...'
First met 4 May 1943
Papers ED 50/197; MH 77/124, 183-193, 204-215
Reports Cmd 6565 1944; Cmd 6727 1945

Economic Policy Committee

Chairman Prime minister
Secretary N Brooks
Terms '(a) To exercise on behalf of the Cabinet a general oversight over the work of economic policy in relation to both external and internal questions (b) to reconcile, subject to the Cabinet, conflicts between the needs of our foreign trading and the requirements of our internal economy (c) to consider questions of external economic policy'
First met 9 October 1947
Papers CAB 21/1724, 2221; CAB 134/215-230, 841-846; LAB 10/695; MAF 83/2505-2507; PREM 11/110; T 238/110-111

Evacuation, Committee on

Chairman Sir John Anderson
Secretary A Johnson
Terms 'to examine the problems of the transference of persons from areas which might be exposed to continuous air attack and to recommend plans for the purpose.'
First met 27 May 1938
Papers AIR 2/3931/844304/38; ED 136/116-117; HO 45/17634-17636
Report Cmd 5837 1938

Food Policy Committee

Chairman Lord privy seal
Secretary R B Howorth
Terms 'to keep under continuous and close review the broader aspects of the problems of food policy'
First met 28 November 1939
Papers CAB 74/1-7; MH 79/63-64

Further Education and Training, Interdepartmental Committee on

Chairman Lord Hankey
Secretary E M H Markham, H F Rossetti
Terms '(1) to consider in the light of the prospects of employment at home and abroad (a) the number of persons who should be encouraged to enter upon courses of education and training above the secondary school or equivalent standard (b) the opportunities for education and training above secondary school or equivalent standard which should be made available to men and women who have been engaged in service or work connected with war, and to co-ordinate these with the

corresponding opportunities to be provided by the services for those still abroad in the services...'

First met   3 June 1943
Papers   ADM 1/16740; BT 60/73/8; CO 877/28/2; ED 136/547, 689; LAB 18/178-181; LAB 30/14

General Practitioners, Interdepartmental Committee on Remuneration of

Chairman   Sir Will Spens
Secretary   A V Kelynack; A L Thompson
Terms   'To consider... what ought to be the range of total professional income of a registered medical practitioner in any publicly organised service of general medical practice; to consider this with due regard to what have been the normal financial expectations of general medical practitioners in the past, and to the desirability of maintaining in the future the proper social and economic status of general medical practitioners and its power to attract a suitable type of recruit to the profession.'
First met   7 March 1945
Papers   MH 77/172-182; T 161/1364/S42032/2
Report   Cmd 6810 1946

Higher Technological Education, Committee on

Chairman   Lord Eustace Percy
Secretary   A R M Maxwell-Hyslop
Terms   'Having regard to the requirements of industry, to consider the needs of higher technological education in England and Wales and the respective contributions to be made thereto by the universities and technical colleges, and to make recommendations, among other things, as to the means for maintaining appropriate collaboration between universities and technological colleges in this field.'
First met   28 April 1944
Papers   ED 46/295-296
Report   *Higher Technological Education*. Report of a special committee, 1945

Home Policy Committee (from 1942 the Legislation Committee)

Chairman   Lord privy seal
Secretary   Sir Rupert Howorth
First met   13 September 1939
Papers   CAB 75

House Construction, Interdepartmental Committee on

Chairman   Sir George Burt
Secretary   J G Ledeboer
Terms   'to consider materials and methods of construction suitable for the building of houses and flats, having regard to efficiency, economy, and speed of erection, and to make recommendations for postwar practice in the light of all relevant findings of the study committee co-ordinated by the Ministry of Works and Planning.'
First met   16 September 1942
Papers   HLG 94
Reports   Post-war building studies Nos 1, 23, 25 (Ministry of Works) 1943-1947

Housing, Central, Advisory Committee

Chairman	Minister of health
Secretary	Enid Russell-Smith
Terms	'to advise the Minister of Health and local House Management Commissioners on specific questions, which may be referred to it and will also be available for consultation by the Minister on any questions connected with housing administration generally'
First met	1935
Papers	HLG 36; HLG 37; HLG 52/780

Investment Programmes Committee

Chairman	E N Plowden, H T Weeks
Secretary	Treasury, Cabinet Office, CEPS
Terms	'(1) To review the size of the total investment programme, both building and plant and machinery, and to make proposals as to the extent to which the programmes of departments require modification (2) To obtain from departments a statement of the steps necessary to carry out these proposals and their effect on their programmes (3) To submit a comprehensive review to Ministers (4) To supervise methods of controlling and reducing the total programme through labour ceilings, expenditure limits, material supplies, licences, or any other methods...'
First met	6 January 1948
Papers	BT 70/143; CAB 130/27; CAB 134/438-454; HLG 52/1574-1577; HLG 71/1571; POWE 37/95-98; T 161/1251/S53555; T 161/1297/S53555/02; T 229/332-333, 344, 455-459

Land Utilization in Rural Areas, Committee on

Chairman	Lord Justice Scott
Secretary	T Sharp, B C Engholm
Terms	'To consider the conditions which should govern building and other constructional development in country areas consistent with the maintenance of agriculture and in particular the factors affecting location of industry, having regard to economic operations, part-time and seasonal employment, the well-being of rural communities, and the preservation of rural amenities'
First met	23 October 1941
Papers	CAB 117/16, 140, 127; CAB 123/44; ED 136/330; HLG 51/924; HLG 80
Report	Cmd 6378 1941-1942

Local Government Manpower Committee

Chairman	P Dennis Proctor
Secretary	D Somerville
Terms	'To review and co-ordinate the existing arrangements for ensuring economy in the use of manpower by local authorities and by government departments which are concerned with local government matters; and to examine in particular the distribution of functions between central and local government and the possibility

of releasing departmental supervision of local authorities and delegating more responsibility to local authorities.'

First met	4 February 1949
Papers	ED 46/751; ED 121/493; HLG 51/980-1036; HLG 52/1278, 1441; HLG 101/420; HLG 71/1457; MH 102/1908-1925
Reports	Cmd 7870 1949; Cmd 8421 1951.

Lord President's Committee

Chairman	Lord president
Secretary	J P R Maud, W S Murrie
Terms	'(i) to keep continuous watch on behalf of the War Cabinet over the general trend of economic development (ii) to concert the work of the economic committees'. In 1945 it took over the function of the Reconstruction Committee, and was temporarily renamed the House Affairs Committee.
First met	1940
Papers	CAB 71 (wartime), CAB 132 (postwar)

National Health Service, Committee on the

Chairman	Prime minister
Secretary	A Johnson
Terms	'(1) To fix limits for the total cost of the NHS in the financial year 1951/1952 and succeeding years; (2) to keep under review the cause of expenditure on this service, on the basis of monthly statements by the health departments, and if cost seems likely to exceed the limits set for the current year, to devise appropriate remedies; (3) generally to assist the Health Minister in securing due economy in the administration of the service.'
First met	22 April 1950
Papers	CAB 21/1733, 2027; CAB 134/518-519

National Insurance Advisory Committee

Chairman	Sir Will Spens
Secretary	E M Kemp-Jones
Terms	'To consider and report on preliminary draft regulations which the Minister would refer to them and to consider special questions involving difficult problems of insurance on which the minister would seek their advice.'
First met	14 November 1947
Papers	LAB 12/440-441, 671; PIN 19/124, 126-136; PIN 44/36; PIN 60/1-168;
Report	Cmd 8446 1951

Poor Law, Interdepartmental Committee on the Breakup of the

Chairman	Sir Arthur Rucker
Secretary	J W M Siberry
First met	11 April 1946
Papers	AST 7/810, 828; CAB 128/6; CAB 134/698; MH 79/313

Postwar Internal Economic Problems, Official Committee on

Chairman Sir George Chrystal, Sir Alfred Hurst (from 25 February 1942)

Terms '(a) to formulate the chief problems of postwar internal economic policy (b) to arrange for preparation of memoranda on these problems (c) to formulate for ministers the considerations which should be borne in mind in framing policy.'

First met 11 November 1941

Papers AVIA 22/176; BT 64/3107; BT 131/62; CAB 21/1589; CAB 87/54-57; CAB 117/4-19; ED 136/333-335, 358; HLG 71/642, 876; HLG 101/377

Production Committee

Chairman Chancellor of the Exchequer

Secretary S E V Luke

Terms 'To supervise the production programme (both for export and the home market) required to give effect to the general economic plan; and to consider questions of internal economic policy.'

First met 13 October 1947

Papers CAB 134/638-652

Reconstruction Committee

Chairman Minister of reconstruction

Secretary J Maud

Terms '(1) To formulate government policy on the social security scheme (2) To review all major reconstruction schemes in terms of principle and cost to the Exchequer.'

First met June 1944

Papers ADM 1/19037; BT 60/77/5; CAB 21/1587; CAB 87/5-10; CAB 124/566; HLG 102/32-33; LAB 8/909; LAB 13/122; MAF 83/2718

Reconstruction Priorities, Committee on

Chairman Lord president; chancellor of the Exchequer (from 29 September 1943)

First met 22 January 1943

Papers CAB 21/1588; CAB 87/12-13; CAB 123/48

Reconstruction Problems, Committee on (reconstituted in March 1942 when it absorbed the Committee on Economic Aspects of Reconstruction)

Chairman Minister without portfolio; paymaster general (from March 1942)

Secretary Sir George Chrystal; Sir Alfred Hurst (from March 1942)

Terms '(a) To arrange for the preparation of practical schemes of reconstruction' having 'as their general aim the perpetuation of national unity achieved in the country during the war (b) To propose a scheme for a postwar European and world system.'

First met 6 March 1941

Papers CAB 87/1-2; CAB 21/779, 1583, 2295; CAB 117/1-2; CAB 127/162; ED 136/353

Social Insurance and Allied Services, Interdepartmental Committee on

Chairman	Sir William Beveridge
Secretary	D H Chester
Terms	'To undertake, with special reference to the inter-relation of the scheme, a survey of the existing national scheme of social insurance and allied services, including workmen's compensation, and to make recommendations.'
First met	8 July 1941
Papers	ACT 1/681-691; AST 7/551; CAB 21/2295; CAB 87/1, 76-82; CAB 123/43, 45, 242-244; LAB 17/125; MH 57/220-221; PIN 8; PIN 21/65
Reports	Cmd 6404 1942; Cmd 6405 1942; *Social insurance and allied services: the Beveridge report in brief*, 1942 (Treasury)

Social Services Committee

Chairman	Lord privy seal
Secretary	W S Murrie
Terms	'(a) To consider questions of policy connected with the completion and bringing into operation of the scheme of national insurance and family allowances. (b) To secure consistency, having regard to the varying character of the scheme, between the rates of payments to be made to individuals under the new schemes of national insurance and payments of similar kind from Exchequer funds.'
First met	29 August 1945
Papers	CAB 21/2028; CAB 134/697-698

Teachers, Committee on the Recruitment and Training of

Chairman	Sir Arnold McNair
Secretary	S H Wood
Terms	'To investigate the present sources of supply and the methods of recruitment and training of teachers and youth leaders and to report what priorities should guide the Board in these matters in the future.'
First met	17 April 1942
Papers	ED 86/94-95; ED 136/608-620
Report	*Teachers and youth leaders*, 1944 (Ministry of Education).

Chairmen of committees

Anderson, Sir John
  Evacuation, Committee on
Athlone, Earl of
  Nursing Services, Interdepartmental
    Committee on

Barlow, Sir Alan
  Further Education of Demobilized
    Soldiers, Committee on the
  Scientific Manpower, Committee on
Barter, Percy
  Evacuation Scheme, Government,
    Committee on the
  Evacuation of the Aged, Committee on
    the
Beveridge, Sir William
  Social Insurance and Allied Services,
    Interdepartmental Committee on
  Unemployment Insurance Statutory
    Committee
Bradlow, R V
  Central Health Services Council: Standing
    Dental Advisory Committee
Bray, Frederick
  Further Education Schemes Committee
Brooke, Henry
  Social Needs and Problems of Families
    living in Large Blocks of Flats
    Subcommittee
Burt, Sir George
  House Construction, Interdepartmental
    Committee on

Champness, Sir William
  British Medical Association: Central
    Emergency Committee
Charles, J A
  Eye Service Committee
Chrystal, Sir George
  Evacuation of School Children, Advisory
    Committee on
  Postwar Internal Economic Problems,
    Official Committee on

Clark Turner, R
  Dental War Committee
Cleary, William C
  Teachers, Uncertified, Committee on
Clyde, Lord
  Homeless Children (Scotland), Committee
    on
Curtis, Myra
  Care of Children Committee

Dale, Edgar T
  Industrial Disease, Departmental
    Committee on
Dalrymple-Champneys, Sir Weldon
  Drugs Requirement Advisory Committee
Davies, Clement
  London Planning Administration
    Committee
  London Regional Planning, Advisory
    Committee for
Delevingne, Sir Malcolm
  Nursing Profession, Central Emergency
    Committee for the
Dick, J W
  Pensions Organization Committee
Dudley, Lord
  Housing, Central, Advisory Committee:
    Design of Flats and Houses
    Subcommittee

Elliott, W
  Day Continuation School Committee
Every, C T
  Reconstruction Committee: Special Needs
    of Particular Areas for Postwar Building
    Subcommittee

Fforde, A F
  Reconstruction Committee: Wartime
    Contraventions of the Building Laws
    Subcommittee
Fife Clarke, T
  Housing Publicity Committee

221

Fleming, A P M
  Teachers, Committee on the Recruitment
    and Training of: Technical Teachers
    Subcommittee
Fleming, Lord
  Public Schools, Committee on
Fletcher, B A
  Teachers, National Advisory Council on
    the Training and Supply of:
    (Sub)committee on Youth Leaders and
    Community Centre Wardens
French, Sir Henry
  Home Information Services, Committee
    on the Cost of

Girdwood, J G
  House Building Costs, Committee on
Goldberg, P
  Domestic Workers for Hospitals,
    Consultative Committee
    on the Recruitment of
Goodfellow, S M E
  Canteen Equipment Committee
Gowers, Sir Ernest
  London Civil Defence Region, Co-
    ordinating Committee
Griffiths, J
  Welsh Youth Committee
Guillebaud, C W
  National Health Service, Committee of
    Enquiry into the Cost of

Hall, G
  Welsh Youth Committee
Hall, Sir Arthur
  Mental Nursing and the Nursing of the
    Mentally Defective Subcommittee
Hancock, Judge
  Disablement due to Specific Injuries,
    Interdepartmental Committee on the
    Assessment of
Hankey, Lord
  Further Education and Training,
    Interdepartmental Committee on
Hardman, David Rennie
  Teachers, Interim Committee for
  Teachers (Wales), Interim Committee for
Harrison, Sir Thomas
  Land, Aquisition of, Subcommittee (of
    the Subcommittee on the Uthwatt
    Report on Compensation and
    Betterment)

Hobhouse, Sir Arthur
  Footpaths and Access to the Countryside
    Special Committee
  National Parks Committee
Hopkins, Sir Richard
  Employment, Postwar, Committee on
Horder, Lord
  Air Raid Shelters, Committee on the
    Conditions of
Horsbrugh, Florence
  Adoption Societies and Agencies,
    Departmental Committee on
Hume, Capt H N
  Housing Costs, Official Committee on
Hurst, Sir Alfred
  Postwar Economic Problems, Official
    Committee on: Uthwatt Report on
    Compensation and Betterment
    Subcommittee
Hutchinson, Sir Robert
  Central Medical War Committee:
    Advisory Emergency Hospital Medical
    Service Committee
Hyde, R R
  Harvest Camps Advisory Committee

Ince, Sir Godfrey
  Juvenile Employment Service, Committee
    on the
  Disabled Persons, Interdepartmental
    Committee on the Rehabilitation and
    Resettlement of
Izard, G
  Approved Societies, Advisory Committee
    on the Absorption of (Committee A)

Jackson, E J W
  Youth Leaders and Community Centre
    Wardens, Committee on the
    Recruitment, Training and Conditions
    of Service of
Jameson, Sir Wilson
  Medical Advisory Committee
  Blood Donors Advisory Committee

Kearn, A W
  London Local Advisory Committee

Lee, A G
  Approved Societies, Advisory Committee
    on the Absorption of (Staffs of)
    Approved Societies (Committee B)

Lidbury, Sir David
  Involuntary Absenteeism in the
    Coalmining Industry, Committee on
Lindsay, K
  National Youth Committee
Loveday, Dr Thomas
  Agricultural Education, Joint Advisory
    Committee on
Luxmoore, Lord Justice
  Agricultural Education in England and
    Wales, Committee on Postwar

MacKintosh, Professor J M
  Scientific Advisory Committee: Building
    Requirements Subcommittee
McNair, Sir Arnold
  Teachers, Committee on the Recruitment
    and Training of
MacNalty, Sir Arthur
  Casualties, Committee on Hospital
    Treatment of
  Nursing, Committee on
Maude, E J
  Dental Policy, Committee on Postwar
Maxwell Fyfe, Sir David
  Central Planning Authority,
    Interdepartmental Committee on a
  Conservative Party: Committee on the
    Uthwatt Report
Messer, Frederick
  Handicapped Children, Advisory
    Committee on
  Medical Advisory Committee:
    Subcommittee on Health Centres
Mitchell, C E
  Housing, Central, Advisory Committee:
    Revision of the Housing Manual
    Subcommittee
Moberly, Sir Walter
  Teachers, National Advisory Council on
    the Training and Supply of: Standing
    Committee A
Monckton, Sir Walter
  Alternative Remedies, Departmental
    Committee on
Montgomerie, H H
  Central Progress Committee
Myrrdin-Evans, Sir Guildhaume
  Social Services in Western Europe,
    Committee on

Neal, L
  Estate Development and Management,
    Central Advisory Committee on
Neville, A W
  Conscription of Doctors in the Public
    Health Services, Committee on the
  Dental Emergency Committee
  Emergency Hospital Scheme, Committee
    on the 'demobilization' of
Nicholson, Mr
  'How to Pay' Committee
Norwood, Sir Cyril
  Curriculum and Examinations, Committee
    on

Oliver, R A C
  Teachers, National Advisory Council on
    the Training and Supply of: Training of
    Teachers of Handicapped Children
    Subcommittee

Padmore, Thomas
  National Insurance, Ministry of, and the
    Assistance Board, Interdepartmental
    Committee on the Organization of
    Local Work of
Palmer, Sir William
  Building Materials Prices Committee
Part, A A
  Building Costs, Committee on
Peake, O
  Workmen's Compensation Advisory
    Committee
Percy, Lord Eustace
  Higher Technological Education,
    Committee on
Phillips, Sir Thomas
  Beveridge Report, Official Committee on
    the
Plowden, E N
  Investment Programmes Committee
Pole, Sir Felix
  Postwar Internal Economic Problems,
    Official Committee on: Private
    Enterprise Housing Subcommittee
Proctor, P Dennis
  Local Government Manpower Committee

Reith, Lord
  New Towns Committee

Ridley, Viscount
  Rent Control, Interdepartmental
    Committee on
Robinson, Sir Arthur
  Medical Personnel, Committee of Enquiry
    on
Robinson, Sir Percival
  Reconstruction Committee: Control of
    Postwar Building Subcommittee
Rootes, W E
  Coventry Reconstruction Co-ordinating
    Committee
Rucker, Sir Arthur
  Poor Law, Interdepartmental Committee
    on the Breakup of the
Rushcliffe, Lord
  Nurses Salaries Committee

Safford, Archibald
  Medical Certificates, Interdepartmental
    Committee on
Schuster, Sir George
  Planners, Committee on the Qualification
    of
Scott, Lord Justice
  Land Utilization in Rural Areas,
    Committee on
Shakespeare, Sir Geoffrey
  Medical Personnel (Priority) Committee
Sharp, Evelyn A
  Physical Planning Committee, Central
    Interdepartmental
Simmonds, Oliver E
  Brick Industry Committee
Simon, Sir Ernest
  Building Materials Distribution
    Committee
  Central Council for Works and Buildings:
    Education Committee
Simpson, J R
  Pensions and Allowances,
    Interdepartmental Committee on the
    Payment of
Soulbery, Lord
  Burnham (Main) Committee
  Teaching Staff of Training Colleges,
    Committee on the Scale of Salaries for
Soutter, H S
  British Medical Association: Central
    Emergency Committee

Spens, Sir Will
  Consultants and Specialists,
    Interdepartmental Committee on the
    Remuneration of
  Dental Practitioners, General,
    Interdepartmental Committee into the
    Remuneration of
  Education, Board of, Consultative
    Committee 1938
  General Practitioners, Interdepartmental
    Enquiry on the Remuneration of
  National Insurance Advisory Committee
Stocks, Mary D
  Nurses and Midwives, National Advisory
    Council for the Recruitment and
    Distribution of Nurses and Midwives:
    Inquiry into Midwives Subcommittee

Taylor, W
  Local Government Manpower Committee:
    Youth Employment Service
    Subcommittee
Teviot, Lord
  Dentistry, Interdepartmental Committee
    on
Tomlinson, George
  Disabled Persons, Interdepartmental
    Committee on the Rehabilitation and
    Re-settlement of
Tristram, W J
  Central Health Services Council: Standing
    Pharmaceutical Advisory Committee

Underwood, J E A
  Maladjusted Children, Committee on
  School Medical Officers, Consultative
    Committee of
Uthwatt, Mr Justice
  Compensation and Betterment, Expert
    Committee on

Valentine, A B
  Satellite and New Towns Committee
  New Towns Corporations, Joint
    Consultative Committee on Financial
    Arrangements for
Vincent, H B
  Reconstruction, Interdepartmental
    Advisory Committee on

Wilson A
  Labour and National Service, Ministry of,
    and Ministry of National Insurance,
    Joint Standing Committee of the
Wilson, C
  Casualty Organization in London,
    Advisory Committee on

Wood, Sir Robert
  Teachers, Office Committee on the
    Postwar Supply and Training of
Wood, S H
  Youth Training Committee

Index

Committees have been indexed under their official names, inverted where appropriate. Appendix C gives the names of chairmen of committees, arranged alphabetically, together with the names of the committees they chaired

Abercrombie, Professor Sir Patrick, 3.3.2.1
  Greater London Plan, 3.3.2.1, 3.4.2
Actuary, Government, 2.2, 2.3.2, 2.3.3
Admiralty, 2.7 records, 6.4.1, 5.2 records
Adoption of Children (Regulations) Act
  1939, 6.4.1
Adoption societies, 6.4.1
Adoption Societies and Agencies,
  Departmental Committee on, 6.4.1
Age Concern, 6.3.1
Aged, Committee on the Evacuation of, *see*
  Evacuation
Agricultural Education, Joint Advisory
  Committee on, 5.4.1.2
Agricultural Education in England and
  Wales, Committee on Postwar, 5.4.1.2
Agriculture and Fisheries, Ministry of, 3.3.1,
  3.3.2.1, 3.3.2.3 records; 5.3.1 records,
  5.4.1.2; Norwich and Oxford Divisional
  Offices, Land Drainage, Water
  Supplies and Building Division, 3.4.4
  records
Air Ministry, 2.7 records
Air Raid Damage, Committee on, 3.2
Air Raid Precautions, 4.2.1, 4.2.3.1
Air Raid Precautions Act 1937, 4.2.3.1
Air Raid Shelters, Committee on the
  Conditions of, 4.2.3.1
Aircraft Production, Ministry of, 3.2, 3.4.3
Allen of Hurtwood, Lady, 6.4.3
Alternative Remedies, Departmental
  Committee on, 2.6 records
Aluminium houses, 3.4.3
Ambulance Service, 4.2.1, 4.2.2.1
  trains, 4.2.2.1
  American Ambulance (GB), 4.2.3.1
Anderson, Sir John, later Viscount
  Waverley, 1.2, 2.2, *see also* Evacuation,
  Committee on
Anglesey multilateral schools system 5.3.2

Appointed Day for the NHS, 1.1, 1.3, 2.3.1,
  4.4.2.2
Approved Societies, Advisory Committees
  on the Absorption of, 2.3.2
Arcon houses, 3.4.3
Armed forces medical services, 4.2.2.1
  records
Assheton, Ralph, 2.2
Assistance Board, 2.2., 2.3.1, 2.3.4, 2.4, 2.5
  records, 2.7, 3.2, 3.4.3, 4.2.3.2 records,
  4.4.3 records, 5.3.5.1 records, 6.3.1,
  6.3.2, 6.4.4. records, 6.5 records, 5.3.1
  records; *see also* National Assistance
  Board
Atlantic Charter, 1.2
Atomic Energy Commission, 3.4.1
Attlee, Clement, later 1st Earl Attlee, 1.2,
  1.3, 3.3.1, 3.4.4, 4.2.3.2, 4.3, 5.3.5.1

Barlow, Sir Montague; *see* Distribution of
  the Industrial Population, Royal
  Commission on
Bedfordshire and Luton Executive Council,
  4.4.2.5 records
Berkshire County Council children's homes,
  6.4.4 records
Bevan, Aneurin, 1.1, 1.3, 3.4.3, 3.4.4, 4.4.1,
  4.4.2.1, 4.4.2.2, 4.4.3
Beveridge Report, Official Committee on
  the, 2.2, 2.4, 2.5, 4.3, 6.3.2; *see also*
  Appendix B
Beveridge, Sir William, later 1st Baron
  Beveridge, Introduction, 2.2, 2.2.3; *see
  also* Social Insurance and Allied
  Services, Interdepartmental Committee
  on
Bevin, Ernest, 1.2, 2.3.3, 2.4, 5.3.4, 5.4.1.3,
  6.4.2.1
Birmingham
  Executive Council, 4.4.2.5 records,
  Housing and rest centres, 3.2. records

227

Birmingham—*contd.*
  Local Advisory Committee, 4.2.2.2
    records
  University, 6.4.4
Blood Donors Advisory Committee, 4.4.2.3
Blood Transfusion Service, National,
    4.2.2.2, 4.4.2.3
  regional offices, 4.4.2.3 records
Board of Control, 4.1, 4.3, 4.4.2.6, 6.4.4
    records
Board of Customs and Excise, 2.4 records
Board of Trade, 1.2, 3.2 records, 3.4.2,
    3.4.6
  compensation scheme, 2.6 records
Bolton
  Municipal College, 5.4.1.1
  schools proposed, 5.3.2
Borstals, 6.4.1
Boundary Commission, 6.2
Boy Scouts, 5.5
Bracken, Brendan, later Viscount Bracken,
    1.2, 2.2
Bradford, proposed comprehensive schools
    in, 5.3.2
Brecon Beacons, 3.3.2.3
Bretton Wood Agreement 3.4.4
Brick Advisory Council, National, 3.2
Brick Industry Committee, 3.4.6
Bridges, Sir Edward, later Baron Bridges,
    1.2, 2.2 records, 3.3.1 records, 4.4.3
    records
British Dental Association, 4.3, 4.4.2.5,
    5.3.5.2
British Employers' Confederation, 2.6
British Hospital Contributory Scheme
    Association, 4.4.2.3
British Industry National Council, 3.4.2
    records
British Medical Association, 2.6, 4.3, 4.4.2.1
  Central Emergency Committee, 4.2.2.2;
  Negotiating Committee, 4.4.1, 4.4.2.1
British restaurants, 6.3.1
British Standard Codes of Practice, 3.2
Broadmoor State Institution, 4.4.2.6
Brocket, 2nd Baron, 3.3.1
Bronsby, Dr E Roy, report on poverty in
    London families, 5.3.1 records
Brook, Norman, later Baron Normanbrook,
    1.2, 1.3
Brown, A Ernest, 4.3; plan 4.3

Building *see also* Central Council for Works
    and Buildings; Postwar Building
    Studies; Reconstruction Committee
Building Brick Council, National, 3.4.6
Building and Civil Engineering Industries,
    Advisory Council of the, 3.2
Building and Civil Engineering Industries,
    National Consultative Council of the,
    3.2
Building Costs, Committee on, 5.3.3
Building Industry, Advisory Committee of
    Specialists and Sub-contractors in the,
    3.2
Building industry *see also* Federation of
    Building Trades Employers; Scientific
    Advisory Committee
Building Laws, contravention of, *see*
    Reconstruction Committee
Building Material Production, National
    Council for, 3.4.6
Building Materials Co-ordinating
    Committee, 3.4.6
Building Materials Distribution Committee,
    3.4.6
Building Materials and Housing Act 1945,
    3.4.6 records
Building Materials Prices Committee, 3.4.6
Building Materials Priority Distribution
    Scheme, 3.4.6
Building requirements *see* Scientific
    Advisory Council
Building Research, Working Party on, 3.4.4
Building Restrictions (Wartime
    Contraventions) Act 1946, 3.3.2.2
Building societies, 3.4.5
Building Trade Employers, National
    Federation of, 3.3.2.2, 3.4.4
Building, Treasury Subcommittee on
    Postwar, 3.4.6
Burnham Committee, 5.3.2 records
Burt, Sir George, 3.4.6; *see also* House
    Construction, Interdepartmental
    Committee on
Butler, Richard Austen, 1.2, 5.1, 5.2, 5.3.2,
    5.3.4, 5.3.5.1

Cabinet Office, 3.3.2.1 records, 4.4.1
    records
  Historical Section, 1.2 records
Camp schools, 5.3.1
Canteen Equipment Committee, 5.3.5.1

228

Cardiff
  Elementary school structure, 5.3.2
  Local Education Authority, 5.1
  University, 6.4.4
Care of Children Committee, 2.7, 6.4.2.2,
  6.4.3, 6.4.4; *see also* Appendix B
Casualties, Committee on the Hospital
  Treatment of, 4.2.2.1, 4.2.2.2
Casualty Organization in London, Advisory
  Committee on, 4.2.2.1
Catholic Workers' College, 5.4.1.4
Central Advisory Council for Education,
  5.4.1.3
Central Council for Health Education,
  4.4.2.4
Central Council for Works and Buildings,
  3.2
  Education Committee 3.4.6
Central Economic Planning Staff, 1.3, 5.3.3
Central Health Services Council, 4.4.2.2,
  4.4.2.5
  Dental, Maternity and Midwifery, Mental
  Health, Nursing, Opthalmic and
  Pharmaceutical standing advisory
  committees, 4.4.2.2 records, 4.4.2.5
  records, 4.4.2.6 records
  Health Centre Committee, 4.4.2.4
Central Land Board, 3.3.2.2
Central Land Owners' Association, 3.3.1
Central Medical Board, 4.3
Central Medical War Committee, 4.2.2.2
  Advisory Emergency Hospital Medical
  Service Committee, 4.2.2.1 records
Central Midwives Board, 4.2.3.2, 4.4.2.4
  records
Central Office of Information, 4.4.2.2
  social surveys on the employment of
  adolescents and on youth leisure time,
  5.5 records
Central Planning Authority,
  Interdepartmental Committee on a,
  3.3.1
Central Progress Committee, 3.4.3 records
Central Statistical Office, 2.3.3 records,
  3.3.2.2, 3.4.3 records, 3.4.4 records,
  4.4.2.5 records
Central Youth Employment Executive, 5.5
Chamberlain, A Neville, 1.2
Chancellor of the Exchequer's Office, 3.3.1
  records
Chemists *see* Guild of British Dispensing
  Chemists; Pharmaceutical Society

Child Care, Advisory Council on, 6.4.4
Child Care, Central Training Council in,
  6.4.3, 6.4.4
Child Care Reserve, 6.4.2.1
Child minding, 6.4.2.1
Children
  fostering of, 6.4.3, 6.4.4
  see also diabetic children; disabled
  children; handicapped children;
  maladjusted children
Children Act 1948, 6.1, 6.2, 6.3.2, 6.4.1,
  6.4.3, 6.4.4
Children, Care of, *see* Care of Children
  Committee
Children, National Society for the
  Prevention of Cruelty to, 6.4.4
Children and Young Persons Act 1933,
  6.4.1, 6.4.4
Children's committees, 6.3.2, 6.4.4
Chrystal, Sir George, 5.3.1 records
Church of England 'Five Points', 5.2
Churches and education, 5.1, 5.2
Churchill, Sir Winston, 1.2, 3.3.1, 3.4.2, 5.1,
  5.2
Chuter-Ede, James, later Baron Chuter-
  Ede, 5.1 records
Citizens Advice Bureaux, 6.4.2.2
Civil Defence Committee, 5.3.1 records
  Government Evacuation Scheme
  Subcommittee, 5.3.1
  Winter Plans Subcommittee, 3.2
Civil Defence regions, regional
  commissioners, 4.2.3.1
Cleary, Sir William, 5.3.4
Clyde, James Latham McDiarmid, Lord
  6.4.3
Colonial Office, 2.6 records
Community Centre Wardens *see* Youth
  Leaders
Compensation and Betterment, Expert
  Committee on (Uthwatt Committee),
  1.2, 3.3.1, 3.3.2.2; Report 3.4.2; *see
  also* Appendix B; Postwar Internal
  Economic Problems, Official Committee
  on; Land Acquisition of, Subcommittee
Conference of Allied Ministers of Education
  (later UNESCO) 5.2
Conscription of Doctors in the Public Health
  Services, Committee on the, 4.2.2.2
  records

Conservative Party
  Committee on the Uthwatt Report, 3.3.1
  Secret committee on the Beveridge
    Report (Assheton Committee), 2.2
Consultants and Specialists,
    Interdepartmental Committee on the
    Remuneration of, 4.4.2.1
Council for the Preservation of Rural
    England, 3.1
  National Parks Standing Committee,
    3.3.2.3
County Councils Association, 4.4.1, 6.2
County Youth Service Corps, 5.5
Coventry
  Local Advisory Committee, 4.2.2.2
    records
  Reconstruction Co-ordinating Committee,
    3.2
  schools proposal, 5.3.2
Cripps, Sir Stafford, 1.3, 4.4.2.3
Curriculum and Examinations, Committee
    on: Norwood Report, 1943, 5.3.2
Customs and Excise see Board of Customs
    and Excise

Dalton, Hugh, later Baron Dalton, 1.3
Dartmoor National Park, 3.3.2.3
Day Continuation School Committee,
    5.4.1.3
Day continuation schools, 5.2, 5.4.1.2
Death grant 2.3.5
De la Warr, 9th Earl, 5.4.1.2
Delinquency, 6.4.1
Demobilization, Interdepartmental
    Committee on the Machinery of, 4.2.2.2
Demobilized Soldiers, see Further Education
    of
Dental Advisory Committee, Standing, see
    Central Health Services Council
Dental committees, local, 4.4.2.5
Dental Emergency Committee, 4.2.2.2
Dental Estimates Board, 4.4.2.5
Dental Policy, Committee on, Postwar, 4.3
Dental Practitioners, General,
    Interdepartmental Committee into the
    Remuneration of, 4.4.2.5
Dental War Committee, 4.2.2.2
Dentists Bill 1952, 4.4.2.5
Dentistry, Interdepartmental Committee on,
    4.3, 4.4.2.5, 5.3.5.2; see also Appendix
    B

Dentistry, Standing Advisory Committee on,
    4.4.2.2 records
Determination of Needs Act 1941, 2.3.4, 2.4
Development Charges, Official Committee
    on, 3.3.2.2
Development Corporations, 3.3.2.1, 3.4.5
Diabetic children, 5.3.5.3
Disabled children, 5.3.5.3
Disabled, National Advisory Council on
    Employment of, 6.5
Disabled Persons (Employment) Act 1944,
    5.3.5.3, 6.1, 6.5
Disabled Persons Employment Corporation
    (later Remploy), 6.5
Disabled Persons, Interdepartmental
    Committee on the Rehabilitation and
    Resettlement of, 6.5
Disablement due to Specified Injuries,
    Interdepartmental Committee on
    Assessment of, 2.6
Distribution of the Industrial Population,
    Royal Commission on, 3.3.1; Report
    3.1, 3.3.2.1, 3.4.2
Directorate of Physical Recreation, 5.5
Dr Barnardo's, 6.4.3
Doctors, Conscription of, see Conscription
Domestic help, 6.3.1
Domestic Workers for Hospitals,
    Consultative Committee on the
    Recruitment of, 4.4.2.3
Dower, John, 3.3.2.3
Drugs see Supply Committee
Drugs Requirement Advisory Committee,
    4.4.2.3
Drummond, Sir Jack, 5.3.5.1

East Kilbride (New Town), 3.3.2.1 records
Economic Information Committee, 1.3
Economic Planning Board, 1.3
Economic Planning, Committee on, 5.3.2
Economic Policy Committee, 1.2, 1.3, 4.4.3;
    see also Appendix B
Ede see Chuter-Ede
Education
  Education after the war, Green Book,
    5.2, 5.3.4, 5.3.5.1, 5.4.1.2, 5.4.1.3
  Education reconstruction, White Paper
    1943, 5.4.1.2
  government survey on, 1945, 5.1
  institutes of, 5.3.4
  local education authorities, 5.1, 5.3.1,
    5.3.2, 5.3.3, 5.3.5.1

Education—*contd.*
  see also Central Advisory Council for
    Education; Central Council for Health
    Education; Central Council for Works
    and Buildings; Schools; Teachers;
    Training colleges
Education Acts
  Education Act 1902, 5.2
  Education Act 1936, 5.3.2, 5.3.3
  Education Act 1944, 5.1, 5.2, 5.3.2, 5.3.3,
    5.3.4, 5.3.5.1, 5.3.5.2, 5.3.5.3, 5.4.1.1,
    5.4.1.3, 5.4.1.4, 6.2, 6.4.2.1
  Education (Provision of Meals) Act 1906,
    5.3.5.1
Education Advisory Service, 5.4.1.2 records
Education, Agricultural, *see* Agricultural
    Education
Education, Board of, 2.5 records, 3.2
    records, 3.3.2.1, 5.1, 5.2, 5.3.1, 5.3.3,
    5.3.5.1, 5.3.5.3, 6.5
  Technical Branch, 5.4.1.1, 5.4.1.2;
  ARP files, 4.2.3.1 records
  school meals, 4.2.3.2
  Consultative Committee 1938, 5.1, 5.2,
    5.4.1.1
Education Committees, Association of, 5.2
Education, Further, *see* Further Education
Education, Higher, *see* Higher Technological
    Education
Education, Ministry of, 2.6 records, 2.7, 5.1,
    5.3.3, 6.4.3, 6.4.4
  Architecture and Building Branch, 5.3.3
Education of Poles, Committee for the,
    5.4.1.4
Education, Postwar, Committee of Senior
    Officials on, 5.2
Education, Technological, *see* Higher
    Technological Education; Technological
    Education
Edwards, John, 6.4.2.1
Elementary Education (Blind and Deaf
    Children) Act 1892, 5.3.5.3
Elliott, William Rowcliffe, 5.4.1.3
Emergency Hospital Scheme, Committee on
    the 'demobilization' of, 4.2.2.1
Emergency schemes and services
  Bed Scheme, 4.4.2.3
  Blood Transfusion Service, 4.2.1, 4.2.2.2,
    4.4.2.3
  Canteen Service, 6.3.1
  Hospital Scheme, 4.2.2.1

Emergency schemes and services—*contd.*
  Medical Service, 1.2, 4.2.1, 4.2.2.1,
    4.2.2.2, 4.3, 4.4.2.3 *see also* British
    Medical Association; Central Medical
    War Committee
  Teacher Training Scheme, 5.3.2, 5.3.3,
    5.3.4
Employment exchanges, 2.3.3
Employment Policy, White Paper 1944, 1.2
Employment, Postwar, Committee on, 1.2
Employment and Training Act 1948, 5.5
Engineering, Consultative Committee on,
    5.4.1.2
Estate Development and Management,
    Central Advisory Committee on, 3.3.1
Evacuation, evacuees, 1.2, 2.4, 5.3.1, 5.3.4,
    5.3.5.1, 5.3.5.2, 6.4.1, 6.4.2.1, 6.4.2.2,
    6.4.3; *see also* Nursery Centre Scheme
  evacuation of the elderly, 6.3.1
Evacuation of the Aged, Committee on the,
    6.3.1
Evacuation, Committee on, 5.3.1; *see also*
    Appendix B
Evacuation Scheme, Government,
    Committee on the, 5.3.1 records; *see
    also* Civil Defence Committee
Evacuation of School Children, Advisory
    Committee on, 5.3.1 records
Executive Councils (local, for practitioner
    services), 4.4.2.5
Exmoor National Park, 3.3.2.3
Eye Service Committee, 4.4.2.5

Family Allowances Act 1945, 2.2, 2.5
Family Allowances Act 1952, 2.3.1
Family Allowances, White Paper 1942, 2.5
Federation of British Industry, 2.2, 3.3.2.2,
    5.4.1.2
Fircroft College, Birmingham, 5.4.1.4
First Aid Nursing Yeomanry, 4.2.3.1
Fitness, National, Council, 5.5
Flats *see* Social Needs and Problems of
    Families Living in
Flats and Houses, Design of, *see* Housing,
    Central, Advisory Committee
Fleming, Sir Arthur, 5.3.4
Food, Ministry of, 2.5, 5.3.1 records, 5.3.5.1
  National Milk Scheme, 4.2.3.2
  Statistics and Intelligence Division, 4.4.2.4
    records
  Welfare Food Scheme, 4.2.3.2

Food Policy Committee, 4.2.3.2, 5.3.5.1; *see also* Appendix B
Foot, Michael, 3.3.1, 4.1
Footpaths and Access to the Countryside Special Committee, 3.3.2.3 records
Fostering, 6.4.3, 6.4.4
Friendly Societies, 2.3.2
Fuel and Power, Ministry of, 3.4.4
Furnished Houses (Rent Control) Act 1946, 3.4.5
Further Education of Demobilised Soldiers, Committee on the, 5.4.1.4
Further Education Schemes Committee, 5.4.1.1 records
Further Education and Training, Interdepartmental Committee on, 3.3.1, 5.4.1.4 records, 5.4.2; See also Appendix B
Further Education and Training Scheme, 5.4.1.4

Gaitskell, Hugh, 3.4.4
Garden City Movement, 3.3.2.1
General Certificate of Education, O and A Level Examinations, 5.3.2
General Nursing Council for England and Wales, 4.2.2.2 records, 4.4.2.3
General Nursing Recruitment Campaign, 4.4.2.3
General Post Office, 2.1, 2.3.1, 2.3.2
General Practitioners, Interdepartmental Committee on the Remuneration of, 4.4.1, 4.4.2.1; *see also* Appendix B
General Register Office, 2.5 records
    Files on Education Act, 5.2 records
Gilbert, Sir Bernard, 2.2, 2.3.3, 2.6
Girl Guides Association, 5.5
Gould, Barbara Ayrton, 6.4.4
Green Belt, 3.3.2.1
Greenwood, Arthur, 1.2
Griffiths, James, 2.3.1
Guild of British Dispensing Chemists: liaison committee, 4.4.2.5 records

Hadow Committee *see* Education, Board of, Consultative Committee of
Hadow, Sir Henry, 5.1
Hale, Sir Edward, 2.3.3, 2.5, 4.4.3, 5.4.2, 6.4.2.1
Handicapped children *see also* Teachers, National Advisory Council on the Training and supply of; Schools, special

Handicapped Children, Advisory Committee on, 5.3.5.3
Handicapped Persons, Advisory Council for the Welfare of, 6.5
Hardman, David Rennie, 5.3.4
Harlech College (Coleg Harlech), 5.4.1.4
Harvest Camps Advisory Committee, 5.3.1 records
Health Centres, 4.4.2.4; *see also* Central Health Service Council; Medical Advisory Committee
Health, Department of, for Scotland, 2.3.1
Health, Ministry of, 2.1, 2.2 records, 2.3.1, 2.3.2, 2.5 records 2.7, 3.3.1, 3.4.3, 3.4.4, 3.4.5, 3.4.6, 4.4.1, 5.3.1, 5.3.5.2, 6.4.2.2, 6.4.3, 6.4.4
    Administrative Division and Medical Section 4.2.2.1
    Chief Medical Officer, 4.3
    paper on the breakup of the Poor Law and the care of children and old people, 6.3.2
    Public Assistance Division, Evacuation Division, 6.3.1
    social welfare files, 6.3.2 records
Health Services *see* Central Health Services Council
Health visitors, 4.1. 4.2.3.2, 4.4.2.4
Henderson, Sir Hubert, 3.2
Hetherington, Sir Hector, 2.6, 5.3.4
Higher Technological Education, Committee on, 5.4.1.2, 5.4.2; *see also* Appendix B
Hill, Charles, 4.3
Hillcroft College, Surbiton, 5.4.1.4
Hobhouse, Sir Arthur, 3.3.2.3
Home Affairs Committee, 1.2
Home Guard, 5.3.4
Home helps, 2.4, 4.4.2.4, 6.3.1
Home Information, Ministerial Committee on, 1.3 records
Home Information, Official Committee on, 1.3 records
Home Information Services, Committee on the Cost of, 1.3
Home Office, 2.1, 2.5 records, 2.7, 3.3.1 records, 3.3.2.3 records, 6.4.3, 6.4.4
    Children's Department, 6.4.1 records
    responsibility for criminally insane, 4.4.2.6
Home Policy Committee, 1.2, 4.2.2.2, 6.5; *see also* Appendix B

Home Security, Ministry of, 2.7 records,
4.2.3.1 5.3.1 records 6.2
  Research and Experimental Department
3.2 records
Homeless Children (Scotland), Committee
on, 6.4.3
Horder, Thomas Jeeves, Baron Horder,
6.3.1
Horsbrugh, Florence later Baroness
Horsbrugh, 6.4.1
Hospital accounts, 4.4.3 records
Hospital Management Committees, 4.4.2.3
Hospital Problems during the Transitional
Period, Committee on, 4.4.2.3
Hospital survey 1938, 4.2.2.1
Hospitals, see also Emergency Hospital
Scheme; Regional Hospital Boards
Hospitals, teaching, 4.4.2.3
Hospitals and Allied Institutions, National
Joint Council for Staff of, 4.4.2.3
House Builders Association of Great
Britain, 3.4.2 records
House Builders, National Federation of
Registered, 3.4.2 records
House Builders Registration Council,
National, 3.4.5
House Building Costs, Committee on, 3.4.4
House Construction, Interdepartmental
Committee on, 3.4.3, 3.4.6; see also
Appendix B
House Construction, Interdepartmental
Committee on Technical Methods of,
3.4.6
Houseworkers, National Institute of, 6.3.1
Household means test see Means test
Houses, Interdepartmental Committee on
the Selling Price of, 3.4.5 records
Housing see also Postwar housing;
International Federation for Housing
and Town Planning
associations, 3.4.2, 3.4.5
local authorities, 5.3.1
White Paper on, 3.4.2
Housing Acts
  Housing Act 1949, 3.4.3, 3.4.4, 3.4.5
  Housing (Building Materials and Housing)
Act 1945, 3.4.3, 3.4.5, 3.4.6
  Housing (Emergency Powers) Act 1939,
3.2
  Housing (Financial and Miscellaneous
Provisions) Act 1946, 3.4.4

Housing Acts—contd.
  Housing (Temporary Accommodation)
Act 1948, 3.4.3
Housing, Central, Advisory Committee,
3.4.2 records, 3.4.3, 3.4.4; see also
Appendix B
  Design of Flats and Houses
Subcommittee, 3.4.4
  Revision of the Housing Manual
Subcommittee, 3.4.4
  Rural Housing Subcommittee, 3.4.4
records
Housing Centre Trust, 3.4.4
Housing Committee, 3.4.4
Housing Committee, Standing, 3.4.4
Housing Costs, Official Committee on, 3.4.6
Housing and Local Government, Ministry
of, 3.3.2.2, 4.4.2.2
Housing, Postwar, Departmental Committee
on, 3.4.2 records
Housing Production Executive, 3.4.4, 3.4.6
Housing Publicity Committee, 3.4.4 records
Housing, Societies, National Federation of,
3.4.5
Housing (War Requirements) Committee,
3.2
'How to Pay' Committee, 2.3.1
Huddersfield Technical College 5.4.1.1
Hull, 3.2 records, executive council, 4.4.2.5
records
Hundred New Towns Association, 3.3.2.1
Hutting Operation for the Raising of the
School Leaving Age (HORSA), 5.3.2,
5.3.3

Immunization and vaccination, 4.2.3.2,
4.4.2.4, 5.3.5.2; see also National Anti-
Vaccination League
Imperial Defence, Committee of, 4.2.2.1
Ince, Sir Godfrey, 5.5
Industrial Assurance and Friendly Society
Act 1948, 2.3.2 records
Industrial Disease, Departmental Committee
on, 2.6
Industrial Population, Royal Commission on
the Distribution of the, 3.3.1; Report
1940, 3.1, 3.3.2.1, 3.4.2
Industry see Federation of British Industry
Industry and Commerce, National Advisory
Council for, 5.4.1.2
Information, Minister of, 2.2, 4.2.3.2
records

Information Services, Committee on, 1.3
  records
Inland Revenue, Board of the, 1.3, 2.6
  records
International Federation for Housing and
  Town Planning, 3.4.4 records
Investment, Committee on the Control of,
  3.4.4 records
Investment Programmes Committee 1.3,
  3.4.1, 4.4.2.3, 5.3.3 records, 5.4.2
  records, 6.4.4 records; *see also*
  Appendix B
Investment Working Party, 1.3 records
Involuntary Absenteeism in the Coalmining
  Industry, Committee on, 2.3.2

Jay, Douglas, later Baron Jay, 3.4.4
John Lewis Partnership, 5.4.1.3
Joint Examination Board, 5.3.4 records
Joint Planning Boards, 3.3.2.2
Joint Town Planning Committees, 3.3.1
Jones, Sir Cyril 4.4.3
Jowitt, Sir William, later 1st Earl Jowitt,
  1.2, 2.3.1, 6.2
Juvenile Employment Service, 5.5
Juvenile Employment Service, Committee
  on the, 5.5

Kent Local Advisory Committee, 4.2.2.2
  records
Keynes, John Maynard, 1st Baron Keynes,
  1.2, 1.3, 2.2

Labour Ministry of, 1.2, 2.1, 3.2, 3.4.6, 5.5,
  6.4.2.1
  correspondence on Education Act, 5.2
  records
Labour and National Service, Ministry of,
  2.3.1, 2.3.3, 3.4.6, 4.2.2.2, 4.2.3.2,
  4.4.2.3, 5.3.4, 5.3.5.3, 5.4.1.2, 6.5
  evacuation scheme 5.3.1 records
Labour and National Service, Ministry of,
  and Ministry of National Insurance,
  Joint Standing Committee of the, 2.3.1
Labour Party
  election manifesto 1945, 5.3.3
  education manifestos 5.3.2
  health service policy 4.3
  Parliamentary, 'Blitzed Areas' Group,
  3.4.3
Labour (Textile Industry) Committee,
  6.4.2.1

Lake District National Park, 3.3.2.3
Land Acquisition Act 1946, 3.4.4
Land, Acquisition of, Subcommittee (of the
  Subcommittee on the Uthwatt Report
  on Compensation and Betterment),
  3.3.1
Land Registry, 2.2 records
Land Tribunal, 3.2 records
Land Use, Control of, White Paper 1944,
  3.3.1, 3.3.2.3
Land Utilization in Rural Areas, Committee
  on, 3.3.1, 3.3.2.3, Report, 3.3.2.1,
  3.4.2; *see also* Appendix B
Landlord and Tenant (Rent Control) Act
  1949, 3.4.5
Landowners' Association, 3.3.2.2
Leeds University, 6.4.4
Legal Aid and Advice Act 1949, 2.4
Legislation Committee, 1.3
Leyland Motors, 3.4.1
Liverpool University, 6.4.4
Local Government Act 1929, 6.2, 6.3.1
Local Government (Boundary Commission)
  Act 1945, 6.2
Local Government Manpower Committee,
  6.4.4 records; *see also* Appendix B
  Education Subcommittee, 5.3.4 records
  Health Panel Subcommittee, 4.4.2.4
  Housing Panel Subcommittee 3.4.6
  records
  Youth Employment Service
  Subcommittee, 5.5
Local government organization, White Paper
  1945, 6.2
Local Government and Planning, Ministry
  of, 3.4.4
Local Loans Act 1945, 3.4.4
London Civil Defence Region, 4.2.3.1
  Co-ordinating Committee, 4.2.3.1
  special commissioner for the homeless, 3.2
London County Council, 3.3.2.2, 4.3, 6.1,
  6.4.1, 6.4.2.2
  Education Scheme 1944, 5.3.2;
  Education Department 6.3.1
London Gazette, 3.3.2.2
London, Greater, Plan 1945, 3.3.2.1
London, Greater, Plan, Interdepartmental
  Committee on the, 3.3.2.1
London Hostels Association Ltd, 6.3.1
London Local Advisory Committee, 4.2.2.2
  records
London Plan 1947, 5.3.2

234

London Planning Administration
Committee, 3.3.2.1
London Regional Planning, Advisory
Committee for, 3.3.2.1
London Repairs Executive, 3.2, 3.4.3
London School of Economics, 6.4.4
Lord Chancellor's Office, 2.5 records, 2.6
records, 3.2 records, 3.3.2.2 records,
3.4.5 records, 3.4.6 records, 6.4.1
records, 6.5 records
Lord President's Committee, 1.2, 1.3, 2.1
records, 3.3.1, 3.3.2.3 records, 3.4.3,
4.4.2.5, 5.2, 5.3.4, 6.4.1; see also
Appendix B
Lord President's Secretariat, 2.2 records,
3.3.1 records, 3.3.2.2 records; 3.4.2
records, 3.4.3 records, 3.4.4 records,
3.4.5 records, 3.4.6 records, 4.4.3
records, 6.4.2.2 records, 6.4.3 records
Loveday, Thomas, vice-chancellor of Bristol
University, 5.4.1.2
Lunacy, Commissioners in, 4.4.2.6
Lunacy and Mental Disorders, Royal
Commission on, Report 1926, 4.4.2.6
Luxmoore, Lord Justice 5.4.1.2

McCorquodale, M M, 4.2.2.2
MacDonald, Malcolm John, 4.3
McNair, Sir Arnold, later 1st Baron McNair,
5.3.4; see also Training of Teachers,
Committee on the
Maladjusted Children, Committee on,
5.3.5.3 records
Manchester children's homes, 6.4.4 records
Margate, nutritional survey of, 1939, 5.3.5.1
Marquand, Hilary, 4.4.2.2
Marriage grant, 2.3.5
Marshall Aid, 1.3, 3.4.4
Maternity allowance, maternity benefit,
2.3.5
Maternity and Child Welfare Act 1918, 6.3.1
Maternity and Child Welfare, National
Council for, 6.4.2.1
Maternity and Midwifery Advisory
Committee, Standing, see Central
Health Services Council
Maude, Sir John, 4.3
Maycock, Sir William, 4.4.2.3 records
Meade, James Edward, 2.2
Meals on wheels, 2.4, 6.3.1
Means test, 1.2, 2.4
Mechanical Transport Corps, 4.2.3.1

Medical Advisory Committee, 4.3 records
Subcommittee on Health Centres, 4.4.2.3
Medical Appeals Tribunal, 2.6 records
Medical Certificates, Interdepartmental
Committee on, 4.4.2.5 records
Medical equipment see Supply Committee
Medical Officers of Health, local, 4.1
Medical Officers of Health, Advisory
Committee of, 4.2.3.1
Medical Personnel, Committee of Enquiry
on 4.2.2.2
Medical Personnel (Priority) Committee,
4.2.2.2
Medical Practices Committee, 4.4.2.5
Medical Research Council, 4.2.2.2
Medical Service Committees, 4.4.2.5 records
Mental Deficiency Act 1913, 4.4.2.6
Mental Health Advisory Committee,
Standing, see Central Health Services
Council
Mental Health Committee, 4.4.2.6 records
Mental Health Emergency Committee,
5.3.5.2
Mental Nursing and the Nursing of the
Mentally Defective Subcommittee,
4.4.2.6
Mental Treatment Act 1930, 4.4.2.6
Merioneth Executive Council, 4.4.2.5
records
Metropolitan Borough Councils, Standing
Joint Committee of, 6.4.2.2
Middlesex
Executive Council, 4.4.2.5 records
proposed comprehensive schools 5.3.2
Midwifery, Standing Advisory Committee
on, see Central Health Services Council
Midwives
certified, 4.1.
recruitment of, 4.4.2.4
see also Nurses and Midwives; Royal
College of Midwives
Milk in Schools Scheme, 4.2.3.2, 5.3.5.1
Milk, subsidized, 1.2; see also National Milk
Scheme
Miners' Charter, 2.3.2
Miners' pensions, 2.3.4 records
Minister without portfolio, 2.2, 6.2
Mobberley Boys School, incident at, 5.3.1
Monckton, Sir Walter, later 1st Viscount
Monckton, 6.4.3
Moran, 1st Baron, 4.4.2.1, 4.4.2.3

Morrison, Herbert, later Baron Morrison,
1.2, 1.3, 3.3.1, 3.3.2.3, 4.4.1, 4.4.2.2,
6.1, 4.3
Moss Side State Institution, 4.4.2.6
Municipal Corporations, Association of, 6.2

National Advisory Councils *see* under
subject
National Anti-Vaccination League, 4.2.3.2
National Assistance Act 1948, 2.2, 2.3.1,
2.4, 6.2, 6.3.2, 6.3.1, 6.3.2, 6.4.1, 6.5
National Assistance Board (1948), 2.4,
3.4.3, 6.2; *see also* Assistance Board
National Coal Board, 3.4.4
National colleges, 5.4.1.2
National Councils *see* under subject
National Expenditure, Select Committee on,
6.4.2.2 records
National Federations *see* under subject
National Health Insurance Benefits, 4.3
National Health Insurance Scheme, 2.3.2,
2.6, 4.1
National Health Service
charges 1.3
prescription charges 4.4.3
superannuation scheme, 2.3.4 records
National Health Service Act 1946, 4.4, 6.2,
6.3.1
National Health Service (Amendment Act)
1949, 4.4.2.5
National Health Service (Amendment) Act
1951, 4.4.3
National Health Service, Committee on the,
4.4.2.3, 4.4.2.4, 4.4.3; *see also*
Appendix B
National Health Service, Committee of
Enquiry into the Cost of, 4.4.3
National Insurance, 1.1
contributions, 2.2
National Insurance Act 1946, 2.2, 2.3.1,
2.3.2, 2.3.4, 2.3.5, 2.4
National Insurance Act 1952, 2.3.1
National Insurance Advisory Committee,
2.3.1, 2.3.3, 2.3.5 records; *see also*
Appendix B
National Insurance Commissioners, 2.3.1,
2.3.2 records, 2.3.4 records, 2.5 records,
2.6 records
National Insurance (Industrial Injuries) Act
1946, 2.3.1, 2.6, 2.7 records
National Insurance Fund, 2.3.4,
surplus, 1950, 2.3.3

National Insurance, Ministry of, 2.1 records,
2.2, 2.3.1, 2.3.2 records, 2.3.3, 2.5, 2.6,
2.7, 4.4.1 records
National Insurance, Ministry of, and the
Assistance Board, Interdepartmental
Committee on the Organization of the
Local Work of, 2.3.1 records
National Juvenile Employment Council, 5.5
National Milk Scheme, 4.2.3.2
National Old People's Welfare Council,
formerly Committee, 6.3.1
National Parks and Access to the
Countryside Act 1949, 3.3.2, 3.3.2.3
National Parks Commission, 3.3.2.3
National Parks Committee: Report 1931,
3.3.2.3
National Parks Committee: Report 1947,
3.3.2.3
National Parks in England and Wales,
report by John Dower, 1945, 3.3.2.3
National Parks, Standing Committee on, *see*
Council for the Protection of Rural
England
National Savings Certificate holders, 2.4
records
National Service (Armed Forces) Act 1939,
4.2.2.2
National Union of Teachers, 5.3.4
National Union of Women Teachers, 5.3.4
National Youth Committee, 5.5
New Zealand, 1.3, 2.2
New Town Corporations, Working Party on
the Financial Arrangements for, 3.3.2.1
New Town Planning Committee 5.3.3
New Towns Act 1946, 3.3.2, 3.3.2.1, 3.3.2.2
New Towns Committee, 3.3.2.1
New Towns Corporations, Joint Consultative
Committee on Financial Arrangements
for, 3.3.2.1
Newcastle upon Tyne Hospital board of
governors, 4.4.2.3 records
Council, The 1940, 3.3.1
North Yorkshire Moors National Park,
3.3.2.3
Northumberland National Park, 3.3.2.3
Nottingham University, 6.4.4
Nuffield College surveys, 1.2
on local government reorganization, 6.2
on social reconstruction, 3.3.1, 3.3.2.1
Nuffield Foundation survey on the problem
of ageing and the care of the elderly,
6.3.2

Nufffield Provincial Hospital Trust, 4.3

Nurse, Area, Training Committees 4.4.2.3

Nurseries, 6.4.2.1, 6.4.2.2; in factories, 6.4.2.1

Nursery Centre Scheme 5.3.1, 6.4.2.1
   Joint Committee of the Ministry of Health and Board of Education, 6.4.2.1

Nurses
   district, 4.1
   see also General Nursing Council, General Nursing Recruitment Campaign

Nurses Act 1943, 4.2.2.2

Nurses Act 1949, 4.4.2.3

Nurses and Midwives, National Advisory Council for the Recruitment and Distribution of, 4.2.2.2, 4.2.3.2, 4.4.2.4 records
   Inquiry into Midwives Subcommittee, 4.4.2.3 records

Nurses' Salaries Committee, 4.2.2.2

Nursing Advisory Committee, Standing, *see* Central Health Services Council

Nursing, Committee on, 4.2.2.2

Nursing Profession, Central Advisory Committee for the, 4.2.2.2.

Nursing Profession, Central Emergency Committee for the, 4.2.2.2

Nursing Reserve, Civil, 4.2.2.2

Nursing Services, Interdepartmental Committee on, 4.2.2.2.

Office of Population Censuses and Surveys inquiry into hospital records systems, 4.4.2.3 records

Old Age Pensioners, National Federation of, 2.3.4

Old Age and Widow's Pension Act 1940, 2.4, 2.7 records, 6.3.1

Old People, *see* National Old People's Welfare Council; Nuffield Foundation Survey

Old peoples' homes, 2.4

Oldham schools proposal, 5.3.2

O'Neill, Denis, 6.4.3

Opthalmic Advisory Committee, Standing, *see* Central Health Services Council

Optical Profession, Joint Emergency Committee for the: liaison committee, 4.4.2.5 records

Opticians, Central Emergency Committee for, (England and Wales) 4.2.2.2

Payment by Results Advisory Panel, 3.2

Peak District National Park, 3.3.2.3

Pembrokeshire Coast National Park, 3.3.2.3

Pension Appeals Tribunal, 2.7 records

Pensions and Allowances, Interdepartmental Committee on the Payment of, 2.3.1

Pensions, Ministry of, 2.1, 2.3.4, 2.5 records, 2.6, 2.7 records, 4.4.3, 6.4.1, 6.4.4.

Pensions and National Insurance, Ministry of, 2.7

Pensions Organization Committee, 2.3.1 records

Percy, Lord Eustace, 5.4.1.2,

Personal Injuries (Civilian) Scheme, 2.4, 2.7

Personal Injuries (Emergency Provisions) Act 1939, 2.7 records

Pharmaceutical, Advisory Committee, Standing, *see* Central Health Services Council

Pharmaceutical Society, 4.3
   Central Pharmaceutical Emergency Committee, 4.2.2.2.

Pharmaceutical Undertakings Act 1942, 4.2.2.2

Phillips, Sir Thomas, 2.2

Physical Planning Committee, Central Interdepartmental, 3.3.1

Physical Reconstruction, Consultative Panel on, 3.3.1

Physical Recreation, Directorate of, 5.5

Physical Training and Recreation Acts 1937, 5.5

Planners, Committee on the Qualification of, 3.3.1

Plowden, Sir Edwin, later Baron Plowden, 1.3

Poles, Committee for the Education of, *see* Education

Polish resettlement, 2.4 records

Polish Resettlement Act 1947, 5.4.1.4

Political and Economic Planning, 1.2

Poor Law, 2.4, 4.1
   Unions 6.3.1

Poor Law Act 1930, 6.4.4.

Poor Law, Interdepartmental Committee on the Breakup of the, 6.3.2, 6.4.3; *see also* Appendix B

Portal house, 3.4.3

Portal, Wyndham, 1st Viscount Portal, 3.3.1

Postwar Building Studies, 3.2

Postwar Building *see also* Reconstruction
Committee
Postwar Internal Economic Problems,
Official Committee on, 3.4.2, 3.4.6, 6.2;
see also Appendix B
Private Enterprise Housing Subcommittee,
3.4.2
Uthwatt Report on Compensation and
Betterment Subcommittee, 3.3.1; *see
also* Land, Acquisition of,
Subcommittee
Prefabricated houses, 3.4.3
Prefabricated Houses, Working Party on,
3.4.3
Prefabricated Housing, Committee on, 3.4.3
Prefabricated school buildings, 5.3.3
Prevention and Relief of Distress Scheme,
2.4
Prime Minister's Office, 3.2 records, 3.3.1
records, 3.3.2.1 records, 3.3.2.2 records,
3.4.2 records, 3.4.3 records, 3.4.4
records, 3.4.6 records, 6.4.4 records
Production Committee, 1.3, 3.4.4, 3,4,6; *see
also* Appendix B
Production Council, 1.2, 3.2
Production Executive, 3.2
Production, Ministry of, 3.2
Property Owners, National Federation of,
3.3.1
Property Owners' Protection Society, 3.3.1
Public Assistance
committees, 2.2, 2.4, 2.6, 3.2, 6.2, 6.3.1,
6.3.2, 6.4.1, 6.4.3, 6.5
institutions, 6.3.1, 6.3.2, 6.4.4
Public Health Act 1936, 6.3.1, 6.4.1
Public Schools, Committee on, 5.3.2, 5.3.4
records
Public Schools Governing Bodies
Association, 5.3.2
Public Works Loan Board, 3.4.4, 6.2

Quaker relief organizations, 6.3.1

Raising of the School Leaving Age Scheme
(ROSLA), 5.3.2
Rampton State Institution, 4.4.2.6
Rationing *see* Appendix A
Reconstruction Committee, 1.1, 1.2, 2.3.2,
records, 3.3.1, 3.4.2, 3.4.3, *see also*
Appendix B
Housing Subcommittee 3.4.2

Reconstructon Committee—*contd.*
Control of Postwar Building
Subcommittee, 3.4.2
Special Needs of Particular Areas for
Postwar Building Subcommittee, 3.4.6
records
Wartime Contravention of the Building
Laws Subcommittee, 3.2
Workmen's Compensation Subcommittee,
2.6
Reconstruction, Interdepartmental Advisory
Committee on, 3.3.1
Reconstruction Joint Advisory Council, 1.2
records
Reconstruction, Ministry of, 1.2, 2.2, 3.4.2
Reconstruction Priorities, Committee on,
1.2, 4.3, 6.3.2, *see also* Appendix B
Reconstruction Problems, Committee on,
1.2, 2.2, 2.5 records, 3.3.1, 3.4.2; *see
also* Appendix B
Reconstruction Secretariat, 1.2, 5.2 records,
6.2 records
Reconstruction of Town and Country,
Committee on the, 3.3.1
Red Cross
American, 6.4.2.2
British, 4.2.2.2, 4.2.3.1
Refugees, 2.4 records
Regional Commissioners, 6.2
Regional Hospital Boards, 4.4.2.3
Registrar General: immunization and
vaccination statistics, 4.2.3.2 records
Registry of Friendly Societies, 2.2, 2.4
records
Reith, lst Baron, 3.3.1, 3.3.2.1
Remand homes, 6.4.1, 6.4.4
Remploy Ltd, 6.5
Rent Control, Interdepartmental Committee
on, 3.4.5
Rent of Furnished Houses Control
(Scotland) Act 1943, 3.2
Rent Tribunals, 3.4.5
Rents and Furnished Lets, *ad hoc*
Committee on the Control of, Scotland,
3.2 records
Rents and Mortgages (Restrictions) Act
1939, 3.2
Residential homes for the elderly, 6.3.2
Rest centres, 3.2
Ridley, 3rd Viscount, 3.4.5
Robinson, Sir Arthur, 4.2.2.2

Rotherhithe evacuated day nurseries, 6.4.2.2
    records
Royal Air Force
    educational service, 5.4.1.4 records
    medical service, 4.2.2.1 records
Royal College of Midwives, 4.2.3.2
Rucker, Sir Arthur, 6.3.2
Ruskin College, Oxford, 5.4.1.4

St John Ambulance, 4.2.3.1
    voluntary blood service, 4.2.2.2.
St Thomas's Hospital, board of governors,
    4.4.2.3 records
Salford Executive Council, 4.4.2.5 records
Satellite and New Towns Committee, 3.3.2.1
Scheme M, 5.4.1.2.
School
    Dental Service, 5.3.5.2
    Eye Service, 5.3.5.2
    Leaving Age, 1.3, 5.3.2, *see also* Hutting
    Meals Service, 2.5, 5.3.5.1
    Medical Service, 4.2.3.2, 5.3.5.2, 5.3.5.3
School, Day Continuation, Committee *see*
    Day Continuation School Committee
School Leaving Age, *ad hoc* Committee on
    the Raising of the, 5.3.2
School Medical Officers, Consultative
    Committee of, 5.3.5.2
School Planning, Committee on, 5.3.3
    records
    Schools
    Approved, 6.4.1, 6.4.4
    Special, 5.3.5.3, 6.5
    Technical, 5.3.2
Scientific Advisory Committee, 3.4.6
    Building Industry Subcommittee, 3.4.6
    Building Requirements Subcommittee,
    3.4.6
Scientific and Industrial Research,
    Department of, 3.2, 3.4.6
    research on air raid shelters, 4.2.3.1
    records
Scientific Manpower, Committee on, Report
    1946, 5.4.2
Scotland, housing in, 3.4.4 records
Scotland, Secretary of state for, 3.3.2.1,
    3.4.4, 5.3.2
Scottish Education Department, 5.5
Secondary Schools Examination Council,
    5.3.2
Sellafield Atomic Energy Commission
    Establishment, 3.4.1

Separation allowance, 2.7
Sheffield health centre, 4.4.2.4
Simon, 1st Viscount, 2.2, 2.4
Smithers, Sir Waldron, 2.2
Snowdonia National Park, 3.3.2.3
Social Insurance and Allied Services,
    Interdepartmental Committee on
    (Beveridge Committee), 1.1, 1.2, 2.1,
    2.2, 2.3.4, 2.6, 2.7, 4.3, 6.3.2; Report,
    1.2, 2.2, 2.3.2, 2.3.3, 2.3.4, 2.3.5, 2.4,
    2.5, 2.6, 5.2, 5.3.5.1, 5.3.5.2; *see also*
    Appendix B
Social Insurance, Ministry of (proposed) 2.7
Social Insurance, White Paper on, 1944,
    2.3.4, 2.4
Social Needs and Problems of Families
    Living in Large Blocks of Flats
    Subcommittee, 3.4.4 records
Social Service, National Council of, 1.2,
    6.3.1
Social Services Committee, 1.3, 2.3.2
    records; *see also* Appendix B
Social Services in Western Europe,
    Committee on, 1.3
Socialist Medical Association, 4.4.2.4
Southend schools proposal, 5.3.2
Spens, Sir Will, 4.4.1, *see also* Appendix C
Spens Report *see* Education, Board of;
    Consultative Committee 1938
Stamp, 1st Baron, 2.5
Stevenage (New Town) 3.3.2.1
Stewart-Lloyd Iron and Steel Production,
    3.4.1
Supply Committee (for drugs and medical
    equipment), 4.2.2.2.
Supply, Ministry of, 3.4.2, 3.4.3 records,
    3.4.6, 4.2.2.1, 4.2.2.2, 6.4.2.2, records
    Medical Directorate 4.2.2.2, 4.4.2.3,
    records
    Central Priority Department, 3.2
    evacuation scheme files, 5.3.1 records
Sussex Local Advisory Committee 4.2.2.2,
    records

Taxation of Profits and Income, Royal
    Commission on the, 1.3
Teachers, Committee on the Recruitment
    and Training of, 5.3.4, 5.4.1.1, 5.4.2,
    5.5; *see also* Appendix B
    Technical Teachers Subcommittee, 5.3.4
Teachers, (Hetherington) committee on the
    training of, 5.3.4

Teachers, Interim Committee for, 5.3.4

Teachers, National Advisory Council on the Training and Supply of, 5.3.4; standing committees and subcommittees on the training of technical teachers, teachers of handicapped children, and youth leaders, 5.3.4

Teachers, National Union of, *see* National Union of Teachers

Teachers, Office Committee on the Postwar Supply and Training of, 5.3.4

Teachers' salaries, *see* Burnham Committee

Teachers' superannuation, 2.3.4 records

Teachers, Uncertified, Committee on, 5.3.4

Teachers (Wales), Interim Committee for, 5.3.4

Teaching Staff of Training Colleges, Committee on the Scales of Salaries for, 5.3.4 records

Technological education, regional advisory councils on, 5.4.1.2, *see also* Higher Technological Education Committee; Schools, technical.

Technology, National Council of, 5.4.1.2

Temple, William, archbishop of Canterbury, 5.2

Timber Development Association, 3.4.3 records

Tomlinson, George, 5.1, 5.3.2, 5.3.4, 6.4.2.1

Tory Reform Committee, 2.2

Town and Country Planning Act 1944, 3.3.1

Town and Country Planning Act 1947, 3.3.2, 3.3.2.1, 3.3.2.2, 3.4.4, 4.4.2.3, 6.2

Town and Country Planning Acts, 5.3.3.

Town and Country Planning Association, 3.3.1, 3.4.2 records 3.3.2.1

Town and Country Planning (Interim Development) Act 1943, 3.3.1, 3.3.3.2, 5.3.5.1

Town and Country Planning, Ministry of, 3.3.1, 3.3.2.1, 3.3.2.3 records, 3.4.1, 3.4.2, 3.4.4, 3.4.5 records

co-operation with local education authorities, 5.3.3

papers on rural schools, 5.3.2 records

Regional Physical Planning Committee, 3.3.1 records

Town Development Act 1952, 3.3.2.1

Trades Union Congress, 2.6

Training colleges, 5.3.4

Training, Ministerial Committee on, 5.4.1.2

Treasury, 2.6 records, 3.3.2.1 records, 3.3.2.2 records, 3.4.2, 3.4.3 records, 3.4.4 records, 3.4.5 records, 3.4.6 records, 4.4.1 records, 6.2 records, 6.4.2.2 records, 6.4.4 records, 6.5 records

Agriculture and Food Divisions, 2.5 records

Land and Building Division, 3.2 records, 3.3.1 records, 3.3.2.2 records

Tube Shelter Committee, 4.2.3.1

Under Fives Panel, 6.4.2.2

Uniseco houses, 3.4.3

Unemployment Assistance, 1.2

Unemployment Assistance Board, 2.1, 2.3.3, 2.3.4, 2.4

Unemployment Insurance Statutory Committee, 2.3.3

United Nations Educational, Scientific and Cultural Organization, 5.2

Universities, Ministerial Committee on, 5.4.2

University Grants Committee, 5.4.2

Uthwatt Report *see* Compensation and Betterment

Vaccination *see* immunization

Vagrants, 2.4

Wales,
county councils, education finance, 5.3.2
rural housing, 3.4.4 records
see also Teachers (Wales); Welsh ...

War Aims Committee, 1.2

War Cabinet
Economic Section, 1.2, 1.3, 2.2
Works and Buildings Priority Subcommittee, 3.2

War Damage Commission, 3.2, 3.3.1 records

War Damage (Compensation) Act 1941, 3.2

War Damage (Compensation) Act 1943, 3.2

War Office, 6.4.1
Medical Branch, 4.2.2.1 records
Service Camps, 3.2

War Orphans Act 1942, 6.4.1

War Pensions Committee, 2.7 records

War Transport, Ministry of, 2.7

Weitzman, Dr S, official history of education in the Second World War, 5.2 records, 5.3.1 records, 5.3.3 records

Welfare Foods Scheme, 4.2.3.2, 4.4.2.4

Welsh Board of Health, 3.2 records, 3.3.1, 3.4.3 records, 3.4.4 records, 4.1 records, 4.4.2.2

Welsh Regional Office, 3.3.1

Welsh Youth Committee, 5.5

Wilkinson, Ellen, 5.1, 5.3.2, 5.3.3, 5.3.4, 5.4.2

Willesden (New Town), 3.3.2.1 records

Willink, Sir Henry, 4.3

Wilson, Sir Harold, later Baron Wilson, 1.1, 4.4.3

Wolverhampton and Staffordshire Technical College, 5.4.1.1.

Wolverhampton Local Advisory Committee, 4.2.2.2 records

Women, National Council of, 2.2

Women's Voluntary Service, 4.2.3.1, 6.3.1, 6.3.2

   Evacuation Department, 6.4.2.2

Wood, Sir Kingsley, 2.2, 4.3, 5.2

Wood, Sir Robert, 5.4.1.2

Wood, Sydney Herbert, 5.3.4

Woolton, Baron, later 1st Earl of, 5.3.5.1, 1.2

Workers' Educational Association, 5.2, 5.4.1.4

Workmen's Compensation Acts, 2.6

   (Stewart) Committee on, 2.6

Workmen's Compensation Advisory Committee, 2.6

Workmen's Compensation, Royal Commission on (Hetherington Commission), 2.1, 2.6

Works, Ministry of, 3.2, 3.3.2.1 records, 3.3.2.3 records, 3.4.2, 3.4.3, 3.4.4, 3.4.6, 5.4.1.2, 5.3.4

   Directorate of Emergency Works 3.2

Regional Building Committees 3.4.3 records

Directorate of Postwar Building, 3.4.6

Hospitals 4.2.2.2 records

ARP files 4.2.3.1

Works and Buildings, Ministry of, 3.3.1, 3.4.2

   Postwar Building Study Division 3.4.2

Works and Buildings Priority Subcommittee *see* War Cabinet

Works and Planning, Ministry of, 3.3.2.3, 3.4.2

Yorkshire

   children's homes, East Riding, 6.4.4 records

   schools proposal, West Riding, 5.3.2

Yorkshire Dales National Park, 3.3.2.3

Yorkshire, North, Moors *see* North Yorkshire Moors

Young Men's Christian Association, 5.5

Young Women's Christian Association, 5.5

Youth

   service squads, 5.5

   see also Central Youth Employment Executive; Local Government Manpower Committee; National Juvenile Employment Council; National Youth Committee; Teachers, National Advisory Council on the Training and Supply of; Welsh Youth Committee

Youth Advisory Council, 5.5

Youth Leaders and Community Centre Wardens, Committee on the Recruitment, Training and Conditions of Service of, 5.5

Youth Training Committee (for youth leaders) 5.5

Printed in the United Kingdom for HMSO at Edinburgh Press
Dd 294207 C15 12/91 (290834)